American
Protest
in
Perspective
Robert W. Uphaus

AMERICAN
PROTEST
IN
PERSPECTIVE

AMERICAN PROTEST IN PERSPECTIVE

Edited by

ROBERT W. UPHAUS
Michigan State University

HARPER & ROW, PUBLISHERS
New York, Evanston, San Francisco, London

AMERICAN PROTEST IN PERSPECTIVE

Copyright © 1971 by Robert W. Uphaus

Standard Book Number: 06-046724-X

Library of Congress Catalog Card Number: 78-144237

B377178

Contents

III. Divided America (1917–1960)

IV. Confrontation (1960–1970)

Acknowledgments

Grateful acknowledgment is made to the publishers and authors who granted permission to reprint the following essays.

Jane Addams, "Survivals of Militarism in Civil Government" from *Newer Ideals of Peace*. Reprinted by permission of Mrs. Stanley R. Linn.

James Baldwin, "Notes of a Native Son" from *Notes of a Native Son*. Reprinted by permission of the Beacon Press, copyright © 1955 by James Baldwin.

Eldridge Cleaver, "Open Letter to Ronald Reagan" from *Eldridge Cleaver: Post-Prison Writings and Speeches*, edited by Robert Scheer. Reprinted by permission of Random House, Inc., copyright © 1969 by Eldridge Cleaver.

Clarence Darrow, "Crime and Criminals" from Arthur Weinberg, *"Attorney for the Damned*. Reprinted by permission of Simon & Schuster, Inc., copyright © 1957 by Arthur Weinberg.

Frederick Douglass, "The Meaning of July Fourth for the Negro" from *The Life and Writings of Frederick Douglass*. Reprinted by permission of International Publishers Co., Inc.

W. E. B. DuBois, "The Souls of White Folk" from *Darkwater*. Reprinted by permission.

Ralph Ellison, "Twentieth-Century Fiction and the Black Mask of Humanity" from *Shadow and Act*. Reprinted by permission of Random House, Inc., copyright © 1953 by Ralph Ellison.

Ralph Waldo Emerson, "The Fugitive Slave Law" from *Miscellanies*. Reprinted by permission of Houghton Mifflin Company.

Timothy Thomas Fortune, "The Negro and the Nation" from *Black and White*. Reprinted from the Arno Press Edition, 1968.

J. William Fulbright, "The Two Americas" from *The Arrogance of Power*. Reprinted by permission of Random House, Inc., copyright © 1966 by J. William Fulbright.

Michael Harrington, "The Invisible Land" from *The Other America*. Reprinted by permission of The Macmillan Company, copyright © 1962 by Michael Harrington.

LeRoi Jones, "Tokenism: 300 Years for Five Cents" from *Home: Social Essays.* Reprinted by permission of William Morrow and Company, Inc., copyright © 1962, 1966 by LeRoi Jones.

Martin Luther King, Jr., "Letter from Birmingham Jail" from *Why We Can't Wait.* Reprinted by permission of Harper & Row, Publishers, copyright © 1963 by Martin Luther King, Jr.

Henry Demarest Lloyd, "What Washington Would Do To-day" from *Lords of Industry.* Reprinted by permission of G. P. Putnam's Sons, copyright by G. P. Putnam's Sons.

Mary McCarthy, "The Contagion of Ideas" from *On the Contrary.* Reprinted by permission of Farrar, Straus & Giroux, Inc., copyright © 1961 by Mary McCarthy.

Dwight Macdonald, "The Bomb." Reprinted by permission of Dwight Macdonald from *Politics* (Sept. 1945).

Norman Mailer, "The Real Meaning of the Right Wing in America" from *The Presidential Papers.* Reprinted by permission of G. P. Putnam's Sons, copyright © 1960, 1961, 1962, 1963 by Norman Mailer.

H. L. Mencken, "Coda" from *Notes on Democracy.* Reprinted by permission of Random House, Inc., copyright © 1926 by Alfred A. Knopf, Inc., renewed 1954 by H. L. Mencken.

Truman Nelson, "No Rights, No Duties" from *The Right of Revolution.* Reprinted by permission of the Beacon Press, copyright © 1968 by Truman Nelson.

Eric Norden, "American Atrocities in Viet-Nam." This article originally appeared in *Liberation* Magazine, 339 Lafayette St., New York, N.Y. 10012.

Jacob Riis, "The Common Herd" from *How the Other Half Lives.* Reprinted by permission of Hill & Wang, Inc., copyright © 1957 by Hill & Wang, Inc.

Henry David Thoreau, "Civil Disobedience." Reprinted from The Norton Critical Edition of *Walden and Civil Disobedience* by Henry David Thoreau, edited by Owen Thomas. Copyright © 1966 by W. W. Norton & Company, Inc., New York, N.Y.

David Walker, "Our Wretchedness In Consequence of Ignorance" from *David Walker's Appeal, in Four Articles; Together with a Preamble to the Coloured Citizens of the World,* edited and with an introduction by Charles M. Wiltse. Reprinted by permission of Hill & Wang, Inc., copyright © 1965 by Hill & Wang, Inc.

Robert Penn Warren, "Conversation Piece" from *Who Speaks for the Negro?* Reprinted by permission of Random House, Inc., copyright © 1965 by Robert Penn Warren.

Richard Wright, "The Ethics of Living Jim Crow" from *Uncle Tom's Children.* Reprinted by permission of Harper & Row, Publishers, copyright © 1937 by Richard Wright.

For Sue

There is nothing more common than to confound the terms American Revolution with those of the late American War. The American War is over, but this is far from being the case with the American Revolution.

Benjamin Rush,
"On the Defects of the Confederation," 1787.

What is a man born for but to be a Reformer, a Remaker of what man has made; a renouncer of lies; a restorer of truth and good, imitating that great Nature which embosoms us all, and which sleeps no moment on an old past, but every hour repairs herself, yielding us every morning a new day, and with every pulsation a new life?

Ralph Waldo Emerson,
"Man the Reformer," 1841.

✿ INTRODUCTION

The publication of another "protest" anthology requires some convincing justification. It is really very easy to appeal to a people's, particularly a *young* people's, sense of injustice and oppression. After all, it is just recently that most citizens under twenty-one have been allowed to vote (although the validity of the 1970 Voting Rights Bill has not been tested in court), yet for years young men under twenty-one have been dying for their country. The young are thrown into jail for smoking marijuana, while many adults regularly get "high" on liquor and a variety of "pain-killers"; the young are encouraged to attend college, but as soon as they become critical and militant, the legislature and administration are quick to take punitive action; and there are a number of other discrepancies which point to our society's arbitrary distinction between adolescence and adulthood. The fact is that many young people and an increasing number of "adults" are living their real life "underground." Many blacks, as Claude Brown so vividly demonstrates in *Manchild in the Promised Land*, necessarily take refuge in a drug culture as a counter-response to the injustices of society. Similarly, a growing number of whites—middle-class whites—now seek a "real" life in drugs, communal sex, and other methods of "marginal" existence that stand in opposition to generally accepted modes of behavior. It is easy enough to say that these expressions of dissatisfaction are not unique—that they are, in effect, just another version of scrawling on lavatory walls—but there is in such protest a sense of urgency and aggressiveness that not only needs to be noticed but also deserves examination. The question is, how do we examine American protest in such a way that we are faithful to the protestors while we are, at the same time, faithful to American history?

1

The temptation to distort—to align oneself either on the side of the protestors or on the side of American history and institutions—is often succumbed to, the end result being, in its mildest form, partisanship or, in its worst form, paranoia. The way to avoid such temptation (a method that, to my knowledge, has not been used in other protest anthologies) is to view American protect in "perspective," namely the perspective of history. We need to realize, in other words, that American protest has a history, that it *is* a history—a history written by some of our country's most distinguished men and women. And while this history, like any other history, does not proceed in a straight line, there is a valid sense in which one can talk about the process of American protest. This process derives from two basic American documents—the Declaration of Independence and the Constitution of the United States (particularly the Bill of Rights); they are the standards against which the authors whose works are represented in this anthology measure their protest.

To the great disappointment and discomfort of many people, the average United States citizen has simply forgotten, or deliberately ignored, the ideals on which this country was founded. Recently, for example, there were individuals in the United States who opposed a commemorative stamp for Henry David Thoreau, and a sample survey conducted by CBS newsmen demonstrated that many citizens were unable to recognize quotations from the Declaration of Independence and the Bill of Rights. One could multiply these cases endlessly, for they are by no means unique in our day. Thomas Paine, one of the great voices of the American Revolution, was denied consecrated ground for burial in New Rochelle, New York; at an earlier time, the American government wanted to deprive him of his citizenship. David Walker, one of the first important black protestors, was poisoned to death. Such a "tradition" of suppression and violence is as much a sign of American ignorance of the rights and duties of citizenship as it is of human intolerance. It is also the major burden of an American's conscience.

We need to understand American protest in perspective, not in order to tame it into a sterile academic subject, but to understand its roots, its dimensions, and its usefulness. We Americans may be an ahistorical people; we forget easily, and perhaps a case could be made that we do so deliberately. (How else can the sudden "discovery" of black literature be explained?) It is the protestors included in this anthology, among other people, who keep our sense of history alive. It is they, among others, who ask the root questions of American life: What is it like to be an American, and how can we, as Americans, best live up to the ideals of the Declaration of Independence and the Constitution? Thomas Paine made the following observation about the American Revolution:

It would be a circumstance ever to be lamented and never to be forgotten, were a single blot, from any cause whatever, suffered to fall on a revolution, which to the end of time must be an honor to the age that accomplished it.

This statement, of course, is vulnerable to the charge of naïveté. How could Paine be so foolish as not to expect a "single blot," especially in light of the many smudges since smeared on the pages of American history? But such a charge, informed only by retrospective complacency, in no way invalidates Paine's admonition. It is the protestors, such as those represented in this anthology, who have heard Paine's warning and who have responded to the call. It is they who simultaneously lament our falling farther and farther away from the ideals of the American Revolution and who yet urge us to restore, as best we can, the honorable ideals of the revolution.

What needs to be understood is that protest is an act of citizenship. William Ellery Channing has stated this position most strikingly:

The citizen has rights as well as duties. Government is instituted for one and a single end, the benefit of the governed, the protection, peace, and welfare of society; and when it is perverted to other objects, to purposes of avarice, ambition, or party spirit, we are authorized and even bound to make such opposition, as is suited to restore it to its proper end, to render it as pure as the imperfection of our nature and state will admit.

Here is the awful dilemma a protestor must live with: the average citizen, a member of what is now known as the "silent majority," wants to push the protestor to the edge and even out of society, when, in fact, the protestor is "authorized and even bound" to voice his opinions when he feels that his American rights and duties are being pandered or threatened. Frequently the protestor is called "un-American" when it is those who oppress *him* who are "un-American." (This brings to mind Dr. Samuel Johnson's remark that "patriotism is the last refuge of scoundrels.") Such is the ahistorical, not to say hypocritical, turn that many American citizens have taken. The very men who wish to restore government to its "proper end" have been summarily dismissed as agitators, anarchists, and "effete intellectual snobs." It is not, however, my intention (nor was it, more importantly, the intent of the authors of the Declaration of Independence and the Constitution) to suggest that any act of protest is automatically legitimate. To do so would be to assert rights to the exclusion of duties, to emphasize our responsibility to ourselves and to neglect our obligations to society at large. This double awareness of rights *and* duties distinguishes effective and mature protest writing from uninformed complaint.

Although there are many authors I would like to have included in this anthology, the limitations of space and my own principles of editorial coherence have prevented me from doing so. Aside from this initial limitation, I have used six criteria (applicable to all the essays), which I think are characteristic of mature protest writing and which have determined the selections in this anthology. First, the essay must prod the reader's conscience; without this minimal response, protest writing will never take hold. Second, the essay must have, for lack of a better term, therapeutic value. It should affect the reader in such a way that it does not elicit a stock response; rather, the essay should release the knowledge or awareness that has been a burden for the reader and lead him to the recognition of responsibility. Third, the essays in this anthology are all written from *within* society (even if, paradoxically, the writer is in prison or about to flee the country). This is not to imply that some of the authors are not alienated from society, but I am saying that the necessary sense of urgency and crisis of effective protest writing does not come from social "dropouts." Fourth, the essays should enlarge a specific feeling, idea, or grievance into a wider significance. The difference between complaint and protest, as I use the term, is that complaint is self-oriented, if not essentially vain, whereas protest writing is directed at society at large, *away* from the self alone. Fifth, all the essays either implicitly or explicitly raise the central question, "What is it like to be an American?" These essays challenge us to measure our own conduct, as well as society's, against the ideals of the Declaration of Independence and the Constitution. The essays do not channel the reader into a narrowly political, religious or philosophical system; they are addressed to us as whole men, as responsible *individuals*. Finally, all the essays are of demonstrable literary merit. By this I do not mean that they employ exactly the same vocabulary, techniques, and perspective. What I *do* mean is that these essays superbly match style and content; the quality of writing and thought is well executed, effective, of permanent interest, and not given to cliché. These essays quicken our imagination rather than blunt it. Their energy substantiates Emerson's assertion that "Liberty is aggressive."

I.
The Roots of Protest
(1776–1865)

The selections in this section examine the period beginning with the signing of the Declaration of Independence and extending to the selections written in the early 1850s by Ralph Waldo Emerson and Frederick Douglass, which plainly anticipate the causes of the Civil War. There is, however, no one selection in this section dealing with the Civil War per se, although they all discuss to some degree the indirect causes of that war. For if one assumes that slavery was the root problem of the war, then it is fair to say that the Civil War began with the failure of American citizens to abide by the pronouncements of the Declaration of Independence and the Bill of Rights. The issue of slavery, then, should be seen within the larger framework of rights and duties, a framework which Orestes Brownson explains in this way:

> Good government demands, not only strict obedience to the laws, but just laws, and wise administration. The justice of the laws, and the wisdom of the administration depend on the virtue and intelligence of the people, not in their capacity of subjects, but in their capacity of citizens.

In this light, slavery should be understood as not only a deprivation of the rights of black men and women, but a failure on the part of the citizens and government to enact their own duties.

Of the eight selections in this section, the first five are directed, in varying ways, toward an understanding of the meaning of the new nation. The authors of these five selections continually raise the focal question, what are the rights and duties of American citizens? On the one hand, William Ellery Channing strikes a delicate balance when he writes, "With a sincere disposition to obey, should be united a firm purpose not to be

7

oppressed." On the other hand, Thoreau takes a more aggressive stand, saying, "I think we should be men first, and subjects afterward." While this important debate is under way, the authors of the last three selections examine the specific problem of slavery, viewing it as an evil that, in the words of Frederick Douglass, appears to be "co-extensive with the star-spangled banner, and American Christianity." The seeds of the Civil War are in Douglass's prophetic statement of black disfranchisement: "This Fourth of July is *yours*, not *mine*."

Thomas Jefferson
(1743–1826)

•

THOMAS JEFFERSON, the third President of the United States (1801–1809), was born in "Shadwell" in Albermarle County, Virginia. He graduated from William and Mary College in 1762 and was admitted to the bar in 1767. He entered the House of Burgesses in 1769 and was twice elected Governor of Virginia (1779–1781). As President, he was largely responsible for the Louisiana Purchase (1803), the Lewis and Clark Expedition (1804–1806), and the Embargo Act (1807). He helped to found and he completely designed the University of Virginia.

The Declaration of Independence derives from Richard Henry Lee's proposed resolution in Congress on June 7, 1776, that "these united Colonies are, and of right ought to be, free and independent states." As a result of this resolution, a committee of five was appointed, and on June 28, 1776, it presented a draft of the Declaration of Independence, which was mainly the work of Thomas Jefferson. Lee's original resolution was passed on July 2, 1776, and two days later a revised draft of the Declaration of Independence was passed.

THE DECLARATION OF INDEPENDENCE

In CONGRESS, July 4, 1776.

THE UNANIMOUS DECLARATION of the thirteen united STATES OF AMERICA

When in the Course of human events, it becomes necessary for one people to dissolve the political bands which have connected them with another, and to assume among the powers of the earth, the separate and equal station to which the Laws of Nature and of Nature's God entitle them, a decent respect to the opinions of mankind requires that they should declare the causes which impel them to the separation.—We hold these truths to be self-evident, that all men are created equal, that they are endowed by their Creator with certain unalienable Rights, that among these are Life, Liberty and the pursuit of Happiness.—That to secure these rights, Governments are instituted among Men, deriving their just powers from the consent of the governed,—That whenever any Form of Government becomes destructive of these ends, it is the Right of the People to alter or to abolish it, and to institute new Government, laying its foundation on such principles and organizing its powers in such form, as to them shall seem most likely to effect their Safety and Happiness. Prudence, indeed, will dictate that Governments long established should not be changed for light and transient causes; and accordingly all experience hath shewn, that mankind are more disposed to suffer, while evils are sufferable, than to right themselves by abolishing the forms to which they are accustomed. But when a long train of abuses and usurpations, pursuing invariably the same Object evinces a design to reduce them under absolute Despotism, it is their right, it is their duty, to throw off such Government, and to provide new Guards for their future security.—Such has been the patient sufferance of these Colonies; and such is now the necessity which constrains them to alter their former Systems of Government. The history of the present King of Great Britain[1] is a history of repeated injuries and usurpations, all having in direct object the establishment of an absolute Tyranny over these States. To prove this, let Facts be submitted to a candid world.—He has refused his Assent to Laws, the most wholesome and necessary for the public good.—He has forbidden his Governors to pass Laws of immediate and pressing importance, unless suspended in their operation till his Assent should be obtained; and when so suspended, he has utterly neglected to attend to them.—He has refused to pass other Laws for the accommodation of large districts of people, unless those people would relinquish the right of Representation in the Legislature, a right inestimable to them and formidable to tyrants only.—He has called together legislative bodies at places unusual, uncomfortable, and distant from the depository of their public Records, for the sole purpose of fatiguing them into compliance with his measures.—He has dissolved Representative Houses repeatedly, for opposing with manly firmness his invasions on the rights of the people.—He has refused for a long time, after such dissolutions, to cause others to be elected; whereby the Legislative powers, incapable of Annihilation, have returned to the People at large for their exercise; the State remaining in the meantime exposed to all the dangers of invasion from without, and convulsions within.—He has endeavoured to prevent the population of these States; for that purpose obstructing the Laws for Naturalization of Foreigners; refusing to pass others to encourage their migrations hither, and raising the conditions of new Appropriations of Lands.—He has obstructed the Administration of Justice, by refusing his Assent to Laws for establishing Judiciary powers.—He has made Judges dependent on his Will alone, for the tenure of their officers, and the amount and payment of their salaries.—He has erected a multitude of New Offices, and sent hither swarms of Officers to harass our people, and eat out their substance.—He has kept among us, in times of peace, Standing Armies without the Consent of our legislatures.—He has affected to render the Military independent of and superior to the Civil power.—He has combined with others[2] to subject us to a jurisdiction foreign to our constitution, and unacknowledged by our laws; giving his Assent to their Acts of pretended Legislation:—For Quartering large bodies of armed troops among us:—For protecting them, by a mock Trial, from punishment for any Murders which they should commit on the Inhabitants of these States:—For cutting off our Trade with all parts of the world:— For imposing Taxes on us without our Consent:—For depriving us in

1. George III reigned as king from 1760 until 1820.—*Editor.*
2. The British Parliament.—*Editor.*

many cases, of the benefits of Trial by Jury:—For transporting us beyond Seas to be tried for pretended offences:—For abolishing the free System of English Laws in a neighbouring Province, establishing therein an Arbitrary government, and enlarging its Boundaries so as to render it at once an example and fit instrument for introducing the same absolute rule into these Colonies:—For taking away our Charters, abolishing our most valuable Laws, and altering fundamentally the Forms of our Governments:— For suspending our own Legislatures and declaring themselves invested with power to legislate for us in all cases whatsoever.—He has abdicated Government here, by declaring us out of his Protection and waging War against us:—He has plundered our seas, ravaged our Coasts, burnt our towns, and destroyed the lives of our people.—He is at this time transporting large Armies of foreign Mercenaries[3] to compleat the works of death, desolation and tyranny, already begun with circumstances of Cruelty & perfidy scarcely paralleled in the most barbarous ages, and totally unworthy the Head of a civilized nation.—He has constrained our fellow Citizens taken Captive on the high Seas to bear Arms against their Country, to become the executioners of their friends and Brethren, or to fall themselves by their Hands.—He has excited domestic insurrections amongst us, and has endeavoured to bring on the inhabitants of our frontiers, the merciless Indian Savages, whose known rule of warfare, is an undistinguished destruction of all ages, sexes and conditions. In every stage of these Oppressions We have Petitioned for Redress in the most humble terms: Our repeated Petitions have been answered only by repeated injury. A Prince, whose character is thus marked by every act which may define a Tyrant, is unfit to be the ruler of a free people. Nor have We been wanting in attentions to our British brethren. We have warned them from time to time of attempts by their legislature to extend an unwarrantable jurisdiction over us. We have reminded them of the circumstances of our emigration and settlement here. We have appealed to their native justice and magnanimity, and we have conjured them by the ties of our common kindred to disavow these usurpations, which, would inevitably interrupt our connections and correspondence. They too have been deaf to the voice of justice and of consanguinity. We must, therefore, acquiesce in the necessity, which denounces our Separation, and hold them, as we hold the rest of mankind, Enemies in War, in Peace Friends.

WE, THEREFORE, the Representatives of the UNITED STATES OF AMERICA, in General Congress Assembled, appealing to the Supreme Judge of the world for the rectitude of our intentions, do, in the Name and by Authority of the good People of these Colonies, solemnly publish and

---

3. German soldiers, principally Hessians, were hired by the British for colonial service. —Editor.

declare, That these United Colonies are, and of Right ought to be FREE AND INDEPENDENT STATES; that they are Absolved from all Allegiance to the British Crown, and that all political connection between them and the State of Great Britain, is and ought to be totally dissolved; and that as Free and Independent States, they have full Power to levy War, conclude Peace, contract Alliances, establish Commerce, and to do all other Acts and Things which Independent States may of right do.—And for the support of this Declaration, with a firm reliance on the protection of divine Providence, we mutually pledge to each other our Lives, our Fortunes and our sacred Honor.

Thomas Paine
(1737–1809)

THOMAS PAINE was born in Thetford, Norfolk County, England, and for many years pursued a variety of jobs and activities. Encouraged by Benjamin Franklin, he came to America and settled in Philadelphia in 1774. Paine soon became one of the great voices of the American Revolution, first as an editor of the *Pennsylvania Journal* (1775–1776), but most notably as the author of *Common Sense* (1776) and *The American Crisis* (1776–1783). Upon the close of the American Revolution, Paine involved himself in the French Revolution and again wrote another significant political essay, *The Rights of Man* (1791–1792). In the last years of his life Paine was the frequent victim of poverty and ostracism; he died in New Rochelle, New York.

"Thoughts on the Peace, and the Probable Advantages Thereof" is the penultimate of sixteen pamphlets collectively known as *The American Crisis*. The first pamphlet originally appeared in the *Pennsylvania Journal* on December 19, 1776. "Thoughts on the Peace" is dated April 19, 1783, which was the eighth anniversary of the Battle of Lexington and Concord, when "the shot heard 'round the world" was fired.

THOUGHTS ON THE PEACE, AND THE PROBABLE ADVANTAGES THEREOF

"The times that tried men's souls,"[1] are over—and the greatest and completest revolution the world ever knew, gloriously and happily accomplished.

But to pass from the extremes of danger to safety—from the tumult of war to the tranquillity of peace, though sweet in contemplation, requires a gradual composure of the senses to receive it. Even calmness has the power of stunning, when it opens too instantly upon us. The long and raging hurricane that should cease in a moment, would leave us in a state rather of wonder than enjoyment; and some moments of recollection must pass, before we could be capable of tasting the felicity of repose. There are but few instances, in which the mind is fitted for sudden transitions: it takes in its pleasures by reflection and comparison and those must have time to act, before the relish for new scenes is complete.

In the present case—the mighty magnitude of the object—the various uncertainties of fate it has undergone—the numerous and complicated dangers we have suffered or escaped—the eminence we now stand on, and the vast prospect before us, must all conspire to impress us with contemplation.

To see it in our power to make a world happy—to teach mankind the art of being so—to exhibit, on the theatre of the universe a character hitherto unknown—and to have, as it were, a new creation intrusted to our hands, are honors that command reflection, and can neither be too highly estimated, nor too gratefully received.

In this pause then of recollection—while the storm is ceasing, and the

---

1. Paine is here referring to the opening sentence of Pamphlet No. 1 of *The American Crisis:* "These are the times that try men's souls."—*Editor.*

long agitated mind vibrating to a rest, let us look back on the scenes we have passed, and learn from experience what is yet to be done.

Never, I say, had a country so many openings to happiness as this. Her setting out in life, like the rising of a fair morning, was unclouded and promising. Her cause was good. Her principles just and liberal. Her temper serene and firm. Her conduct regulated by the nicest steps, and everything about her wore the mark of honor. It is not every country (perhaps there is not another in the world) that can boast so fair an origin. Even the first settlement of America corresponds with the character of the revolution. Rome, once the proud mistress of the universe, was originally a band of ruffians. Plunder and rapine made her rich, and her oppression of millions made her great. But America need never be ashamed to tell her birth, nor relate the stages by which she rose to empire.

The remembrance, then, of what is past, if it operates rightly, must inspire her with the most laudable of all ambition, that of adding to the fair fame she began with. The world has seen her great in adversity; struggling, without a thought of yielding, beneath accumulated difficulties, bravely, nay proudly, encountering distress, and rising in resolution as the storm increased. All this is justly due to her, for her fortitude has merited the character. Let, then, the world see that she can bear prosperity: and that her honest virtue in time of peace, is equal to the bravest virtue in time of war.

She is now descending to the scenes of quiet and domestic life. Not beneath the cypress shade of disappointment, but to enjoy in her own land, and under her own vine, the sweet of her labors, and the reward of her toil.—In this situation, may she never forget that a fair national reputation is of as much importance as independence. That it possesses a charm that wins upon the world, and makes even enemies civil. That it gives a dignity which is often superior to power, and commands reverence where pomp and splendor fail.

It would be a circumstance ever to be lamented and never to be forgotten, were a single blot, from any cause whatever, suffered to fall on a revolution, which to the end of time must be an honor to the age that accomplished it: and which has contributed more to enlighten the world, and diffuse a spirit of freedom and liberality among mankind, than any human event (if this may be called one) that ever preceded it.

It is not among the least of the calamities of a long continued war, that it unhinges the mind from those nice sensations which at other times appear so amiable. The continual spectacle of woe blunts the finer feelings, and the necessity of bearing with the sight, renders it familiar. In like manner, are many of the moral obligations of society weakened, till the custom of acting by necessity becomes an apology, where it is truly a crime. Yet let but a nation conceive rightly of its character, and it will be chastely just in protecting it. None ever began with a fairer than America and none can be under a greater obligation to preserve it.

The debt which America has contracted, compared with the cause she has gained, and the advantages to flow from it, ought scarcely to be mentioned. She has it in her choice to do, and to live as happily as she pleases. The world is in her hands. She has no foreign power to monopolize her commerce, perplex her legislation, or control her prosperity. The struggle is over, which must one day have happened, and, perhaps, never could have happened at a better time.[2] And instead of a domineering master, she has gained an *ally* whose exemplary greatness, and universal liberality, have extorted a confession even from her enemies.

With the blessings of peace, independence, and an universal commerce, the states, individually and collectively, will have leisure and opportunity to regulate and establish their domestic concerns, and to put it beyond the power of calumny to throw the least reflection on their honor. Character is much easier kept than recovered, and that man, if any such there be, who, from sinister views, or littleness of soul, lends unseen his hand to injure it, contrives a wound it will never be in his power to heal.

As we have established an inheritance for posterity, let that inheritance descend, with every mark of an honorable conveyance. The little it will cost, compared with the worth of the states, the greatness of the object, and the value of the national character, will be a profitable exchange.

But that which must more forcibly strike a thoughtful, penetrating mind, and which includes and renders easy all inferior concerns, is the UNION OF THE STATES. On this our great national character depends. It is this which must give us importance abroad and security at home. It is through this only that we are, or can be, nationally known in the world; it is the flag of the United States which renders our ships and commerce safe on the seas, or in a foreign port. Our Mediterranean passes must be

2. That the revolution began at the exact period of time best fitted to the purpose, is sufficiently proved by the event.—But the great hinge on which the whole machine turned, is the *Union of the States:* and this union was naturally produced by the inability of any one state to support itself against any foreign enemy without the assistance of the rest.

Had the states severally been less able than they were when the war began, their united strength would not have been equal to the undertaking, and they must in all human probability have failed.—And, on the other hand, had they severally been more able, they might not have seen, or, what is more, might not have felt the necessity of uniting: and, either by attempting to stand alone or in small confederacies, would have been separately conquered.

Now, as we cannot see a time (and many years must pass away before it can arrive) when the strength of any one state, or several united, can be equal to the whole of the present United States, and as we have seen the extreme difficulty of collectively prosecuting the war to a successful issue, and preserving our national importance in the world, therefore, from the experience we have had, and the knowledge we have gained, we must, unless we make a waste of wisdom, be strongly impressed with the

obtained under the same style. All our treaties, whether of alliance, peace, or commerce, are formed under the sovereignty of the United States, and Europe knows us by no other name or title.

The division of the empire into states is for our own convenience, but abroad this distinction ceases. The affairs of each state are local. They can go on further than to itself. And were the whole worth of even the richest of them expended in revenue, it would not be sufficient to support sovereignty against a foreign attack. In short, we have no other national sovereignty than as United States. It would even be fatal for us if we had— too expensive to be maintained, and impossible to be supported. Individuals, or individual states, may call themselves what they please; but the world, and especially the world of enemies, is not to be held in awe by the whistling of a name. Sovereignty must have power to protect all the parts that compose and constitute it: and as UNITED STATES we are equal to the importance of the title, but otherwise we are not. Our union, well and wisely regulated and cemented, is the cheapest way of being great—the easiest way of being powerful, and the happiest invention in government which the circumstances of America can admit of.—Because it collects from each state, that which, by being inadequate, can be of no use to it, and forms an aggregate that serves for all.

The states of Holland are an unfortunate instance of the effects of individual sovereignty. Their disjointed condition exposes them to numerous intrigues, losses, calamities, and enemies; and the almost impossibility of bringing their measures to a decision, and that decision into execution, is to them, and would be to us, a source of endless misfortune.

It is with confederated states as with individuals in society; something must be yielded up to make the whole secure. In this view of things we gain by what we give, and draw an annual interest greater than the capital. —I ever feel myself hurt when I hear the union, that great palladium of

---

advantage, as well as the necessity of strengthening that happy union which had been our salvation, and without which we should have been a ruined people.

While I was writing this note, I cast my eye on the pamphlet, *Common Sense*, from which I shall make an extract, as it exactly applies to the case. It is as follows:

"I have never met with a man, either in England, or America, who has not confessed it as his opinion that a separation between the countries would take place one time or other; and there is no instance in which we have shown less judgment, than in endeavoring to describe what we call the ripeness or fitness of the continent for independence.

"As all men allow the measure, and differ only in their opinion of the time, let us, in order to remove mistakes, take a general survey of things, and endeavor, if possible, to find out the *very time*. But we need not to go far, the inquiry ceases at once, for, *the time has found us*. The general concurrence, the glorious union of all things prove the fact.

"It is not in numbers, but in a union, that our great strength lies. The continent is just arrived at that pitch of strength, in which no single colony is able to support itself, and the whole, when united, can accomplish the matter; and either more or less than this, might be fatal in its effects."—*Author*.

our liberty and safety, the least irreverently spoken of. It is the most sacred thing in the constitution of America, and that which every man should be most proud and tender of. Our citizenship in the United States is our national character. Our citizenship in any particular state is only our local distinction. By the latter we are known at home, by the former to the world. Our great title is AMERICANS—our inferior one varies with the place.

So far as my endeavors could go, they have all been directed to conciliate the affections, unite the interests, and draw and keep the mind of the country together; and the better to assist in this foundation work of the revolution, I have avoided all places of profit or office, either in the state I live in, or in the United States;[3] kept myself at a distance from all parties and party connections, and even disregarded all private and inferior concerns: and when we take into view the great work which we have gone through, and feel, as we ought to feel, the just importance of it, we shall then see, that the little wranglings and indecent contentions of personal parley, are as dishonorable to our characters, as they are injurious to our repose.

It was the cause of America that made me an author. The force with which it struck my mind, and the dangerous condition the country appeared to me in, by courting an impossible and an unnatural reconciliation with those who were determined to reduce her, instead of striking out into the only line that could cement and save her, A DECLARATION OF INDEPENDENCE, made it impossible for me, feeling as I did, to be silent: and if, in the course of more than seven years, I have rendered her any service, I have likewise added something to the reputation of literature, by freely and disinterestedly employing it in the great cause of mankind, and showing that there may be genius without prostitution.

Independence always appeared to me practicable and probable, provided the sentiment of the country could be formed and held to the object: and there is no instance in the world, where a people so extended, and wedded to former habits of thinking, and under such a variety of circumstances, were so instantly and effectually pervaded, by a turn in politics, as in the case of independence; and who supported their opinions, undiminished, through such a succession of good and ill fortune, till they crowned it with success.

But as the scenes of war are closed, and every man preparing for home and happier times, I therefore take my leave of the subject. I have most sincerely followed it from beginning to end, and through all its turns and windings: and whatever country I may hereafter be in, I shall always feel an honest pride at the part I have taken and acted, and a gratitude to nature and providence for putting it in my power to be of some use to mankind.

3. Some years earlier Paine had served as the Secretary of the Congressional Committee of Foreign Affairs and Clerk of the Pennsylvania legislature.—*Editor.*

William Ellery Channing
(1780–1842)

WILLIAM ELLERY CHANNING was born in Newport, Rhode Island, and graduated from Harvard College in 1798. A leading advocate of Unitarianism, he served as pastor of the Federal Street Church in Boston from 1803 until his death. His sermons and pamphlets were continually directed to the major social issues of his time.

The title "Sermon on the War of 1812" has been assigned to this selection by the editor. On June 18, 1812, the United States declared war on Great Britain. The issues, both varied and complex, were summed up in the slogan "Free Trade and Sailor's Rights." In 1814, the Treaty of Ghent was signed, ending two and a half years of war.

SERMON ON
THE WAR OF 1812

In all circumstances, at all times, war is to be deprecated. The evil passions which it excites, its ravages, its bloody conflicts, the distress and terror which it carries into domestic life, the tears which it draws from the widow and fatherless, all render war a tremendous scourge.

There are indeed conditions in which war is justifiable, is necessary. It may be the last and only method of repelling lawless ambition, and of defending invaded liberty and essential rights. It may be the method which God's providence points out by furnishing the means of success. In these cases we must not shrink from war; though even in these we should deeply lament the necessity of shedding human blood. In such wars our country claims and deserves our prayers, our cheerful services, the sacrifice of wealth and even of life. In such wars, we have one consolation, when our friends fall on the field of battle; we know that they have fallen in a just cause. Such conflicts, which our hearts and consciences approve, are suited to call forth generous sentiments, to breathe patriotism and fortitude through a community. Could I view the war in which we are engaged in this light, with what different feelings, my friends, should I address you! We might then look up to God and commit to him our country with a holy confidence. But, in our present state, what can I say to you? I would, but I cannot address you in the language of encouragement. We are precipitated into a war, which, I think, cannot be justified, and a war which promises not a benefit, that I can discover, to this country or to the world.

A solemn question now offers itself. What conduct belongs to a good citizen in our present trying condition? To this subject I call your serious attention.

Our condition induces me to begin with urging on you the important duty of cherishing respect for civil government, and a spirit of obedience to the laws. I am sensible, that many whom I address consider themselves as called to oppose the measures of our present rulers. Let this opposition breathe nothing of insubordination, impatience of authority, or love of change. It becomes you to remember, that government is a divine institution, essential to the improvement of our nature, the spring of industry and enterprise, the shield of property and life, the refuge of the weak and oppressed. It is to the security which laws afford, that we owe the successful application of human powers. Government, though often perverted by ambition and other selfish passions, still holds a distinguished rank among those influences by which man has been rescued from barbarism, and conducted through the ruder stages of society to the habits of order, the diversified employments and dependencies, the refined and softened manners, the intellectual, moral, and religious improvements of the age in which we live. We are bound to respect government, as the great security for social happiness; and we should carefully cherish that habit of obedience to the laws, without which the ends of government cannot be accomplished. All wanton opposition to the constituted authorities; all censures of rulers, originating in a factious, aspiring, or envious spirit; all unwillingness to submit to laws which are directed to the welfare of the community, should be rebuked and repressed by the frown of public indignation.

It is impossible that all the regulations of the wisest government should equally benefit every individual; and sometimes the general good will demand arrangements, which will interfere with the interests of particular members or classes of the nation. In such circumstances, the individual is bound to regard the inconveniences under which he suffers, as inseparable from a social, connected state, as the result of the condition which God has appointed, and not as the fault of his rulers; and he should cheerfully submit, recollecting how much more he receives from the community than he is called to resign to it. Disaffection towards a government which is administered with a view to the general welfare, is a great crime; and such opposition, even to a bad government, as springs from and spreads a restless temper, and unwillingness to yield to wholesome and necessary restraint, deserves no better name. In proportion as a people want a conscientious regard to the laws, and are prepared to evade them by fraud, or to arrest their operation by violence,—in that proportion they need and deserve an arbitrary government, strong enough to crush at a blow every symptom of opposition.

These general remarks on the duty of submission, are by no means designed to teach that rulers are never to be opposed. Because I wish to guard you against that turbulent and discontented spirit, which precipitates free communities into an anarchy, and thus prepares them for chains, you will not consider me as asserting that all opposition to government, whatever be the occasion, or whatever the form, is to be branded as a crime. The citizen has rights as well as duties. Government is instituted for one and a single end, the benefit of the governed, the protection, peace, and welfare of society; and when it is perverted to other objects, to purposes of avarice, ambition, or party spirit, we are authorized and even bound to make such opposition, as is suited to restore it to its proper end, to render it as pure as the imperfection of our nature and state will admit.

The Scriptures have sometimes been thought to enjoin an unqualified, unlimited subjection to the "higher powers"; but in the passages which seem so to teach, it is supposed that these powers are "ministers of God for good," are a terror to evil doers, and an encouragement to those that do well. When a government wants this character, when it becomes an engine of oppression, the Scriptures enjoin subjection no longer. Expediency may make it our duty to obey, but the government has lost its rights; it can no longer urge its claims as an ordinance of God.

There have, indeed, been times, when sovereigns have demanded subjection as an inalienable right, and when the superstition of subjects has surrounded them with a mysterious sanctity, with a majesty approaching the divine. But these days have past. Under the robe of office, we, my hearers, have learned to see a man like ourselves. There is no such sacredness in rulers, as forbids scrutiny into their motives, or condemnation of their measures. In leaving the common walks of life, they leave none of their imperfections behind them. Power has even a tendency to corrupt, to feed an irregular ambition, to harden the heart against the claims and sufferings of mankind. Rulers are not to be viewed with a malignant jealousy; but they ought to be inspected with a watchful, undazzled eye. Their virtues and services are to be rewarded with generous praise; and their crimes, and arts, and usurpations, should be exposed with a fearless sincerity, to the indignation of an injured people. We are not to be factious, and neither are we to be servile. With a sincere disposition to obey, should be united a firm purpose not to be oppressed.

So far is an existing government from being clothed with an inviolable sanctity, that the citizen, in particular circumstances, acquires the right, not only of remonstrating, but of employing force for its destruction. This right accrues to him, when a government wantonly disregards the ends of social union; when it threatens the subversion of national liberty and happiness; and when no relief but force remains to the suffering community. This, however, is a right which cannot be exercised with too much deliberation. Subjects should very slowly yield to the conviction, that rulers have that settled hostility to their interests, which authorizes violence. They must not indulge a spirit of complaint, and suffer their passions to pronounce on their wrongs. They must remember, that the best government will partake the imperfection of all human institutions, and that if the ends of the social compact are in any tolerable degree accomplished, they will be mad indeed to hazard the blessings they possess, for the possibility of greater good.

Resistance of established power is so great an evil, civil commotion excites such destructive passions, the result is so tremendously uncertain, that every milder method of relief should first be tried, and fairly tried. The last dreadful resort is never justifiable, until the injured members of the community are brought to despair of other relief, and are so far united in views and purposes as to be authorized in the hope of success. Civil commotion should be viewed as the worst of national evils, with the single exception of slavery. I know that this country has passed through one civil war, without experiencing the calamitous consequences of which I have spoken. But let us not forget, that this was a civil war of a very peculiar character. The government which we shook off was not seated in the midst of us. Our struggle was that of nation with nation, rather than of fellow-citizens with one another. Our manners and habits tended to give a considerateness and a stability to the public mind, which can hardly be expected in a future struggle. And, in addition to these favorable circumstances, we were favored by Heaven with a leader of incorruptible integrity, of unstained purity; a patriot who asked no glory, but that of delivering his country, who desired to reign only in the hearts of a free and happy people, whose disinterestedness awed and repressed the selfish and ambitious, who inspired universal confidence, and thus was a centre and bond of union to the minds of men in the most divided and distracted periods of our country. The name of WASHINGTON I may pronounce with reverence even in the temple of the Almighty; and it is a name which revives the sinking spirits in this day of our declining glory. From a revolution, conducted by such a man, under such circumstances, let no conclusions be hastily drawn on the subject of civil commotion.

It becomes us to rejoice, my friends, that we live under a constitution, one great design of which is, to prevent the necessity of appealing to force, to give the people an opportunity of removing, without violence, those rulers from whom they suffer or apprehend an invasion of rights. This is one of the principal advantages of a republic over an absolute government. In a despotism, there is no remedy for oppression but force. The subject cannot influence public affairs, but by convulsing the state. With us, rulers may be changed, without the horrors of a revolution. A republican government secures to its subjects this immense privilege, by confirming to them two most important rights,—the right of suffrage, and the right of discussing with freedom the conduct of rulers. The value of these rights in affording a peaceful method of redressing public grievances, cannot be expressed, and the duty of maintaining them, of never surrendering them, cannot be too strongly urged. Resign either of these, and no way of escape from oppression will be left you, but civil commotion.

From the important place which these rights hold in a republican government, you should consider yourselves bound to support every citizen in the lawful exercise of them, especially when an attempt is made to wrest them from any by violent means. At the present time, it is particularly your duty to guard, with jealousy, the right of expressing with freedom your honest convictions respecting the measures of your rulers. Without this, the right of election is not worth possessing. If public abuses may not be exposed, their authors will never be driven from power. Freedom of opinion, of speech, and of the press, is our most valuable privilege, the very soul of republican institutions, the safeguards of all other rights. We may learn its value if we reflect that there is nothing which tyrants so much dread. They anxiously fetter the press; they scatter spies through society, that the murmurs, anguish, and indignation of their oppressed subjects may be smothered in their own breasts; that no generous sentiment may be nourished by sympathy and mutual confidence. Nothing awakens and improves men so much as free communication of thoughts and feelings. Nothing can give to public sentiment that correctness which is essential to the prosperity of a Commonwealth, but the free circulation of truth, from the lips and pens of the wise and good. If such men abandon the right of free discussion; if, awed by threats, they suppress their convictions; if rulers succeed in silencing every voice but that which approves them; if nothing reaches the people but what will lend support to men in power,—farewell to liberty. The form of a free government may remain, but the life, the soul, the substance is fled.

If these remarks be just, nothing ought to excite greater indignation and alarm than the attempts which have lately been made, to destroy the freedom of the press. We have lived to hear the strange doctrine, that to expose the measures of rulers is treason; and we have lived to see this doctrine carried into practice. We have seen a savage populace excited and let loose on men whose crime consisted in bearing testimony against the present war; and let loose, not merely to waste their property, but to tear them from the refuge which the magistrate had afforded, and to shed their blood. In this, and in other events, there have been symptoms of a purpose to terrify into silence those who disapprove the calamitous war under which we suffer; to deprive us of the only method which is left, of obtaining a wiser and better government. The cry has been, that war is declared, and all opposition should therefore be hushed. A sentiment more unworthy of a free country can hardly be propagated. If this doctrine be admitted, rulers have only to declare war, and they are screened at once from scrutiny. At the very time when they have armies at command, when their patronage is most extended, and their power most formidable, not a word of warning, of censure, of alarm must be heard. The press, which is to expose inferior abuses, must not utter one rebuke, one indignant complaint, although our best interests and most valuable rights are put to hazard, by an unnecessary war! Admit this doctrine, let rulers once know, that, by placing the country in a state of war, they place themselves beyond the only power they dread, the power of free discussion, and we may expect war without end. Our peace and all our interests require, that a different sentiment should prevail. We should teach our present and all future rulers, that there is no measure for which they must render so solemn an account to their constituents, as for a declaration of war; that no measure will be so freely, so fully discussed; and that no administration can succeed in persuading this people to exhaust their treasure and blood in supporting war, unless it be palpably necessary and just. In war, then, as in peace, assert the freedom of speech and of the press. Cling to this as the bulwark of all your rights and privileges.

But, my friends, I should not be faithful, were I only to call you to hold fast this freedom. I would still more earnestly exhort you not to abuse it. Its abuse may be as fatal to our country as its relinquishment. If undirected, unrestrained by principle, the press, instead of enlightening, depraves the public mind; and, by its licentiousness, forges chains for itself and for the community. The right of free discussion is not the right of uttering what we please. Let nothing be spoken or written but truth. The influence of the press is exceedingly diminished by its gross and frequent misrepresentations. Each party listens with distrust to the statements of the other; and the consequence is, that the progress of truth is slow, and sometimes wholly obstructed. Whilst we encourage the free expression of opinion, let us unite in fixing the brand of infamy on falsehood and slander, wherever they originate, whatever be the cause they are designed to maintain.

But it is not enough that truth be told. It should be told for a good end; not to irritate, but to convince; not to inflame the bad passions, but to sway the judgment and to awaken sentiments of patriotism. Unhappily the press seems now to be chiefly prized as an instrument of exasperation. Those who have embraced error, are hardened in their principles by the reproachful epithets heaped on them by their adversaries. I do not mean by this, that political discussion is to be conducted tamely, that no sensibility is to be expressed, no indignation to be poured forth on wicked men and wicked deeds. But this I mean—that we shall deliberately inquire, whether indignation be deserved, before we express it; and the object of expressing it should ever be, not to infuse ill will, rancor, and fury into the minds of men, but to excite an enlightened and conscientious opposition to injurious measures.

Every good man must mourn that so much is continually published among us, for no other apparent end than to gratify the malevolence of one party, by wounding the feelings of the opposite. The consequence is, that an alarming degree of irritation exists in our country. Fellow-citizens burn with mutual hatred, and some are evidently ripe for outrage and violence. In this feverish state of the public mind, we are not to relinquish free discussion, but every man should feel the duty of speaking and writing with deliberation. It is the time to be firm without passion. No menace should be employed to provoke opponents, no defiance hurled, no language used, which will, in any measure, justify the ferocious in appealing to force.

The sum of my remarks is this. It is your duty to hold fast and to assert with firmness those truths and principles on which the welfare of your country seems to depend, but do this with calmness, with a love of peace, without ill will and revenge. Use every opportunity of allaying animosities. Discourage, in decided and open language, that rancor, malignity, and unfeeling abuse, which so often find their way into our public prints. Remember, that in proportion as a people become enslaved to their passions, they fall into the hands of the aspiring and unprincipled; and that a corrupt government, which has an interest in deceiving the people, can desire nothing more favorable to their purposes, than a frenzied state of the public mind.

My friends, in this day of discord, let us cherish and breathe around us the benevolent spirit of Christianity. Let us reserve to ourselves this consolation, that we have added no fuel to the flames, no violence to the storms, which threaten to desolate our country. Though dishonored, though endangered, it is still our country. Let us not forsake it in this evil day. Let us hold fast the inheritance of our civil and religious liberties, which we have received from our fathers, sealed and hallowed by their blood. That these blessings may not be lost, let us labor to improve public sentiment, and to exalt men of wisdom and virtue to power. Let it be our labor to establish in ourselves and in our fellow-citizens the empire of true religion. Let us remember that there is no foundation of public liberty, but public virtue, that there is no method of obtaining God's protection but adherence to his laws.

Let us not despair of our country. If all that we wish cannot be done for the state, still something may be done. In the good principles, in the love of order and liberty, by which so many of our citizens are distinguished; in the tried virtue, deliberate prudence, and unshaken firmness of the Chief Magistrate, whom God in his great goodness has given to this Commonwealth; in the value of the blessings which are at stake; in the peculiar kindness which God has manifested towards our fathers and ourselves, we have motives, encouragements, and solemn obligations to resolute, persevering exertion in our different spheres, and according to our different capacities, for the public good. Thus faithful to ourselves and our country, and using vigorously every righteous means for restoring peace and confirming freedom, we may confidently leave the issue to the wise and holy providence of Him who cannot err, and who, we are assured, will accept and reward every conscientious effort for his own glory and the good of mankind.

Orestes Brownson
(1803–1876)

ORESTES BROWNSON was born in Stockbridge, Vermont. He experimented with a number of religious views, finally settling on his own kind of Catholicism. Most of his life was devoted to an analysis of a wide range of social and religious questions, first as editor of the *Democratic Review* (1842–1844), and most importantly as the editor of *Brownson's Quarterly Review* (1844–1864, 1873–1875).

"Demagoguism" was first published in *Brownson's Quarterly Review* in January of 1844.

DEMAGOGUISM

It is universally conceded, that republics, especially democracies, can subsist only by means of the virtue and intelligence of the people; but it does not appear to have been very generally considered, that democracies, or popular forms of government, which, through suffrage and eligibility, admit the great mass of the population to a share in the administration, have a strong tendency to counteract the very virtues on which their permanence and utility depend.

Our political history, we think, demonstrates this latter position, beyond the reach of cavil or doubt, to all who have accustomed themselves to look a little below the surface of things. Here, in this matter, the boasted maxim of political economy, that demand creates a supply, does not hold good. Looking at what we were in the beginning, and at what we now are, it may well be doubted, whether another country in Christendom has so rapidly declined as we have, in the stern and rigid virtues, in the high-toned and manly principles of conduct, essential to the stability and wise administration of popular government.

We commenced our national existence with many peculiar advantages, and advantages wholly independent of our peculiar political institutions. We began our labors on a virgin soil, in a new country, of vast extent, great internal resources, and remote from the vicious and corrupting examples of the Old World. We were, for the most part, an agricultural people, sparse, not crowded into towns and cities, with plenty of new and fertile lands, easy to be obtained, and yielding a rich and immediate reward to the cultivator. Our wants were few, our manners and tastes were simple, and life with us was uniform, and little exposed to vicious temptations. Government had little to do, for all moved on harmoniously, as it were, of itself. It must have been a bad government, indeed, that could at once, have corrupted us, and hindered our growth and prosperity. So were we in the outset; but so are we no longer. Our population has become comparatively dense; our new lands are exhausted, or have receded so far in the distance as to be no longer of easy access, or attainable at all by the inhabitants of the older states, who have not some little capital in advance. We have become a populous and a wealthy country, a great manufacturing and trading people, as well as a great agricultural people; we are separating more and more, capital and labor, and have the beginnings of a constantly increasing *operative* class, unknown to our fathers, and doomed always to be dependent on employment by the class who represent the capital of the country, for the means of subsistence, and therefore to die of hunger and nakedness, when employment fails them; we are brought, by improvements in steam navigation, alongside of the Old World, into immediate contact with its vicious and corrupt civilization; we are no longer isolated, no longer a simple, primitive people; our old manners have passed, or are rapidly passing, away; our increasing wealth brings in with it luxury, poverty, and distress, as well as refinement and a more general culture.

Here is what we have become. It is now, under these altered circumstances both of the country and the people, that the virtues of our institutions are put to the test. These institutions have as yet had no severe trial. The peculiar advantages of our position are sufficient to account for all the superiority, under a moral and social point of view, we have hitherto exhibited. But if, with these advantages, our institutions have suffered us so to deteriorate, will they suffice to restore us to our former elevation? Nay, if with these advantages, we have, under these institutions, fallen nearly to a level with the Old World, and shown a rapid decline in the stern and rigid virtues, in the high-toned and manly qualities we are accustomed to boast in our ancestors, unparalleled in other Christian nations, not excepting even England, to what can we attribute so lamentable a fact, but to our peculiar institutions themselves? The result, to which we have come, is attributable to no slight or accidental cause, but to a deep-seated and constantly operating cause, and this cause can be found nowhere, but in our peculiar form of government.

In speaking of the decline we have experienced in the stern, rigid, high-toned virtues of our population, we are far from implying, or wishing to imply, that we have fallen below even the more advanced nations of the Old World; and, in assuming that our political institutions, taken independently of the accidental advantages of our position, have not produced such unmixed good as our noisy politicians pretend, we are equally far from implying, or wishing to imply, that we are not even yet in a moral and social condition much superior to that of any other people. What we mean to assert is that, under a moral and social point of view, we have not maintained our former relative superiority. We are still in advance of the Old World, but by no means so far in advance as we were in the out-set; and considering the many obstacles the several nations of the Old World have had to encounter, and the much we have had in our peculiar position in our favor, we have, relatively speaking, fallen behind them, and show a deterioration, of which they set us no example. France, Germany, England, even Spain, have, during the period of our national existence, made no inconsiderable efforts at national regeneration, and each and all of them have, we believe, commenced the upward movement, while we alone have actually deteriorated.

Assuming this to be a fact, there must be, in the nature of our peculiar institutions, some inherent and permanent cause of this deterioration. And this we solemnly believe to be the case. In this world, good and evil grow together, and often spring from the same root. The matter of virtue and vice, as Milton has remarked, is not unfrequently the same. As you recede from one evil, you strike upon another; and as you secure a new advan-tage, you expose yourself to a new danger. This has been our experience as a people. We have escaped many, perhaps the heaviest, of the political evils of the Old World; but, in return, have exposed ourselves to evils, from which the Old World is comparatively free. These evils, to which we have exposed ourselves, are by no means so great, or so difficult to guard against, or to counteract, as to induce us, for a moment, to balance our institutions with those of any other people; or to ask ourselves, if we have done wisely in adopting, or shall do wisely in sustaining them. With all the evils to which they expose us, they are the best, at least for us, that the world has ever seen, or that we can even conceive of. All we insist on is, that they do expose us to evils, which demand our sleepless vigilance, and all our wisdom and energy, to counteract. They will not, as it were, go of themselves, of themselves create all the virtue essential to their wise and just administration.

A delusion had seized the world about the time of our national birth, that all the evils the human race suffers are owing to bad government, and that a wisely constituted government will, as it were, of itself cure them. Hence we fell into the mistake of feeling that our institutions would take care of themselves, and work out for us, without any special agency of our own, that higher social good towards which our minds and hearts were turned. But bad government itself must have a cause, and can have no cause but the ignorance, the vice, the selfishness, and the indolence of the people; and the best of institutions will produce only mischievous results, if not wisely and virtuously administered; and wisdom and virtue, in our case, to secure the right sort of administration, must not only be generally diffused among the people, but be brought to bear directly on the adminis-tration itself.

Another delusion, at the same epoch, seized the more advanced nations of Christendom, namely, that the people could MAKE the constitution, and that nothing was wanting to secure its successful practical working, but to intrust it to the care of the people. The desideratum of the time was to get rid of bad governments, of tyrannical and oppressive rulers. It was felt that the people, if admitted into the government, would have so deep an interest in good government, that they would never submit to bad government, or suffer the government to become bad, and that their own interest would lead them to resist all tyrannical and oppressive magistrates, and to invest none with power who would not exercise it for the common good. All this was plausible, and taking; but it obviously placed the dependence for good government, not on the virtue of the people, on their sense of duty, and power of sacrifice, but on their *sense of interest*. Their own sense of their own interest would lead them to institute good government, and to insist on wise and equitable administration. But, in throwing a people back upon their sense of their own interest, leaving them, nay, teaching them, to be governed by their own views of their own interest, do we not necessarily destroy the very virtues essential to the maintenance of wise and good government? Do we not set up interest as the ruling motive? And when interest becomes the ruling motive of a people, will not each individual struggle, not to administer the government for the good of all, but to make it a machine for promoting his own private ends?

The principle of the political order sought to be introduced, and on which the statesmen and politicians relied for securing the practical benefits to be expected from government, was to pit the selfishness of one against the equal selfishness of another; or, as we may express it, UNIVERSAL COMPETITION. The principle of competition is selfishness. Leave, then, free scope to the selfishness of all, and the selfishness of each will neutralize the selfishness of each, and we shall have for result—eternal justice, wise and equitable government, shedding its blessings, like the dews of heaven, upon all, without distinction of rank or condition! Truly, this were putting vice to a noble use, and proposing a transmutation of the base metals into the precious, far surpassing that dreamed of by the old alchymists, in their insane pursuit of the philosopher's stone. But the success of the theory would not have given the result anticipated. From absolute negation, how obtain an affirmative? Assuming the absolute equality of all, and that in all cases the selfishness of one will exactly balance the selfishness of another, the result will be zero, that is to say, absolutely nothing. But assuming the *inequality* of the social elements, and that the selfishness of one is not in all cases the exact measure of the selfishness of another, then they in whom selfishness is the strongest will gain the preponderance, and, having the power, must, being governed only by selfishness, wield the government for their own private ends. And this is precisely what has happened, and which a little reflection might have enabled any one to have foretold. The attempt to obtain wise and equitable government by means of universal competition, then, must always fail. But this is not the worst. It, being a direct appeal to selfishness, promotes the growth of selfishness, and therefore increases the very evil from which government is primarily needed to protect us.

Nor is this all. Alongside of this principle of universal competition, lay that of RESPONSIBILITY TO THE PEOPLE. Responsibility of the civil magistrate to the people was, no doubt, asserted with a good motive, for the purpose of establishing the right of the people to divest the agents of authority of all power, in case they abused it; and also as a restraint on these agents themselves, who, knowing that if they abused their trusts, the people could dismiss them, would be induced, by all their love of power and place, to use their power for the common good. Here, again, the same attempt to convert the base metals into the precious, to make selfishness produce the effects of the loftiest virtue. But the old alchymists did not discover the philosopher's stone. We have not yet discovered any method by which lead can be converted into silver or gold. Selfishness is selfishness, and will be selfish, say or do what we will. And therefore instead of taking care not to abuse its trusts, so as not to lose place or power, it only sets its wits at work to secure the confidence of the people, by professing the greatest respect for their virtue and intelligence, and a willingness at all times to bow to their will, and to do all their bidding. Selfishness became a courtier, and sought to gain its end by flattering the sovereign people, and *seeming* to have no interest but theirs. It would not tyrannize and oppress with the strong hand, by bidding defiance to popular power; but it would do it by sly cunning, by subtle arts, and plunder the people, and enrich itself, by their own consent, at least with their own hands. If it pleased the people and gained their confidence, it was enough; no matter by what means.

The result, therefore, of making all officers of government, and all aspirants to office, feel their responsibility to the people, has been simply to encourage DEMAGOGUISM, and to cover the land with swarms of greedy and unprincipled demagogues. To gain place or power, I must please the people; and the readiest way of pleasing the people, the only way practicable to selfishness, is to flatter them, to defer to them, to adopt their opinions, to take the law from them, and never to resist them, or seek to change their course, let it lead where it may. Selfishness then becomes a TIME-SERVER; seeks not for truth and justice, but for what is popular; asks not, What is right? but simply, What will the people say? It has no opinions of its own. It runs athwart no popular prejudice; treads on none of the people's corns; is non-committal on all points on which the public mind has not declared itself; and is tolerant to all incipient errors, for they may become popular to-morrow. It is prudent, sleek, decorous. It has no rough edges, no angular points, and thrusts its elbow into no man's ribs. Its face has a settled smile; and its voice is soft, gentle, insinuating. It is calm, dispassionate, mild, deliberate. It is free from rage, from hurry, and "bides its time." If it fails to-day, it will succeed to-morrow. "The sober second thought of the people" will set all right, and place it at the top of the ladder. Hence, all manly devotion to truth, all earnestness in the defence of the right, all firm resistance to popular error and delusion, all bold and vigorous efforts to advance the people, and carry on individual and social progress, are out of place, and must be quietly left by the way; for they might endanger our popularity, offend perhaps the majority, and prevent us from securing the objects of our ambition.

We draw here no fancy sketch; we are, unhappily, painting from the life. One sees the original everywhere. The evil has become great and menacing. We have lost our manliness; we have sacrificed our independence; we have become tame and servile, afraid to say that our souls are our own, till we have obtained permission of the public to say so, or at least till we have pretty well ascertained that it will not be *unpopular* to say so. The tameness and servility of American literature are almost universally admitted. It has no manliness, no reach, no depth, no aspiration. It seeks to win popular favor, not to correct public sentiment; to echo public opinion, not to form it.

Now this, we contend is a natural result of the principle of *responsibility to the people,* contended for by our politicians. If you repeat always to your statesmen "Remember your accountability to the *people*," you must expect them to ask always, not, What is right? but, What is popular? And when you have led your statesmen to do so, made popular opinion their guide, you have made it so for all who aspire to place or power; and then you have made it so for the great body of your whole community, and not in relation to politics only, but in relation to every department of life. Popularity will become the leading object of ambition, and popular opinion the standard of morality. The public will intervene everywhere. The minister of religion will court the public, and the pulpit will soften or suppress the unpopular truth. All will be done with a view to immediate popular effect; and what will not tend to secure immediate popularity will be looked upon as a blunder, or, at best, as a crime. In such a state as this, how can there be the virtue necessary to sustain wise, equitable, and efficient government? In such a state as this we indisputably are, and to such a state as this, if not our institutions themselves, at least our doctrines in regard to them, with which we commenced our political career, have a direct, if not an inevitable, tendency to reduce us. Here is the weak side of our political order, and here is what must always be the result of a political order, which rests for its support on selfishness, on interest, on universal competition, and responsibility to the popular will. Here is the danger to which we are particularly exposed, and against which, if we love our country, and desire the prevalence of justice, we must be always on our guard.

It is useless to undertake to deny what we have here stated, and useless to undertake to prove that popular governments have not a direct tendency to create a multitude of demagogues, and to make what is popular the standard of what is right or proper to be undertaken. Popular governments are favorable, by the freedom of competition they maintain, to commerce, to industry, to great material prosperity, *for a time*, so long as there remains a large body of the people as yet uncorrupted,—so long as the selfish principle they foster has not yet become universal. But as soon as this principle, on which they are founded, reaches the heart of the community, and the scramble for wealth, for place, and for power, affects all classes, and becomes universal, all sorts of prosperity come to a standstill, and the state falls to pieces by its own internal vice and rottenness. What are called free states are always marked by a sudden and surprising activity, by a sudden and surprising prosperity, and by almost as sudden and surprising a decline and fall. And this lies in the nature of things, unless, independent of the government proper, there be in the community a counteracting and conservative principle. On this point, if we will neglect the lessons of antiquity (for our experiment is not so new as we sometimes boast), we do not well to neglect the lessons of our own experience. No man can attentively study our political history, and analyze with some care our popular institutions, but must perceive and admit that our state contains the seeds of its own dissolution, and seeds which have already begun to germinate. Unless the tendency we have thus far obeyed can be arrested, and a stronger and more conservative principle be brought in to our relief, all hopes of a successful issue must be abandoned.

We feel how very unpalatable all this must be to our countrymen, and how ill it must be received. It will be easy to ascribe it to our diseased imagination, or disappointed ambition; it will be easy to ascribe it to a growing distrust of our institutions, to a hankering after other forms of government, or to a love of singularity, or of notoriety. All this it is easy to say, and all this unquestionably will be said, and believed by not a few. There are a thousand voices interested in silencing the still small voice of truth; and may do so. But, alas! the truth remains the same, and the evil exists not the less, conceal we it never so effectually from the eyes of the spectator. The evil is there. The cancer eats into the very vitals, and death must sooner or later ensue. We may say what we will of the physician who warns us of our danger, who bids us seize time by the forelock, and apply the remedy before it has become formidable; we may dismiss him and call in another who will tell us smooth things, that there is no danger, that we may eat, drink, dance, sing, and be merry as usual; but this will avail us nothing. The cancer is there, and eats, eats, never the less.

But we have not closed the catalogue of our dangers. The root of all is in the attempt, with a mere negative quantity to obtain a positive, out of selfishness to bring forth virtue. This attempt, as we have seen, makes selfishness the ruling principle of the whole community. The great object of action, then, so far as government is concerned, is to make it the means of promoting, not the public good, but private interest. But to suppose that it can promote equally the private interest of all, is absurd; or even of a majority. It can, in the nature of things, promote the private interest of only the few. Then there must be some contrivance by which the few can control its operations, and secure to themselves its advantages, in the language of the day, "the spoils." This contrivance we may express by the word PARTY. There may still be in the country some remains of virtue, some reminiscences of the doctrine, that we ought to seek the public good. They who share these reminiscences might, if free to act according to their own convictions and sense of duty, trouble us and thwart our schemes. We must control them by means of party organization and party usages, and substitute devotion to party for devotion to the public, and thus make even the virtues of the people subservient to our selfish purposes. Hence springs up a system of party tactics, from which this country has more to fear, than from any other cause whatever.

This system, if we have rightly learned it,—and we have learned it from the intimate personal associates of the distinguished man[1] who is at present its most brilliant representative,—is in substance this: In a republican government everything must be done by means of party. Our first effort therefore must be to get, and keep, our party in the majority. We must never propose any measure likely to throw it, or to keep it, in the minority. If we keep our party in the majority, we can from time to time through it propose and carry such measures as we may judge to be proper or expedient. Mark this. The *first* object is, not to find out and support what is for the public good, but by organization and discipline to get and keep our party in the ascendency. *After this*, if we can serve the public without falling into the minority, well and good; if not, why just as well and good, provided we only hold on—*to the offices*. Nothing can be worse than this. Regular organized parties, in a republican government, organized with a view to permanence, so as to make it the primary duty of the citizen to support them, are fraught with the greatest danger to liberty. They are contrivances to override the constitution, and to enable a minority to rule the majority. They are machines constructed for the express purpose of

---

1. The reference is to Martin Van Buren, eighth President of the United States (1837–1841).—*Editor.*

centralizing power for the express benefit of intriguing politicians, who by getting hold of the crank may work them as they please. The only parties really defensible in a free government are such as naturally and spontaneously spring up, and group themselves around different views of government policy. These come when they should, last as long as the difference of policy lasts, and then dissolve of themselves. They come, accomplish their object, and disappear.

But having determined that all is to be done by and through party, and that our primary duty is to labor for the organization and ascendency of our party, the next thing to be insisted on is, *Fidelity to the party, and strict adherence to its usages*,—the surrender of all individual opinions, convictions, and preferences to the decision of the party, which decision, be it understood, is always to be effected by the aforesaid politicians who have hold of the crank. This throws the whole business into the hands of central committees, and deprives the great mass of the citizens of all free voice in the determination of measures, or in the selection of candidates. These committees, often self-constituted, or, if not, chosen by a feeble minority, arrange every thing, and leave to the citizens at large, or to the great mass of the party, nothing to do but to accept their arrangements and support their nominations, or to assume the responsibility of throwing the government into the hands of the opposing party.

To keep the ranks of the party full, to prevent members from breaking away and asserting their independence, appeals are now made to the lowest and most corrupting passions of the human heart. The individual, who shows himself a little uneasy, or disposed to kick at the party traces, must be denounced, thrown over, and declared to be an enemy, and no longer entitled to the confidence of the party. Thus men must be kept in the party and faithful to its usages, decisions, and nominations, not by attachment to its principles and measures, but through fear that, if they assert their independence, they will lose their share of the "spoils."

Now, fasten this doctrine on the country, and let it become our settled mode of disposing of all political matters, and our liberties, and the whole action of the government, will be at the mercy of the sly, cunning, adroit, intriguing, selfish demagogues, whom our country, as we have seen, has a direct and strong tendency to multiply.

And here, we must be permitted to say, is a strong reason why the American people should pause and deliberate long before restoring Mr. Van Buren to the high office from which, in 1840, they so indignantly ejected him.[2] It cannot be denied that Mr. Van Buren is the most conspicuous representative of this system of party management, in the country.

---

2. James K. Polk, not Van Buren, received the nomination of the Democratic Party and became the eleventh President of the United States (1845–1849).—*Editor*

The system itself has been perfected, and to no inconsiderable extent was founded, by him and his more immediate political associates. He is intimately connected with it; owes to it all the political elevation he has ever received, and relies on it alone for his restoration to the presidency. He has no hope but in its influence; his restoration would therefore be a direct sanction of the system by the American people, and go far towards fastening it upon the country beyond the reach of future redress. In this view of the case, the reelection of Mr. Van Buren, whatever his personal worth, would be a dangerous precedent, and a most serious public calamity.

In 1840, such was the state of certain great public questions, and such Mr. Van Buren's position, that all those of us, who felt deeply the importance of completing the financial policy commenced under his administration, were obliged either to vote for him, or to vote against our principles. But there is no necessity of driving us again to this severe alternative. Moreover, his defeat was not an unmixed evil, for it was not wholly owing to the opposition of the American people to the leading measures, or rather *measure*—for it had but one—of his administration; but to no inconsiderable extent, to the obnoxious system of party management he represented. We are not sure but the determination to get rid of that system—the caucus system—had as much to do in effecting his defeat, as opposition to the independent treasury. Men had grown weary of party tyranny, and disgusted with its machinery. That this gave to the opposition no little of their strength, is pretty clearly evinced by the fact, that no sooner were Mr. Van Buren and his caucus system believed to be out of the way, than the Republican party was stronger than ever. State after state returned and gave their votes for the principles and measures of government, they had persisted, under him and his tactics, in voting down. The whole party throughout the Union gave a sudden spring, as if freed from some superincumbent weight, which had hitherto oppressed it to the earth, and prevented all free movement. It was a general jubilee, and men seemed to say, "Now Republican principles can have a free development, and a certain triumph."

Considerate men, who had stood by Mr. Van Buren, and made no inconsiderable sacrifices to sustain him, felt, after all, that his defeat had its good side, in that it might tend to break up the old party organization, demolish its machinery, and leave men a measure of freedom to labor for the public good. They felt that all was not lost; nay, that the gain might possibly in the long run overbalance the loss. Mr. Van Buren, they felt, was out of the way; and this, in itself, was no trifling gain. Hope sprang up afresh, and in the buoyancy of their hearts they were disposed to treat him with all tenderness, to tread lightly on his faults, to forget the injuries he had inflicted on the Republican cause, and to magnify as much as possible his virtues and public services. His defeat softened prejudice, and disarmed hostility, and all were disposed to follow him to private life with marked respect, if not with gratitude. They felt that, since he was no longer in the field, the disasters of the campaign could be easily repaired; and that the Republican forces, marshalled again, under new leaders, with fresh hopes, and the natural stimulus of recently recovered freedom, would be in no danger of a future defeat. There was reason and justice in all this. But the reappearance of Mr. Van Buren upon the stage changes the whole aspect of affairs. He comes not alone, but as the chief of a band, which the country had devoutly hoped was dispersed, never to be collected again. He comes as the representative of the same old corrupt and corrupting system of party tactics, followed by the same swarm of greedy spoilsmen, with their appetite for plunder sharpened by the few years' abstinence they have been forced, through the remains of the original virtue and patriotism of the country, to practice. Gratify his wishes, restore him to the place he is personally soliciting, and we lose all that was good in the defeat of the Republican party in 1840, and retain only the evil. We restore what, with an almost unheard-of effort, the country had thrown off, and place the Republican party in the condition in which it must be defeated again, or the country be inevitably ruined.

These are no doubt hard things to say of a man who has once filled the high office of president of these United States; but if Mr. Van Buren had been at all worthy of that high office, they never would have been said; for he would on his defeat have retired and remained thenceforth in private life. The fact that he is now before the public, soliciting to be restored to that office from which the country ejected him with indignation and disgust, is a proof of his moral unfitness for the place to which he aspires, and of the justice and wisdom of the people in ejecting him. He loses all the sympathy his defeat excited, forfeits all the respect with which generous hearts follow the fallen, and all the sacredness that ordinarily belongs to those who have filled high office. He stands before us simply as an aspirant for the highest honor in the gift of the American people, and not an aspirant relying on his own personal merits and eminent public services, but on a system of party tactics and caucus machinery, which cannot be countenanced for a moment, without the most serious detriment to liberty, and the grossest indignity to civil virtue. Under these circumstances, he must expect to have hard things said of him, at least hard things to be *thought* of him, by every man capable of distinguishing between the virtue of the citizen and the virtues of the partisan. He voluntarily provokes the severest censure from every enlightened friend of his country and of her republican institutions. It is too much to ask us to restore the old caucus system, the old party machinery, and reinstate all the old drill-sergeants, by whose means our liberties have been jeopardized and our republic brought to the very verge of the precipice. It is too much to expect us quietly, now after so much has been done to clear the onward path of republicanism; now after Providence has so signally intervened in our favor against those who had for so long a time provoked its indignation, to replace the old impediments swept away by the whirlwind of 1840, by rallying again around the very man, who, of all others in the Union, relies most on these very impediments for success, and who cannot be ignorant that, if it were not for the party contrivances which stifle the free voice of the people, he would never be solicited to leave, even for a moment, the classic shades of Lindenwold.

We have spoken of the peculiar dangers to which institutions like ours are exposed. These dangers are great and threatening; they have already acquired an alarming force, and seem almost ready to break upon us with overwhelming fury; but we do not look upon them as inevitable, or irremediable. We may guard against them, and shelter ourselves almost, if not wholly, against all ill consequences. But our protection against them is in the virtue of the people, in their firmness to resist the tendency to selfishness, which our institutions themselves naturally generate; and we must add, in their virtue, not merely as *subjects* of the government, but as *citizens.*

Here, where, suffrage is so nearly universal, the great body of the adult male population sustain to the government a two-fold relation—the relation of *subject,* and the relation of *citizen.* As subjects, they are held to allegiance; their virtue is loyalty, and their duty, obedience; as citizens, they are constituent elements of the government itself, and share in the administration.

A faithful discharge of all their duties as subjects will not secure the ends of good government. Good government demands, not only strict obedience to the laws, but just laws, and wise administration. The justice of the laws, and the wisdom of the administration depend on the virtue and intelligence of the people, not in their capacity of subjects, but in their capacity of citizens. The republican form of government will prove a total failure, unless the citizens, acting as constituent elements of the government, carry into its administration loyalty to eternal justice; that stern integrity, and disinterested devotion to the public, which will force the government in all its practical workings to seek, always and everywhere, the greatest good of each individual subject, whether high or low, rich or poor.

The chief danger, to which our republican institutions are exposed, does not lie in the disloyalty of the people when acting as subjects, but in their venality and corruption when acting as citizens—in their increasing want of devotion to the public good, and increasing efforts to convert the government into a machine for promoting their own purely private and selfish ends—each regardless of the evils he may cause it to inflict on others.

This distinction has not, we apprehend, been always made, nor sufficiently insisted on. The teachers of morality, whether from the pulpit or the press, when insisting on the necessity of popular virtue to sustain popular government, have confined themselves mainly to the virtue of the subject, that is, obedience to the laws, and the faithful discharge of the several duties involved in the various private relations of man with man; and it is still this obedience, and these private virtues, that our clergy have chiefly in view when they speak of the necessity of religion as the support of popular government. Here is one great reason why we have so many tolerable subjects, who are grossly corrupt citizens; and why, with no mean share of private morality, we have scarcely the semblance of civic virtue. There has been with us, in a deeper sense than is commonly implied, a total separation of church and state. Religion and morality, in a political point of view, afford us little or no protection, because they are seldom brought to bear upon the people in their capacity of citizens. They will be sufficient for our wants, only when we are made to feel by our moral and religious teachers, that we must carry with us, in our capacity of citizens, all the singleness of purpose, all the firmness to resist temptation, and all the self-denial and disinterested devotion to the supreme law, that we are required to have in our capacity of subjects or private individuals.

Doubtless the cultivation and growth of our virtues as subjects will tend to strengthen and confirm our virtues as citizens; but, on the other hand, the neglect of our virtues as citizens will tend to corrupt and destroy our virtues as subjects. I carry my selfishness with me into the discharge of my duties as a citizen, and I seek to make laws, or to administer the government, for my own private benefit. But I make the laws. If they are against my interest, why should I obey them? If I obey selfishness in making the laws, I shall be very apt to obey it in keeping them; and if I am corrupt in what concerns the public, I shall not long remain pure in what concerns individuals. We would not underrate the virtues of the subject, but, in their effects, the virtues of the citizen, in a country like ours, are of far more vital importance. The former affect few, and those only for a short period; the latter affect millions, and it may be through a thousand generations. Our religious and moral teachers should, then, bring the whole force of religion and morality to bear upon our conduct as citizens. The citizen, as distinguished from the subject, is a public officer; in voting, he acts in a public capacity; exercises, not a private right, but a public trust; and, therefore, is bound to vote, not according to his private interests or feelings, but according to his most solemn convictions of the public good. No citizen has a right to say, "My vote is my own, and I may give it for whom I please." The consequences of his vote do not concern himself alone. In voting, he acts for others, no less than for himself. It is not, then, what he is willing to submit to for himself, that should govern him, but what he has the right to fasten upon others with whom he is associated. The citizen, who deposits his vote, should, then, do it under a deep and solemn feeling of his accountability, both to his fellow-citizens or subjects and to the great moral Governor of the universe. He who trifles with his vote, trifles with a sacred trust; he who gives his vote for the party, or the man, he cannot in conscience approve, and thus aids in fastening, what he cannot but believe an injury, on his country, is worse than a thief and a robber. He is a traitor to his God, his country, and his race. Here, no more than elsewhere, can there be the least compromise with duty, without guilt. To the citizen, as to the man, God says, "My son, give me thy heart." We must be made as citizens to feel this, and to act accordingly, or all is lost. Wise and just government cannot long coexist with the utter profligacy of the great mass of our citizens, as citizens. The citizens will impress upon the government their own want of public spirit and integrity. Our great danger lies here—in our want of high-toned, stern, and uncompromising civic virtue.

It is not our design, in this journal, which is devoted mainly to the discussion of first principles, to mingle in the party strife about special measures or particular men; but there are times, when men and principles are so interlinked, that it is impossible to disjoin them, and treat them separately. Such is, in our view, the present. We have reached such a crisis in our political affairs, that almost every thing depends, not on the party which now succeeds, but on the *man* we elect president. The great labor should now be to elect a president of the country, not the mere chief of a party—a man who will go into office, and reform the administration, and wield the whole force of the government against the spoilsmen, and do all that he can constitutionally to arrest the tendency to suffer the politics of the country to lie under the control of the demagogues, as they have been for the last fifteen years. We want a man of high moral integrity, of a high order of intellect, of great firmness, decision, and energy of character, who shall look more than four years ahead; a man who is above all party trickery, and who disdains all appeal to party machinery as the means of his elevation; a man, in one word, the very opposite, in all his moral qualities and party relations, of Mr. Van Buren. We want a man at the head of the government who is a man, feeling his accountability to his Maker, and his duty to sacrifice himself, if need be, for the good of his country, and the moral and social elevation of his countrymen.

Now, it strikes us, is the time for the sound portion of the people, disregarding all old party lines, and laying aside for the moment even favorite party measures, to rally around some such man, whether he has heretofore been called a Democrat or a Whig. Greater questions are at stake than Bank or No-bank, Tariff or Free Trade. The very existence of our republic, the very existence of our government, as it existed in the minds and the hearts of our fathers, and as capable of being a guaranty of individual liberty and public prosperity, is at stake. If the right man, if a statesman, instead of a politician, be placed now in the presidential chair, the circumstances of the country are such, that he can give to the political action of the country a healthy direction, and aid in our restoration to civic virtue. He can dash the hopes of the spoilsmen, and rescue the government from those who would make it an instrument of plundering the many for the benefit of the few. We have carried our ultraism, on both sides, far enough, and go we with the *extreme right*, or the *extreme left*, ruin alike awaits us.

We trust this appeal does not come too late. Sensible men, in all parts of the country, are beginning to feel, that the success of the partisans of Mr. Van Buren, or those of Mr. Clay,[3] representing as they do the opposite extremes, would be fraught with the most serious injury. Corruption has spread far and wide; the two armies of demagogues are marshalled, their drill-sergeants are at work day and night; but it is to be hoped that there is yet a sufficient number not enrolled in either of these divisions, to save the republic. Let these men, who want justice and free government, make themselves heard before it is too late; let them select their man; let them rally to his support; and they will succeed. If not, if they fail, they will have the imperishable glory of having failed in a noble effort for a righteous cause. But they will not fail. There is a moral majesty in the movements of honest men and firm patriots, before which the unprincipled and corrupt cannot stand a moment. They will succeed. The moral forces of the universe are all with those who contend for the right, and let it not be said, that already the chains of party are so firmly riveted on our limbs, and our lips so closely fastened with its padlocks, that we cannot move nor speak.

3. Henry Clay, running as the Whig candidate, lost to James K. Polk.—*Editor.*

Henry David Thoreau
(1817–1862)

THOREAU was born in Concord, Massachusetts. After his graduation from Harvard College in 1837, he taught for a brief time. He lived with Ralph Waldo Emerson for several years and resided at Walden Pond from 1845 to 1847. Thoreau was an immensely versatile man, combining interests in literature, philosophy, politics, and his own version of scientific observation. He is the author of *A Week on the Concord and Merrimack Rivers* (1849), *Walden* (1854), and numerous other works published posthumously.

"Civil Disobedience" first appeared in the anthology *Aesthetic Essays* (1849), edited by Elizabeth Palmer Peabody, under the title "Resistance to Civil Government." The essay was later published with its present title in the posthumous collections *A Yankee in Canada* (1866) and *Miscellanies* (1893).

CIVIL DISOBEDIENCE

I heartily accept the motto,—"That government is best which governs least;"[1] and I should like to see it acted up to more rapidly and systematically. Carried out, it finally amounts to this, which also I believe,— "That government is best which governs not at all;" and when men are prepared for it, that will be the kind of government which they will have. Government is at best but an expedient; but most governments are usually, and all governments are sometimes, inexpedient. The objections which have been brought against a standing army, and they are many and weighty, and deserve to prevail, may also at last be brought against a standing government. The standing army is only an arm of the standing government. The government itself, which is only the mode which the people have chosen to execute their will, is equally liable to be abused and perverted before the people can act through it. Witness the present Mexican war,[2] the work of comparatively a few individuals using the standing government as their tool; for, in the outset, the people would not have consented to this measure.

This American government,—what is it but a tradition, though a recent one, endeavoring to transmit itself unimpaired to posterity, but each instant losing some of its integrity? It has not the vitality and force of a single living man; for a single man can bend it to his will. It is a sort of wooden gun to the people themselves; and, if ever they should use it in

1. This is the motto of the *United States Magazine and Democratic Review*, a monthly literary-political journal; a similar statement occurs in Emerson's essay, "Politics."— *Editor.*
2. The war between Mexico and the United States (1846–1848); the issues included slavery and the annexation of Texas.—*Editor.*

earnest as a real one against each other, it will surely split. But it is not the less necessary for this; for the people must have some complicated machinery or other, and hear its din, to satisfy that idea of government which they have. Governments show thus how successfully men can be imposed on, even impose on themselves, for their own advantage. It is excellent, we must all allow; yet this government never of itself furthered any enterprise, but by the alacrity with which it got out of its way. It does not keep the country free. It does not settle the West. It does not educate. The character inherent in the American people has done all that has been accomplished; and it would have done somewhat more, if the government had not sometimes got in its way. For government is an expedient by which men would fain succeed in letting one another alone; and, as has been said, when it is most expedient, the governed are most let alone by it. Trade and commerce, if they were not made of India rubber, would never manage to bounce over the obstacles which legislators are continually putting in their way; and, if one were to judge these men wholly by the effects of their actions, and not partly by their intentions, they would deserve to be classed and punished with those mischievous persons who put obstructions on the railroads.

But, to speak practically and as a citizen, unlike those who call themselves no-government men, I ask for, not at once no government, but *at once* a better government. Let every man make known what kind of government would command his respect, and that will be one step toward obtaining it.

After all, the practical reason why, when the power is once in the hands of the people, a majority are permitted, and for a long period continue to rule, is not because they are most likely to be in the right, nor because this seems fairest to the minority, but because they are physically the strongest. But a government in which the majority rule in all cases cannot be based on justice, even as far as men understand it. Can there not be a government in which majorities do not virtually decide right and wrong, but conscience?—in which majorities decide only those questions to which the rule of expediency is applicable? Must the citizen ever for a moment, or in the least degree, resign his conscience to the legislator? Why has every man a conscience, then? I think that we should be men first, and subjects afterward. It is not desirable to cultivate a respect for the law, so much as for the right. The only obligation which I have a right to assume, is to do at any time what I think right. It is truly enough said, that a corporation has no conscience; but a corporation of conscientious men is a corporation *with* a conscience. Law never made men a whit more just; and, by means of their respect for it, even the well-disposed are daily made the agents of injustice. A common and natural result of an undue respect for law is, that you may see a file of soldiers, colonel, captain, corporal, privates, powdermonkeys and all, marching in admirable order over hill and dale to the wars, against their wills, aye, against their common sense and consciences, which makes it very steep marching indeed, and produces a palpitation of the heart. They have no doubt that it is a damnable business in which they are concerned; they are all peaceably inclined. Now, what are they? Men at all? or small moveable forts and magazines, at the service of some unscrupulous man in power? Visit the Navy Yard, and behold a marine, such a man as an American government can make, or such as it can make a man with its black arts, a mere shadow and reminiscence of humanity, a man laid out alive and standing, and already, as one may say, buried under arms with funeral accompaniments, though it may be

"Not a drum was heard, nor a funeral note,
    As his corse to the ramparts we hurried;
Not a soldier discharged his farewell shot
    O'er the grave where our hero we buried."

The mass of men serve the State thus, not as men mainly, but as machines, with their bodies. They are the standing army, and the militia, jailers, constables, *posse comitatus*, &c. In most cases there is no free exercise whatever of the judgment or of the moral sense; but they put themselves on a level with wood and earth and stones; and wooden men can perhaps be manufactured that will serve the purpose as well. Such command no more respect than men of straw, or a lump of dirt. They have the same sort of worth only as horses and dogs. Yet such as these even are commonly esteemed good citizens. Others, as most legislators, politicians, lawyers, ministers, and office-holders, serve the State chiefly with their heads; and, as they rarely make any moral distinctions, they are as likely to serve the devil, without intending it, as God. A very few, as heroes, patriots, martyrs, reformers in the great sense, and *men*, serve the State with their consciences also, and so necessarily resist it for the most part; and they are commonly treated by it as enemies. A wise man will only be useful as a man, and will not submit to be "clay," and "stop a hole to keep the wind away,"[3] but leave that office to his dust at least:—

"I am too high-born to be propertied,
To be a secondary at control,
Or useful serving-man and instrument
To any sovereign state throughout the world."[4]

3. Shakespeare, *Hamlet*, V. i. 236–237.—*Editor*.
4. Shakespeare, *King John*, V. ii. 79–82.—*Editor*.

He who gives himself entirely to his fellow-men appears to them useless and selfish; but he who gives himself partially to them is pronounced a benefactor and philanthropist.

How does it become a man to behave toward this American government to-day? I answer that he cannot without disgrace be associated with it. I cannot for an instant recognize that political organization as *my* government which is the *slave's* government also.

All men recognize the right of revolution; that is, the right to refuse allegiance to and to resist the government, when its tyranny or its inefficiency are great and unendurable. But almost all say that such is not the case now. But such was the case, they think, in the Revolution of '75. If one were to tell me that this was a bad government because it taxed certain foreign commodities brought to its ports, it is most probable that I should not make an ado about it, for I can do without them: all machines have their friction; and possibly this does enough good to counterbalance the evil. At any rate, it is a great evil to make a stir about it. But when the friction comes to have its machine, and oppression and robbery are organized, I say, let us not have such a machine any longer. In other words, when a sixth of the population of a nation which has undertaken to be the refuge of liberty are slaves, and a whole country is unjustly overrun and conquered by a foreign army, and subjected to military law, I think that it is not too soon for honest men to rebel and revolutionize. What makes this duty the more urgent is the fact, that the country so overrun is not our own, but ours is the invading army.

Paley,[5] a common authority with many on moral questions, in his chapter on the "Duty of Submission to Civil Government," resolves all civil obligation into expediency; and he proceeds to say, "that so long as the interest of the whole society requires it, that is, so long as the established government cannot be resisted or changed without public inconveniency, it is the will of God that the established government be obeyed, and no longer."—"This principle being admitted, the justice of every particular case of resistance is reduced to a computation of the quantity of the danger and grievance on the one side, and of the probability and expense of redressing it on the other."[6] Of this, he says, every man shall judge for himself. But Paley appears never to have contemplated those cases to which the rule of expediency does not apply, in which a people, as well as an individual, must do justice, cost what it may. If I have unjustly wrested a plank from a drowning man, I must restore it to him though I drown myself. This, according to Paley, would be inconvenient. But he that would save his life, in such a case, shall lose it. This people

5. William Paley (1743–1805), British philosopher.—*Editor.*
6. The quotation is from Paley's *Principles of Moral and Political Philosophy.*—*Editor.*

must cease to hold slaves, and to make war on Mexico, though it cost them their existence as a people.

In their practice, nations agree with Paley; but does any one think that Massachusetts does exactly what is right at the present crisis?

> "A drab of state, a cloth-o'-silver slut,
> To have her train borne up, and her soul trail in the dirt."[7]

Practically speaking, the opponents to a reform in Massachusetts are not a hundred thousand politicians at the South, but a hundred thousand merchants and farmers here, who are more interested in commerce and agriculture than they are in humanity, and are not prepared to do justice to the slave and to Mexico, *cost what it may*. I quarrel not with far-off foes, but with those who, near at home, co-operate with, and do the bidding of those far away, and without whom the latter would be harmless. We are accustomed to say, that the mass of men are unprepared; but improvement is slow, because the few are not materially wiser or better than the many. It is not so important that many should be as good as you, as that there be some absolute goodness somewhere; for that will leaven the whole lump. There are thousands who are *in opinion* opposed to slavery and to the war, who yet in effect do nothing to put an end to them; who, esteeming themselves children of Washington and Franklin, sit down with their hands in their pockets, and say that they know not what to do, and do nothing; who even postpone the question of freedom to the question of free-trade, and quietly read the prices-current along with the latest advices from Mexico, after dinner, and, it may be, fall asleep over them both. What is the price-current of an honest man and patriot to-day? They hesitate, and they regret, and sometimes they petition; but they do nothing in earnest and with effect. They will wait, well disposed, for others to remedy the evil, that they may no longer have it to regret. At most, they give only a cheap vote, and a feeble countenance and God-speed, to the right, as it goes by them. There are nine hundred and ninety-nine patrons of virtue to one virtuous man; but it is easier to deal with the real possessor of a thing than with the temporary guardian of it.

All voting is a sort of gaming, like chequers or backgammon, with a slight moral tinge to it, a playing with right and wrong, with moral questions; and betting naturally accompanies it. The character of the voters is not staked. I cast my vote, perchance, as I think right; but I am not vitally concerned that that right should prevail. I am willing to leave it to the majority. Its obligation, therefore, never exceeds that of expediency. Even voting *for the right* is *doing* nothing for it. It is only expressing to men

---

7. Cyril Tourneur (1575?–1626), *The Revengers Tragaedie*, IV. iv.—*Editor.*

feebly your desire that it should prevail. A wise man will not leave the right to the mercy of chance, nor wish it to prevail through the power of the majority. There is but little virtue in the action of masses of men. When the majority shall at length vote for the abolition of slavery, it will be because they are indifferent to slavery, or because there is but little slavery left to be abolished by their vote. They will then be the only slaves. Only his vote can hasten the abolition of slavery who asserts his own freedom by his vote.

I hear of a convention to be held at Baltimore, or elsewhere, for the selection of a candidate for the Presidency, made up chiefly of editors, and men who are politicians by profession; but I think, what is it to any independent, intelligent, and respectable man what decision they may come to, shall we not have the advantage of his wisdom and honesty, nevertheless? Can we not count upon some independent votes? Are there not many individuals in the country who do not attend conventions? But no: I find that the respectable man, so called, has immediately drifted from his position, and despairs of his country, when his country has more reason to despair of him. He forthwith adopts one of the candidates thus selected as the only *available* one, thus proving that he is himself *available* for any purposes of the demagogue. His vote is of no more worth than that of any unprincipled foreigner or hireling native, who may have been bought. Oh for a man who is a *man*, and, as my neighbor says, has a bone in his back which you cannot pass your hand through! Our statistics are at fault: the population has been returned too large. How many *men* are there to a square thousand miles in this country? Hardly one. Does not America offer any inducement for men to settle here? The American has dwindled into an Odd Fellow—one who may be known by the development of his organ of gregariousness, and a manifest lack of intellect and cheerful self-reliance; whose first and chief concern, on coming into the world, is to see that the alms-houses are in good repair; and, before yet he has lawfully donned the virile garb, to collect a fund for the support of the widows and orphans that may be; who, in short, ventures to live only by the aid of the mutual insurance company, which has promised to bury him decently.

It is not a man's duty, as a matter of course, to devote himself to the eradication of any, even the most enormous wrong; he may still properly have other concerns to engage him; but it is his duty, at least, to wash his hands of it, and, if he gives it no thought longer, not to give it practically his support. If I devote myself to other pursuits and contemplations, I must first see, at least, that I do not pursue them sitting upon another man's shoulders. I must get off him first, that he may pursue his contemplations too. See what gross inconsistency is tolerated. I have heard some of my townsmen say, "I should like to have them order me out to help put down

an insurrection of the slaves, or to march to Mexico,—see if I would go,"
and yet these very men have each, directly by their allegiance, and so
indirectly, at least, by their money, furnished a substitute. The soldier is
applauded who refuses to serve in an unjust war by those who do not
refuse to sustain the unjust government which makes the war; is applauded
by those whose own act and authority he disregards and sets at nought;
as if the State were penitent to that degree that it hired one to scourge it
while it sinned, but not to that degree that it left off sinning for a moment.
Thus, under the name of order and civil government, we are all made at
last to pay homage to and support our own meanness. After the first blush
of sin, comes its indifference; and from immoral it becomes, as it were,
*un*moral, and not quite unnecessary to that life which we have made.

The broadest and most prevalent error requires the most disinterested
virtue to sustain it. The slight reproach to which the virtue of patriotism
is commonly liable, the noble are most likely to incur. Those who, while
they disapprove of the character and measures of a government, yield to
it their allegiance and support, are undoubtedly its most conscientious
supporters, and so frequently the most serious obstacles to reform. Some
are petitioning the State to dissolve the Union, to disregard the requisitions
of the President. Why do they not dissolve it themselves,—the union between themselves and the State,—and refuse to pay their quota into its
treasury? Do not they stand in the same relation to the State, that the
State does to the Union? And have not the same reasons prevented the
State from resisting the Union, which have prevented them from resisting
the State?

How can a man be satisfied to entertain an opinion merely, and enjoy
it? Is there any enjoyment in it, if his opinion is that he is aggrieved? If
you are cheated out of a single dollar by your neighbor, you do not rest
satisfied with knowing that you are cheated, or with saying that you are
cheated, or even with petitioning him to pay you your due; but you take
effectual steps at once to obtain the full amount, and see that you are never
cheated again. Action from principle,—the perception and the performance
of right,—changes things and relations; it is essentially revolutionary, and
does not consist wholly with any thing which was. It not only divides
states and churches, it divides families; aye, it divides the *individual*,
separating the diabolical in him from the divine.

Unjust laws exist: shall we be content to obey them, or shall we endeavor
to amend them, and obey them until we have succeeded, or shall we trans-
gress them at once? Men generally, under such a government as this, think
that they ought to wait until they have persuaded the majority to alter
them. They think that, if they should resist, the remedy would be worse
than the evil. But it is the fault of the government itself that the remedy *is*
worse than the evil. *It* makes it worse. Why is it not more apt to anticipate

and provide for reform? Why does it not cherish its wise minority? Why does it cry and resist before it is hurt? Why does it not encourage its citizens to be on the alert to point out its faults, and *do* better than it would have them? Why does it always crucify Christ, and excommunicate Copernicus and Luther, and pronounce Washington and Franklin rebels?

One would think, that a deliberate and practical denial of its authority was the only offence never contemplated by government; else, why has it not assigned its definite, its suitable and proportionate penalty? If a man who has no property refuses but once to earn nine shillings for the State, he is put in prison for a period unlimited by any law that I know, and determined only by the discretion of those who placed him there; but if he should steal ninety times nine shillings from the State, he is soon permitted to go at large again.

If the injustice is part of the necessary friction of the machine of government, let it go, let it go: perchance it will wear smooth,—certainly the machine will wear out. If the injustice has a spring, or a pulley, or a rope, or a crank, exclusively for itself, then perhaps you may consider whether the remedy will not be worse than the evil; but if it is of such a nature that it requires you to be the agent of injustice to another, then, I say, break the law. Let your life be a counter friction to stop the machine. What I have to do is to see, at any rate, that I do not lend myself to the wrong which I condemn.

As for adopting the ways which the State has provided for remedying the evil, I know not of such ways. They take too much time, and a man's life will be gone. I have other affairs to attend to. I came into this world, not chiefly to make this a good place to live in, but to live in it, be it good or bad. A man has not everything to do, but something; and because he cannot do *every thing*, it is not necessary that he should do *something* wrong. It is not my business to be petitioning the governor or the legislature any more than it is theirs to petition me, and, if they should not hear my petition, what should I do then? But in this case the State has provided no way: its very Constitution is the evil. This may seem to be harsh and stubborn and unconciliatory; but it is to treat with the utmost kindness and consideration the only spirit that can appreciate or deserves it. So is all change for the better, like birth and death which convulse the body.

I do not hesitate to say, that those who call themselves abolitionists should at once effectually withdraw their support, both in person and property, from the government of Massachusetts, and not wait till they constitute a majority of one, before they suffer the right to prevail through them. I think that it is enough if they have God on their side, without waiting for that other one. Moreover, any man more right than his neighbors, constitutes a majority of one already.

I meet this American government, or its representative the State government, directly, and face to face, once a year, no more, in the person of its tax-gatherer; this is the only mode in which a man situated as I am necessarily meets it; and it then says distinctly, Recognize me; and the simplest, the most effectual, and, in the present posture of affairs, the indispensablest mode of treating with it on this head, of expressing your little satisfaction with and love for it, is to deny it then. My civil neighbor, the tax-gatherer, is the very man I have to deal with,—for it is, after all, with men and not with parchment that I quarrel,—and he has voluntarily chosen to be an agent of the government. How shall he ever know well what he is and does as an officer of the government, or as a man, until he is obliged to consider whether he shall treat me, his neighbor, for whom he has respect, as a neighbor and well-disposed man, or as a maniac and disturber of the peace, and see if he can get over this obstruction to his neighborliness without a ruder and more impetuous thought or speech corresponding with his action? I know this well, that if one thousand, if one hundred, if ten men whom I could name,—if ten *honest* men only,— aye, if *one* HONEST man, in this State of Massachusetts, *ceasing to hold slaves,* were actually to withdraw from this copartnership, and be locked up in the county jail therefore, it would be the abolition of slavery in America. For it matters not how small the beginning may seem to be: what is once well done is done for ever. But we love better to talk about it: that we say is our mission. Reform keeps many scores of newspapers in its service, but not one man. If my esteemed neighbor, the State's ambas- sador, who will devote his days to the settlement of the question of human rights in the Council Chamber, instead of being threatened with the prisons of Carolina, were to sit down the prisoner of Massachusetts, that State which is so anxious to foist the sin of slavery upon her sister,—though at present she can discover only an act of inhospitality to be the ground of a quarrel with her,—the Legislature would not wholly waive the subject the following winter.

Under a government which imprisons any unjustly, the true place for a just man is also a prison. The proper place to-day, the only place which Massachusetts has provided for her freer and less desponding spirits, is in her prisons, to be put out and locked out of the State by her own act, as they have already put themselves out by their principles. It is there' that the fugitive slave, and the Mexican prisoner on parole, and the Indian come to plead the wrongs of his race, should find them; on that separate, but more free and honorable ground, where the State places those who are not *with* her but *against* her,—the only house in a slave-state in which a free man can abide with honor. If any think that their influence would be lost there, and their voices no longer afflict the ear of the State, that they would not be as an enemy within its walls, they do not know by how much truth is stronger than error, nor how much more eloquently and effectively he can combat injustice who has experienced a little in his own person. Cast your whole vote, not a strip of paper merely, but your whole influence. A minority is powerless while it conforms to the majority; it is not even a minority then; but it is irresistible when it clogs by its whole weight. If the alternative is to keep all just men in prison, or give up war and slavery, the State will not hesitate which to choose. If a thousand men were not to pay their tax-bills this year, that would not be a violent and bloody measure, as it would be to pay them, and enable the State to commit violence and shed innocent blood. This is, in fact, the definition of a peaceable revolution, if any such is possible. If the tax-gatherer, or any other public officer, asks me, as one has done, "But what shall I do?" my answer is, "If you really wish to do any thing, resign your office." When the subject has refused allegiance, and the officer has resigned his office, then the revolution is accomplished. But even suppose blood should flow. Is there not a sort of blood shed when the conscience is wounded? Through this wound a man's real manhood and immortality flow out, and he bleeds to an everlasting death. I see this blood flowing now.

I have contemplated the imprisonment of the offender, rather than the seizure of his goods,—though both will serve the same purpose,—because they who assert the purest right, and consequently are most dangerous to a corrupt State, commonly have not spent much time in accumulating property. To such the State renders comparatively small service, and a slight tax is wont to appear exorbitant, particularly if they are obliged to earn it by special labor with their hands. If there were one who lived wholly without the use of money, the State itself would hesitate to demand it of him. But the rich man—not to make any invidious comparison—is always sold to the institution which makes him rich. Absolutely speaking, the more money, the less virtue; for money comes between a man and his objects, and obtains them for him; and it was certainly no great virtue to obtain it. It puts to rest many questions which he would otherwise be taxed to answer; while the only new question which it puts is the hard but superfluous one, how to spend it. Thus his moral ground is taken from under his feet. The opportunities of living are diminished in proportion as what are called the "means" are increased. The best thing a man can do for his culture when he is rich is to endeavor to carry out those schemes which he entertained when he was poor. Christ answered the Herodians according to their condition. "Show me the tribute-money," said he;—and one took a penny out of his pocket;—If you use money which has the image of Caesar on it, and which he has made current and valuable, that is, *if you are men of the State*, and gladly enjoy the advantages of Caesar's government, then pay him back some of his own when he demands it; "Render therefore to Caesar that which is Caesar's, and to God those things which are God's,"—leaving them no wiser than before as to which was which; for they did not wish to know.

When I converse with the freest of my neighbors, I perceive that, whatever they may say about the magnitude and seriousness of the question, and their regard for the public tranquillity, the long and the short of the matter is, that they cannot spare the protection of the existing government, and they dread the consequences of disobedience to it to their property and families. For my own part, I should not like to think that I ever rely on the protection of the State. But, if I deny the authority of the State when it presents its tax-bill, it will soon take and waste all my property, and so harass me and my children without end. This is hard. This makes it impossible for a man to live honestly and at the same time confortably in outward respects. It will not be worth the while to accumulate property; that would be sure to go again. You must hire or squat somewhere, and raise but a small crop, and eat that soon. You must live within yourself, and depend upon yourself, always tucked up and ready for a start, and not have many affairs. A man may grow rich in Turkey even, if he will be in all respects a good subject of the Turkish government. Confucius said,—"If a state is governed by the principles of reason, poverty and misery are subjects of shame; if a State is not governed by the principles of reason, riches and honors are the subjects of shame." No: until I want the protection of Massachusetts to be extended to me in some distant southern port, where my liberty is endangered, or until I am bent solely on building up an estate at home by peaceful enterprise, I can afford to refuse allegiance to Massachusetts, and her right to my property and life. It costs me less in every sense to incur the penalty of disobedience to the State, than it would to obey. I should feel as if I were worth less in that case.

Some years ago, the State met me in behalf of the church, and commanded me to pay a certain sum toward the support of a clergyman whose preaching my father attended, but never I myself. "Pay it," it said, "or be locked up in the jail." I declined to pay. But, unfortunately, another man saw fit to pay it. I did not see why the schoolmaster should be taxed to support the priest, and not the priest the schoolmaster; for I was not the State's schoolmaster, but I supported myself by voluntary subscription. I did not see why the lyceum should not present its tax-bill, and have the State to back its demand, as well as the church. However, at the request of the selectmen, I condescended to make some such statement as this in writing:—"Know all men by these presents, that I, Henry Thoreau, do not wish to be regarded as a member of any incorporated society which I have not joined." This I gave to the town-clerk; and he has it. The State, having thus learned that I did not wish to be regarded as a member of that church, has never made a like demand on me since; though it said that it must adhere to its original presumption that time. If I had known how to name them, I should then have signed off in detail from all the societies which I never signed on to; but I did not know where to find a complete list.

I have paid no poll-tax for six years. I was put into a jail once on this account, for one night; and, as I stood considering the walls of solid stone, two or three feet thick, the door of wood and iron, a foot thick, and the iron grating which strained the light, I could not help being struck with the foolishness of that institution which treated me as if I were mere flesh and blood and bones, to be locked up. I wondered that it should have concluded at length that this was the best use it could put me to, and had never thought to avail itself of my services in some way. I saw that, if there was a wall of stone between me and my townsmen, there was a still more difficult one to climb or break through, before they could get to be as free as I was. I did not for a moment feel confined, and the walls seemed a great waste of stone and mortar. I felt as if I alone of all my townsmen had paid my tax. They plainly did not know how to treat me, but behaved like persons who are underbred. In every threat and in every compliment there was a blunder; for they thought that my chief desire was to stand the other side of that stone wall. I could not but smile to see how industriously they locked the door on my meditations, which followed them out again without let or hinderance, and *they* were really all that was dangerous. As they could not reach me, they had resolved to punish my body; just as boys, if they cannot come at some person against whom they have a spite, will abuse his dog. I saw that the State was half-witted, that it was timid as a lone woman with her silver spoons, and that it did not know its friends from its foes, and I lost all my remaining respect for it, and pitied it.

Thus the State never intentionally confronts a man's sense, intellectual or moral, but only his body, his senses. It is not armed with superior wit or honesty, but with superior physical strength. I was not born to be forced. I will breathe after my own fashion. Let us see who is the strongest. What force has a multitude? They only can force me who obey a higher law than I. They force me to become like themselves. I do not hear of *men* being *forced* to live this way or that by masses of men. What sort of life were that to live? When I meet a government which says to me, "Your money or your life," why should I be in haste to give it my money? It may be in a great strait, and not know what to do: I cannot help that. It must help itself; do as I do. It is not worth the while to snivel about it. I am not responsible for the successful working of the machinery of society. I am not the son of the engineer. I perceive that, when an acorn and a chestnut fall side by side, the one does not remain inert to make way for the other, but both obey their own laws, and spring and grow and flourish as best they can, till one, perchance, overshadows and destroys the other. If a plant cannot live according to its nature, it dies; and so a man.

The night in prison was novel and interesting enough. The prisoners in their shirt-sleeves were enjoying a chat and the evening air in the doorway, when I entered. But the jailer said, "Come, boys, it is time to lock up;" and so they dispersed, and I heard the sound of their steps returning into the hollow apartments. My room-mate was introduced to me by the jailer, as "a first-rate fellow and a clever man." When the door was locked, he showed me where to hang my hat, and how he managed matters there. The rooms were whitewashed once a month; and this one, at least, was the whitest, most simply furnished, and probably the neatest apartment in the town. He naturally wanted to know where I came from, and what brought me there; and, when I had told him, I asked him in my turn how he came there, presuming him to be an honest man, of course; and, as the world goes, I believe he was. "Why," said he, "they accuse me of burning a barn; but I never did it." As near as I could discover, he had probably gone to bed in a barn when drunk, and smoked his pipe there; and so a barn was burnt. He had the reputation of being a clever man, had been there some three months waiting for his trial to come on, and would have to wait as much longer; but he was quite domesticated and contented, since he got his board for nothing, and thought that he was well treated.

He occupied one window, and I the other; and I saw, that if one stayed there long, his principal business would be to look out the window. I had soon read all the tracts that were left there, and examined where former prisoners had broken out, and where a grate had been sawed off, and heard the history of the various occupants of that room; for I found that even here there was a history and a gossip which never circulated beyond the walls of the jail. Probably this is the only house in the town where verses are composed, which are afterward printed in a circular form, but not published. I was shown quite a long list of verses which were composed by some young men who had been detected in an attempt to escape, who avenged themselves by singing them.

I pumped my fellow-prisoner as dry as I could, for fear I should never see him again; but at length he showed me which was my bed, and left me to blow out the lamp.

It was like travelling into a far country, such as I had never expected to behold, to lie there for one night. It seemed to me that I never had heard the town-clock strike before, nor the evening sounds of the village; for we slept with the windows open, which were inside the grating. It was to see my native village in the light of the middle ages, and our Concord was turned into a Rhine stream, and visions of knights and castles passed before me. They were the voices of old burghers that I heard in the streets. I was an involuntary spectator and auditor of whatever was done and said in the kitchen of the adjacent village-inn,—a wholly new and rare experience to me. It was a closer view of my native town. I was fairly inside of it. I never had seen its institutions before. This is one of its peculiar institutions; for it is a shire town. I began to comprehend what its inhabitants were about.

In the morning, our breakfasts were put through the hole in the door, in small oblong-square tin pans, made to fit, and holding a pint of chocolate, with brown bread, and an iron spoon. When they called for the vessels again, I was green enough to return what bread I had left; but my comrade seized it, and said that I should lay that up for lunch or dinner. Soon after, he was let out to work at haying in a neighboring field, whither he went every day, and would not be back till noon; so he bade me good-day, saying that he doubted if he should see me again.

When I came out of prison,—for some one interfered, and paid the tax,—I did not perceive that great changes had taken place on the common, such as he observed who went in a youth, and emerged a tottering and gray-headed man; and yet a change had to my eyes come over the scene,— the town, and State, and country,—greater than any that mere time could effect. I saw yet more distinctly the State in which I lived. I saw to what extent the people among whom I lived could be trusted as good neighbors and friends; that their friendship was for summer weather only; that they did not greatly purpose to do right; that they were a distinct race from me by their prejudices and superstitions, as the Chinamen and Malays are; that, in their sacrifices to humanity, they ran no risks, not even to their property; that, after all, they were not so noble but they treated the thief as he had treated them, and hoped, by a certain outward observance and a few prayers, and by walking in a particular straight though useless path from time to time, to save their souls. This may be to judge my neighbors harshly; for I believe that most of them are not aware that they have such an institution as the jail in their village.

It was formerly the custom in our village, when a poor debtor came out of jail, for his acquaintances to salute him, looking through their fingers, which were crossed to represent the grating of a jail window, "How do ye do?" My neighbors did not thus salute me, but first looked at me, and then at one another, as if I had returned from a long journey. I was put into jail as I was going to the shoemaker's to get a shoe which was mended. When I was let out the next morning, I proceeded to finish my errand, and, having put on my mended shoe, joined a huckleberry party, who were impatient to put themselves under my conduct; and in half an hour,—for the horse was soon tackled,—was in the midst of a huckleberry field, on one of our highest hills, two miles off; and then the State was nowhere to be seen.

This is the whole history of "My Prisons."[8]

I have never declined paying the highway tax, because I am as desirous of being a good neighbor as I am of being a bad subject; and, as for supporting schools, I am doing my part to educate my fellow-countrymen now. It is for no particular item in the tax-bill that I refuse to pay it. I simply wish to refuse allegiance to the State, to withdraw and stand aloof from it effectually. I do not care to trace the course of my dollar, if I could, till it buys a man, or a musket to shoot one with,—the dollar is innocent,—but I am concerned to trace the effects of my allegiance. In fact, I quietly declare war with the State, after my fashion, though I will still make what use and get what advantage of her I can, as is usual in such cases.

If others pay the tax which is demanded of me, from a sympathy with the State, they do but what they have already done in their own case, or rather they abet injustice to a greater extent than the State requires. If they pay the tax from a mistaken interest in the individual taxed, to save his property or prevent his going to jail, it is because they have not considered wisely how far they let their private feelings interfere with the public good.

This, then, is my position at present. But one cannot be too much on his guard in such a case, lest his action be biassed by obstinacy, or an undue regard for the opinions of men. Let him see that he does only what belongs to himself and to the hour.

I think sometimes, Why, this people mean well; they are only ignorant; they would do better if they knew how: why give your neighbors this pain to treat you as they are not inclined to? But, I think, again, this is no reason why I should do as they do, or permit others to suffer much greater pain of a different kind. Again, I sometimes say to myself, When many millions of men, without heat, without ill-will, without personal feeling of any kind, demand of you a few shillings only, without the possibility, such is their constitution, of retracting or altering their present demand, and without the possibility, on your side, of appeal to any other millions, why expose yourself to this overwhelming brute force? You do not resist cold and hunger, the winds and the waves, thus obstinately; you quietly submit to a thousand similar necessities. You do not put your head into the fire. But just in proportion as I regard this as not wholly a brute force, but partly a human force, and consider that I have relations to those millions as to so many millions of men, and not of mere brute or inanimate

---

8. A reference to *Le Mie Prigioni*, the memoirs of the Italian patriot, Silvio Pellico (1789–1854).—*Editor.*

things, I see that appeal is possible, first and instantaneously, from them to the Maker of them, and, secondly, from them to themselves. But, if I put my head deliberately into the fire, there is no appeal to fire or to the Maker of fire, and I have only myself to blame. If I could convince myself that I have any right to be satisfied with men as they are, and to treat them accordingly, and not according, in some respects, to my requisitions and expectations of what they and I ought to be, then, like a good Mussulman[9] and fatalist, I should endeavor to be satisfied with things as they are, and say it is the will of God. And, above all, there is this difference between resisting this and a purely brute or natural force, that I can resist this with some effect; but I cannot expect, like Orpheus, to change the nature of the rocks and trees and beasts.

I do not wish to quarrel with any man or nation. I do not wish to split hairs, to make fine distinctions, or set myself up as better than my neighbors. I seek rather, I may say, even an excuse for conforming to the laws of the land. I am but too ready to conform to them. Indeed I have reason to suspect myself on this head; and each year, as the tax-gatherer comes around, I find myself disposed to review the acts and position of the general and state governments, and the spirit of the people, to discover a pretext for conformity. I believe that the State will soon be able to take all my work of this sort out of my hands, and then I shall be no better a patriot than my fellow-countrymen. Seen from a lower point of view, the Constitution, with all its faults, is very good; the law and the courts are very respectable; even this State and this American government are, in many respects, very admirable and rare things, to be thankful for, such as a great many have described them; but seen from a point of view a little higher, they are what I have described them; seen from a higher still, and the highest, who shall say what they are, or that they are worth looking at or thinking of at all?

However, the government does not concern me much, and I shall bestow the fewest possible thoughts on it. It is not many moments that I live under a government, even in this world. If a man is thought-free, fancy-free, imagination-free, that which *is not* never for a long time appearing *to be* to him, unwise rulers or reformers cannot fatally interrupt him.

I know that most men think differently from myself; but those whose lives are by profession devoted to the study of these or kindred subjects, content me as little as any. Statesmen and legislators, standing so completely within the institution, never distinctly and nakedly behold it. They speak of moving society, but have no resting-place without it. They may be men of a certain experience and discrimination, and have no doubt invented ingenious and even useful systems, for which we sincerely thank

9. A Moslem.—*Editor.*

them; but all their wit and usefulness lie within certain not very wide limits. They are wont to forget that the world is not governed by policy and expediency. Webster never goes behind government, and so cannot speak with authority about it. His words are wisdom to those legislators who contemplate no essential reform in the existing government; but for thinkers, and those who legislate for all time, he never once glances at the subject. I know of those whose serene and wise speculations on this theme would soon reveal the limits of his mind's range and hospitality. Yet, compared with the cheap professions of most reformers, and the still cheaper wisdom and eloquence of politicians in general, his are almost the only sensible and valuable words, and we thank Heaven for him. Comparatively, he is always strong, original, and, above all, practical. Still his quality is not wisdom, but prudence. The lawyer's truth is not Truth, but consistency, or a consistent expediency. Truth is always in harmony with herself, and is not concerned chiefly to reveal the justice that may consist with wrong-doing. He well deserves to be called, as he has been called, the Defender of the Constitution. There are really no blows to be given by him but defensive ones. He is not a leader, but a follower. His leaders are the men of '87.[10] "I have never made an effort," he says, "and never propose to make an effort; I have never countenanced an effort, and never mean to countenance an effort, to disturb the arrangement as originally made, by which the various States came into the Union." Still thinking of the sanction which the Constitution gives to slavery, he says, "Because it was a part of the original compact,—let it stand." Notwithstanding his special acuteness and ability, he is unable to take a fact out of its merely political relations, and behold it as it lies absolutely to be disposed of by the intellect,—what, for instance, it behoves a man to do here in America to-day with regard to slavery, but ventures, or is driven, to make some such desperate answer as the following, while professing to speak absolutely, and as a private man,—from which what new and singular code of social duties might be inferred?—"the manner," says he, "in which the government of those States where slavery exists are to regulate it, is for their own consideration, under their responsibility to their constituents, to the general laws of propriety, humanity and justice, and to God. Associations formed elsewhere, springing from a feeling of humanity, or any other cause, have nothing whatever to do with it. They have never received any encouragement from me, and they never will."

They who know of no purer source of truth, who have traced up its stream no higher, stand, and wisely stand, by the Bible and the Constitution, and drink at it there with reverence and humility; but they who

10. Members of the Federal Constitutional Convention, held in Philadelphia in 1787 and presided over by George Washington. The quotations that follow are from Webster's speech in the Senate on the admission of Texas as a state.—*Editor.*

behold where it comes trickling into this lake or that pool, gird up their loins once more, and continue their pilgrimage toward its fountain-head.

No man with a genius for legislation has appeared in America. They are rare in the history of the world. There are orators, politicians, and eloquent men, by the thousand; but the speaker has not yet opened his mouth to speak, who is capable of settling the much-vexed questions of the day. We love eloquence for its own sake, and not for any truth which it may utter, or any heroism it may inspire. Our legislators have not yet learned the comparative value of free-trade and of freedom, of union, and of rectitude, to a nation. They have no genius or talent for comparatively humble questions of taxation and finance, commerce and manufactures and agriculture. If we were left solely to the wordy wit of legislators in Congress for our guidance, uncorrected by the seasonable experience and the effectual complaints of the people, America would not long retain her rank among the nations. For eighteen hundred years, though perchance I have no right to say it, the New Testament has been written; yet where is the legislator who has wisdom and practical talent enough to avail himself of the light which it sheds on the science of legislation?

The authority of government, even such as I am willing to submit to,— for I will cheerfully obey those who know and can do better than I, and in many things even those who neither know nor can do so well,—is still an impure one: to be strictly just, it must have the sanction and consent of the governed. It can have no pure right over my person and property but what I concede to it. The progress from an absolute to a limited monarchy, from a limited monarchy to a democracy, is a progress toward a true respect for the individual. Is a democracy, such as we know it, the last improvement possible in government? Is it not possible to take a step further towards recognizing and organizing the rights of man? There will never be a really free and enlightened State, until the State comes to recognize the individual as a higher and independent power, from which all its own power and authority are derived, and treats him accordingly. I please myself with imagining a State at last which can afford to be just to all men, and to treat the individual with respect as a neighbor; which even would not think it inconsistent with its own repose, if a few were to live aloof from it, not meddling with it, nor embraced by it, who fulfilled all the duties of neighbors and fellowmen. A State which bore this kind of fruit, and suffered it to drop off as fast as it ripened, would prepare the way for a still more perfect and glorious State, which also I have imagined, but not yet anywhere seen.

David Walker
(1785–1830)

DAVID WALKER was born a slave in North Carolina, but because his mother was a free Negro he traveled widely in the United States, finally settling in Boston during the 1820s. Here Walker's lectures on the evils of slavery culminated in 1829 in the private printing of his *Appeal*, regarded as a decisive event in the crusade against slavery. It is said to have marked the transition from Quaker persuasiveness to a more militant form of social protest. He was much abused for the publication of this pamphlet, and even many abolitionists, including William Lloyd Garrison, opposed its circulation. Walker was found dead—the apparent victim of poison—on June 28, 1830.

"Our Wretchedness in Consequence of Ignorance" appears as Article II of the *Appeal*.

OUR WRETCHEDNESS
IN CONSEQUENCE
OF IGNORANCE

Ignorance, my brethren, is a mist, low down into the very dark and almost impenetrable abyss in which, our fathers for many centuries have been plunged. The Christians, and enlightened of Europe, and some of Asia, seeing the ignorance and consequent degradation of our fathers, instead of trying to enlighten them, by teaching them that religion and light with which God had blessed them, they have plunged them into wretchedness ten thousand times more intolerable, than if they had left them entirely to the Lord, and to add to their miseries, deep down into which they have plunged them tell them, that they are an *inferior* and *distinct race* of beings, which they will be glad enough to recall and swallow by and by. Fortune and misfortune, two inseparable companions, lay rolled up in the wheel of events, which have from the creation of the world, and will continue to take place among men until God shall dash worlds together.

When we take a retrospective view of the arts and sciences—the wise legislators—the Pyramids, and other magnificent buildings—the turning of the channel of the river Nile, by the sons of Africa or of Ham, among whom learning originated, and was carried thence into Greece, where it was improved upon and refined. Thence among the Romans, and all over the then enlightened parts of the world, and it has been enlightening the dark and benighted minds of men from then, down to this day. I say, when I view retrospectively, the renown of that once mighty people, the children of our great progenitor I am indeed cheered. Yea further, when I view that mighty son of Africa, HANNIBAL, one of the greatest generals of antiquity, who defeated and cut off so many thousands of the white Romans or murderers, and who carried his victorious arms, to the very gate of Rome, and I give it as my candid opinion, that had Carthage been well united and had given him good support, he would have carried that cruel and barbarous city by storm. But they were dis-united, as the coloured people are now, in the United States of America, the reason our natural enemies are enabled to keep their feet on our throats.

Beloved brethren—here let me tell you, and believe it, that the Lord our God, as true as he sits on his throne in heaven, and as true as our Saviour died to redeem the world, will give you a Hannibal, and when the Lord shall have raised him up, and given him to you for your possession, O my suffering brethren! remember the divisions and consequent sufferings of *Carthage* and of *Hayti*. Read the history particularly of Hayti, and see how they were butchered by the whites, and do you take warning. The person whom God shall give you, give him your support and let him go his length, and behold in him the salvation of your God. God will indeed, deliver you through him from your deplorable and wretched condition under the Christians of America. I charge you this day before my God to lay no obstacle in his way, but let him go.

The whites want slaves, and want us for their slaves, but some of them will curse the day they ever saw us. As true as the sun ever shone in its meridian splendor, my colour will root some of them out of the very face of the earth. They shall have enough of making slaves of, and butchering, and murdering us in the manner which they have. No doubt some may say that I write with a bad spirit, and that I being a black, wish these things to occur. Whether I write with a bad or a good spirit, I say if these things do not occur in their proper time, it is because the world in which we live does not exist, and we are deceived with regard to its existence.—It is immaterial however to me, who believe, or who refuse— though I should like to see the whites repent peradventure God may have mercy on them, some however, have gone so far that their cup must be filled.

But what need have I to refer to antiquity, when Hayti, the glory of the blacks and terror of tyrants, is enough to convince the most avaricious and stupid of wretches—which is at this time, and I am sorry to say it, plagued with that scourge of nations, the Catholic religion; but I hope and pray God that she may yet rid herself of it, and adopt in its stead the Protestant faith; also, I hope that she may keep peace within her borders and be united, keeping a strict look out for tyrants, for if they get the least chance to injure her, they will avail themselves of it, as true as the Lord lives in heaven. But one thing which gives me joy is, that they are men who would be cut off to a man, before they would yield to the combined forces of the whole world—in fact, if the whole world was combined against them, it could not do any thing with them, unless the Lord delivers them up.

Ignorance and treachery one against the other—a grovelling servile and abject submission to the lash of tyrants, we see plainly, my brethren, are not the natural elements of the blacks, as the Americans try to make us believe; but these are misfortunes which God has suffered our fathers to be enveloped in for many ages, no doubt in consequence of their disobedience to their Maker, and which do, indeed, reign at this time among us, almost to the destruction of all other principles: for I must truly say, that ignorance, the mother of treachery and deceit, gnaws into our very vitals. Ignorance, as it now exists among us, produces a state of things, Oh my Lord! too horrible to present to the world. Any man who is curious to see the full force of ignorance developed among the coloured people of the United States of America, has only to go into the southern and western states of this confederacy, where, if he is not a tyrant, but has the feelings of a human being, who can feel for a fellow creature, he may see enough to make his very heart bleed! He may see there, a son take his mother, who bore almost the pains of death to give him birth, and by the command of a tyrant, strip her as naked as she came into the world, and apply the cow-hide to her, until she falls a victim to death in the road! He may see a husband take his dear wife, not unfrequently in a pregnant state, and perhaps far advanced, and beat her for an unmerciful wretch, until his infant falls a lifeless lump at her feet! Can the Americans escape God Almighty? If they do, can he be to us a God of Justice? God is just, and I know it—for he has convinced me to my satisfaction—I cannot doubt him. My observer may see fathers beating their sons, mothers their daughters, and children their parents, all to pacify the passions of unrelenting tyrants. He may also, see them telling news and lies, making mischief one upon another. These are some of the productions of ignorance, which he will see practised among my dear brethren, who are held in unjust slavery and wretchedness, by avaricious and unmerciful tyrants, to whom, and their hellish deeds, I would suffer my life to be taken before I would submit. And when my curious observer comes to take notice of those who are said to be free, (which assertion I deny) and who are making some frivolous pretentions to common sense, he will see that branch of ignorance among the slaves assuming a more cunning and deceitful course of procedure.—He may see some of my brethren in league with tyrants, selling their own brethren into *hell upon earth,* not dissimilar to the exhibitions in Africa, but in a more secret, servile and abject manner. Oh Heaven! I am full!!! I can hardly move my pen!!!! and as I expect some will try to put me to death to strike terror into others, and to obliterate from their minds the notion of freedom, so as to keep my brethren the more secure in wretchedness, where they will be permitted to stay but a short time (whether tyrants believe it or not)—I shall give the world a development of facts, which are already witnessed in the courts of heaven. My observer may see some of those ignorant and treacherous creatures (coloured people) sneaking about in the large cities, endeavoring to find out all strange coloured people, where they work and where they reside, asking them questions, and trying to ascertain whether they are runaways or not, telling them, at the same time, that they always have been, are, and always will be, friends to their brethren; and, perhaps, that they themselves are absconders, and a thousand such treacherous lies to get the better information of the more ignorant!!! There have been and are at this day in Boston, New-York, Philadelphia, and Baltimore, coloured men, who are in league with tyrants, and who receive a great portion of their daily bread, of the moneys which they acquire from the blood and tears of their more miserable brethren, whom they scandalously delivered into the hands of our *natural enemies!!!!!!*

To show the force of degraded ignorance and deceit among us some farther, I will give here an extract from a paragraph, which may be found in the Columbian Centinel of this city, for September 9, 1829, on the first page of which, the curious may find an article, headed

"AFFRAY AND MURDER."

Portsmouth (Ohio), Aug. 22, 1829.

"A most shocking outrage was committed in Kentucky, about eight miles from this place, on 14th inst. A negro driver, by the name of Gordon, who had purchased in Maryland about sixty negroes, was taking them, assisted by an associate named Allen, and the wagoner who conveyed the baggage, to the Mississippi. The men were hand-cuffed and chained together, in the usual manner for driving those poor wretches, while the women and children were suffered to proceed without incumbrance. It appears that, by means of a file the negroes, unobserved, had succeeded in separating the iron which bound their hands, in such a way as to be able to throw them off at any moment. About 8 o'clock in the morning, while proceeding on the state road leading from Greenup to Vanceburg, two of them dropped their shackles and commenced a fight, when the wagoner (Petit) rushed in with his whip to compel them to desist. At this moment, every negro was found to be perfectly at liberty; and one of them seizing a club, gave Petit a violent blow on the head, and laid him dead at his feet; and Allen, who came to his assistance, met a similar fate, from the contents of a pistol fired by another of the gang. Gordon was then attacked, seized and held by one of the negroes, whilst another fired twice at him with a pistol, the ball of which each time grazed his head, but not proving effectual, he was beaten with clubs, and left for dead. They then commenced pillaging the wagon, and with an axe split open the trunk of Gordon, and rifled it of the money, about $2,400. Sixteen of the negroes then took to the woods; Gordon, in the mean time, not being materially injured, was enabled, by the assistance of one of the women, to mount his horse and flee; pursued,

however, by one of the gang on another horse, with a drawn pistol; fortunately he escaped with his life bacely, arriving at a plantation, as the
negro came in sight; who then turned about and retreated.

"The neighborhood was immediately rallied, and a hot pursuit given—
which, we understand, has resulted in the capture of the whole gang and
the recovery of the greatest part of the money. Seven of the negro men
and one woman, it is said were engaged in the murders, and will be
brought to trial at the next court in Greenupsburg."

Here my brethren, I want you to notice particularly in the above article,
the *ignorant* and *deceitful actions* of this coloured woman. I beg you to
view it candidly, as for ETERNITY!!!! Here a *notorious wretch,* with
two other confederates had SIXTY of them in a gang, driving them like
brutes—the men all in chains and hand-cuffs, and by the help of God
they got their chains and hand-cuffs thrown off, and caught two of the
wretches and put them to death, and beat the other until they thought he
was dead, and left him for dead; however, he deceived them, and rising
from the ground, this *servile woman* helped him upon his horse, and he
made his escape. Brethren, what do you think of this? Was it the natural
fine feelings of this woman, to save such a wretch alive? I know that the
blacks, take them half enlightened and ignorant, are more humane and
merciful than the most enlightened and refined European that can be
found in all the earth. Let no one say that I assert this because I am
prejudiced on the side of my colour, and against the whites or Europeans.
For what I write, I do it candidly, for my God and the good of both
parties: Natural observations have taught me these things; there is a
solemn awe in the hearts of the blacks, as it respects *murdering* men:[1]
whereas the whites, (though they are great cowards) where they have the
advantage, or think that there are any prospects of getting it, they murder
all before them, in order to subject men to wretchedness and degradation
under them. This is the natural result of pride and avarice. But I declare,
the actions of this black woman are really insupportable. For my own
part, I cannot think it was any thing but servile deceit, combined with
the most gross ignorance: for we must remember that *humanity, kindness*
and the *fear of the Lord,* does not consist in protecting *devils.* Here is a
set of wretches, who had SIXTY of them in a gang, driving them around
the country like *brutes,* to dig up gold and silver for them, (which they
will get enough of yet.) Should the lives of such creatures be spared? Are
God and Mammon in league? What has the Lord to do with a gang of
desperate wretches, who go *sneaking about the country like robbers*—light
upon his people wherever they can get a chance, binding them with chains
and hand-cuffs, beat and murder them as they would *rattle-snakes?* Are

1. Which is the reason the whites take the advantage of us.—*Author.*

they not the Lord's enemies? Ought they not to be destroyed? Any person who will save such wretches from destruction, is fighting against the Lord, and will receive his just recompense. The black men acted like *blockheads*. Why did they not make sure of the wretch? He would have made sure of them, if he could. It is just the way with black men—eight white men can frighten fifty of them; whereas, if you can only get courage into the blacks, I do declare it, that one good black man can put to death six white men; and I give it as a fact, let twelve black men get well armed for battle, and they will kill and put to flight fifty whites.—The reason is, the blacks, once you get them started, they glory in death. The whites have had us under them for more than three centuries, murdering, and treating us like brutes; and, as Mr. Jefferson wisely said, they have never *found us out*—they do not know, indeed, that there is an unconquerable disposition in the breasts of the blacks, which, when it is fully awakened and put in motion, will be subdued, only with the destruction of the animal existence. Get the blacks started, and if you do not have a gang of tigers and lions to deal with, I am a deceiver of the blacks and of the whites. How sixty of them could let that wretch escape unkilled, I cannot conceive—they will have to suffer as much for the two whom, they secured, as if they had put one hundred to death: if you commence, make sure work—do not trifle, for they will not trifle with you—they want us for their slaves, and think nothing of murdering us in order to subject us to that wretched condition—therefore, if there is an *attempt* made by us, kill or be killed. Now, I ask you, had you not rather be killed than to be a slave to a tyrant, who takes the life of your mother, wife, and dear little children? Look upon your mother, wife and children, and answer God Almighty; and believe this, that it is no more harm for you to kill a man, who is trying to kill you, than it is for you to take a drink of water when thirsty; in fact, the man who will stand still and let another murder him, is worse than an infidel, and, if he has common sense, ought not to be pitied. The actions of this deceitful and ignorant coloured woman, in saving the life of a desperate wretch, whose avaricious and cruel object was to drive her, and her companions in miseries, through the country like cattle, to make his fortune on their carcasses, are but too much like that of thousands of our brethren in these states: if any thing is whispered by one, which has any allusion to the melioration of their dreadful condition, they run and tell tyrants, that they may be enabled to keep them the longer in wretchedness and miseries. Oh! coloured people of these United States, I ask you, in the name of that God who made us, have we, in consequence of oppression, nearly lost the spirit of man, and, in no very trifling degree, adopted that of brutes? Do you answer, no?—I ask you, then, what set of men can you point me to, in all the world, who are so abjectly employed by their oppressors, as we are by our *natural enemies?* How can, Oh! how can those enemies but say that we and our children are not of the HUMAN FAMILY, but were made by our Creator to be an inheritance to them and theirs for ever? How can the slaveholders but say that they can bribe the best coloured person in the country, to sell his brethren for a trifling sum of money, and take that atrocity to confirm them in their avaricious opinion, that we were made to be slaves to them and their children? How could Mr. Jefferson but say,[2] "I advance it therefore as a suspicion only, that the blacks, whether originally a distinct race, or made distinct by time and circumstances, are *inferior* to the whites in the endowments both of body and mind?"—"It," says he, "is not against experience to suppose, that different species of the same genus, or varieties of the same species, may possess different qualifications." [Here, my brethren, listen to him.] "Will not a lover of natural history, then, one who views the gradations in all the races of *animals* with the eye of philosophy, excuse an effort to keep those in the department of MAN as *distinct* as nature has formed them?"—I hope you will try to find out the meaning of this verse—its widest sense and all its bearings: whether you do or not, remember the whites do. This very verse, brethren, having emanated from Mr. Jefferson, a much greater philosopher the world never afforded, has in truth injured us more, and has been as great a barrier to our emancipation as any thing that has ever been advanced against us. I hope you will not let it pass unnoticed. He goes on further, and says: "This *unfortunate* difference of colour, and *perhaps* of *faculty*, is a powerful obstacle to the emancipation of these people. Many of their advocates, while they wish to vindicate the liberty of human nature are anxious also to preserve its *dignity* and *beauty*. Some of these, embarrassed by the question, 'What further is to be done with them?' join themselves in opposition with those who are actuated by sordid avarice only." Now I ask you candidly, my suffering brethren in time, who are candidates for the eternal worlds, how could Mr. Jefferson but have given the world these remarks respecting us, when we are so submissive to them, and so much servile deceit prevail among ourselves—when we so *meanly* submit to their murderous lashes, to which neither the Indians nor any other people under Heaven would submit? No, they would die to a man, before they would suffer such things from men who are no better than themselves, and *perhaps not so good.* Yes, how can our friends but be embarrassed, as Mr. Jefferson says, by the question, "What further is to be done with these people?" For while they are working for our emancipation, we are, by our treachery, wickedness, and deceit, working against ourselves and our children—helping ours, and the enemies of God, to keep us and our

2. See his *Notes on Virginia*, page 213.—*Author.*

dear little children in their infernal chains of slavery!!! Indeed, our friends cannot but relapse and join themselves "with those who are actuated by *sordid avarice* only!!!!" For my own part, I am glad Mr. Jefferson has advanced his positions for your sake; for you will either have to contradict or confirm him by your own actions, and not by what our friends have said or done for us; for those things are other men's labours, and do not satisfy the Americans, who are waiting for us to prove to them ourselves, that we are MEN, before they will be willing to admit the fact; for I pledge you my sacred word of honour, that Mr. Jefferson's remarks respecting us, have sunk deep into the hearts of millions of the whites, and never will be removed this side of eternity.—For how can they, when we are confirming him every day, by our *groveling submissions* and *treachery*? I aver, that when I look over these United States of America, and the world, and see the ignorant deceptions and consequent wretchedness of my brethren, I am brought oftimes solemnly to a stand, and in the midst of my reflections I exclaim to my God, "Lord didst thou make us to be slaves to our brethren, the whites?" But when I reflect that God is just, and that millions of my wretched brethren would meet death with glory—yea, more, would plunge into the very mouths of cannons and be torn into particles as minute as the atoms which compose the elements of the earth, in preference to a mean submission to the lash of tyrants, I am with streaming eyes, compelled to shrink back into nothingness before my Maker, and exclaim again, thy will be done, O Lord God Almighty.

Men of colour, who are also of sense, for you particularly is my APPEAL designed. Our more ignorant brethren are not able to penetrate its value. I call upon you therefore to cast your eyes upon the wretchedness of your brethren, and to do your utmost to enlighten them—*go to work and enlighten your brethren!*—Let the Lord see you doing what you can to rescue them and yourselves from degradation. Do any of you say that you and your family are free and happy, and what have you to do with the wretched slaves and other poeple? So can I say, for I enjoy as much freedom as any of you, if I am not quite as well off as the best of you. Look into our freedom and happiness, and see of what kind they are composed!! They are of the very lowest kind—they are the very *dregs!*— they are the most servile and abject kind, that ever a people was in possession of! If any of you wish to know how FREE you are, let one of you start and go through the southern and western States of this country, and unless you travel as a slave to a white man (a servant is a *slave* to the man whom he serves) or have your free papers, (which if you are not careful they will get from you) if they do not take you up and put you in jail, and if you cannot give good evidence of your freedom, sell you into eternal slavery, I am not a living man: or any man of colour, immaterial who he is, or where he came from, if he is not *the fourth from the negro race!!* (as we are called) the white Christians of America will serve him the same they will sink him into wretchedness and degradation for ever while he lives. And yet some of you have the hardihood to say that you are free and happy! May God have mercy on your freedom and happiness!! I met a coloured man in the street a short time since, with a string of boots on his shoulders; we fell into conversation, and in course of which, I said to him, what a miserable set of people we are! He asked, why?—Said I, we are so subjected under the whites, that we cannot obtain the comforts of life, but by cleaning their boots and shoes, old clothes, waiting on them, shaving them &c. Said he, (with the boots on his shoulders) "I am completely happy!!! I never want to live any better or happier than when I can get a plenty of boots and shoes to clean!!!" Oh, how can those who are actuated by avarice only, but think, that our Creator made us to be an inheritance to them for ever, when they see that our greatest glory is centered in such mean and low objects? Understand me, brethren, I do not mean to speak against the occupations by which we acquire enough and sometimes scarcely that, to render ourselves and families comfortable through life. I am subjected to the same inconvenience, as you all.—My objections are, to our *glorying* and being *happy* in such low employments; for if we are men, we ought to be thankful to the Lord for the past, and for the future. Be looking forward with thankful hearts to higher attainments than *wielding the razor* and *cleaning boots and shoes.* The man whose aspirations are not *above,* and even *below* these, is indeed, ignorant and wretched enough. I advanced it therefore to you, not as a *problematical,* but as an unshaken and for ever immovable *fact,* that your full glory and happiness, as well as all other coloured people under Heaven, shall never be fully consummated, but with the *entire emancipation of your enslaved brethren all over the world.* You may therefore, go to work and do what you can to rescue, or join in with tyrants to oppress them and yourselves, until the Lord shall come upon you all like a thief in the night. For I believe it is the will of the Lord that our greatest happiness shall consist in working for the salvation of our whole body. When this is accomplished a burst of glory will shine upon you, which will indeed astonish you and the world. Do any of you say this never will be done? I assure you that God will accomplish it—if nothing else will answer, he will hurl tyrants and devils into *atoms* and make way for his people. But O my brethren I say unto you again, you must go to work and prepare the way of the Lord.

There is a great work for you to do, as trifling as some of you may think of it. You have to prove to the Americans and the world, that we are MEN, and not *brutes,* as we have been represented, and by millions treated. Remember, to let the aim of your labours among your brethren, and particularly the youths, be the dissemination of education and religion.[3] It is lamentable, that many of our children go to school, from four until they are eight or ten, and sometimes fifteen years of age, and leave school knowing but a little more about the grammar of their language than a horse does about handling a musket—and not a few of them are really so ignorant, that they are unable to answer a person correctly, general questions in geography, and to hear them read, would only be to disgust a man who has a taste for reading; which, to do well, as trifling as it may appear to some, (to the ignorant in particular) is a great part of learning. Some few of them, may make out to scribble tolerably well, over a half sheet of paper, which I believe has hitherto been a powerful obstacle in our way, to keep us from acquiring knowledge. An ignorant father, who knows no more than what nature has taught him together with what little he acquires by the senses of hearing and seeing, finding his son able to write a neat hand, sets it down for granted that he has as good learning as any body; the young, ignorant gump, hearing his father or mother, who perhaps may be ten times more ignorant, in point of literature, than himself, extolling his learning, struts about, in the full assurance, that his attainments in literature are sufficient to take him through the world, when, in fact, he has scarcely any learning at all!!!!

I promiscuously fell in conversation once, with an elderly coloured man on the topics of education, and of the great prevalency of ignorance among us: Said he, "I know that our people are very ignorant but my son has a good education: I spent a great deal of money on his education: he can write as well as any white man, and I assure you that no one can fool him," &c. Said I, what else can your son do, besides writing a good hand? Can he post a set of books in a mercantile manner? Can he write a neat piece of composition in prose or in verse? To these interrogations he answered in the negative. Said I, did your son learn, while he was at school, the width and depth of English Grammar? To which he also replied in the negative, telling me his son did not learn those things. Your son said I, then, has hardly any learning at all—he is almost as ignorant, and more so, than many of those who never went to school one day in all their lives. My friend got a little put out, and so walking off, said that his son could write as well as any white man. Most of the coloured people, when they speak of the education of one among us who can write a neat hand,

3. Never mind what the ignorant ones among us may say, many of whom when you speak to them for their good, and try to enlighten their minds, laugh at you, and perhaps tell you plump to your face, that they want no instruction from you or any other Nigger, and all such aggravating language. Now if you are a man of understanding and sound sense, I conjure you in the name of the Lord, and of all that is good, to impute their actions to ignorance, and wink at their follies, and do your very best to get around them some way or other, for remember they are your brethren; and I declare to you that it is for your interests to teach and enlighten them.—*Author.*

and who perhaps knows nothing but to scribble and puff pretty fair on a small scrap of paper, immaterial whether his words are grammatical, or spelt correctly, or not; if it only looks beautiful, they say he has as good an education as any white man—he can write as well as any white man, &c. The poor, ignorant creature, hearing this, he is ashamed, forever after, to let any person see him humbling himself to another for knowledge but going about trying to deceive those who are more ignorant than himself, he at last falls an ignorant victim to death in wretchedness. I pray that the Lord may undeceive my ignorant brethren, and permit them to throw away pretensions, and seek after the substance of learning. I would crawl on my hands and knees through mud and mire, to the feet of a learned man, where I would sit and humbly supplicate him to instill into me, that which neither devils nor tyrants could remove, only with my life —for coloured people to acquire learning in this country, makes tyrants quake and tremble on their sandy foundation. Why, what is the matter? Why, they know that their infernal deeds of cruelty will be made known to the world. Do you suppose one man of good sense and learning would submit himself, his father, mother, wife and children to be slaves to a wretched man like himself, who, instead of compensating him for his labours, chains, hand-cuffs and beats him and family almost to death, leaving life enough in them, however, to work for, and call him master? No! no! he would cut his devilish throat from ear to ear, and well do slave-holders know it. The bare name of educating the coloured people, scares our cruel oppressors almost to death. But if they do not have enough to be frightened for yet, it will be, because they can always keep us ignorant, and because God approbates their cruelties, with which they have been for centuries murdering us. The whites shall have enough of the blacks, yet, as true as God sits on his throne in Heaven.

Some of our brethren are so very full of learning, that you cannot mention any thing to them which they do not know better than yourself!! —nothing is strange to them!!—they knew every thing years ago!—if any thing should be mentioned in company where they are, immaterial how important it is respecting us or the world, if they had not divulged it; they make light of it, and affect to have known it long before it was mentioned and try to make all in the room, or wherever you may be, believe that your conversation is nothing!!—not worth hearing! All this is the result of ignorance and ill-breeding; for a man of good-breeding, sense and penetration, if he had heard a subject told twenty times over, and should happen to be in company where one should commence telling it again, he would wait with patience on its narrator, and see if he would tell it as it was told in his presence before—paying the most strict attention to what is said, to see if any more light will be thrown on the subject: for all men are not gifted alike in telling, or even hearing the most simple narration. These ignorant, vicious, and wretched men, contribute almost as much injury to our body as tyrants themselves, by doing so much for the promotion of ignorance amongst us; for they, making such pretensions to knowledge, such of our youth as are seeking after knowledge, and can get access to them, take them as criterions to go by, who will lead them into a channel, where, unless the Lord blesses them with the privilege of seeing their folly, they will be irretrievably lost forever, while in time!!!

I must close this article by relating the very heartrending fact, that I have examined school-boys and young men of colour in different parts of the country, in the most simple parts of Murray's English Grammar, and not more than one in thirty was able to give a correct answer to my interrogations. If any one contradicts me, let him step out of his door into the streets of Boston, New-York, Philadelphia, or Baltimore, (no use to mention any other, for the Christians are too charitable further south or west!)—I say, let him who disputes me, step out of his door into the streets of either of those four cities, and promiscuously collect one hundred school-boys, or young men of colour, *who have been to school,* and who are considered by the coloured people to have received an excellent education, because, perhaps, some of them can write a good hand, but who, notwithstanding their neat writing, may be almost as ignorant, in comparison, as a horse.—And, I say it, he will hardly find (in this enlightened day, and in the midst of this *charitable* people) five in one hundred, who, are able to correct the false grammar of their language.—The cause of this almost universal ignorance among us, I appeal to our schoolmasters to declare. Here is a fact, which I this very minute take from the mouth of a young colored man, who has been to school in this state (Massachusetts) nearly nine years, and who knows grammar this day, *nearly* as well as he did the day he first entered the schoolhouse, under a white master. This young man says: "My master would never allow me to study grammar." I asked him, why? "The school committee," said he "forbid the coloured children learning grammar—they would not allow any but the white children to study grammar." It is a notorious fact, that the major part of the white Americans, have, ever since we have been among them, tried to keep us ignorant, and make us believe that God made us and our children to be slaves to them and theirs. *Oh! my God, have mercy on Christian Americans!!!*

Ralph Waldo Emerson
(1803–1882)

EMERSON was born in Boston and graduated from Harvard College in 1821, after which he taught for a short time. In 1829, after studying at Harvard Divinity School, he became a Unitarian minister of the Old South Church in Boston but resigned three years later. The remainder of his life was mainly devoted to speaking and writing on the major social and intellectual issues of his day. An early advocate of Transcendentalism, he is chiefly famous as the author of *Nature* (1836), *Essays* (1841), and *Essays: Second Series* (1844).

"The Fugitive Slave Law" was first delivered as a lecture in New York City on March 7, 1854, on the fourth anniversary of Daniel Webster's speech in favor of the Fugitive Slave Law. It was subsequently published in Emerson's *Miscellanies.*

THE FUGITIVE SLAVE LAW*

I do not often speak to public questions;—they are odious and hurtful, and it seems like meddling or leaving your work. I have my own spirits in prison;—spirits in deeper prisons, whom no man visits if I do not. And then I see what havoc it makes with any good mind, a dissipated philanthropy. The one thing not to be forgiven to intellectual persons is, not to know their own task, or to take their ideas from others. From this want of manly rest in their own and rash acceptance of other people's watchwords, come the imbecility and fatigue of their conversation. For they cannot affirm these from any original experience, and of course not with the natural movement and total strength of their nature and talent, but only from their memory, only from their cramped position of standing for their teacher. They say what they would have you believe, but what they do not quite know.

My own habitual view is to the well-being of students or scholars. And it is only when the public event affects them, that it very seriously touches me. And what I have to say is to them. For every man speaks mainly to a class whom he works with and more or less fully represents. It is to these I am beforehand related and engaged, in this audience or out of it— to them and not to others. And yet, when I say the class of scholars or students,—that is a class which comprises in some sort all mankind, comprises every man in the best hours of his life; and in these days not only virtually but actually. For who are the readers and thinkers of 1854? Owing to the silent revolution which the newspaper has wrought, this class

* Two fugitive slave laws were passed, one in 1793, the other in 1850, both of which provided for the return of escaped Negro slaves to their owners. According to the law of the land (a view which was reaffirmed in the Dred Scott Case of 1857), Negroes were not citizens and hence lacked the rights of white Americans.—*Editor.*

has come in this country to take in all classes. Look into the morning trains which, from every suburb, carry the business men into the city to their shops, counting-rooms, work-yards and warehouses. With them enters the car—the newsboy, that humble priest of politics, finance, philosophy, and religion. He unfolds his magical sheets,—twopence a head his bread of knowledge costs—and instantly the entire rectangular assembly, fresh from their breakfast, are bending as one man to their second breakfast. There is, no doubt, chaff enough in what he brings; but there is fact, thought, and wisdom in the crude mass, from all regions of the world.

I have lived all my life without suffering any known inconvenience from American Slavery. I never saw it; I never heard the whip; I never felt the check on my free speech and action, until, the other day, when Mr. Webster, by his personal influence, brought the Fugitive Slave Law on the country. I say Mr. Webster, for though the Bill was not his, it is yet notorious that he was the life and soul of it, that he gave it all he had: it cost him his life, and under the shadow of his great name inferior men sheltered themselves, threw their ballots for it and made the law. I say inferior men. There were all sorts of what are called brilliant men, accomplished men, men of high station, a President of the United States, Senators, men of eloquent speech, but men without self-respect, without character, and it was strange to see that office, age, fame, talent, even a repute for honesty, all count for nothing. They had no opinions, they had no memory for what they had been saying like the Lord's Prayer all their lifetime: they were only looking to what their great Captain did: if he jumped, they jumped, if he stood on his head, they did. In ordinary, the supposed sense of their district and State is their guide, and that holds them to the part of liberty and justice. But it is always a little difficult to decipher what this public sense is; and when a great man comes who knots up into himself the opinions and wishes of the people, it is so much easier to follow him as an exponent of this. He too is responsible; they will not be. It will always suffice to say,—"I followed him."

I saw plainly that the great show their legitimate power in nothing more than in their power to misguide us. I saw that a great man, deservedly admired for his powers and their general right direction, was able,—fault of the total want of stamina in public men,—when he failed, to break them all with him, to carry parties with him.

In what I have to say of Mr. Webster I do not confound him with vulgar politicians before or since. There is always base ambition enough, men who calculate on the immense ignorance of the masses; that is their quarry and farm: they use the constituencies at home only for their shoes. And, of course, they can drive out from the contest any honorable man. The low can best win the low, and all men like to be made much of. There are those too who have power and inspiration only to do ill. Their talent or their faculty deserts them when they undertake any thing right. Mr. Webster had a natural ascendency of aspect and carriage which distinguished him over all his contemporaries. His countenance, his figure, and his manners were all in so grand a style, that he was, without effort, as superior to his most eminent rivals as they were to the humblest; so that his arrival in any place was an event which drew crowds of people, who went to satisfy their eyes, and could not see him enough. I think they looked at him as the representative of the American Continent. He was there in his Adamitic capacity, as if he alone of all men did not disappoint the eye and the ear, but was a fit figure in the landscape.

I remember his appearance at Bunker's Hill. There was the Monument, and here was Webster. He knew well that a little more or less of rhetoric signified nothing: he was only to say plain and equal things,—grand things if he had them, and, if he had them not, only to abstain from saying unfit things,—and the whole occasion was answered by his presence. It was a place for behavior more than for speech, and Mr. Webster walked through his part with entire success. His excellent organization, the perfection of his elocution and all that thereto belongs,—voice, accent, intonation, attitude, manner,—we shall not soon find again. Then he was so thoroughly simple and wise in his rhetoric; he saw through his matter, hugged his fact so close, went to the principle or essential, and never indulged in a weak flourish, though he knew perfectly well how to make such exordiums, episodes and perorations as might give perspective to his harangues without in the least embarrassing his march or confounding his transitions. In his statement things lay in daylight; we saw them in order as they were. Though he knew very well how to present his own personal claims, yet in his argument he was intellectual,—stated his fact pure of all personality, so that his splendid wrath, when his eyes became lamps, was the wrath of the fact and the cause he stood for.

His power, like that of all great masters, was not in excellent parts, but was total. He had a great and everywhere equal propriety. He worked with that closeness of adhesion to the matter in hand which a joiner or a chemist uses, and the same quiet and sure feeling of right to his place that an oak or a mountain have to theirs. After all his talents have been described, there remains that perfect propriety which animated all the details of the action or speech with the character of the whole, so that his beauties of detail are endless. He seemed born for the bar, born for the senate, and took very naturally a leading part in large private and in public affairs; for his head distributed things in their right places, and what he saw so well he compelled other people to see also. Great is the privilege of eloquence. What gratitude does every man feel to him who speaks well for the right,—who translates truth into language entirely plain and clear!

The history of this country has given a disastrous importance to the defects of this great man's mind. Whether evil influences and the corruption of politics, or whether original infirmity, it was the misfortune of his country that with this large understanding he had not what is better than intellect, and the source of its health. It is a law of our nature that great thoughts come from the heart. If his moral sensibility had been proportioned to the force of his understanding, what limits could have been set to his genius and beneficent power? But he wanted that deep source of inspiration. Hence a sterility of thought, the want of generalization in his speeches, and the curious fact that, with a general ability which impresses all the world, there is not a single general remark, not an observation on life and manners, not an aphorism that can pass into literature from his writings.

Four years ago to-night, on one of those high critical moments in history when great issues are determined, when the powers of right and wrong are mustered for conflict, and it lies with one man to give a casting vote,—Mr. Webster, most unexpectedly, threw his whole weight on the side of Slavery, and caused by his personal and official authority the passage of the Fugitive Slave Bill.[1]

It is remarked of the Americans that they value dexterity too much, and honor too little; that they think they praise a man more by saying that he is "smart" than by saying that he is right. Whether the defect be national or not, it is the defect and calamity of Mr. Webster; and it is so far true of his countrymen, namely, that the appeal is sure to be made to his physical and mental ability when his character is assailed. His speeches on the seventh of March, and at Albany, at Buffalo, at Syracuse and Boston are cited in justification. And Mr. Webster's literary editor believes that it was his wish to rest his fame on the speech of the seventh of March. Now, though I have my own opinions on this seventh of March discourse[2] and those others, and think them very transparent and very open to criticism,—yet the secondary merits of a speech, namely, its logic, its illustrations, its points, etc., are not here in question. Nobody doubts that Daniel Webster could make a good speech. Nobody doubts that there were good and plausible things to be said on the part of the South. But this is not a question of ingenuity, not a question of syllogisms, but of ideas. *How came he there?*

There are always texts and thoughts and arguments. But it is the genius and temper of the man which decides whether he will stand for right or for might. Who doubts the power of any fluent debater to defend either of our political parties, or any client in our courts? There was the same

1. Daniel Webster, known as one of America's great political orators, was instrumental in the passage of the Fugitive Slave Law of 1850.—*Editor.*
2. On March 7, 1850, in a speech entitled "The Constitution and the Union," Webster defended the constitutional rights of slaveholders.—*Editor.*

law in England for Jeffries and Talbot and Yorke to read slavery out of, and for Lord Mansfield to read freedom. And in this country one sees that there is always margin enough in the statute for a liberal judge to read one way and a servile judge another.

But the question which History will ask is broader. In the final hour when he was forced by the peremptory necessity of the closing armies to take a side,—did he take the part of great principles, the side of humanity and justice, or the side of abuse and oppression and chaos?

Mr. Webster decided for Slavery, and that, when the aspect of the institution was no longer doubtful, no longer feeble and apologetic and proposing soon to end itself, but when it was strong, aggressive, and threatening an illimitable increase. He listened to State reasons and hopes, and left, with much complacency we are told, the testament of his speech to the astonished State of Massachusetts, *vera pro gratis;* a ghastly result of all those years of experience in affairs, this, that there was nothing better for the foremost American man to tell his countrymen than that Slavery was now at that strength that they must beat down their conscience and become kidnappers for it.

This was like the doleful speech falsely ascribed to the patriot Brutus: "Virtue, I have followed thee through life, and I find thee but a shadow." Here was a question of an immoral law; a question agitated for ages, and settled always in the same way by every great jurist, that an immoral law cannot be valid. Cicero, Grotius, Coke, Blackstone, Burlamaqui, Vattel, Burke, Jefferson, do all affirm this, and I cite them, not that they can give evidence to what is indisputable, but because, though lawyers and practical statesmen, the habit of their profession did not hide from them that this truth was the foundation of States.

Here was the question, Are you for man and for the good of man; or are you for the hurt and harm of man? It was questioned whether man shall be treated as leather? whether the Negroes shall be as the Indians were in Spanish America, a piece of money? Whether this system, which is a kind of mill or factory for converting men into monkeys, shall be upheld and enlarged? And Mr. Webster and the country went for the application to these poor men of quadruped law.

People were expecting a totally different course from Mr. Webster. If any man had in that hour possessed the weight with the country which he had acquired, he could have brought the whole country to its senses. But not a moment's pause was allowed. Angry parties went from bad to worse, and the decision of Webster was accompanied with everything offensive to freedom and good morals. There was something like an attempt to debauch the moral sentiment of the clergy and of the youth. Burke said he "would pardon something to the spirit of liberty." But by Mr. Webster the opposition to the law was sharply called treason, and prosecuted so. He told the

people at Boston "they must conquer their prejudices"; that "agitation of
the subject of Slavery must be suppressed." He did as immoral men usually
do, made very low bows to the Christian Church, and went through all the
Sunday decorums; but when allusion was made to the question of duty
and the sanctions of morality, he very frankly said, at Albany, "Some
higher law, something existing somewhere between here and the third
heaven,—I do not know where." And if the reporters say true, this
wretched atheism found some laughter in the company.

I said I had never in my life up to this time suffered from the Slave
Institution. Slavery in Virginia or Carolina was like Slavery in Africa or
the Feejees, for me. There was an old fugitive law, but it had become or
was fast becoming a dead letter, and, by the genius and laws of Massachusetts, inoperative. The new Bill made it operative, required me to hunt
slaves, and it found citizens in Massachusetts willing to act as judges and
captors. Moreover, it discloses the secret of the new times, that Slavery
was no longer mendicant, but was become aggressive and dangerous.

The way in which the country was dragged to consent to this, and the
disastrous defection (on the miserable cry of Union) of the men of letters,
of the colleges, of educated men, nay, of some preachers of religion,—
was the darkest passage in the history. It showed that our prosperity had
hurt us, and that we could not be shocked by crime. It showed that the
old religion and the sense of the right had faded and gone out; that while
we reckoned ourselves a highly cultivated nation, our bellies had run away
with our brains, and the principles of culture and progress did not exist.

For I suppose that liberty is an accurate index, in men and nations, of
general progress. The theory of personal liberty must always appeal to
the most refined communities and to the men of the rarest perception and
of delicate moral sense. For there are rights which rest on the finest sense
of justice, and, with every degree of civility, it will be more truly felt and
defined. A barbarous tribe of good stock will, by means of their best heads,
secure substantial liberty. But where there is any weakness in a race, and
it becomes in a degree matter of concession and protection from their
stronger neighbors, the incompatibility and offensiveness of the wrong
will of course be most evident to the most cultivated. For it is,—is it not?
—the essence of courtesy, of politeness, of religion, of love, to prefer another, to postpone oneself, to protect another from oneself? That is the
distinction of the gentleman, to defend the weak and redress the injured,
as it is of the savage and the brutal to usurp and use others.

In Massachusetts, as we all know, there has always existed a predominant conservative spirit. We have more money and value of every kind
than other people, and wish to keep them. The plea on which freedom
was resisted was Union. I went to certain serious men, who had a little
more reason than the rest, and inquired why they took this part? They

answered that they had no confidence in their strength to resist the Demo-cratic party; that they saw plainly that all was going to the utmost verge of license; each was vying with his neighbor to lead the party, by propos-ing the worst measure, and they threw themselves on the extreme con-servatism, as a drag on the wheel: that they knew Cuba would be had, and Mexico would be had, and they stood stiffly on conservatism, and as near to monarchy as they could, only to moderate the velocity with which the car was running down the precipice. In short, their theory was despair; the Whig wisdom was only reprieve, a waiting to be last devoured. They side with Carolina, or with Arkansas, only to make a show of Whig strength, wherewith to resist a little longer this general ruin.

I have a respect for conservatism. I know how deeply founded it is in our nature, and how idle are all attempts to shake ourselves free from it. We are all conservatives, half Whig, half Democrat, in our essences: and might as well try to jump out of our skins as to escape from our Whiggery. There are two forces in Nature, by whose antagonism we exist; the power of Fate, Fortune, the laws of the world, the order of things, or however else we choose to phrase it, the material necessities, on the one hand,—and Will or Duty or Freedom on the other.

May and Must, and the sense of right and duty, on the one hand, and the material necessities on the other: May and Must. In vulgar politics the Whig goes for what has been, for the old necessities,—the Musts. The reformer goes for the Better, for the ideal good, for the Mays. But each of these parties must of necessity take in, in some measure, the principles of the other. Each wishes to cover the whole ground; to hold fast *and* to advance. Only, one lays the emphasis on keeping, and the other on advanc-ing. I too think the *musts* are a safe company to follow, and even agree-able. But if we are Whigs, let us be Whigs of nature and science, and so for all the necessities. Let us know that, over and above all the *musts* of poverty and appetite, is the instinct of man to rise, and the instinct to love and help his brother.

Now, Gentlemen, I think we have in this hour instruction again in the simplest lesson. Events roll, millions of men are engaged, and the result is the enforcing of some of those first commandments which we heard in the nursery. We never got beyond our first lesson, for, really, the world exists, as I understand it, to teach the science of liberty, which begins with liberty from fear.

The events of this month are teaching one thing plain and clear, the worthlessness of good tools to bad workmen; that official papers are of no use; resolutions of public meetings, platforms of conventions, no, nor laws, nor constitutions, any more. These are all declaratory of the will of the moment, and are passed with more levity and on grounds far less honorable than ordinary business transactions of the street.

You relied on the constitution. It has not the word *slave* in it; and very good argument has shown that it would not warrant the crimes that are done under it; that, with provisions so vague for an object not named, and which could not be availed of to claim a barrel of corn,—the robbing of a man and of all his posterity is effected. You relied on the Supreme Court. The law was right, excellent law for the lambs. But what if unhappily the judges were chosen from the wolves, and give to all the law a wolfish interpretation? You relied on the Missouri Compromise. That is ridden over. You relied on State sovereignty in the Free States to protect their citizens. They are driven with contempt out of the courts and out of the territory of the Slave States,—if they are so happy as to get out with their lives,—and now you relied on these dismal guaranties infamously made in 1850; and, before the body of Webster is yet crumbled, it is found that they have crumbled. This eternal monument of his fame and of the Union is rotten in four years. They are no guaranty to the Free States. They are a guaranty to the Slave States that, as they have hitherto met with no repulse, they shall meet with none.

I fear there is no reliance to be put on any kind or form of covenant, no, not on sacred forms, none on churches, none on bibles. For one would have said that a Christian would not keep slaves;—but the Christians keep slaves. Of course they will not dare to read the Bible? Won't they? They quote the Bible, quote Paul, quote Christ to justify slavery. If slavery is good, then is lying, theft, arson, homicide, each and all good, and to be maintained by Union societies.

These things show that no forms, neither constitutions, nor laws, nor covenants, nor churches, nor bibles, are of any use in themselves. The Devil nestles comfortably into them all. There is no help but in the head and heart and hamstrings of a man. Covenants are of no use without honest men to keep them; laws of none, but with loyal citizens to obey them. To interpret Christ it needs Christ in the heart. The teachings of the Spirit can be apprehended only by the same spirit that gave them forth. To make good the cause of Freedom, you must draw off from all foolish trust in others. You must be citadels and warriors, yourselves, declarations of Independence, the charter, the battle and the victory. Cromwell said, "We can only resist the superior training of the King's soldiers, by enlisting godly men." And no man has a right to hope that the laws of New York will defend him from the contamination of slaves another day until he has made up his mind that he will not owe his protection to the laws of New York, but to his own sense and spirit. Then he protects New York. He only who is able to stand alone is qualified for society. And that I understand to be the end for which a soul exists in this world, —to be himself the counterbalance of all falsehood and all wrong. "The army of unright is encamped from pole to pole, but the road of victory is known to the just." Everything may be taken away; he may be poor, he may be houseless, yet he will know out of his arms to make a pillow, and out of his breast a bolster. Why have the minority no influence? Because they have not a real minority of one.

I conceive that thus to detach a man and make him feel that he is to owe all to himself, is the way to make him strong and rich; and here the optimist must find, if anywhere, the benefit of Slavery. We have many teachers; we are in this world for culture, to be instructed in realities, in the laws of moral and intelligent nature; and our education is not conducted by toys and luxuries, but by austere and rugged masters, by poverty, solitude, passions, War, Slavery; to know that Paradise is under the shadow of swords; that divine sentiments which are always soliciting us are breathed into us from on high, and are an offset to a Universe of suffering and crime; that self-reliance, the height and perfection of man, is reliance on God. The insight of the religious sentiment will disclose to him unexpected aids in the nature of things. The Persian Saadi said, "Beware of hurting the orphan. When the orphan sets a-crying, the throne of the Almighty is rocked from side to side."

Whenever a man has come to this mind, that there is no Church for him but his believing prayer; no Constitution but his dealing well and justly with his neighbor; no liberty but his invincible will to do right,— then certain aids and allies will promptly appear: for the constitution of the Universe is on his side. It is of no use to vote down gravitation or morals. What is useful will last, whilst that which is hurtful to the world will sink beneath all the opposing forces which it must exasperate. The terror which the Marseillaise struck into oppression, it thunders again to-day,

"Tout est soldat pour vous combattre."

Everything turns soldier to fight you down. The end for which man was made is not crime in any form, and a man cannot steal without incurring the penalties of the thief, though all the legislatures vote that it is virtuous, and though there be a general conspiracy among scholars and official persons to hold him up, and to say, "Nothing is good but stealing." A man who commits a crime defeats the end of his existence. He was created for benefit, and he exists for harm; and as well-doing makes power and wisdom, ill-doing takes them away. A man who steals another man's labor steals away his own faculties; his integrity, his humanity is flowing away from him. The habit of oppression cuts out the moral eyes, and, though the intellect goes on simulating the moral as before, its sanity is gradually destroyed. It takes away the presentiments.

I suppose in general this is allowed, that if you have a nice question of right and wrong, you would not go with it to Louis Napoleon, or to a political hack; or to a slave-driver. The habit of mind of traders in power would not be esteemed favorable to delicate moral perception. American slavery affords no exception to this rule. No excess of good nature or of tenderness in individuals has been able to give a new character to the system, to tear down the shipping-house. The plea that the negro is an inferior race sounds very oddly in my ear in the mouth of a slave-holder. "The masters of slaves seem generally anxious to prove that they are not of a race superior in any noble quality to the meanest of their bondmen." And indeed when the Southerner points to the anatomy of the negro, and talks of chimpanzee,—I recall Montesquieu's remark, "It will not do to say that negroes are men, lest it should turn out that whites are not."

Slavery is disheartening; but Nature is not so helpless but it can rid itself at last of every wrong. But the spasms of Nature are centuries and ages, and will tax the faith of short-lived men. Slowly, slowly the Avenger comes, but comes surely. The proverbs of the nations affirm these delays, but affirm the arrival. They say, "God may consent, but not forever." The delay of the Divine Justice—this was the meaning and soul of the Greek Tragedy; this the soul of their religion. "There has come, too, one to whom lurking warfare is dear, Retribution, with a soul full of wiles; a violator of hospitality; guileful without the guilt of guile; limping, late in her arrival." They said of the happiness of the unjust, that "at its close it begets itself an offspring and does not die childless, and instead of good fortune, there sprouts forth for posterity ever-ravening calamity":

> "For evil word shall evil word be said,
> For murder-stroke a murder-stroke be paid.
> Who smites must smart."

These delays, you see them now in the temper of the times. The national spirit in this country is so drowsy, preoccupied with interest, deaf to principle. The Anglo-Saxon race is proud and strong and selfish. They believe only in Anglo-Saxons. In 1825 Greece found America deaf, Poland found America deaf, Italy and Hungary found her deaf. England maintains trade, not liberty; stands against Greece; against Hungary; against Schleswig Holstein; against the French Republic, whilst it was a republic.

To faint hearts the times offer no invitation, and torpor exists here throughout the active classes on the subject of domestic slavery and its appalling aggressions. Yes, that is the stern edict of Providence, that liberty shall be no hasty fruit, but that event on event, population on population, age on age, shall cast itself into the opposite scale, and not until liberty has slowly accumulated weight enough to countervail and preponderate against all this, can the sufficient recoil come. All the great cities, all the refined circles, all the statesmen, Guizot, Palmerston, Webster, Calhoun, are sure to be found befriending liberty with their words, and crushing it with their votes. Liberty is never cheap. It is made difficult, because freedom is the accomplishment and perfectness of man. He is a finished man; earning and bestowing good; equal to the world; at home in nature and dignifying that; the sun does not see anything nobler, and has nothing to teach him. Therefore mountains of difficulty must be surmounted, stern trials met, wiles of seduction, dangers, healed by a quarantine of calamities to measure his strength before he dare say, I am free.

Whilst the inconsistency of slavery with the principles on which the world is built guarantees its downfall, I own that the patience it requires is almost too sublime for mortals, and seems to demand of us more than mere hoping. And when one sees how fast the rot spreads,—it is growing serious—I think we demand of superior men that they be superior in this, —that the mind and the virtue shall give their verdict in their day, and accelerate so far the progress of civilization. Possession is sure to throw its stupid strength for existing power, and appetite and ambition will go for that. Let the aid of virtue, intelligence and education be cast where they rightfully belong. They are organically ours. Let them be loyal to their own. I wish to see the instructed class here know their own flag, and not fire on their comrades. We should not forgive the clergy for taking on every issue the immoral side; nor the Bench, if it put itself on the side of the culprit; nor the Government, if it sustain the mob against the laws.

It is a potent support and ally to a brave man standing single, or with a few, for the right, and out-voted and ostracized, to know that better men in other parts of the country appreciate the service and will rightly report him to his own and the next age. Without this assurance, he will sooner sink. He may well say, If my countrymen do not care to be defended, I too will decline the controversy, from which I only reap invectives and hatred. Yet the lovers of liberty may with reason tax the coldness and indifferentism of scholars and literary men. They are lovers of liberty in Greece and Rome and in the English Commonwealth, but they are lukewarm lovers of the liberty of America in 1854. The Universities are not, as in Hobbes's time, "the core of rebellion," no, but the seat of inertness. They have forgotten their allegiance to the Muse, and grown worldly and political. I listened, lately, on one of those occasions when the University chooses one of its distinguished sons returning from the political arena, believing that Senators and Statesmen would be glad to throw off the harness and to dip again in the Castalian pools. But if audiences forget themselves, statesmen do not. The low bows to all the crockery gods of the day were duly made:—only in one part of the discourse the orator allowed to transpire rather against his will a little sober sense. It was this. "I am as you see a man virtuously inclined, and only corrupted by my profession of politics. I should prefer the right side. You, gentlemen of these literary and scientific schools, and the important class you represent, have the power to make your verdict clear and prevailing. Had you done so, you would have found me its glad organ and champion. Abstractly, I should have preferred that side. But you have not done it. You have not spoken out. You have failed to arm me. I can only deal with masses as I find them. Abstractions are not for me. I go then for such parties and opinions as have provided me with a working apparatus. I give you my word, not without regret, that I was first for you; and though I am now to deny and condemn you, you see it is not my will but the party necessity." Having made this manifesto and professed his adoration for liberty in the time of his grandfathers, he proceeded with his work of denouncing freedom and freemen at the present day, much in the tone and spirit in which Lord Bacon prosecuted his benefactor Essex. He denounced every name and aspect under which liberty and progress dare show themselves in this age and country, but with a lingering conscience which qualified each sentence with a recommendation to mercy.

But I put it to every noble and generous spirit, to every poetic, every heroic, every religious heart, that not so is our learning, our education, our poetry, our worship to be declared. Liberty is aggressive, Liberty is the crusade of all brave and conscientious men, the Epic Poetry, the new religion, the chivalry of all gentlemen. This is the oppressed Lady whom true knights on their oath and honor must rescue and save.

Now at last we are disenchanted and shall have no more false hopes. I respect the Anti-Slavery Society. It is the Cassandra that has foretold all that has befallen, fact for fact, years ago; foretold all, and no man laid it to heart. It seemed, as the Turks say, "Fate makes that a man should not believe his own eyes." But the Fugitive Law did much to unglue the eyes of men, and now the Nebraska Bill leaves us staring.[3] The Anti-Slavery Society will add many members this year. The Whig Party will join it: the Democrats will join it. The population of the Free States will join it. I doubt not, at last, the Slave States will join it. But be that sooner or later, and whoever comes or stays away, I hope we have reached the end of our unbelief, have come to a belief that there is a divine Providence in the world, which will not save us but through our own co-operation.

3. It was the Kansas-Nebraska Act of 1854 that occasioned Emerson's lecture. This act repealed the Missouri Compromise, which, among other things, forbade slavery in the Louisiana Territory north of latitude $36°30'$; and, in turn, the Kansas-Nebraska Act permitted the territories of Kansas and Nebraska, rather than Congress itself, to decide whether they would have slavery or not.—*Editor.*

Frederick Douglass
(1817?–1895)

FREDERICK DOUGLASS was born a slave in Maryland. He fled North in 1838, and there became one of the most articulate opponents of slavery. He lectured both in the United States and abroad, and established in Rochester, New York, the antislavery weekly *North Star* (1847–1864), later called *Frederick Douglass's Paper*. Douglass held several positions in government and is the author of a classic autobiography, *Narrative of the Life of Frederick Douglass*, first published in 1845 and revised and enlarged in 1855 and 1892.

"The Meaning of July Fourth for the Negro" was first delivered as a speech in Rochester, New York, on July 5, 1852.

THE MEANING OF JULY
FOURTH FOR THE NEGRO

Mr. President, Friends and Fellow Citizens:

He who could address this audience without a quailing sensation, has
stronger nerves than I have. I do not remember ever to have appeared as
a speaker before any assembly more shrinkingly, nor with greater distrust
of my ability, than I do this day. A feeling has crept over me quite un-
favorable to the exercise of my limited powers of speech. The task before
me is one which requires much previous thought and study for its proper
performance. I know that apologies of this sort are generally considered
flat and unmeaning. I trust, however, that mine will not be so considered.
Should I seem at ease, my appearance would much misrepresent me. The
little experience I have had in addressing public meetings, in country
school houses, avails me nothing on the present occasion.

The papers and placards say that I am to deliver a Fourth of July
Oration. This certainly sounds large, and out of the common way, for me.
It is true that I have often had the privilege to speak in this beautiful
Hall, and to address many who now honor me with their presence. But
neither their familiar faces, nor the perfect gage I think I have of Corin-
thian Hall seems to free me from embarrassment.

The fact is, ladies and gentlemen, the distance between this platform and
the slave plantation, from which I escaped, is considerable—and the
difficulties to be overcome in getting from the latter to the former are by
no means slight. That I am here to-day is, to me, a matter of astonishment
as well as of gratitude. You will not, therefore, be surprised, if in what I
have to say I evince no elaborate preparation, nor grace my speech with
any high sounding exordium. With little experience and with less learning,
I have been able to throw my thoughts hastily and imperfectly together;

and trusting to your patient and generous indulgence, I will proceed to lay them before you.

This, for the purpose of this celebration, is the Fourth of July. It is the birthday of your National Independence, and of your political freedom. This, to you, is what the Passover was to the emancipated people of God. It carries your minds back to the day, and to the act of your great deliverance; and to the signs, and to the wonders, associated with that act, and that day. This celebration also marks the beginning of another year of your national life; and reminds you that the Republic of America is now 76 years old. I am glad, fellow-citizens, that your nation is so young. Seventy-six years, though a good old age for a man, is but a mere speck in the life of a nation. Three score years and ten is the allotted time for individual men; but nations number their years by thousands. According to this fact, you are, even now, only in the beginning of your national career, still lingering in the period of childhood. I repeat, I am glad this is so. There is hope in the thought, and hope is much needed, under the dark clouds which lower above the horizon. The eye of the reformer is met with angry flashes, portending disastrous times; but his heart may well beat lighter at the thought that America is young, and that she is still in the impressible stage of her existence. May he not hope that high lessons of wisdom, of justice and of truth, will yet give direction to her destiny? Were the nation older, the patriot's heart might be sadder, and the reformer's brow heavier. Its future might be shrouded in gloom, and the hope of its prophets go out in sorrow. There is consolation in the thought that America is young.—Great streams are not easily turned from channels, worn deep in the course of ages. They may sometimes rise in quiet and stately majesty, and inundate the land, refreshing and fertilizing the earth with their mysterious properties. They may also rise in wrath and fury, and bear away, on their angry waves, the accumulated wealth of years of toil and hardship. They, however, gradually flow back to the same old channel, and flow on as serenely as ever. But, while the river may not be turned aside, it may dry up, and leave nothing behind but the withered branch, and the unsightly rock, to howl in the abyss-sweeping wind, the sad tale of departed glory. As with rivers so with nations.

Fellow-citizens, I shall not presume to dwell at length on the associations that cluster about this day. The simple story of it is, that, 76 years ago, the people of this country were British subjects. The style and title of your "sovereign people" (in which you now glory) was not then born. You were under the British Crown. Your fathers esteemed the English Government as the home government; and England as the fatherland. This home government, you know, although a considerable distance from your home, did, in the exercise of its parental prerogatives, impose upon its colonial children, such restraints, burdens and limitations, as, in its mature judgment, it deemed wise, right and proper.

But your fathers, who had not adopted the fashionable idea of this day, of the infallibility of government, and the absolute character of its acts, presumed to differ from the home government in respect of the wisdom and the justice of some of those burdens and restraints. They went so far in their excitement as to pronounce the measures of government unjust, unreasonable, and oppressive, and altogether such as ought not to be quietly submitted to. I scarcely need say, fellow-citizens, that my opinion of those measures fully accords with that of your fathers. Such a declaration of agreement on my part would not be worth much to anybody. It would certainly prove nothing as to what part I might have taken had I lived during the great controversy of 1776. To say now that America was right, and England wrong, is exceedingly easy. Everybody can say it; the dastard, not less than the noble brave, can flippantly discant on the tyranny of England towards the American Colonies. It is fashionable to do so; but there was a time when, to pronounce against England, and in favor of the cause of the colonies, tried men's souls. They who did so were accounted in their day plotters of mischief, agitators and rebels, dangerous men. To side with the right against the wrong, with the weak against the strong, and with the oppressed against the oppressor! here lies the merit, and the one which, of all others, seems unfashionable in our day. The cause of liberty may be stabbed by the men who glory in the deeds of your fathers. But, to proceed.

Feeling themselves harshly and unjustly treated, by the home government, your fathers, like men of honesty, and men of spirit, earnestly sought redress. They petitioned and remonstrated; they did so in a decorous, respectful, and loyal manner. Their conduct was wholly unexceptionable. This, however, did not answer the purpose. They saw themselves treated with sovereign indifference, coldness and scorn. Yet they persevered. They were not the men to look back.

As the sheet anchor takes a firmer hold, when the ship is tossed by the storm, so did the cause of your fathers grow stronger as it breasted the chilling blasts of kingly displeasure. The greatest and best of British statesmen admitted its justice, and the loftiest eloquence of the British Senate came to its support. But, with that blindness which seems to be the unvarying characteristic of tyrants, since Pharaoh and his hosts were drowned in the Red Sea, the British Government persisted in the exactions complained of.

The madness of this course, we believe, is admitted now, even by England; but we fear the lesson is wholly lost on our present rulers.

Oppression makes a wise man mad. Your fathers were wise men, and if they did not go mad, they became restive under this treatment. They felt themselves the victims of grievous wrongs, wholly incurable in their colonial capacity. With brave men there is always a remedy for oppression. Just here, the idea of a total separation of the colonies from the crown was born! It was a startling idea, much more so than we, at this distance of time, regard it. The timid and the prudent (as has been intimated) of that day were, of course, shocked and alarmed by it.

Such people lived then, had lived before, and will, probably, ever have a place on this planet; and their course, in respect to any great change (no matter how great the good to be attained, or the wrong to be redressed by it), may be calculated with as much precision as can be the course of the stars. They hate all changes, but silver, gold and copper change! Of this sort of change they are always strongly in favor.

These people were called Tories in the days of your fathers; and the appellation, probably, conveyed the same idea that is meant by a more modern, though a somewhat less euphonious term, which we often find in our papers, applied to some of our old politicians.

Their opposition to the then dangerous thought was earnest and powerful; but, amid all their terror and affrighted vociferations against it, the alarming and revolutionary idea moved on, and the country with it.

On the 2d of July, 1776, the old Continental Congress, to the dismay of the lovers of ease, and the worshipers of property, clothed that dreadful idea with all the authority of national sanction. They did so in the form of a resolution; and as we seldom hit upon resolutions, drawn up in our day, whose transparency is at all equal to this, it may refresh your minds and help my story if I read it.

> "Resolved, That these united colonies are, and of right, ought to be free and Independent States; that they are absolved from all allegiance to the British Crown; and that all political connection between them and the State of Great Britain is, and ought to be, dissolved."

Citizens, your fathers made good that resolution. They succeeded; and to-day you reap the fruits of their success. The freedom gained is yours; and you, therefore, may properly celebrate this anniversary. The 4th of July is the first great fact in your nation's history—the very ring bolt in the chain of your yet undeveloped destiny.

Pride and patriotism, not less than gratitude, prompt you to celebrate and to hold it in perpetual remembrance. I have said that the Declaration of Independence is the ring bolt to the chain of your nation's destiny; so, indeed, I regard it. The principles contained in that instrument are saving principles. Stand by those principles, be true to them on all occasions, in all places, against all foes, and at whatever cost.

From the round top of your ship of state, dark and threatening clouds may be seen. Heavy billows, like mountains in the distance, disclose to the leeward huge forms of flinty rocks! That bolt drawn, that chain broken, and all is lost. Cling to this day—cling to it, and to its principles, with the grasp of a storm-tossed mariner to a spar at midnight.

The coming into being of a nation, in any circumstances, is an interesting event. But, besides general considerations, there were peculiar circumstances which make the advent of this republic an event of special attractiveness.

The whole scene, as I look back to it, was simple, dignified and sublime. The population of the country, at the time, stood at the insignificant number of three millions. The country was poor in the munitions of war. The population was weak and scattered, and the country a wilderness unsubdued. There were then no means of concert and combination, such as exist now. Neither steam nor lightning had then been reduced to order and discipline. From the Potomac to the Delaware was a journey of many days. Under these, and innumerable other disadvantages, your fathers declared for liberty and independence and triumphed.

Fellow Citizens, I am not wanting in respect for the fathers of this republic. The signers of the Declaration of Independence were brave men. They were great men, too—great enough to give frame to a great age. It does not often happen to a nation to raise, at one time, such a number of truly great men. The point from which I am compelled to view them is not, certainly, the most favorable; and yet I cannot contemplate their great deeds with less than admiration. They were statesmen, patriots and heroes, and for the good they did, and the principles they contended for, I will unite with you to honor their memory.

They loved their country better than their own private interests; and, though this is not the highest form of human excellence, all will concede that it is a rare virtue, and that when it is exhibited it ought to command respect. He who will, intelligently, lay down his life for his country is a man whom it is not in human nature to despise. Your fathers staked their lives, their fortunes, and their sacred honor, on the cause of their country. In their admiration of liberty, they lost sight of all other interests.

They were peace men; but they preferred revolution to peaceful submission to bondage. They were quiet men; but they did not shrink from agitating against oppression. They showed forbearance; but that they knew its limits. They believed in order; but not in the order of tyranny. With them, nothing was "settled" that was not right. With them, justice, liberty and humanity were "final"; not slavery and oppression. You may well cherish the memory of such men. They were great in their day and generation. Their solid manhood stands out the more as we contrast it with these degenerate times.

How circumspect, exact and proportionate were all their movements! How unlike the politicians of an hour! Their statesmanship looked beyond the passing moment, and stretched away in strength into the distant future. They seized upon eternal principles, and set a glorious example in their defence. Mark them!

Fully appreciating the hardships to be encountered, firmly believing in the right of their cause, honorably inviting the scrutiny of an on-looking world, reverently appealing to heaven to attest their sincerity, soundly comprehending the solemn responsibility they were about to assume, wisely measuring the terrible odds against them, your fathers, the fathers of this republic, did, most deliberately, under the inspiration of a glorious patriotism, with a sublime faith in the great principles of justice and freedom, lay deep, the corner-stone of the national super-structure, which has risen and still rises in grandeur around you.

Of this fundamental work, this day is the anniversary. Our eyes are met with demonstrations of joyous enthusiasm. Banners and pennants wave exultingly on the breeze. The din of business, too, is hushed. Even mammon seems to have quitted his grasp on this day. The ear-piercing fife and the stirring drum unite their accents with the ascending peal of a thousand church bells. Prayers are made, hymns are sung, and sermons are preached in honor of this day; while the quick martial tramp of a great and multitudinous nation, echoed back by all the hills, valleys and mountains of a vast continent, bespeak the occasion one of thrilling and universal interest—a nation's jubilee.

Friends and citizens, I need not enter further into the causes which led to this anniversary. Many of you understand them better than I do. You could instruct me in regard to them. That is a branch of knowledge in which you feel, perhaps, a much deeper interest than your speaker. The causes which led to the separation of the colonies from the British crown have never lacked for a tongue. They have all been taught in your common schools, narrated at your firesides, unfolded from your pulpits, and thundered from your legislative halls, and are as familiar to you as household words. They form the staple of your national poetry and eloquence.

I remember, also, that, as a people, Americans are remarkably familiar with all facts which make in their own favor. This is esteemed by some as a national trait—perhaps a national weakness. It is a fact, that whatever makes for the wealth or for the reputation of Americans and can be had cheap! will be found by Americans. I shall not be charged with slandering Americans if I say I think the American side of any question may be safely left in American hands.

I leave, therefore, the great deeds of your fathers to other gentlemen whose claim to have been regularly descended will be less likely to be disputed than mine!

My business, if I have any here to-day, is with the present. The accepted time with God and His cause is the ever-living now.

> Trust no future, however pleasant,
> Let the dead past bury its dead;
> Act, act in the living present,
> Heart within, and God overhead.

We have to do with the past only as we can make it useful to the present and to the future. To all inspiring motives, to noble deeds which can be gained from the past, we are welcome. But now is the time, the important time. Your fathers have lived, died, and have done their work, and have done much of it well. You live and must die, and you must do your work. You have no right to enjoy a child's share in the labor of your fathers, unless your children are to be blest by your labors. You have no right to wear out and waste the hard-earned fame of your fathers to cover your indolence. Sydney Smith tells us that men seldom eulogize the wisdom and virtues of their fathers, but to excuse some folly or wickedness of their own. This truth is not a doubtful one. There are illustrations of it near and remote, ancient and modern. It was fashionable, hundreds of years ago, for the children of Jacob to boast, we have "Abraham to our father," when they had long lost Abraham's faith and spirit. That people contented themselves under the shadow of Abraham's great name, while they repudiated the deeds which made his name great. Need I remind you that a similar thing is being done all over this country to-day? Need I tell you that the Jews are not the only people who built the tombs of the prophets, and garnished the sepulchers of the righteous? Washington could not die till he had broken the chains of his slaves. Yet his monument is built up by the price of human blood, and the traders in the bodies and souls of men shout—"We have Washington to our father."—Alas! that it should be so; yet so it is.

> The evil that men do, lives after them,
> The good is oft interred with their bones.

Fellow-citizens, pardon me, allow me to ask, why am I called upon to speak here to-day? What have I, or those I represent, to do with your national independence? Are the great principles of political freedom and of natural justice, embodied in that Declaration of Independence, extended to us? and am I, therefore, called upon to bring our humble offering to the national altar, and to confess the benefits and express devout gratitude for the blessings resulting from your independence to us?

Would to God, both for your sakes and ours, that an affirmative answer could be truthfully returned to these questions! Then would my task be light, and my burden easy and delightful. For *who* is there so cold, that a nation's sympathy could not warm him? Who so obdurate and dead to the claims of gratitude, that would not thankfully acknowledge such priceless benefits? Who so stolid and selfish, that would not give his voice to swell the hallelujahs of a nation's jubilee, when the chains of servitude had been torn from his limbs? I am not that man. In a case like that, the dumb might eloquently speak, and the "lame man leap as an hart."

But such is not the state of the case. I say it with a sad sense of the disparity between us. I am not included within the pale of this glorious anniversary! Your high independence only reveals the immeasurable distance between us. The blessings in which you, this day, rejoice, are not enjoyed in common.—The rich inheritance of justice, liberty, prosperity and independence, bequeathed by your fathers, is shared by you, not by me. The sunlight that brought light and healing to you, has brought stripes and death to me. This Fourth of July is *yours,* not *mine. You* may rejoice, *I* must mourn. To drag a man in fetters into the grand illuminated temple of liberty, and call upon him to join you in joyous anthems, were inhuman mockery and sacrilegious irony. Do you mean, citizens, to mock me, by asking me to speak to-day? If so, there is a parallel to your conduct. And let me warn you that it is dangerous to copy the example of a nation whose crimes, towering up to heaven, were thrown down by the breath of the Almighty, burying that nation in irrevocable ruin! I can to-day take up the plaintive lament of a peeled and woe-smitten people!

"By the rivers of Babylon, there we sat down. Yea! we wept when we remembered Zion. We hanged our harps upon the willows in the midst thereof. For there, they that carried us away captive, required of us a song; and they who wasted us required of us mirth, saying, Sing us one of the songs of Zion. How can we sing the Lord's song in a strange land? If I forget thee, O Jerusalem, let my right hand forget her cunning. If I do not remember thee, let my tongue cleave to the roof of my mouth."

Fellow-citizens, above your national, tumultuous joy, I hear the mournful wail of millions! whose chains, heavy and grievous yesterday, are, to-day, rendered more intolerable by the jubilee shouts that reach them. If I do forget, if I do not faithfully remember those bleeding children of sorrow this day, "may my right hand forget her cunning, and may my tongue cleave to the roof of my mouth!" To forget them, to pass lightly over their wrongs, and to chime in with the popular theme, would be treason most scandalous and shocking, and would make me a reproach before God and the world. My subject, then, fellow-citizens, is American slavery. I shall see this day and its popular characteristics from the slave's point of view. Standing there identified with the American bondman, making his wrongs mine, I do not hesitate to declare, with all my soul, that the character and conduct of this nation never looked blacker to me than on this 4th of July! Whether we turn to the declarations of the past, or to the professions of the present, the conduct of the nation seems equally hideous and revolting. America is false to the past, false to the present, and solemnly binds herself to be false to the future. Standing with God and the crushed and bleeding slave on this occasion, I will, in the name of humanity which is outraged, in the name of liberty which is fettered, in the name of the constitution and the Bible which are disregarded and trampled upon, dare to call in question and to denounce, with all the emphasis I can command, everything that serves to perpetuate slavery—the great sin and shame of America! "I will not equivocate; I will not excuse";[1] I will use the severest language I can command; and yet not one word shall escape me that any man, whose judgment is not blinded by prejudice, or who is not at heart a slaveholder, shall not confess to be right and just.

But I fancy I hear some one of my audience say, "It is just in this circumstance that you and your brother abolitionists fail to make a favorable impression on the public mind. Would you argue more, and denounce less; would you persuade more, and rebuke less; your cause would be much more likely to succeed." But, I submit, where all is plain there is nothing to be argued. What point in the anti-slavery creed would you have me argue? On what branch of the subject do the people of this country need light? Must I undertake to prove that the slave is a man? That point is conceded already. Nobody doubts it. The slaveholders themselves acknowledge it in the enactment of laws for their government. They acknowledge it when they punish disobedience on the part of the slave. There are seventy-two crimes in the State of Virginia, which, if committed by a black man (no matter how ignorant he be), subject him to the punishment of death; while only two of the same crimes will subject a white man to the like punishment. What is this but the acknowledgment that the slave is a moral, intellectual, and responsible being? The manhood of the slave is conceded. It is admitted in the fact that Southern statute books are covered with enactments forbidding, under severe fines and penalties, the teaching of the slave to read or to write. When you can point to any such laws in reference to the beasts of the field, then I may consent to argue the manhood of the slave. When the dogs in your streets, when the fowls of the air, when the cattle on your hills, when the fish of the sea, and the reptiles that crawl, shall be unable to distinguish the slave from a brute, *then* will I argue with you that the slave is a man!

For the present, it is enough to affirm the equal manhood of the Negro race. Is it not astonishing that, while we are ploughing, planting, and reaping, using all kinds of mechanical tools, erecting houses, constructing

---

1. These are the words of William Lloyd Garrison, a famous Abolitionist, in the first issue of his abolitionist weekly, *The Liberator* (1831–1865).—*Editor.*

bridges, building ships, working in metals of brass, iron, copper, silver and gold; that, while we are reading, writing and ciphering, acting as clerks, merchants, and secretaries, having among us lawyers, doctors, ministers, poets, authors, editors, orators and teachers; that, while we are engaged in all manner of enterprises common to other men, digging gold in California, capturing the whale in the Pacific, feeding sheep and cattle on the hill-side, living, moving, acting, thinking, planning, living in families as husbands, wives and children, and, above all, confessing and worshipping the Christian's God, and looking hopefully for life and immortality beyond the grave, we are called upon to prove that we are men!

Would you have me argue that man is entitled to liberty? That he is the rightful owner of his own body? You have already declared it. Must I argue the wrongfulness of slavery? Is that a question for Republicans? Is it to be settled by the rules of logic and argumentation, as a matter beset with great difficulty, involving a doubtful application of the principle of justice, hard to be understood? How should I look to-day, in the presence of Americans, dividing, and subdividing a discourse, to show that men have a natural right to freedom? speaking of it relatively and positively, negatively and affirmitively. To do so, would be to make myself ridiculous, and to offer an insult to your understanding.—There is not a man beneath the canopy of heaven that does not know that slavery is wrong *for him*.

What, am I to argue that it is wrong to make men brutes, to rob them of their liberty, to work them without wages, to keep them ignorant of their relations to their fellow men, to beat them with sticks, to flay their flesh with the lash, to load their limbs with irons, to hunt them with dogs, to sell them at auction, to sunder their families, to knock out their teeth, to burn their flesh, to starve them into obedience and submission to their masters? Must I argue that a system thus marked with blood, and stained with pollution, is *wrong?* No! I will not. I have better employment for my time and strength than such arguments would imply.

What, then, remains to be argued? Is it that slavery is not divine; that God did not establish it; that our doctors of divinity are mistaken? There is blasphemy in the thought. That which is inhuman, cannot be divine! *Who* can reason on such a proposition? They that can, may; I cannot. The time for such argument is passed.

At a time like this, scorching irony, not convincing argument, is needed. O! had I the ability, and could reach the nation's ear, I would, to-day, pour out a fiery stream of biting ridicule, blasting reproach, withering sarcasm, and stern rebuke. For it is not light that is needed, but fire; it is not the gentle shower, but thunder. We need the storm, the whirlwind, and the earthquake. The feeling of the nation must be quickened; the conscience of the nation must be roused; the propriety of the nation must be startled; the hypocrisy of the nation must be exposed; and its crimes against God and man must be proclaimed and denounced.

What, to the American slave, is your 4th of July? I answer; a day that reveals to him, more than all other days in the year, the gross injustice and cruelty to which he is the constant victim. To him, your celebration is a sham; your boasted liberty, an unholy license; your national greatness, swelling vanity; your sounds of rejoicing are empty and heartless; your denunciation of tyrants, brass fronted impudence; your shouts of liberty and equality, hollow mockery; your prayers and hymns, your sermons and thanksgivings, with all your religious parade and solemnity, are, to Him, mere bombast, fraud, deception, impiety, and hypocrisy—a thin veil to cover up crimes which would disgrace a nation of savages. There is not a nation on the earth guilty of practices more shocking and bloody than are the people of the United States, at this very hour.

Go where you may, search where you will, roam through all the monarchies and despotisms of the Old World, travel through South America, search out every abuse, and when you have found the last, lay your facts by the side of the everyday practices of this nation, and you will say with me, that, for revolting barbarity and shameless hypocrisy, America reigns without a rival.

Take the American slave-trade, which we are told by the papers, is especially prosperous just now. Ex-Senator Benton tells us that the price of men was never higher than now.[2] He mentions the fact to show that slavery is in no danger. This trade is one of the peculiarities of American institutions. It is carried on in all the large towns and cities in one-half of this confederacy; and millions are pocketed every year by dealers in this horrid traffic. In several states this trade is a chief source of wealth. It is called (in contradistinction to the foreign slave-trade) *"the internal slave-trade."* It is, probably, called so, too, in order to divert from it the horror with which the foreign slave-trade is contemplated. That trade has long since been denounced by this government as piracy. It has been denounced with burning words from the high places of the nation as an execrable traffic. To arrest it, to put an end to it, this nation keeps a squadron, at immense cost, on the coast of Africa. Everywhere, in this country, it is safe to speak of this foreign slave-trade as a most inhuman traffic, opposed alike to the laws of God and of man. The duty to extirpate and destroy it, is admitted even by our doctors of divinity. In order to put an end to it, some of these last have consented that their colored brethren (nominally free) should leave this country, and establish themselves on the western coast of Africa! It is, however, a notable fact that,

2. Thomas Hart Benton (1782–1858) served in the United States Senate from 1820 to 1850. A rigid hard-money man, he was known as "Old Bullion" Benton.—*Editor.*

while so much execration is poured out by Americans upon all those engaged in the foreign slave-trade, the men engaged in the slave-trade between the states pass without condemnation, and their business is deemed honorable.

Behold the practical operation of this internal slave-trade, the American slave-trade, sustained by American politics and American religion. Here you will see men and women reared like swine for the market. You know what is a swine-drover? I will show you a man-drover. They inhabit all Southern States. They perambulate the country, and crowd the highways of the nation, with droves of human stock. You will see one of these human flesh jobbers, armed with pistol, whip, and bowie-knife, driving a company of a hundred men, women, and children, from the Potomac to the slave market at New Orleans. These wretched people are to be sold singly, or in lots, to suit purchasers. They are food for the cotton-field and the deadly sugar-mill. Mark the sad procession, as it moves wearily along, and the inhuman wretch who drives them. Hear his savage yells and his blood-curdling oaths, as he hurries on his affrighted captives! There, see the old man with locks thinned and gray. Cast one glance, if you please, upon that young mother, whose shoulders are bare to the scorching sun, her briny tears falling on the brow of the babe in her arms. See, too, that girl of thirteen, weeping, yes! weeping, as she thinks of the mother from whom she has been torn! The drove moves tardily. Heat and sorrow have nearly consumed their strength; suddenly you hear a quick snap, like the discharge of a rifle; the fetters clank, and the chain rattles simultaneously; your ears are saluted with a scream, that seems to have torn its way to the centre of your soul! The crack you heard was the sound of the slave-whip; the scream you heard was from the woman you saw with the babe. Her speed had faltered under the weight of her child and her chains! that gash on her shoulder tells her to move on. Follow this drove to New Orleans. Attend the auction; see men examined like horses; see the forms of women rudely and brutally exposed to the shocking gaze of American slave-buyers. See this drove sold and separated forever; and never forget the deep, sad sobs that arose from that scattered multitude. Tell me, citizens, where, under the sun, you can witness a spectacle more fiendish and shocking. Yet this is but a glance at the American slave-trade, as it exists, at this moment, in the ruling part of the United States.

I was born amid such sights and scenes. To me the American slave-trade is a terrible reality. When a child, my soul was often pierced with a sense of its horrors. I lived on Philpot Street, Fell's Point, Baltimore, and have watched from the wharves the slave ships in the Basin, anchored from the shore, with their cargoes of human flesh, waiting for favorable winds to waft them down the Chesapeake. There was, at that time, a grand slave mart kept at the head of Pratt Street, by Austin Woldfolk. His agents were sent into every town and county in Maryland, announcing their arrival, through the papers, and on flaming *"hand-bills,"* headed cash for Negroes. These men were generally well dressed men, and very captivating in their manners; ever ready to drink, to treat, and to gamble. The fate of many a slave has depended upon the turn of a single card; and many a child has been snatched from the arms of its mother by bargains arranged in a state of brutal drunkenness.

The flesh-mongers gather up their victims by dozens, and drive them, chained, to the general depot at Baltimore. When a sufficient number has been collected here, a ship is chartered for the purpose of conveying the forlorn crew to Mobile, or to New Orleans. From the slave prison to the ship, they are usually driven in the darkness of night; for since the anti-slavery agitation, a certain caution is observed.

In the deep, still darkness of midnight, I have been often aroused by the dead, heavy footsteps, and the piteous cries of the chained gangs that passed our door. The anguish of my boyish heart was intense; and I was often consoled, when speaking to my mistress in the morning, to hear her say that the custom was very wicked; that she hated to hear the rattle of the chains and the heart-rending cries. I was glad to find one who sympathized with me in my horror.

Fellow-citizens, this murderous traffic is, to-day, in active operation in this boasted republic. In the solitude of my spirit I see clouds of dust raised on the highways of the South; I see the bleeding footsteps; I hear the doleful wail of fettered humanity on the way to the slave-markets, where the victims are to be sold like *horses, sheep,* and *swine,* knocked off to the highest bidder. There I see the tenderest ties ruthlessly broken, to gratify the lust, caprice and rapacity of the buyers and sellers of men. My soul sickens at the sight.

> Is this the land your Fathers loved,
>   The freedom which they toiled to win?
> Is this the earth whereon they moved?
>   Are these the graves they slumber in?

But a still more inhuman, disgraceful, and scandalous state of things remains to be presented. By an act of the American Congress, not yet two years old, slavery has been nationalized in its most horrible and revolting form. By that act, Mason and Dixon's line has been obliterated; New York has become as Virginia; and the power to hold, hunt, and sell men, women and children, as slaves, remains no longer a mere state institution, but is now an institution of the whole United States. The power is co-extensive with the star-spangled banner, and American Christianity. Where these go, may also go the merciless slave-hunter. Where these are, man is not sacred. He is a bird for the sportsman's gun. By that most foul and fiendish of all human decrees, the liberty and person of every man are put in peril. Your broad republican domain is hunting ground for *men*. *Not* for thieves and robbers, enemies of society, merely, but for men guilty of no crime. Your law-makers have commanded all good citizens to engage in this hellish sport. Your President, your Secretary of State, your *lords, nobles,* and ecclesiastics enforce, as a duty you owe to your free and glorious country, and to your God, that you do this accursed thing. Not fewer than forty Americans have, within the past two years, been hunted down and, without a moment's warning, hurried away in chains, and consigned to slavery and excruciating torture. Some of these have had wives and children, dependent on them for bread; but of this, no account was made. The right of the hunter to his prey stands superior to the right of marriage, and to *all* rights in this republic, the rights of God included! For black men there is neither law nor justice, humanity nor religion. The Fugitive Slave *Law* makes mercy to them a crime; and bribes the judge who tries them. An American judge gets ten dollars for every victim he consigns to slavery, and five, when he fails to do so. The oath of any two villains is sufficient, under this hell-black enactment, to send the most pious and exemplary black man into the remorseless jaws of slavery! His own testimony is nothing. He can bring no witnesses for himself. The minister of American justice is bound by the law to hear but *one* side; and *that* side is the side of the oppressor. Let this damning fact be perpetually told. Let it be thundered around the world that in tyrant-killing, king-hating, people-loving, democratic, Christian America the seats of justice are filled with judges who hold their offices under an open and palpable *bribe,* and are bound, in deciding the case of a man's liberty, *to hear only his accusers!*

In glaring violation of justice, in shameless disregard of the forms of administering law, in cunning arrangement to entrap the defenceless, and in diabolical intent this Fugitive Slave Law stands alone in the annals of tyrannical legislation. I doubt if there be another nation on the globe having the brass and the baseness to put such a law on the statute-book. If any man in this assembly thinks differently from me in this matter, and feels able to disprove my statements, I will gladly confront him at any suitable time and place he may select.

I take this law to be one of the grossest infringements of Christian Liberty, and, if the churches and ministers of our country were not stupidly blind, or most wickedly indifferent, they, too, would so regard it.

At the very moment that they are thanking God for the enjoyment of civil and religious liberty, and for the right to worship God according to the dictates of their own consciences, they are utterly silent in respect to a law which robs religion of its chief significance and makes it utterly worthless to a world lying in wickedness. Did this law concern the *"mint, anise, and cummin"*—abridge the right to sing psalms, to partake of the sacrament, or to engage in any of the ceremonies of religion, it would be smitten by the thunder of a thousand pulpits. A general shout would go up from the church demanding *repeal, repeal, instant repeal!*—And it would go hard with that politician who presumed to solicit the votes of the people without inscribing this motto on his banner. Further, if this demand were not complied with, another Scotland would be added to the history of religious liberty, and the stern old covenanters would be thrown into the shade. A John Knox would be seen at every church door and heard from every pulpit, and Fillmore[3] would have no more quarter than was shown by Knox to the beautiful, but treacherous, Queen Mary of Scotland. The fact that the church of our country (with fractional exceptions) does not esteem "the Fugitive Slave Law" as a declaration of war against religious liberty, implies that that church regards religion simply as a form of worship, an empty ceremony, and *not* a vital principle, requiring active benevolence, justice, love, and good will towards man. It esteems sacrifice above mercy; psalm singing above right doing; solemn meetings above practical righteousness. A worship that can be conducted by persons who refuse to give shelter to the houseless, to give bread to the hungry, clothing to the naked, and who enjoin obedience to a law forbidding these acts of mercy is a curse, not a blessing to mankind. The Bible addresses all such persons as "scribes, pharisees, hypocrites, who pay tithe of *mint, anise,* and *cummin,* and have omitted the weightier matters of the law, judgment, mercy, and faith."

But the church of this country is not only indifferent to the wrongs of the slave, it actually takes sides with the oppressors. It has made itself the bulwark of American slavery, and the shield of American slave-hunters. Many of its most eloquent Divines, who stand as the very lights of the church, have shamelessly given the sanction of religion and the Bible to the whole slave system. They have taught that man may, properly, be a slave; that the relation of master and slave is ordained of God; that to send back an escaped bondman to his master is clearly the duty of all the followers of the Lord Jesus Christ; and this horrible blasphemy is palmed off upon the world for Christianity.

For my part, I would say, welcome infidelity! welcome atheism! welcome anything! in preference to the gospel, *as preached by those Divines!* They convert the very name of religion into an engine of tyranny and barbarous cruelty, and serve to confirm more infidels, in this age, than all the infidel writings of Thomas Paine, Voltaire, and Bolingbroke put

3. Millard Fillmore (1800–1874) was the thirteenth President of the United States (1850–1853). Fillmore was a strong advocate of the fugitive slave laws.—*Editor.*

together have done! These ministers make religion a cold and flinty-hearted thing, having neither principles of right action nor bowels of compassion. They strip the love of God of its beauty and leave the throne of religion a huge, horrible, repulsive form. It is a religion for oppressors, tyrants, manstealers, and *thugs*. It is not that *"pure and undefiled religion"* which is from above, and which is *"first pure, then peaceable, easy to be entreated*, full of mercy and good fruits, *without partiality, and without hypocrisy."* But a religion which favors the rich against the poor; which exalts the proud above the humble; which divides mankind into two classes, tyrants and slaves; which says to the man in chains, *stay there;* and to the oppressor, *oppress on;* it is a religion which may be professed and enjoyed by all the robbers and enslavers of mankind; it makes God a respecter of persons, denies his fatherhood of the race, and tramples in the dust the great truth of the brotherhood of man. All this we affirm to be true of the popular church, and the popular worship of our land and nation—a religion, a church, and a worship which, on the authority of inspired wisdom, we pronounce to be an abomination in the sight of God. In the language of Isaiah, the American church might be well addressed, "Bring no more vain oblations; incense is an abomination unto me: the new moons and Sabbaths, the calling of assemblies, I cannot away with; it is iniquity, even the solemn meeting. Your new moons, and your ap-pointed feasts my soul hateth. They are a trouble to me; I am weary to bear them; and when ye spread forth your hands I will hide mine eyes from you. Yea! when ye make many prayers, I will not hear. Your hands are full of blood; cease to do evil, learn to do well; seek judgment; re-lieve the oppressed; judge for the fatherless; plead for the widow."

The American church is guilty, when viewed in connection with what it is doing to uphold slavery; but it is superlatively guilty when viewed in its connection with its ability to abolish slavery.

The sin of which it is guilty is one of omission as well as of commission. Albert Barnes but uttered what the common sense of every man at all observant of the actual state of the case will receive as truth, when he declared that "There is no power out of the church that could sustain slavery an hour, if it were not sustained in it."

Let the religious press, the pulpit, the Sunday School, the conference meeting, the great ecclesiastical, missionary, Bible and tract associations of the land array their immense powers against slavery, and slave-holding; and the whole system of crime and blood would be scattered to the winds, and that they do not do this involves them in the most awful responsibility of which the mind can conceive.

In prosecuting the anti-slavery enterprise, we have been asked to spare the church, to spare the ministry; but *how*, we ask, could such a thing be done? We are met on the threshold of our efforts for the redemption of the slave, by the church and ministry of the country, in battle arrayed against us; and we are compelled to fight or flee. From *what* quarter, I beg to know, has proceeded a fire so deadly upon our ranks, during the last two years, as from the Northern pulpit? As the champions of oppressors, the chosen men of American theology have appeared—men honored for their so-called piety, and their real learning. The Lords of Buffalo, the Springs of New York, the Lathrops of Auburn, the Coxes and Spencers of Brooklyn, the Gannets and Sharps of Boston, the Deweys of Washington, and other great religious lights of the land have, in utter denial of the authority of *Him* by whom they professed to be called to the ministry, deliberately taught us, against the example of the Hebrews, and against the remonstrance of the Apostles, *that we ought to obey men's law before the law of God.*

My spirit wearies of such blasphemy; and how such men can be supported, as the "standing types and representatives of Jesus Christ," is a mystery which I leave others to penetrate. In speaking of the American church, however, let it be distinctly understood that I mean the *great mass* of the religious organizations of our land. There are exceptions, and I thank God that there are. Noble men may be found, scattered all over these Northern States, of whom Henry Ward Beecher, of Brooklyn; Samuel J. May, of Syracuse; and my esteemed friend (Rev. R. R. Raymond) on the platform, are shining examples; and let me say further, that, upon these men lies the duty to inspire our ranks with high religious faith and zeal, and to cheer us on in the great mission of the slave's redemption from his chains.

One is struck with the difference between the attitude of the American church towards the anti-slavery movement, and that occupied by the churches in England towards a similar movement in that country. There, the church, true to its mission of ameliorating, elevating and improving the condition of mankind, came forward promptly, bound up the wounds of the West Indian slave, and restored him to his liberty. There, the question of emancipation was a high religious question. It was demanded in the name of humanity, and according to the law of the living God. The Sharps, the Clarksons, the Wilberforces, the Buxtons, the Burchells, and the Knibbs were alike famous for their piety and for their philanthropy. The anti-slavery movement *there* was not an anti-church movement, for the reason that the church took its full share in prosecuting that movement: and the anti-slavery movement in this country will cease to be an anti-church movement, when the church of this country shall assume a favorable instead of a hostile position towards that movement.

Americans! your republican politics, not less than your republican religion, are flagrantly inconsistent. You boast of your love of liberty, your superior civilization, and your pure Christianity, while the whole political power of the nation (as embodied in the two great political parties) is solemnly pledged to support and perpetuate the enslavement of three millions of your countrymen. You hurl your anathemas at the crowned headed tyrants of Russia and Austria and pride yourselves on your Democratic institutions, while you yourselves consent to be the mere *tools* and *body-guards* of the tyrants of Virginia and Carolina. You invite to your shores fugitives of oppression from abroad, honor them with banquets, greet them with ovations, cheer them, toast them, salute them, protect them, and pour out your money to them like water; but the fugitives from your own land you advertise, hunt, arrest, shoot, and kill. You glory in your refinement and your universal education; yet you maintain a system as barbarous and dreadful as ever stained the character of a nation —a system begun in avarice, supported in pride, and perpetuated in cruelty. You shed tears over fallen Hungary, and make the sad story of her wrongs the theme of your poets, statesmen, and orators, till your gallant sons are ready to fly to arms to vindicate her cause against the oppressor; but, in regard to the ten thousand wrongs of the American slave, you would enforce the strictest silence, and would hail him as an enemy of the nation who dares to make those wrongs the subject of public discourse! You are all on fire at the mention of liberty for France or for Ireland; but are as cold as an iceberg at the thought of liberty for the enslaved of America. You discourse eloquently on the dignity of labor; yet, you sustain a system which, in its very essence, casts a stigma upon labor. You can bare your bosom to the storm of British artillery to throw off a three-penny tax on tea; and yet wring the last hard earned farthing from the grasp of the black laborers of your country. You profess to believe "that, of one blood, God made all nations of men to dwell on the face of all the earth," and hath commanded all men, everywhere, to love one another; yet you notoriously hate (and glory in your hatred) all men whose skins are not colored like your own. You declare before the world, and are understood by the world to declare that you *"hold these truths to be self-evident, that all men are created equal; and are endowed by their Creator with certain inalienable rights; and that among these are, life, liberty and the pursuit of happiness"*; and yet, you hold securely, in a bondage which, according to your own Thomas Jefferson, *"is worse than ages of that which your fathers rose in rebellion to oppose,"* a *seventh part* of the inhabitants of your country.

Fellow-citizens, I will not enlarge further on your national inconsistencies. The existence of slavery in this country brands your republicanism as a sham, your humanity as a base pretense, and your Christianity as a lie. It destroys your moral power abroad: it corrupts your politicians at home. It saps the foundation of religion; it makes your name a hissing and a bye-word to a mocking earth. It is the antagonistic force in your government, the only thing that seriously disturbs and endangers your *Union*. It fetters your progress; it is the enemy of improvement; the deadly foe of education; it fosters pride; it breeds insolence; it promotes vice; it shelters crime; it is a curse to the earth that supports it; and yet you cling to it as if it were the sheet anchor of all your hopes. Oh! be warned! a horrible reptile is coiled up in your nation's bosom; the venomous creature is nursing at the tender breast of your youthful republic; *for the love of God, tear away*, and fling from you the hideous monster, and *let the weight of twenty millions crush and destroy it forever!*

But it is answered in reply to all this, that precisely what I have now denounced is, in fact, guaranteed and sanctioned by the Constitution of the United States; that, the right to hold, and to hunt slaves is a part of that Constitution framed by he illustrious Fathers of this Republic.

Then, I dare to affirm, notwithstanding all I have said before, your fathers stooped, basely stooped

> To palter with us in a double sense:
> And keep the word of promise to the ear,
> But break it to the heart.

And instead of being the honest men I have before declared them to be, they were the veriest impostors that ever practised on mankind. This is the inevitable conclusion, and from it there is no escape; but I differ from those who charge this baseness on the framers of the Constitution of the United States. It is a slander upon their memory, at least, so I believe. There is not time now to argue the constitutional question at length; nor have I the ability to discuss it as it ought to be discussed. The subject has been handled with masterly power by Lysander Spooner, Esq., by William Goodell, by Samuel E. Sewall, Esq., and last, though not least, by Gerrit Smith, Esq. These gentlemen have, as I think, fully and clearly vindicated the Constitution from any design to support slavery for an hour.

Fellow-citizens! there is no matter in respect to which the people of the North have allowed themselves to be so ruinously imposed upon as that of the pro-slavery character of the Constitution. In that instrument I hold there is neither warrant, license, nor sanction of the hateful thing; but interpreted, as it ought to be interpreted, the Constitution is a glorious liberty document. Read its preamble, consider its purposes. Is slavery among them? Is it at the gateway? or is it in the temple? it is neither. While I do not intend to argue this question on the present occasion, let me ask, if it be not somewhat singular that, if the Constitution were intended to be, by its framers and adopters, a slaveholding instrument, why neither slavery, slaveholding, nor slave can anywhere be found in it. What would be thought of an instrument, drawn up, legally drawn up, for the purpose of entitling the city of Rochester to a tract of land, in which no mention of land was made? Now, there are certain rules of interpretation for the proper understanding of all legal instruments. These rules are well established. They are plain, common-sense rules, such as you and I, and all of us, can understand and apply, without having passed years in the study of law. I scout the idea that the question of the constitutionality, or unconstitutionality of slavery, is not a question for the people. I hold that every American citizen has a right to form an opinion of the constitution, and to propagate that opinion, and to use all honorable means to make his opinion the prevailing one. Without this right, the liberty of an American citizen would be as insecure as that of a Frenchman. Ex-Vice-President Dallas tells us that the constitution is an object to which no American mind can be too attentive, and no American heart too devoted. He further says, the Constitution, in its words, is plain and intelligible, and is meant for the home-bred, unsophisticated understandings of our fellow-citizens. Senator Berrien tells us that the Constitution is the fundamental law, that which controls all others. The charter of our liberties, which every citizen has a personal interest in understanding thoroughly. The testimony of Senator Breese, Lewis Cass, and many others that might be named, who are everywhere esteemed as sound lawyers, so regard the constitution. I take it, therefore, that it is not presumption in a private citizen to form an opinion of that instrument.

Now, take the Constitution according to its plain reading, and I defy the presentation of a single pro-slavery clause in it. On the other hand, it will be found to contain principles and purposes, entirely hostile to the existence of slavery.

I have detained my audience entirely too long already. At some future period I will gladly avail myself of an opportunity to give this subject a full and fair discussion.

Allow me to say, in conclusion, notwithstanding the dark picture I have this day presented, of the state of the nation, I do not despair of this country. There are forces in operation which must inevitably work the downfall of slavery. "The arm of the Lord is not shortened," and the doom of slavery is certain. I, therefore, leave off where I began, with hope. While drawing encouragement from "the Declaration of Independence," the great principles it contains, and the genius of American Institutions, my spirit is also cheered by the obvious tendencies of the age. Nations do not now stand in the same relation to each other that they did ages ago. No nation can now shut itself up from the surrounding world and trot round in the same old path of its fathers without interference. The time was when such could be done. Long established customs of hurtful character could formerly fence themselves in, and do their evil work with social impunity. Knowledge was then confined and enjoyed by the privileged few, and the multitude walked on in mental darkness. But a change has now come over the affairs of mankind. Walled cities and empires have become unfashionable. The arm of commerce has borne away the gates of the strong city. Intelligence is penetrating the darkest corners of the globe. It makes its pathway over and under the sea, as well as on the earth. Wind, steam, and lightning are its chartered agents. Oceans no longer divide, but link nations together. From Boston to London is now a holiday excursion. Space is comparatively annihilated.—Thoughts expressed on one side of the Atlantic are distinctly heard on the other.

The far off and almost fabulous Pacific rolls in grandeur at our feet. The Celestial Empire, the mystery of ages, is being solved. The fiat of the Almighty, "Let there be Light," has not yet spent its force. No abuse, no outrage whether in taste, sport or avarice, can now hide itself from the all-pervading light. The iron shoe, and crippled foot of China must be seen in contrast with nature. Africa must rise and put on her yet unwoven garment. "Ethiopia shall stretch out her hand unto God." In the fervent aspirations of William Lloyd Garrison, I say, and let every heart join in saying it:

> God speed the year of jubilee
>   The wide world o'er!
> When from their galling chains set free,
> Th' oppress'd shall vilely bend the knee,
> And wear the yoke of tyranny
>   Like brutes no more.
> That year will come, and freedom's reign,
> To man his plundered rights again
>   Restore.
>
> God speed the day when human blood
>   Shall cease to flow!
> In every clime be understood,
> The claims of human brotherhood,
> And each return for evil, good,
>   Not blow for blow;
> That day will come all feuds to end,
> And change into a faithful friend
>   Each foe.
>
> God speed the hour, the glorious hour,
>   When none on earth
> Shall exercise a lordly power,
> Nor in a tyrant's presence cower;
> But to all manhood's stature tower,
>   By equal birth!
> That hour will come, to each, to all,
> And from his prison-house, to thrall
>   Go forth.

Until that year, day, hour, arrive,
With head, and heart, and hand I'll strive,
To break the rod, and rend the gyve,
The spoiler of his prey deprive—
So witness Heaven!
And never from my chosen post,
What'er the peril or the cost,
Be driven.

II.
Reconstruction and
the Disfranchised
(1865–1917)

Although the Civil War ostensibly freed the black man, the fact is that such "freedom" was really an introduction to a more subtle, though no less vicious and degrading, form of deprivation. Timothy Thomas Fortune, himself a black man, saw this as clearly as anyone:

> To tell a man he is free when he has neither money nor the opportunity to make it, is simply to mock him. To tell him he has no master when he cannot live except by permission of the man who, under favorable conditions, monopolizes all the land, is to deal in the most tantalizing contradiction of terms.

And this contradiction victimized many whites who, lacking land and therefore genuine freedom, slumped into the cruel anonymity of rural, and more strikingly urban poverty. Henry George called the "new" slavery (a slavery affecting both blacks and whites) "the robbery of labor." The question which echoes throughout this section is, what is freedom without land or money? For in a country of such enormous wealth, land, or the ability to buy land, is a prerequisite for political power.

All of the selections, moreover, pose this question within the general context of urban life. It became increasingly clear to these authors that government was not responding to the country's shift from a rural to an urban society; government largely ignored the plight of the disfranchised, who found themselves starving at the doorstep of the monopolies. Henry Demarest Lloyd saw it this way: "Divine rights have been succeeded by vested rights which look on government as a kind of cow which no one has the right to milk but themselves." Clarence Darrow reiterated this view: "Those men who own the earth make the laws to protect what they have." It was Jane Addams, however, who confronted the widest implications of this dilemma: "We have failed to work out a democratic government which should include the experiences and hopes of all the varied peoples among us." And this statement about the failure of democratic government becomes all the more bitterly ironic when, in 1917, the United States entered World War I "to make the world safe for Democracy."

Timothy Thomas Fortune
(1856–1928)

TIMOTHY THOMAS FORTUNE was born a slave in Florida but left the state in 1875. He eventually attended Howard University, then taught school for two years, and went to New York City. Fortune is best known as the editor of an important Negro weekly, first called the *New York Globe*, and later known as the *New York Age*. He was also the founder of the Afro-American League (1887) and edited the black nationalist *Negro World*.

"The Negro and the Nation" is the third chapter of Fortune's book, *Black and White: Land, Labor, and Politics in the South*, published in 1884.

THE NEGRO AND
THE NATION

The war of the Rebellion settled only one question: It forever settled the question of chattel slavery[1] in this country. It forever choked the life out of the infamy of the Constitutional right of one man to rob another, by purchase of his person, or of his honest share of the produce of his own labor. But this was not the only question permanently and irrevocably settled. Nor was this *the* all-absorbing question involved. The right of a State to secede from the so-called *Union* remains where it was when the treasonable shot upon Fort Sumter aroused the people to all the horrors of internecine war. And the measure of protection which the National government owes the individual members of States, a right imposed upon it by the adoption of the XIVth Amendment[2] to the Constitution, remains still to be affirmed.

It was not sufficient that the Federal government should expend its blood and treasure to unfetter the limbs of four millions of people. There can be a slavery more odious, more galling, than mere chattel slavery. It has been declared to be an act of charity to enforce ignorance upon the slave, since to inform his intelligence would simply be to make his unnatural lot all the more unbearable. Instance the miserable existence of

1. Neither slavery nor involuntary survitude, except as a punishment for crime, whereof the party shall have been duly convicted, shall exist within the United States, or any place subject to their jurisdiction.—Art. XIII, sec. 1 of the Constitution.—*Author*.
2. All persons born or naturalized in the United States, and subject to the jurisdiction thereof, are citizens of the United States and of the State in which they reside. No State shall make or enforce any law which shall abridge the privileges or immunities of citizens of the United States; *nor shall any State deprive any person of life, liberty, or property without due process of law, nor deny to any person within its jurisdiction the equal protection of the laws*—XIVth Amendment, sec. 1.—*Author*.

Aesop, the great black moralist. But this is just what the manumission of the black people of this country has accomplished. They are more absolutely under the control of the Southern whites; they are more systematically robbed of their labor; they are more poorly housed, clothed and fed, than under the slave regime; and they enjoy, practically, less of the protection of the laws of the State or of the Federal government. When they appeal to the Federal government they are told by the Supreme Court to go to the State authorities—as if they would have appealed to the one had the other given them that protection to which their sovereign citizenship entitles them!

Practically, there is no law in the United States which extends its protecting arm over the black man and his rights. He is, like the Irishman in Ireland, an alien in his native land. There is no central or auxiliary authority to which he can appeal for protection. Wherever he turns he finds the strong arm of constituted authority powerless to protect him. The farmer and the merchant rob him with absolute immunity, and irresponsible ruffians murder him without fear of punishment, undeterred by the law, or by public opinion—which connives at, if it does not inspire, the deeds of lawless violence. Legislatures of States have framed a code of laws which is more cruel and unjust than any enforced by a former slave State.

The right of franchise[3] has been practically annulled in every one of the former slave States, in not one of which, to-day, can a man vote, think or act as he pleases. He must conform his views to the views of the men who have usurped every function of government—who, at the point of the dagger, and with shot-gun, have made themselves masters in defiance of every law or precedent in our history as a government. They have usurped government with the weapons of the coward and assassin, and they maintain themselves in power by the most approved practices of the most odious of tyrants. These men have shed as much innocent blood as the bloody triumvirate of Rome. Today, red-handed murderers and assassins sit in the high places of power, and bask in the smiles of innocence and beauty.

The newspapers of the country, voicing the sentiments of the people, literally hiss into silence any man who has the courage to protest against the prevailing tendency to lawlessness[4] and bare-faced usurpation; while

3. The right of citizens of the United States to vote shall not be denied or abridged by the United States, or by any State, on account of race, color, or previous condition of servitude.—XVth Amendment, sec. 1.—*Author.*
4. While I write these lines, the daily newspapers furnish the following paragraph. It is but one of the *waifs* that are to be found in the newspapers day by day. There is always some circumstance which justifies the murder and exculpates the murderer. The black always deserves his fate. I give the paragraph:
"SPEAR, MITCHELL CO., N.C., March 19, 1884.—Col. J. M. English, a farmer and prominent citizen living at Plumtree, Mitchell County, N.C., shot and killed a

parties have ceased to deal with the question for other than purposes of political capital. Even this fruitful mine is well-nigh exhausted. A few more years, and the usurper and the man of violence will be left in undisputed possession of his blood-stained inheritance. No man will attempt to deter him from sowing broadcast the seeds of revolution and death. Brave men are powerless to combat this organized brigandage, complaint of which, in derision, has been termed "waving the bloody shirt."

Men organize themselves into society for mutual protection. Government justly derives its just powers from the consent of the governed. But what shall we say of that society which is incapable of extending the protection which is inherent in it? What shall we say of that government which has not power or inclination to insure the exercise of those solemn rights and immunities which it guarantees? To declare a man to be free, and equal with his fellow, and then to refrain from enacting laws powerful to insure him in such freedom and equality, is to trifle with the most sacred of all the functions of sovereignty. Have not the United States done this very thing? Have they not conferred freedom and the ballot, which are necessary the one to the other? And have they not signally failed to make omnipotent the one and practicable the other? The questions hardly require an answer. The measure of freedom the black man enjoys can be gauged by the power he has to vote. He has, practically, no voice in the government under which he lives. His property is taxed and his life is jeopardized, by states on the one hand and inefficient police regulations on

---

mulatto named Jack Mathis at that place Saturday, March 1. There had been difficulty between them for several months.

"Mathis last summer worked in one of Col. English's mica mines. Evidence pointed to him as being implicated in the systematic stealing of mica from the mine. Still it was not direct enough to convict him, but he was discharged by English. Mathis was also a tenant of one of English's houses and lots. In resentment he damaged the property by destroying fences, tearing off weather boards from the house, and injuring the fruit trees. For this Col. English prosecuted the negro, and on Feb. 9, before a local Justice, ex-Sheriff Wiseman, he got a judgment for $100. On the date stated, during a casual meeting, hot words grew into an altercation, and Col. English shot the negro. Mathis was a powerful man. English is a cripple, being lame in a leg from a wound received in the Mexican war.

"A trial was had before a preliminary court recently, Col. S. C. Vance appearing for Col. English. After a hearing of all the testimony the court reached a decision of justifiable homicide and English was released. The locality of the shooting is in the mountains of western North Carolina, and not far from the Flat Rock mica mine, the scene of the brutal midnight murder, Feb. 17, of Burleson, Miller, and Horton by Rae and Anderson, two revenue officers, who took this means to gain possession of the mica mine."

My knowledge of such affairs in the South is, that, the black man and the white have an altercation over some trivial thing, and the white to end the argument shoots the black man down. The negro is always a "powerful fellow" and the white man a "weak sickly man." The law and public opinion always side with the white man.— Author.

the other, and no question is asked or expected of him. When he protests, when he cries out against this flagrant nullification of the very first principles of a republican form of government, the insolent question is asked: "What are you going to do about it?" And here lies the danger.

You may rob and maltreat a slave and ask him what he is going to do about it, and he can make no reply. He is bound hand and foot; he is effectually gagged. Despair is his only refuge. He knows it is useless to appeal from tyranny unto the designers and apologists of tyranny. Ignominious death alone can bring him relief. This was the case of thousands of men doomed by the institution of slavery. *But such is not the case with free men.* You cannot oppress and murder freemen as you would slaves: you cannot so insult them with the question, "What are you going to do about it?" When you ask free men that question you appeal to men who, though sunk to the verge of despair, yet are capable of uprising and ripping hip and thigh those who deemed them incapable of so rising above their condition. The history of mankind is fruitful of such uprisings of races and classes reduced to a condition of absolute despair. The American negro is no better and no worse than the Haytian revolutionists headed by Toussaint l'Overture, Christophe and the bloody Dessalaines.

I do not indulge in the luxury of prophecy when I declare that the American people are fostering in their bosoms a spirit of rebellion which will yet shake the pillars of popular government as they have never before been shaken, unless a wiser policy is inaugurated and honestly enforced. All the indications point to the fulfilment of such declaration.

The Czar of Russia squirms upon his throne, not because he is necessarily a bad man, but because he is the head and center of a condition of things which squeezes the life out of the people. His subjects hurl infernal machines at the tyrant because he represents the system which oppresses them. But the evil is far deeper than the throne, and cannot be remedied by striking the occupant of it—*the throne itself must be rooted out and demolished.* So the Irish question has a more powerful motive to foment agitation and murder than the landlord and landlordism. The landlord simply stands out as the representative of the real grievance. To remove *him* would not remove the evil; agitation would not cease; murder would still stalk abroad at noon-day. *The real grievance is the false system which makes the landlord possible.* The appropriation of the fertile acres of the soil of Ireland, which created and maintains a privileged class, a class that while performing no labor, wrings from the toiler, in the shape of rents, so much of the produce of his labor that he cannot on the residue support himself and those dependent upon him aggravates the situation. It is this system which constitutes the real grievance and makes the landlord an odious loafer with abundant cash and the laborer a constant toiler always upon the verge of starvation. Evidently, therefore, to remove the landlord and leave the system of land monopoly would not remove the evil. Destroy the latter and the former would be compelled to go.

Herein lies the great social wrong which has turned the beautiful roses of freedom into thorns to prick the hands of the black men of the South; which made slavery a blessing, paradoxical as it may appear, and freedom a curse. It is this great wrong which has crowded the cities of the South with an ignorant pauper population, making desolate fields that once bloomed "as fair as a garden of the Lord," where now the towering oak and pine-tree flourish, instead of the corn and cotton which gladdened the heart and filled the purse. It was this gigantic iniquity which created that arrogant class who have exhausted the catalogue of violence to obtain power and the lexicon of sophistry for arguments to extenuate the exceeding heinousness of crime. How could it be otherwise? To tell a man he is free when he has neither money nor the opportunity to make it, is simply to mock him. To tell him he has no master when he cannot live except by permission of the man who, under favorable conditions, monopolizes all the land, is to deal in the most tantalizing contradiction of terms. But this is just what the United States did for the black man. And yet because he has not grown learned and wealthy in twenty years, because he does not own broad acres and a large bank account, people are not wanting who declare he has no capacity, that he is improvident by nature and mendacious from inclination.

Henry George
(1839-1897)

HENRY GEORGE was raised in Philadelphia and settled in San Francisco in 1857, where he worked as a printer and newspaperman. His knowledge of the city and his awareness of the degradation of poverty led him to publish his classic work, *Progress and Poverty*, in 1879. In 1880 he moved to New York, where he twice ran for mayor in 1886 and again in 1897. For the remainder of his life, he lectured on social issues and sought to reform the corruptions of city government.

"Slavery and Slavery" is the fifteenth chapter of George's book, *Social Problems*, published in 1883.

SLAVERY AND SLAVERY

I must leave it to the reader to carry on in other directions, if he choose, such inquiries as those to which the last three chapters have been devoted. The more carefully he examines, the more fully will he see that at the root of every social problem lies a social wrong,[1] that "ignorance, neglect or contempt of human rights are the causes of public misfortunes and corruptions of government." Yet, in truth, no elaborate examination is necessary. To understand why material progress does not benefit the masses requires but a recognition of the self-evident truth that man cannot live without land; that it is only on land and from land that human labor can produce.

Robinson Crusoe, as we all know, took Friday as his slave. Suppose, however, that instead of taking Friday as his slave, Robinson Crusoe had welcomed him as a man and a brother, had read him a Declaration of Independence, an Emancipation Proclamation and a Fifteenth Amendment, and informed him that he was a free and independent citizen, entitled to vote and hold office; but had at the same time also informed him that that particular island was his (Robinson Crusoe's) private and exclusive property. What would have been the difference? Since Friday could not fly up into the air nor swim off through the sea, since if he lived at all he must live on the island, he would have been in one case as much a slave as in the other. Crusoe's ownership of the island would be equivalent to his ownership of Friday.

Chattel slavery is, in fact, merely the rude and primitive mode of property in man. It only grows up where population is sparse; it never, save by

1. George deals with this idea most thoroughly in *Progress and Poverty* (1879).—
Editor.

124

virtue of special circumstances, continues where the pressure of population gives land a high value, for in that case the ownership of land gives all the power that comes from the ownership of men, in more convenient form. When in the course of history we see the conquerors making chattel slaves of the conquered, it is always where population is sparse and land of little value, or where they want to carry off their human spoil. In other cases, the conquerors merely appropriate the lands of the conquered, by which means they just as effectually, and much more conveniently, compel the conquered to work for them. It was not until the great estates of the rich patricians began to depopulate Italy that the importation of slaves began. In Turkey and Egypt, where chattel slavery is yet legal, it is confined to the inmates and attendants of harems. English ships carried negro slaves to America, and not to England or Ireland, because in America land was cheap and labor was valuable, while in western Europe land was valuable and labor was cheap. As soon as the possibility of expansion over new land ceased, chattel slavery would have died out in our Southern States. As it is, Southern planters do not regret the abolition of slavery. They get out of the freedmen as tenants as much as they got out of them as slaves. While as for predial slavery—the attachment of serfs to the soil—the form of chattel slavery which existed longest in Europe, it is only of use to the proprietor where there is little competition for land. Neither predial slavery nor absolute chattel slavery could have added to the Irish landlord's virtual ownership of *men*—to his power to make them work for him without return. Their own competition for the means of livelihood insured him all they possibly could give. To the English proprietor the ownership of slaves would be only a burden and a loss, when he can get laborers for less than it would cost to maintain them as slaves, and when they are become ill or infirm can turn them on the parish. Or what would the New England manufacturer gain by the enslavement of his operatives? The competition with each other of so-called freemen, who are denied all right to the soil of what is called *their* country, brings him labor cheaper and more conveniently than would chattel slavery.

That a people can be enslaved just as effectually by making property of their lands as by making property of their bodies, is a truth that conquerors in all ages have recognized, and that, as society developed, the strong and unscrupulous who desired to live off the labor of others, have been prompt to see. The coarser form of slavery, in which each particular slave is the property of a particular owner, is fitted only for a rude state of society, and with social development entails more and more care, trouble and expense upon the owner. But by making property of the land instead of the person, much care, supervision and expense are saved the proprietors; and though no particular slave is owned by a particular master, yet the one class still appropriates the labor of the other class as before.

That each particular slave should be owned by a particular master would in fact become, as social development went on, and industrial organization grew complex, a manifest disadvantage to the masters. They would be at the trouble of whipping, or otherwise compelling the slaves to work; at the cost of watching them, and of keeping them when ill or unproductive; at the trouble of finding work for them to do, or of hiring them out, as at different seasons or at different times, the number of slaves which different owners or different contractors could advantageously employ would vary. As social development went on, these inconveniences might, were there no other way of obviating them, have led slave-owners to adopt some such device for the joint ownership and management of slaves, as the mutual convenience of capitalists has led to in the management of capital. In a rude state of society, the man who wants to have money ready for use must hoard it, or, if he travels, carry it with him. The man who has capital must use it himself or lend it. But mutual convenience has, as society developed, suggested methods of saving this trouble. The man who wishes to have his money accessible turns it over to a bank, which does not agree to keep or hand him back that particular money, but money to that amount. And so by turning over his capital to savings-banks or trust companies, or by buying the stock or bonds of corporations, he gets rid of all trouble of handling and employing it. Had chattel slavery continued, some similar device for the ownership and management of slaves would in time have been adopted. But by changing the form of slavery—by freeing men and appropriating land—all the advantages of chattel slavery can be secured without any of the disadvantages which in a complex society attend the owning of a particular man by a particular master.

Unable to employ themselves, the nominally free laborers are forced by their competition with each other to pay as rent all their earnings above a bare living, or to sell their labor for wages which give but a bare living; and as landowners the ex-slaveholders are enabled as before, to appropriate to themselves the labor or the produce of the labor of their former chattels, having in the value which this power of appropriating the proceeds of labor gives to the ownership of land, a capitalized value equivalent, or more than equivalent, to the value of their slaves. They no longer have to drive their slaves to work; want and the fear of want do that more effectually than the lash. They no longer have the trouble of looking out for their employment or hiring out their labor, or the expense of keeping them when they cannot work. That is thrown upon the slaves. The tribute that they still wring from labor seems like voluntary payment. In fact, they take it as their honest share of the rewards of production—since *they* furnish the land! And they find so-called political economists, to say nothing of so-called preachers of Christianity, to tell them it is so.

We of the United States take credit for having abolished slavery. Passing the question of how much credit the majority of us are entitled to for the abolition of negro slavery, it remains true that we have abolished only one form of slavery—and that a primitive form which had been abolished in the greater portion of the country by social development, and that, notwithstanding its race character gave it peculiar tenacity, would in time have been abolished in the same way in other parts of the country. We have not really abolished slavery; we have retained it in its most insidious and widespread form—in a form which applies to whites as to blacks. So far from having abolished slavery, it is extending and intensifying, and we make no scruple of selling into it our own children—the citizens of the Republic yet to be. For what else are we doing in selling the land on which future citizens must live, if they are to live at all?

The essence of slavery is the robbery of labor. It consists in compelling men to work, yet taking from them all the produce of their labor except what suffices for a bare living. Of how many of our "free and equal American citizens" is that already the lot? And of how many more is it coming to be the lot?

In all our cities there are, even in good times, thousands and thousands of men who would gladly go to work for wages that would give them merely board and clothes—that is to say, who would gladly accept the wages of slaves. As I have previously stated, the Massachusetts Bureau of Labor Statistics and the Illinois Bureau of Labor Statistics both declare that in the majority of cases the earnings of wage-workers will not maintain their families, and must be pieced out by the earnings of women and children. In our richest States are to be found men reduced to a virtual peonage—living in their employers' houses, trading at their stores, and for the most part unable to get out of their debt from one year's end to the other. In New York, shirts are made for thirty-five cents a dozen, and women working from fourteen to sixteen hours a day average three dollars or four dollars a week. There are cities where the prices of such work are lower still. As a matter of dollars and cents, no master could afford to work slaves so hard and keep them so cheaply.

But it may be said that the analogy between our industrial system and chattel slavery is only supported by the consideration of extremes. Between those who get but a bare living and those who can live luxuriously on the earnings of others, are many gradations, and here lies the great middle class. Between all classes, moreover, a constant movement of individuals is going on. The millionaire's grandchildren may be tramps, while even the poor man who has lost hope for himself may cherish it for his son. Moreover, it is not true that all the difference between what labor fairly earns and what labor really gets goes to the owners of land. And with us, in the United States, a great many of the owners of land are small owners

—men who own the homesteads in which they live or the soil which they till, and who combine the characters of laborer and landowner.

These objections will be best met by endeavoring to imagine a well-developed society, like our own, in which chattel slavery exists without distinction of race. To do this requires some imagination, for we know of no such case. Chattel slavery had died out in Europe before modern civilization began, and in the New World has existed only as race slavery, and in communities of low industrial development.

But if we do imagine slavery without race distinction in a progressive community, we shall see that society, even if starting from a point where the greater part of the people were made the chattel slaves of the rest, could not long consist of but the two classes, masters and slaves. The indolence, interest and necessity of the masters would soon develop a class of intermediaries between the completely enslaved and themselves. To supervise the labor of the slaves, and to keep them in subjection, it would be necessary to take, from the ranks of the slaves, overseers, policemen, etc., and to reward them by more of the produce of slave labor than goes to the ordinary slave. So, too, would it be necessary to draw out special skill and talent. And in the course of social development a class of traders would necessarily arise, who, exchanging the products of slave labor, would retain a considerable portion; and a class of contractors, who, hiring slave labor from the masters, would also retain a portion of its produce. Thus, between the slaves forced to work for a bare living and the masters who lived without work, intermediaries of various grades would be developed, some of whom would doubtless acquire large wealth.

And in the mutations of fortune, some slaveholders would be constantly falling into the class of intermediaries, and finally into the class of slaves, while individual slaves would be rising. The conscience, benevolence or gratitude of masters would lead them occasionally to manumit slaves; their interest would lead them to reward the diligence, inventiveness, fidelity to themselves, or treachery to their fellows, of particular slaves. Thus, as has often occurred in slave countries, we would find slaves who were free to make what they could on condition of paying so much to their masters every month or every quarter; slaves who had partially bought their freedom, for a day or two days or three days in the week, or for certain months in the year, and those who had completely bought themselves, or had been presented with their freedom. And, as has always happened where slavery had not race character, some of these ex-slaves or their children would, in the constant movement, be always working their way to the highest places, so that in such a state of society the apologists of things as they are would triumphantly point to these examples, saying, "See how beautiful a thing is slavery! Any slave can become a slave-holder himself if he is only faithful, industrious and prudent! It is only their own ignorance and dissipation and laziness that prevent all slaves from becoming masters!" And then they would indulge in a moan for human nature. "Alas!" they would say, "the fault is not in slavery; it is in human nature"— meaning, of course, other human nature than their own. And if any one hinted at the abolition of slavery, they would charge him with assailing the sacred rights of property, and of endeavoring to rob poor blind widow women of the slaves that were their sole dependence; call him a crank and a communist; an enemy of man and a defier of God!

Consider, furthermore, the operation of taxation in an advanced society based on chattel slavery; the effect of the establishment of monopolies of manufacture, trade and transporation; of the creation of public debts, etc., and you will see that in reality the social phenomena would be essentially the same if men were made property as they are under the system that makes land property.

It must be remembered, however, that the slavery that results from the appropriation of land does not come suddenly, but insidiously and progressively. Where population is sparse and land of little value, the institution of private property in land may exist without its effects being much felt. As it becomes more and more difficult to get land, so will the virtual enslavement of the laboring-classes go on. As the value of land rises, more and more of the earnings of labor will be demanded for the use of land, until finally nothing is left to laborers but the wages of slavery—a bare living.

But the degree as well as the manner in which individuals are affected by this movement must vary very much. Where the ownership of land has been much diffused, there will remain, for some time after the mere laborer has been reduced to the wages of slavery, a greater body of smaller landowners occupying an intermediate position, and who, according to the land they hold, and the relation which it bears to their labor, may, to make a comparison with chattel slavery, be compared, in their gradations, to the owners of a few slaves; to those who own no slaves but are themselves free; or to partial slaves, compelled to render service for one, two, three, four or five days in the week, but for the rest of the time their own masters. As land becomes more and more valuable this class will gradually pass into the ranks of the completely enslaved. The independent American farmer working with his own hands on his own land is doomed as certainly as two thousand years ago his prototype of Italy was doomed. He must disappear, with the development of the private ownership of land, as the English yeoman has already disappeared.

We have abolished negro slavery in the United States. But how small is the real benefit to the slave. George M. Jackson writes me from St. Louis, under date of August 15, 1883:

During the war I served in a Kentucky regiment in the Federal army. When the war broke out, my father owned sixty slaves. I had not been back to my old Kentucky home for years until a short time ago, when I was met by one of my father's old negroes, who said to me: "Mas George, you say you sot us free; but 'fore God, I'm wus off than when I belonged to your father." The planters, on the other hand, are contented with the change. They say: "How foolish it was in us to go to war for slavery. We get labor cheaper now than when we owned the slaves." How do they get it cheaper? Why, in the shape of rents they take more of the labor of the negro than they could under slavery, for then they were compelled to return him sufficient food, clothing, and medical attendance to keep him well, and were compelled by conscience and public opinion, as well as by law, to keep him when he could no longer work. Now their interest and responsibility cease when they have got all the work out of him they can.

In one of his novels, Capt. Marryat tells of a schoolmaster who announced that he had abandoned the use of the rod. When tender mothers, tempted by this announcement, brought their boys to his institution, he was eloquent in his denunciations of the barbarism of the rod; but no sooner had the doors closed upon them than the luckless pupils found that the master had only abandoned the use of the rod for the use of the cane! Very much like this is our abolition of negro slavery.

The only one of our prominent men who had any glimmering of what was really necessary to the abolition of slavery was Thaddeus Stevens, but it was only a glimmering.[2] "Forty acres and a mule" would have been a measure of scant justice to the freedmen, and it would for a while have given them something of that personal independence which is necessary to freedom. Yet only for a while. In the course of time, and as the pressure of population increased, the forty acres would, with the majority of them, have been mortgaged, and the mule sold, and they would soon have been, as now, competitors for a foothold upon the earth and for the means of making a living from it. Such a measure would have given the freedom a fairer start, and for many of them would have postponed the evil day; but that is all. Land being private property, that evil day *must* come.

I do not deny that the blacks of the South have in some things gained by the abolition of chattel slavery. I will not even insist that, on the whole, their material condition has not been improved. But it must be remembered that the South is yet but sparsely settled, and is behindhand in industrial development. The continued existence of slavery there was partly the effect and partly the cause of this. As population increases, as industry is developed, the condition of the freedmen must become harder and harder.

2. Thaddeus Stevens (1792–1868) served in Congress from 1849–1853 and from 1859–1868. A strong opponent of slavery, he was instrumental in the development and passage of the thirteenth and fourteenth amendments.—*Editor.*

As yet, land is comparatively cheap in the South, and there is much not only unused but unclaimed. The consequence is, that the freedmen are not yet driven into that fierce competition which must come with denser population; there is no seeming surplus of labor seeking employment on any terms, as in the North. The freedmen merely get a living, as in the days of slavery, and in many cases not so good a living; but still there is little or no difficulty in getting that. To compare fairly the new estate of the freedmen with the old, we must wait until in population and industrial development the South begins to approach the condition of the North.

But not even in the North (nor, for that matter, even in Europe) has that form of slavery which necessarily results from the disinheritance of labor by the monopolization of land, yet reached its culmination. For the vast area of unoccupied land on this continent has prevented the full effects of modern development from being felt. As it becomes more and more difficult to obtain land, so will the virtual enslavement of the laboring-classes go on. As the value of land rises, more and more of the earnings of labor will be demanded for the use of land—that is to say, laborers must give a greater and greater portion of their time up to the service of the landlord, until, finally, no matter how hard they work, nothing is left them but a bare living.

Of the two systems of slavery, I think there can be no doubt that upon the same moral level, that which makes property of persons is more humane than that which results from making private property of land. The cruelties which are perpetrated under the system of chattel slavery are more striking and arouse more indignation because they are the conscious acts of individuals. But for the suffering of the poor under the more refined system no one in particular seems responsible. That one human being should be deliberately burned by other human beings excites our imagination and arouses our indignation much more than the great fire or railroad accident in which a hundred people are roasted alive. But this very fact permits cruelties that would not be tolerated under the one system to pass almost unnoticed under the other. Human beings are overworked, are starved, are robbed of all the light and sweetness of life, are condemned to ignorance and brutishness, and to the infection of physical and moral disease; are driven to crime and suicide, not by other individuals, but by iron necessities for which it seems that no one in particular is responsible.

To match from the annals of chattel slavery the horrors that day after day transpire unnoticed in the heart of Christian civilization it would be necessary to go back to ancient slavery, to the chronicles of Spanish conquest in the New World, or to stories of the Middle Passage.

That chattel slavery is not the worst form of slavery we know from the fact that in countries where it has prevailed irrespective of race distinctions, the ranks of chattel slaves have been recruited from the ranks of the free poor, who, driven by distress, have sold themselves or their children. And I think no one who reads our daily papers can doubt that even already, in the United States, there are many who, did chattel slavery, without race distinction, exist among us, would gladly sell themselves or their children, and who would really make a good exchange for their nominal freedom in doing so.

We have not abolished slavery. We never can abolish slavery, until we honestly accept the fundamental truth asserted by the Declaration of Independence and secure to all the equal and unalienable rights with which they are endowed by their Creator. If we cannot or will not do that, then, as a matter of humanity and social stability, it might be well, would it avail, to consider whether it were not wise to amend our constitution and permit poor whites and blacks alike to sell themselves and their children to good masters. If we must have slavery, it were better in the form in which the slave knows his owner, and the heart and conscience and pride of that owner can be appealed to. Better breed children for the slaves of good, Christian, civilized people, than breed them for the brothel or the penitentiary. But alas! that recourse is denied. Supposing we did legalize chattel slavery again, who would buy men when men can be hired so cheaply?

Jacob Riis
(1849–1914)

RIIS, who was born in Denmark, came to the United States in 1870. He soon established a reputation as a journalist and gained prominence with the publication of *How the Other Half Lives* (1890), a book which lay bare the slum conditions of American city life. Among other published works, his autobiography, *The Making of An American* (1901), is considered an important document of its time.

"The Common Herd" is the fourteenth chapter of Riis's book on the New York slums, *How the Other Half Lives*.

THE COMMON HERD

There is another line not always so readily drawn in the tenements, yet the real boundary line of the Other Half: the one that defines the "flat." The law does not draw it at all, accounting all flats tenements without distinction. The health officer draws it from observation, lumping all those which in his judgment have nothing, or not enough, to give them claim upon the name, with the common herd, and his way is, perhaps, on the whole, the surest and best. The outside of the building gives no valuable clew. Brass and brown-stone go well sometimes with dense crowds and dark and dingy rooms; but the first attempt to enter helps draw the line with tolerable distinctness. A locked door is a strong point in favor of the flat. It argues that the first step has been taken to secure privacy, the absence of which is the chief curse of the tenement. Behind a locked door the hoodlum is not at home, unless there be a jailor in place of a janitor to guard it. Not that the janitor and the door-bell are infallible. There may be a tenement behind a closed door; but never a "flat" without it. The hall that is a highway for all the world by night and by day is the tenement's proper badge. The Other Half ever receives with open doors.

With this introduction we shall not seek it long anywhere in the city. Below Houston Street the door-bell in our age is as extinct as the dodo. East of Second Avenue, and west of Ninth Avenue as far up as the Park, it is practically an unknown institution. The nearer the river and the great workshops the more numerous the tenements. The kind of work carried on in any locality to a large extent determines their character. Skilled and well-paid labor puts its stamp on a tenement even in spite of the open door, and usually soon supplies the missing bell. Gas-houses, slaughter-houses and the docks, that attract the roughest crowds and support the vilest saloons, invariably form slum-centres. The city is full of such above the line of Fourteenth Street, that is erroneously supposed by some to fence off the good from the bad, separate the chaff from the wheat. There is nothing below that line that can outdo in wickedness Hell's Kitchen, in the region of three-cent whiskey, or its counterpoise at the other end of Thirty-ninth Street, on the East River, the house of the infamous Rag Gang. Cherry Street is not "tougher" than Battle Row in East Sixty-third Street, or "the village" at Twenty-ninth Street and First Avenue, where stores of broken bricks, ammunition for the nightly conflicts with the police, are part of the regulation outfit of every tenement. The Mulberry Street Bend is scarce dirtier than Little Italy in Harlem. Even across the Harlem River, Frog Hollow challenges the admiration of the earlier slums for the boldness and pernicious activity of its home gang. There are enough of these sore spots. We shall yet have occasion to look into the social conditions of some of them; were I to draw a picture of them here as they are, the subject, I fear, would outgrow alike the limits of this book and the reader's patience.

It is true that they tell only one side of the story; that there is another to tell. A story of thousands of devoted lives, laboring earnestly to make the most of their scant opportunities for good; of heroic men and women striving patiently against fearful odds and by their very courage coming off victors in the battle with the tenement; of womanhood pure and undefiled. That it should blossom in such an atmosphere is one of the unfathomable mysteries of life. And yet it is not an uncommon thing to find sweet and innocent girls, singularly untouched by the evil around them, true wives and faithful mothers, literally "like jewels in a swine's snout," in the worst of the infamous barracks. It is the experience of all who have intelligently observed this side of life in a great city, not to be explained—unless on the theory of my friend, the priest in the Mulberry Street Bend, that inherent purity revolts instinctively from the naked brutality of vice as seen in the slums—but to be thankfully accepted as the one gleam of hope in an otherwise hopeless desert.

But the relief is not great. In the dull content of life bred on the tenement-house dead level there is little to redeem it, or to calm apprehension for a society that has nothing better to offer its toilers; while the patient efforts of the lives finally attuned to it to render the situation tolerable, and the very success of these efforts, serve only to bring out in stronger contrast the general gloom of the picture by showing how much farther they might have gone with half a chance. Go into any of the "respectable" tenement neighborhoods—the fact that there are not more than two saloons on the corner, nor over three or four in the block will serve as a fair guide—where live the great body of hard-working Irish and German immigrants and their descendants, who accept naturally the conditions of tenement life, because for them there is nothing else in New York; be with and among its people until you understand their ways, their aims, and the quality of their ambitions, and unless you can content yourself with the scriptural promise that the poor we shall have always with us, or with the menagerie view that, if fed, they have no cause or complaint, you shall come away agreeing with me that, humanly speaking, life there does not seem worth the living. Take at random one of these uptown tenement blocks, not of the worst nor yet of the most prosperous kind, within hail of what the newspapers would call a "fine residential section." These houses were built since the last cholera scare made people willing to listen to reason. The block is not like the one over on the East Side in which I actually lost my way once. There were thirty or forty rear houses in the heart of it, three or four on every lot, set at all sorts of angles, with odd, winding passages, or no passage at all, only "runways" for the thieves and toughs of the neighborhood. These yards are clear. There is air there, and it is about all there is. The view between brick walls outside is that of a stony street; inside, of rows of unpainted board fences, a bewildering maze of clothes-posts and lines; underfoot, a desert of brown, hard-baked soil from which every blade of grass, every stray weed, every speck of green, has been trodden out, as must inevitably be every gentle thought and aspiration above the mere wants of the body in those whose moral natures such home surroundings are to nourish. In self-defence, you know, all life eventually accommodates itself to its environment, and human life is no exception. Within the house there is nothing to supply the want thus left unsatisfied. Tenement-houses have no aesthetic resources. If any are to be brought to bear on them, they must come from the outside. There is the common hall with doors opening softly on every landing as the strange step is heard on the stairs, the air-shaft that seems always so busy letting out foul stenches from below that it has no time to earn its name by bringing down fresh air, the squeaking pumps that hold no water, and the rent that is never less than one week's wages out of the four, quite as often half of the family earnings.

Why complete the sketch? It is drearily familiar already. Such as it is, it is the frame in which are set days, weeks, months, and years of unceasing toil, just able to fill the mouth and clothe the back. Such as it is, it is the world, and all of it, to which these weary workers return nightly to feed heart and brain after wearing out the body at the bench, or in the shop. To it come the young with their restless yearnings, perhaps to pass on the threshold one of the daughters of sin, driven to the tenement by the police when they raided her den, sallying forth in silks and fine attire after her day of idleness. These in their coarse garments—girls with the love of youth for beautiful things, with this hard life before them—who shall save them from the tempter? Down in the street the saloon, always bright and gay, gathering to itself all the cheer of the block, beckons the boys. In many such blocks the census-taker found two thousand men, women, and children, and over, who called them home.

The picture is faithful enough to stand for its class wherever along both rivers the Irish brogue is heard. As already said, the Celt falls most readily victim to tenement influences since shanty-town and its original free-soilers have become things of the past. If he be thrifty and shrewd his progress thenceforward is along the plane of the tenement, on which he soon assumes to manage without improving things. The German has an advantage over his Celtic neighbor in his strong love for flowers, which not all the tenements on the East Side have power to smother. His garden goes with him wherever he goes. Not that it represents any high moral principle in the man; rather perhaps the capacity for it. He turns his saloon into a shrubbery as soon as his back-yard. But wherever he puts it in a tenement block it does the work of a dozen police clubs. In proportion as it spreads the neighborhood takes on a more orderly character. As the green dies out of the landscape and increases in political importance, the police find more to do. Where it disappears altogether from sight, lapsing into a mere sentiment, police-beats are shortened and the force patrols double at night. Neither the man nor the sentiment is wholly responsible for this. It is the tenement unadorned that is. The changing of Tompkins Square from a sand lot into a beautiful park put an end for good and all to the Bread and Blood riots of which it used to be the scene, and transformed a nest of dangerous agitators into a harmless, beer-craving band of Anarchists. They have scarcely been heard of since. Opponents of the small parks system as a means of relieving the congested population of tenement districts, please take note.

With the first hot nights in June police despatches, that record the killing of men and women by rolling off roofs and window-sills while asleep, announce that the time of greatest suffering among the poor is at hand. It is in hot weather, when life indoors is well-nigh unbearable with cooking, sleeping, and working, all crowded into the small room together, that the tenement expands, reckless of all restraint. Then a strange and picturesque life moves upon the flat roofs. In the day and early evening mothers air their babies there, the boys fly their kites from the house-tops, undismayed by police regulations, and the young men and girls court and pass the growler. In the stifling July nights, when the big barracks are like fiery furnaces, their very walls giving out absorbed heat, men and women lie in restless, sweltering rows, panting for air and sleep. Then every truck in the street, every crowded fire-escape, becomes a bedroom, infinitely preferable to any the house affords. A cooling shower on such a night is hailed as a heaven-sent blessing in a hundred thousand homes.

Life in the tenements in July and August spells death to an army of little ones whom the doctor's skill is powerless to save. When the white badge of mourning flutters from every second door, sleepless mothers walk the streets in the gray of the early dawn, trying to stir a cooling breeze to fan the brow of the sick baby. There is no sadder sight than this patient devotion striving against fearfully hopeless odds. Fifty "summer doctors," especially trained to this work, are then sent into the tenements by the Board of Health, with free advice and medicine for the poor. Devoted women follow in their track with care and nursing for the sick. Fresh-air excursions run daily out of New York on land and water; but despite all efforts the grave-diggers in Calvary work over-time, and little coffins are stacked mountains high on the deck of the Charity Commissioners' boat when it makes its semi-weekly trips to the city cemetery.

Under the most favorable circumstances, an epidemic, which the well-to-do can afford to make light of as a thing to be got over or avoided by reasonable care, is excessively fatal among the children of the poor, by reason of the practical impossibility of isolating the patient in a tenement. The measles, ordinarily a harmless disease, furnishes a familiar example. Tread it ever so lightly on the avenues, in the tenements it kills right and left. Such an epidemic ravaged three crowded blocks in Elizabeth Street on the heels of the grippe last winter, and, when it had spent its fury, the death-maps in the Bureau of Vital Statistics looked as if a black hand had been laid across those blocks, over-shadowing in part the contiguous tenements in Mott Street, and with the thumb covering a particularly packed settlement of half a dozen houses in Mulberry Street. The track of the epidemic through these teeming barracks was as clearly defined as the track of a tornado through a forest district. There were houses in which as many as eight little children had died in five months. The records showed that respiratory diseases, the common heritage of the grippe and the measles, had caused death in most cases, discovering the trouble to be, next to the inability to check the contagion in those crowds, in the poverty of the parents and the wretched home conditions that made proper care of the sick impossible. The fact was emphasized by the occurrence here and there of a few isolated deaths from diphtheria and scarlet fever. In the case of these diseases, considered more dangerous to the public health, the health officers exercised summary powers of removal to the hospital where proper treatment could be had, and the result was a low death-rate.

These were tenements of the tall, modern type. A little more than a year ago, when a census was made of the tenements and compared with the mortality tables, no little surprise and congratulation was caused by the discovery that as the buildings grew taller the death-rate fell. The reason is plain, though the reverse had been expected by most people. The biggest tenements have been built in the last ten years of sanitary reform rule, and have been brought, in all but the crowding, under its laws. The old houses that from private dwellings were made into tenements, or were run up to house the biggest crowds in defiance of every moral and physical law, can be improved by no device short of demolition. They will ever remain the worst.

That ignorance plays its part, as well as poverty and bad hygienic surroundings, in the sacrifice of life is of course inevitable. They go usually hand in hand. A message came one day last spring summoning me to a Mott Street tenement in which lay a child dying from some unknown disease. With the "charity doctor" I found the patient on the top floor, stretched upon two chairs in a dreadfully stifling room. She was gasping in the agony of peritonitis that had already written its death-sentence on her wan and pinched face. The whole family, father, mother, and four ragged children, sat around looking on with the stony resignation of helpless despair that had long since given up the fight against fate as useless. A glance around the wretched room left no doubt as to the cause of the child's condition. "Improper nourishment," said the doctor, which, translated to suit the place, meant starvation. The father's hands were crippled from lead poisoning. He had not been able to work for a year. A contagious disease of the eyes, too long neglected, had made the mother and one of the boys nearly blind. The children cried with hunger. They had not broken their fast that day, and it was then near noon. For months the family had subsisted on two dollars a week from the priest, and a few loaves and a piece of corned beef which the sisters sent them on Saturday. The doctor gave direction for the treatment of the child, knowing that it was possible only to alleviate its sufferings until death should end them, and left some money for food for the rest. An hour later, when I returned, I found them feeding the dying child with ginger ale, bought for two cents a bottle at the pedlar's cart down the street. A pitying neighbor had proposed it as the one thing she could think of as likely to make the child forget its misery. There was enough in the bottle to go round to the rest of the family. In fact, the wake had already begun; before night it was under way in dead earnest.

Every once in a while a case of downright starvation gets into the newspapers and makes a sensation. But this is the exception. Were the whole truth known, it would come home to the community with a shock that would rouse it to a more serious effort than the spasmodic undoing of its purse-strings. I am satisfied from my own observation that hundreds of men, women, and children are every day slowly starving to death in the tenements with my medical friend's complaint of "improper nourishment." Within a single week I have had this year three cases of insanity, provoked directly by poverty and want. One was that of a mother who in the middle of the night got up to murder her child, who was crying for food; another was the case of an Elizabeth Street truck-driver whom the newspapers never heard of. With a family to provide for, he had been unable to work for many months. There was neither food, nor a scrap of anything upon which money could be raised, left in the house; his mind gave way under the combined physical and mental suffering. In the third case I was just in time with the police to prevent the madman from murdering his whole family. He had the sharpened hatchet in his pocket when we seized him. He was an Irish laborer, and had been working in the sewers until the poisonous gases destroyed his health. Then he was laid off, and scarcely anything had been coming in all winter but the oldest child's earnings as cash-girl in a store, $2.50 a week. There were seven children to provide for, and the rent of the Mulberry Street attic in which the family lived was $10 a month. They had borrowed as long as anybody had a cent to lend. When at last the man got an odd job that would just buy the children bread, the week's wages only served to measure the depth of their misery. "It came in so on the tail-end of everything," said his wife in telling the story, with unconscious eloquence. The outlook worried him through sleepless nights until it destroyed his reason. In his madness he had only one conscious thought: that the town should not take the children. "Better that I take care of them myself," he repeated to himself as he ground the axe to an edge. Help came in abundance from many almost as poor as they when the desperate straits of the family became known through his arrest. The readiness of the poor to share what little they have with those who have even less is one of the few moral virtues of the tenements. Their enormous crowds touch elbow in a closeness of sympathy that is scarcely to be understood out of them, and has no parallel except among the unfortunate women whom the world scorns as outcasts. There is very little professed sentiment about it to draw a sentimental tear from the eye of romantic philanthropy. The hard fact is that the instinct of self-preservation impels them to make common cause against the common misery.

No doubt intemperance bears a large share of the blame for it; judging from the stand-point of the policeman perhaps the greater share. Two such entries as I read in the police returns on successive days last March, of mothers in West Side tenements, who, in their drunken sleep, lay upon and killed their infants, go far to support such a position. And they are far from uncommon. But my experience has shown me another view of it, a view which the last report of the Society for Improving the Condition of the Poor seems more than half inclined to adopt in allotting to "intemperance the cause of distress, or distress the cause of intemperance," forty per cent of the cases it is called upon to deal with. Even if it were all true, I should still load over upon the tenement the heaviest responsibility. A single factor, the scandalous scarcity of water in the hot summer when the thirst of the million tenants must be quenched, if not in that in something else, has in the past years more than all other causes encouraged drunkenness among the poor. But to my mind there is a closer connection between the wages of the tenements and the vices and improvidence of those who dwell in them than, with the guilt of the tenement upon our heads, we are willing to admit even to ourselves. Weak tea with a dry crust is not a diet to nurse moral strength. Yet how much better might the fare be expected to be in the family of this "widow with seven children, very energetic and prudent"—I quote again from the report of the Society for the Improvement of the Condition of the Poor—whose "eldest girl was employed as a learner in a tailor's shop at small wages, and one boy had a place as 'cash' in a store. There were two other little boys who sold papers and sometimes earned one dollar. The mother finishes pantaloons and can do three pairs in a day, thus earning thirty-nine cents. Here is a family of eight persons with rent to pay and an income of less than six dollars a week."

And yet she was better off in point of pay than this Sixth Street mother, who "had just brought home four pairs of pants to finish, at seven cents a pair. She was required to put the canvas in the bottom, basting and sewing three times around; to put the linings in the waistbands; to tack three pockets, three corners to each; to put on two stays and eight buttons, and make six buttonholes; to put the buckle on the back strap and sew on the ticket, all for seven cents." Better off than the "church-going mother of six children," and with a husband sick to death, who to support the family made shirts, averaging an income of one dollar and twenty cents a week, while her oldest girl, aged thirteen, was "employed downtown cutting out Hamburg edgings at one dollar and a half a week—two and a half cents per hour for ten hours of steady labor—making the total income of the family two dollars and seventy cents per week." Then the Harlem woman, who was "making a brave effort to support a sick husband and two children by taking in washing at thirty-five cents for the lot of fourteen large pieces, finding coal, soap, starch, and bluing herself, rather than depend on charity in any form." Specimen wages of the tenements these, seemingly inconsistent with the charge of improvidence.

But the connection on second thought is not obscure. There is nothing in the prospect of a sharp, unceasing battle for the bare necessaries of life, to encourage looking ahead, everything to discourage the effort. Improvidence and wastefulness are natural results. The instalment plan secures to the tenant who lives from hand to mouth his few comforts; the evil day of reckoning is put off till a to-morrow that may never come. When it does come, with failure to pay and the loss of hard-earned dollars, it simply adds another hardship to a life measured from the cradle by such incidents. The children soon catch the spirit of this sort of thing. I remember once calling at the home of a poor washer-woman, living in an East Side tenement, and finding the door locked. Some children in the hallway stopped their play and eyed me attentively while I knocked. The biggest girl volunteered the information that Mrs. Smith was out; but while I was thinking of how I was to get a message to her, the child put a question of her own: "Are you the spring man or the clock man?" When I assured her that I was neither one nor the other, but had brought work for her mother, Mrs. Smith, who had been hiding from the instalment collector, speedily appeared.

Perhaps of all the disheartening experiences of those who have devoted lives of unselfish thought and effort, and their number is not so small as often supposed, to the lifting of this great load, the indifference of those they would help is the most puzzling. They will not be helped. Dragged by main force out of their misery, they slip back again on the first opportunity, seemingly content only in the old rut. The explanation was supplied by two women of my acquaintance in an Elizabeth Street tenement, whom the city missionaries had taken from their wretched hovel and provided with work and a decent home somewhere in New Jersey. In three weeks they were back, saying that they preferred their dark rear room to the stumps out in the country. But to me the oldest, the mother, who had struggled along with her daughter making cloaks at half a dollar apiece, twelve long years since the daughter's husband was killed in a street accident and the city took the children, made the bitter confession: "We do get so kind o'downhearted living this way, that we have to be where something is going on, or we just can't stand it." And there was sadder pathos to me in her words than in the whole long story of their struggle with poverty; for unconsciously she voiced the sufferings of thousands, misjudged by a happier world, deemed vicious because they are human and unfortunate.

It is a popular delusion, encouraged by all sorts of exaggerated stories when nothing more exciting demands public attention, that there are more evictions in the tenements of New York every year "than in all Ireland." I am not sure that it is doing much for the tenant to upset this fallacy. To my mind, to be put out of a tenement would be the height of good luck. The fact is, however, that evictions are not nearly as common in New York as supposed. The reason is that in the civil courts, the judges of which are elected in their districts, the tenant-voter has solid ground to stand upon at last. The law that takes his side to start with is usually twisted to the utmost to give him time and save him expense. In the busiest East Side court, that has been very appropriately dubbed the "Poor Man's Court," fully five thousand dispossess warrants are issued in a year, but probably not fifty evictions take place in the district. The landlord has only one vote, while there may be forty voters hiring his rooms in the house, all of which the judge takes into careful account as elements that have a direct bearing on the case. And so they have—on his case. There are sad cases, just as there are "rounders" who prefer to be moved at the landlord's expense and save the rent, but the former at least are unusual enough to attract more than their share of attention.

If his very poverty compels the tenant to live at a rate if not in a style that would beggar a Vanderbilt, paying four prices for everything he needs, from his rent and coal down to the smallest item in his housekeeping account, fashion, no less inexorable in the tenements than on the avenue, exacts of him that he must die in a style that is finally and utterly ruinous. The habit of expensive funerals—I know of no better classification for it than along with the opium habit and similar grievous plagues of mankind—is a distinctively Irish inheritance, but it has taken root among all classes of tenement dwellers, curiously enough most firmly among the Italians, who have taken amazingly to the funeral coach, perhaps because it furnishes the one opportunity of their lives for a really grand turn-out with a free ride thrown in. It is not at all uncommon to find the hoards of a whole lifetime of hard work and self-denial squandered on the empty show of a ludicrous funeral parade and a display of flowers that ill comports with the humble life it is supposed to exalt. It is easier to understand the wake as a sort of consolation cup for the survivors for whom there is—as one of them, doubtless a heathenish pessimist, put it to me once—"no such luck." The press and the pulpit have denounced the wasteful practice that often entails bitter want upon the relatives of the one buried with such pomp, but with little or no apparent result. Rather, the undertaker's business prospers more than ever in the tenements since the genius of politics has seen its way clear to make capital out of the dead voter as well as of the living, by making him the means of a useful "show of strength" and count of noses.

One free excursion awaits young and old whom bitter poverty has denied the poor privilege of the choice of the home in death they were denied in life, the ride up the Sound to the Potter's Field, charitably styled the City Cemetery. But even there they do not escape their fate. In the common trench of the Poor Burying Ground they lie packed three stories deep, shoulder to shoulder, crowded in death as they were in life, to "save space"; for even on that desert island the ground is not for the exclusive possession of those who cannot afford to pay for it. There is an odd coincidence in this, that year by year the lives that are begun in the gutter, the little nameless waifs whom the police pick up and the city adopts as its wards, are balanced by the even more forlorn lives that are ended in the river. I do not know how or why it happens, or that it is more than a mere coincidence. But there it is. Year by year the balance is struck—a few more, a few less—substantially the same when the record is closed.

Henry Demarest Lloyd
(1847–1903)

LLOYD was born in New York City. He was graduated from Columbia University in 1867 and passed his Bar examinations in 1869. He worked on the editorial staff of the *Chicago Tribune* (1872–1885) and subsequently resigned to devote more time to the pressing social issues of his day. His major book, *Wealth Against Commonwealth* (1894), dramatically portrayed the corruption of business monopolies.

Lloyd delivered the address "What Washington Would Do Today" at Chicago Central Music Hall, February 22, 1890. It was later published in Lloyd's *Lords of Industry* (1910).

WHAT WASHINGTON
WOULD DO TO-DAY

If Washington were with us he would not spend much of his time in celebrating Washington's birthday but would set about doing a Washington's work. He would not fight over again the battles of Stillwater and Brandywine. He would seek out the new measures demanded of new men by the new times. Washington was a republican when there was no republic except that which has kept the flag of human freedom and personal rights flying above the Alps of Switzerland for five hundred glorious years in the face of the kings of Europe. He was a republican when to be a republican was to be odious and an outcast from all the genteel society of the world. In Washington's day the republic was an experiment and an innovation and the boldest scheme of social regeneration under debate. Monarchy was law and order then, but in the words of the Declaration of Independence, he staked his "life, his fortune, and his sacred honor" on the ability of the people to get along without the kind of law and order which had to be imposed upon them from without by an authority foreign to them, and which they hated.

What Washington's head believed, his hand did. In reform he practised the principle that Charles H. Ham calls Manual Training. Like Jefferson and many other leaders of that day he advocated the abolition of slavery by law. But he did not wait for the laws. Of his own free will he did what the law did under bloody compulsion nearly a century later. He freed his slaves, and he did for his enfranchised what this nation has not yet done for its freedmen, black or white, he provided for the support of all the old and the helpless, and the education of the ignorant. We preach the equal rights of all to life, liberty, and the pursuit of happiness, but we practise an undemocratic, unrepublican, unchristian, and inhuman luxury and monopoly created for us by the people at the cost of dehumanizing hardship and poverty for countless thousands. We do not dare look straight into the honest eyes of Washington. That was not the way he lived his belief. Before the war of the Revolution, he was, as Edwin D. Mead says, "admired by everybody; he was famous; he was rich; he was happy; he was the most successful and fortunate of all young Virginia squires." Four years later the rebellion was at its darkest hour; he, the arch-rebel, was as near despair as such a man could go. It is at this moment history credits him with the only humorous remark he is known to have made. Putting his hand to his neck, he said: "I wonder how it would feel to have a rope around here." His neck was the forfeit this gallant Virginia squire was willing to pay for living up to his belief that the Americans were fit for a social system far in advance of that they or any other people had hitherto enjoyed.

As usual, the dreadful and despised heresy of the last century has become the fashionable opinion of to-day. We see an Empire dissolve into a Republic in a night. We hear whispers of a Spanish Republic, a Portuguese Republic, a Latin Republic. We see the Kaiser running a race with the Socialists for votes at the polls of Germany, and we hope for a German Republic. We speculate whether the next ruler of our elder brother across the sea will be the Prince—or a President. To some of us it is not an impossible dream that the day may come of the United States of Europe. But Washington, and those who made him their head in peace and war trod this path plain for the world a hundred years ago. They made this republican egg stand up. These men, whom Gladstone declares to have been the most remarkable group that ever appeared together in history, if they were here to-day would be republicans, but they would be a good deal more. They would be republicans plus a hundred years' growth in their belief in liberty; in their belief that if one people are fit for it, all people are fit for it, because no people are fit for anything else; in their belief that if liberty is good in one thing it is good in all things.

Washington and the Fathers saw that the Americans had outgrown monarchy. If under monarchy men could grow to be fit for the Republic, for what still more glorious destiny is the Republic educating us? Political liberty is but the beginning of liberty. The freeman like the farmer must plant afresh every year if the world is not to starve. Our fathers put an end to the abuse of government by kings. We must put an end to the abuse of government by classes. If the Presbyterians—the Elect—can revise their creed, the charter that regulates their relations with God, we common people can revise the creeds, constitutions, and contracts which regulate our relations with the Lords of Industry. America it was seen a century ago had become too wise, too good, too strong, to endure any longer the abuse of the kingly power. Who will be the Washington to believe—and live his belief—that America has grown too wise, too good, too strong, to endure any longer the abuse of the money-power—the King George of our day? Caesar had his Brutus, Charles I his Cromwell, George III his Washington, and the money-power may profit by their example. Divine rights have been succeeded by vested rights which look on government as a kind of cow which no one has the right to milk but themselves. As long as it fills their pails with special privileges, land grants, contracts, railroad charters, tax bounties, we hear nothing about the old saw that that government is the best which governs least. But when the people want to get hold of the teats to squeeze out a few drops of justice, to prevent the new wealth and power of the new industry from oppressing the weak, and to establish a broader co-operation for the common good, then vested rights discover that a government which does anything is very dangerous. The only government which the new patriotism will tolerate is that which uses the cooperation of all to enfranchise the individual. Let the individual do what the individual can do best. Let the government do what the government can do best.

When Washington was being educated, every gentleman wore a sword. Now the nation wears the sword. The defence of the frontier and the maintenance of internal order are better done, and the rest of us are free to do other things. In the roads, the post-office, the public school, the people have set free an immense volume of individual power—of individualism—by co-operating to do what had anciently been done by each for himself. A traveller who has visited all parts of the world declares that in no other country do the faces of the people show so much intelligence and cheerfulness as in America. America has produced the highest type of individualism because its social co-operation is the completest. The greater the co-operation, the higher the individualism. And this co-operation of all for the enfranchisement of all is the Union, which must and shall be preserved. But the co-operation of all for the benefit of the few we are going to put into the rag-bag where Reform keeps the other old clothes of history. Government is but one branch of industry. It is the social industry. True government is the union of the labor of all for the protection of the life, liberty, and happiness of all. But living under a high death-rate in tenement houses, in full view of the unoccupied prairies, with wife and children forced to work to get enough food for the family, is not life; working ten to twelve hours a day, when the citizen wants to work but eight, signing ironclad contracts because he is hungry, and going without justice because justice is too dear for the poor, is not liberty; and getting a taste of concert music, and protection against accident, poverty, and old age only by the charity of the rich is not happiness.

The Fathers renounced the King George who taxed them on their tea without their consent. What would they do to-day when they found that there was a King George in every important industry, taxing the people without representation or consent? A sugar King George, whose sugar puckers a free man's mouth; an oil King George, a very slippery monarch; and a coal King George, quite a different fellow from old King Cole, who was a merry old soul; and a whiskey King George, who does not distill the spirit of freedom; and a steel King George, who is a great thief; and a twine King George, who will have rope enough left on hand some day to hang himself with; and so many other King Georges that we begin to understand the ancient fable of the Hydra which got two new heads whenever one was cut off. Washington cut off one head, but King George will not stay killed until it is finally settled in all industry as well as in the industry of government that no human being has a right to share in the product of another's life and labor without his consent, and that there is no consent where there is not a perfect understanding and as perfect freedom to say No, as to say Yes, as perfect freedom to withhold as to give.

In their remonstrance to the government of Great Britain, the Continental Congress said: "We will never submit to be hewers of wood or drawers of water for any ministry or nation in the world." For ministry substitute monopolist, trust or privilege, capitalist, and you have the battle-cry of this generation.

"The Parliament of Great Britain," said Washington, "have no more right to put their hands into my pocket without my consent than I have to put my hands into yours for money." Now almost every business has its Parliament which asserts its right to tax us without representation and to-day he would use precisely the same language regarding these persons or combinations of persons who are putting their hands into our pockets without our consent. Faint hearts who doubted the people proposed to Washington to make things right by getting a good king instead of a bad one. But his principle was the very simple one that there could not be a good king. Andrew Carnegie says to the monopolists of the world: Let us be good monopolists and we can reign forever. But the world replies: There can be no good monopolists. It is we the people, not you the privileged, who have the right to decide what is "good" for us, and to do it for ourselves. No comparison can be made between the arbitrary power against which our forefathers rebelled, and that which is grinding us. That was one tax without consent. Now scores of such taxes are laid upon us. That was not burdensome. These are driving the farmers and working men and business men of small capital to desperation. That was foreign oppression; this is worse because it is a domestic oppression by brothers who have been rocked in the same cradle of Liberty with the rest of us. Oppression is oppression whether it is foreign or domestic. King George was as hateful to Chatham and Fox and Burke as to Washington and Adams. The English cut off Charles I.'s head, although he was an Englishman. "Give a man power," said Alexander Hamilton, "over my subsistence, and he has power over the whole of my moral nature." That power the Fathers declared they would not submit to, and they would rebel against it to-day all the more quickly because it was sought to be enforced by Americans against Americans.

King George defended himself on the ground of cheapness. Threepence a pound on tea was nothing to make a fuss about. Cheapness is the defence made by our King Georges of the markets. Washington's healthy conscience and common-sense told him that if a thing was wrong it could not be cheap. When we buy these so-called cheap things the sellers make us throw in our honor and liberties "to boot" and that makes the bargain very bad and very dear. Monopoly we are told is economy. The destruction of free competition, the seizure by usurpation of irresponsible power, whether in government or other industry, the possession of privilege through force and fraud never have had and never could have any other effect than to enable the ruler to abuse his subjects. There never has been a monopoly which was not formed for the express purpose of arresting and reversing the tendency to cheapness. There is not in existence a monopoly, from the Western Union Telegraph Company to the Coffin Trust, which cannot be shown on overwhelming evidence to be drawing its dividends from dearness instead of cheapness. It is an insult to the intelligence of the American people to suppose that they believe that these buccaneers of trade are blowing up competitors, as the oil monopoly has done; shutting up works and throwing working men out of employment, as the sugar monopoly has done; selling the machinery of rivals for junk, as the nail monopoly has done; paying big bonuses to others not to run, as the steel monopoly has done; restricting production, as the coal monopoly has done; buying up and suppressing new patents, as the telephone monopoly has done; and conspiring in dark closets every month or so about price lists as they all do, with the intention or with the result of making things cheaper to the people than they would be if there were a fair field for every one. In the days of honest competition there was a certain rough justice in the maxim, The devil take the hindmost. The kind of competition the monopolies give us demands a change in its wording. Nowadays the devil ought to take the foremost. The men who succeed are just the kind of men the devil wants. And we who are the hindmost can well spare them.

The tax on tea did not make tea dearer in the American colonies than it had been. It was cheaper after the tax than before. But George Washington said: What is it we are contending against? Is it against paying the duty of threepence a pound on tea because burdensome? No, it is the right only we have all along disputed. The plea of cheapness made for our monopolies, even if true, would still be morally monstrous. It condones any crime which may be committed by those who conquer supremacy in a trade provided they let us share the proceeds. It says to the merchant, the manufacturer, the common carrier, Take possession of the property and business of your rival by any means you find handy. We will ask no questions provided you will sell us cheap what you get. The conscience which can be satisfied by this argument of cheapness would applaud King Ahab in murdering Naboth, and stealing his vineyard provided he would sell the stolen grapes at five cents a pound.

The Americans loved Washington because he loved them. It was said of Peter Cartwright, the revivalist, who shook the lightnings of Sinai over the campmeetings of the Great West—when there was a West—that it was not so certain that he loved God as that he hated the devil. The Americans love their country and hate those who are working its ruin. The Americans love their country, their government, the memory of the Fathers, and with rising wrath they are keeping watch over the treasonable practices which now threaten the sanctity and perpetuity of these memories and institutions. As intensely as they love Washington they hate those who would now destroy his work, and desecrate the glories of his Republic by making its dignities the decorations of their ill-gotten, worse-spent wealth. Deep into the hearts of his people have sunk his words: "The preservation of the sacred fire of liberty and . . . the Republican form of government are . . . finally staked on the experiment . . . of the American people." And his warning: "The dangers to it come from ourselves!" The uprising of 1861[1] will be nothing to the whirlwind in which the American people will descend upon the new brood of traitors, when once they comprehend their purposes of destruction.

The rotten-ripe prosperity of America has bred a swarm of millionaire microbes, pestilence germs of plutocracy, the worst kind of grip, which are eating out the heart of our liberties. "You are a villain," said Othello to Iago. "You," replied Iago, "are a—senator." Before our eyes we see beginning to revolve again, as before in human history, the vicious circle in which liberty turns in upon itself to be self-consumed. Liberty produces wealth, wealth destroys liberty. Ingersoll said lately that what a republic has most to fear is mobs. All the mobs that have ever raged in all the cities of America have not done half the damage to life, liberty, and property that is wrought every year by the coal conspirators of Pennsylvania who rob mankind of the stored-up sunshine of millions of years of the past. "The real enemy of the Republic is the foreigner," cries Know-nothingism.[2] All Americans are foreigners more or less; America was discovered by a foreigner, the founders of the government, when it was at its weakest and when the world did not know what a republic was,

1. The reference, of course, is to the Civil War.—*Editor.*
2. The Know-Nothing party was organized in 1849 in New York City as a secret society known as the Order of the Star-Spangled Banner. The Know-Nothings were pro-slavery and anti-immigrant—in short, racist.—*Editor.*

found foreigners good enough material to build up the Union with. Now we are told all our troubles are due to the foreigners. There is one comfort in such statements. They prove that those who make them are forced at last to confess something is wrong in the social life of America. The guilty conscience characteristically puts it on the foreigners, the most innocent, the most helpless, the weakest class of our people. The railroads of Chicago, nullifying the law at their crossings, killed more people, destroyed more values, and practised more anarchy than all the foreigners who ever came to America. The men who fought to destroy the Union were natives. Foreigners fought Americans to save it. One of our great pulpit orators said in this hall last Sunday: "The foreigners cry, 'Down with the law,'" and he continued, "What law? We have none that impedes men or interferes with their liberty. Such laws went down in 1776." But the guns of 1861 called our attention to some laws that had not gone down in 1776. To-day the discontent mingling with the hum of toil in field and shop gives notice that the growing people find themselves shut in on all sides by class laws which make our currency, roads, lands, franchises, labor, like the Roman provinces which were put at the mercy of a few proconsuls. If we are true Americans we must sustain all citizens whether of native or foreign birth in their right to cry, Down with such laws. And we who have been Americans for hundreds of years ought to have the courage to admit that these class laws are practically all the creation of Yankee greed, and that their most helpless and most numerous victims are our foreign fellow-citizens. A foreigner is an alien. The real aliens of America are not the poor and oppressed of other nations who accept our promise of protection and liberty and become Americans by choice. The real aliens of America are the natives, who, reared at the breast of liberty and endowed with all the treasures of freedom, are betraying their country for a few pieces of silver, and in our courts, legislatures, and markets are playing the parts of Judas and Benedict Arnold. These natives are the real foreigners, for they are alien by choice; the immigrant who becomes a citizen by choice because he loves and believes in liberty is the real citizen and brother. Our American Judases use the name of American as a trademark "for revenue only." They are the only foreigners whom the American Republic has to fear.

The conscience of the world has been appalled by the scandals which have of late years disgraced the politics, the finances, the administration of justice, the markets of this country. In not one of them has the leading part been taken by a foreigner. It is not the lawless foreigners, it is the lawless Americans who gave us the Pacific Railroad swindles,[3] the Erie

3. Lloyd is here alluding to the misuse of land and funds arising from the passage of the Pacific Railways Acts of 1862 and 1864.—*Editor.*

and Tweed rings,[4] and all the others of that dreadful list. The central fire in the faith of the Fathers was that a free republic could absorb and assimilate and ennoble all the down-trodden, poor, and ignorant who sought its shelter. If our Republic has no longer this power it is no longer the Republic of Washington. A country in which the little boycotter, the working man who distributes circulars, goes to jail, while the big boycotters who suppress entire industries run the government, is not the Republic of Washington. A country in which the miners of Illinois and Pennsylvania are forbidden to dig coal, and grow thin for the want of corn, while the farmers burn corn to keep warm, is not the Republic of Washington. A country in which the public highways are private property operated for private profit and public robbery is not the Republic of Washington. A country which is owned by 250,000 millionaires is not the country of Washington.

A country in which more than one king has an income of hundreds of dollars an hour, day and night, weekdays and Sundays, while the farmers of Kansas get only fifteen cents a bushel for the grain it takes a year's hard work to raise, is not the Republic of Washington. A country in which the hired man of the Union Pacific Railroad, chartered, built, and supported by the people, dares to say to the people of Nebraska: "Don't you farmers make us railroad men mad," is not the Republic of Washington. A country in which the people have at the elections only the right to be crucified between two thieves—who are not crucified—is not the Republic of Washington. A country in which so much as one office is bought and the sellers and buyers go unpunished, is not the Republic of Washington. A country in which seven railroads have by force and fraud become the owners of all the anthracite coal, and in which half a dozen men meet once a month to determine how much of the coal shall be dug for 60,-000,000 free men, and how much tribute the free men must pay the coal barons for their artificial winter, is not the Republic of Washington.

A country in which the right of free speech and free assembly are regulated by the private temper of the policeman instead of the public policy of centuries of constitutional freedom is not the Republic of Washington. A country where people submit to industrial piracy, because the pirates sell their stolen goods cheap, is not the Republic of Washington.

What the people of America believe in, what the people of Europe came here for, is the Republic of Washington. And they mean to get it back from the plutocrats who are stealing it away like thieves in the night. They

4. By the "Erie ring" Lloyd is referring to the dubious financial manuverings, involving Daniel Drew, Jay Gould and James Fisk, which occurred when Cornelius Vanderbilt sought control of the Erie Railroad. The "Tweed ring" (1869–71), led by William Marcy Tweed, was a political organization which through various corrupt means robbed the city of New York of an estimated $100,000,000.—*Editor.*

mean to get back the old and they mean to win the new. In what Lowell beautifully calls "that angel heart of all—the heart of man" is growing a new sympathy; a new susceptibility to wrongs hitherto unfelt, done by brother to brother, a new science which declares that these wrongs are a social evil which can be righted by social efforts, a new conscience which says since they can be, they must be so righted. There is rising a consciousness of a new social power which can do for the common good many things hitherto done for private greed only. With malice towards none, with charity for all, the union of the people, ever resistless, ever rising, moves forward to pay the debt it owes God and mankind for its hundred years of freedom and happiness. It goes to express the new pity, the new self-interest, the new patriotism in a Commonwealth fit to be the child of the Republic of Washington—more glorious than any the world has yet seen. When the American militia ran away from the British at Kip's Landing, Washington called out to Heaven in anguish: "Are these the men with whom I am to defend America!" Yes, the gods replied, you shall make them such. To-day as he looks down to see us whom he loved so well passing by on the other side the poor, crushed by a new oppression, and holding our craven hands while the old enemy in a new dress destroys his Republic, we can hear him cry: "Are these the men with whom I am to defend America?" From millions of throats will come the answer. Yes. We will defend America. The eternal fires of your love and sacrifice lead us on.

Clarence Darrow
(1857–1938)

DARROW was born in Kinsman, Ohio. He was admitted to legal practice in 1878. From the time he defended Eugene V. Debs in the Pullman Strike (1894), he became associated with many controversial legal cases—among them, the Leopold and Loeb case (1924) and the Scopes Trial (1925). Two of his best known books are *Crime, Its Causes and Treatment* (1925) and *Story of My Life* (1932).

Darrow delivered the address "Crime and Criminals" to the prisoners in the Cook County Jail in Chicago in 1902. It appears in a collection of his writings entitled *Attorney for the Damned* (1957).

CRIME AND CRIMINALS

If I looked at jails and crimes and prisoners in the way the ordinary person does, I should not speak on this subject to you. The reason I talk to you on the question of crime, its cause and cure, is that I really do not in the least believe in crime. There is no such thing as a crime as the word is generally understood. I do not believe there is any sort of distinction between the real moral conditions of the people in and out of jail. One is just as good as the other. The people here can no more help being here than the people outside can avoid being outside. I do not believe that people are in jail because they deserve to be. They are in jail simply because they cannot avoid it on account of circumstances which are entirely beyond their control and for which they are in no way responsible.

I suppose a great many people on the outside would say I was doing you harm if they should hear what I say to you this afternoon, but you cannot be hurt a great deal anyway, so it will not matter. Good people outside would say that I was really teaching you things that were calculated to injure society, but it's worth while now and then to hear something different from what you ordinarily get from preachers and the like. These will tell you that you should be good and then you will get rich and be happy. Of course we know that people do not get rich by being good, and that is the reason why so many of you people try to get rich some other way, only you do not understand how to do it quite as well as the fellow outside.

There are people who think that everything in this world is an accident. But really there is no such thing as an accident. A great many folks admit that many of the people in jail ought to be there, and many who are outside ought to be in. I think none of them ought to be here. There ought

155

to be no jails; and if it were not for the fact that the people on the outside are so grasping and heartless in their dealings with the people on the inside, there would be no such institution as jails.

I do not want you to believe that I think all you people here are angels. I do not think that. You are people of all kinds, all of you doing the best you can—and that is evidently not very well. You are people of all kinds and conditions and under all circumstances. In one sense everybody is equally good and equally bad. We all do the best we can under the circumstances. But as to the exact things for which you are sent here, some of you are guilty and did the particular act because you needed the money. Some of you did it because you are in the habit of doing it, and some of you because you are born to it, and it comes to be as natural as it does, for instance, for me to be good.

Most of you probably have nothing against me, and most of you would treat me the same as any other person would, probably better than some of the people on the outside would treat me, because you think I believe in you and they know I do not believe in them. While you would not have the least thing against me in the world, you might pick my pockets. I do not think all of you would, but I think some of you would. You would not have anything against me, but that's your profession, a few of you. Some of the rest of you, if my doors were unlocked, might come in if you saw anything you wanted—not out of any malice to me, but because that is your trade. There is no doubt there are quite a number of people in this jail who would pick my pockets. And still I know this—that when I get outside pretty nearly everybody picks my pocket. There may be some of you who would hold up a man on the street, if you did not happen to have something else to do, and needed the money; but when I want to light my house or my office the gas company holds me up. They charge me one dollar for something that is worth twenty-five cents. Still all these people are good people; they are pillars of society and support the churches, and they are respectable.

When I ride on the streetcars I am held up—I pay five cents for a ride that is worth two and a half cents, simply because a body of men have bribed the city council and the legislature, so that all the rest of us have to pay tribute to them.

If I do not want to fall into the clutches of the gas trust and choose to burn oil instead of gas, then good Mr. Rockefeller holds me up, and he uses a certain portion of his money to build universities and support churches which are engaged in telling us how to be good.

Some of you are here for obtaining property under false pretenses— yet I pick up a great Sunday paper and read the advertisements of a merchant prince—"Shirtwaists for 39 cents, marked down from $3.00."

When I read the advertisements in the paper I see they are all lies. When

I want to get out and find a place to stand anywhere on the face of the earth, I find that it has all been taken up long ago before I came here, and before you came here, and somebody says, "Get off, swim into the lake, fly into the air; go anywhere, but get off." That is because these people have the police and they have the jails and the judges and the lawyers and the soldiers and all the rest of them to take care of the earth and drive everybody off that comes in their way.

A great many people will tell you that all this is true, but that it does not excuse you. These facts do not excuse some fellow who reaches into my pocket and takes out a five-dollar bill. The fact that the gas company bribes the members of the legislature from year to year, and fixes the law, so that all you people are compelled to be "fleeced" whenever you deal with them; the fact that the streetcar companies and the gas companies have control of the streets; and the fact that the landlords own all the earth —this, they say, has nothing to do with you.

Let us see whether there is any connection between the crimes of the respectable classes and your presence in the jail. Many of you people are in jail because you have really committed burglary; many of you, because you have stolen something. In the meaning of the law, you have taken some other person's property. Some of you have entered a store and carried off a pair of shoes because you did not have the price. Possibly some of you have committed murder. I cannot tell what all of you did. There are a great many people here who have done some of these things who really do not know themselves why they did them. I think I know why you did them —every one of you; you did these things because you were bound to do them. It looked to you at the time as if you had a chance to do them or not, as you saw fit; but still, after all, you had no choice. There may be people here who had some money in their pockets and who still went out and got some more money in a way society forbids. Now, you may not yourselves see exactly why it was you did this thing, but if you look at the question deeply enough and carefully enough you will see that there were circumstances that drove you to do exactly the thing which you did. You could not help it any more than we outside can help taking the positions that we take. The reformers who tell you to be good and you will be happy, and the people on the outside who have property to protect—they think that the only way to do it is by building jails and locking you up in cells on weekdays and praying for you Sundays.

I think that all of this has nothing whatever to do with right conduct. I think it is very easily seen what has to do with right conduct. Some so-called criminals—and I will use this word because it is handy, it means nothing to me—I speak of the criminals who get caught as distinguished from the criminals who catch them—some of these so-called criminals are in jail for their first offenses, but nine tenths of you are in jail because you did not have a good lawyer and, of course, you did not have a good lawyer because you did not have enough money to pay a good lawyer. There is no very great danger of a rich man going to jail.

Some of you may be here for the first time. If we would open the doors and let you out, and leave the laws as they are today, some of you would be back tomorrow. This is about as good a place as you can get anyway. There are many people here who are so in the habit of coming that they would not know where else to go. There are people who are born with the tendency to break into jail every chance they get, and they cannot avoid it. You cannot figure out your life and see why it was, but still there is a reason for it; and if we were all wise and knew the facts, we could figure it out.

In the first place, there are a good many more people who go to jail in the wintertime than in summer. Why is this? Is it because people are more wicked in winter? No, it is because the coal trust begins to get in its grip in the winter. A few gentlemen take possession of the coal, and unless the people will pay seven or eight dollars a ton for something that is worth three dollars, they will have to freeze. Then there is nothing to do but to break into jail, and so there are many more in jail in the winter than in summer. It costs more for gas in the winter because the nights are longer, and people go to jail to save gas bills. The jails are electric-lighted. You may not know it, but these economic laws are working all the time, whether we know it or do not know it.

There are more people who go to jail in hard times than in good times —few people, comparatively, go to jail except when they are hard up. They go to jail because they have no other place to go. They may not know why, but it is true all the same. People are not more wicked in hard times. That is not the reason. The fact is true all over the world that in hard times more people go to jail than in good times, and in winter more people go to jail than in summer. Of course it is pretty hard times for people who go to jail at any time. The people who go to jail are almost always poor people—people who have no other place to live, first and last. When times are hard, then you find large numbers of people who go to jail who would not otherwise be in jail.

Long ago, Mr. Buckle, who was a great philosopher and historian, collected facts, and he showed that the number of people who are arrested increased just as the price of food increased. When they put up the price of gas ten cents a thousand, I do not know who will go to jail, but I do know that a certain number of people will go. When the meat combine raises the price of beef, I do not know who is going to jail, but I know that a large number of people are bound to go. Whenever the Standard Oil Company raises the price of oil, I know that a certain number of girls who are seamstresses, and who work night after night long hours for somebody else, will be compelled to go out on the streets and ply another trade, and I know that Mr. Rockefeller and his associates are responsible and not the poor girls in the jails.

First and last, people are sent to jail because they are poor. Sometimes, as I say, you may not need money at the particular time, but you wish to have thrifty forehanded habits, and do not always wait until you are in absolute want. Some of you people are perhaps plying the trade, the profession, which is called burglary. No man in his right senses will go into a strange house in the dead of night and prowl around with a dark lantern through unfamiliar rooms and take chances of his life, if he has plenty of the good things of the world in his own home. You would not take any such chances as that. If a man had clothes in his clothes-press and beefstake in his pantry and money in the bank, he would not navigate around nights in houses where he knows nothing about the premises whatever. It always requires experience and education for this profession, and people who fit themselves for it are no more to blame than I am for being a lawyer. A man would not hold up another man on the street if he had plenty of money in his own pocket. He might do it if he had one dollar or two dollars, but he wouldn't if he had as much money as Mr. Rockefeller has. Mr. Rockefeller has a great deal better hold-up game than that.

The more that is taken from the poor by the rich, who have the chance to take it, the more poor people there are who are compelled to resort to these means for a livelihood. They may not understand it, they may not think so at once, but after all they are driven into that line of employment.

There is a bill before the legislature of this state to punish kidnaping children with death. We have wise members of the legislature. They know the gas trust when they see it and they always see it—they can furnish light enough to be seen; and this legislature thinks it is going to stop kidnaping children by making a law punishing kidnapers of children with death. I don't believe in kidnaping children, but the legislature is all wrong. Kidnaping children is not a crime, it is a profession. It has been developed with the times. It has been developed with our modern industrial conditions. There are many ways of making money—many new ways that our ancestors knew nothing about. Our ancestors knew nothing about a billion-dollar trust; and here comes some poor fellow who has no other trade and he discovers the profession of kidnapping children.

This crime is born, not because people are bad; people don't kidnap other people's children because they want the children or because they are devilish, but because they see a chance to get some money out of it. You cannot cure this crime by passing a law punishing by death kidnapers of children. There is one way to cure it. There is one way to cure all these offenses, and that is to give the people a chance to live. There is no other way, and there never was any other way since the world began; and the world is so blind and stupid that it will not see. If every man and woman and child in the world had a chance to make a decent, fair, honest living, there would be no jails and no lawyers and no courts. There might be some persons here or there with some peculiar formation of their brain, like Rockefeller, who would do these things simply to be doing them; but they would be very, very few, and those should be sent to a hospital and treated, and not sent to jail; and they would entirely disappear in the second generation, or at least in the third generation.

I am not talking pure theory. I will just give you two or three illustrations.

The English people once punished criminals by sending them away. They would load them on a ship and export them to Australia. England was owned by lords and nobles and rich people. They owned the whole earth over there, and the other people had to stay in the streets. They could not get a decent living. They used to take their criminals and send them to Australia—I mean the class of criminals who got caught. When these criminals got over there, and nobody else had come, they had the whole continent to run over, and so they could raise sheep and furnish their own meat, which is easier than stealing it. These criminals then became decent, respectable people because they had a chance to live. They did not commit any crimes. They were just like the English people who sent them there, only better. And in the second generation the descendants of those criminals were as good and respectable a class of people as there were on the face of the earth, and then they began building churches and jails themselves.

A portion of this country was settled in the same way, landing prisoners down on the southern coast; but when they got here and had a whole continent to run over and plenty of chances to make a living, they became respectable citizens, making their own living just like any other citizen in the world. But finally the descendants of the English aristocracy who sent the people over to Australia found out they were getting rich, and so they went over to get possession of the earth as they always do, and they organized land syndicates and got control of the land and ores, and then they had just as many criminals in Australia as they did in England. It was not because the world had grown bad; it was because the earth had been taken away from the people.

Some of you people have lived in the country. It's prettier than it is here. And if you have ever lived on a farm you understand that if you put a lot of cattle in a field, when the pasture is short they will jump over the fence; but put them in a good field where there is plenty of pasture, and they will be law-abiding cattle to the end of time. The human animal is just like the rest of the animals, only a little more so. The same thing that governs in the one governs in the other.

Everybody makes his living along the lines of least resistance. A wise man who comes into a country early sees a great undeveloped land. For instance, our rich men twenty-five years ago saw that Chicago was small and knew a lot of people would come here and settle, and they readily saw that if they had all the land around here it would be worth a good deal, so they grabbed the land. You cannot be a landlord because somebody has got it all. You must find some other calling. In England and Ireland and Scotland less than five per cent own all the land there is, and the people are bound to stay there on any kind of terms the landlords give. They must live the best they can, so they develop all these various professions— burglary, picking pockets and the like.

Again, people find all sorts of ways of getting rich. These are diseases like everything else. You look at people getting rich, organizing trusts and making a million dollars, and somebody gets the disease and he starts out. He catches it just as a man catches the mumps or the measles; he is not to blame, it is in the air. You will find men speculating beyond their means, because the mania of money-getting is taking possession of them. It is simply a disease—nothing more, nothing less. You cannot avoid catching it; but the fellows who have control of the earth have the advantage of you. See what the law is: when these men get control of things, they make the laws. They do not make the laws to protect anybody; courts are not instruments of justice. When your case gets into court it will make little difference whether you are guilty or innocent, but it's better if you have a smart lawyer. And you cannot have a smart lawyer unless you have money. First and last it's a question of money. Those men who own the earth make the laws to protect what they have. They fix up a sort of fence or pen around what they have, and they fix the law so the fellow on the outside cannot get in. The laws are really organized for the protection of the men who rule the world. They were never organized or enforced to do justice. We have no system for doing justice, not the slightest in the world.

Let me illustrate: Take the poorest person in this room. If the community had provided a system of doing justice, the poorest person in this room would have as good a lawyer as the richest, would he not? When you went into court you would have just as long a trial and just as fair a trial as the richest person in Chicago. Your case would not be tried in fifteen or twenty minutes, whereas it would take fifteen days to get through with a rich man's case.

Then if you were rich and were beaten, your case would be taken to the Appellate Court. A poor man cannot take his case to the Appellate Court;

he has not the price. And then to the Supreme Court. And if he were beaten there he might perhaps go to the United States Supreme Court. And he might die of old age before he got into jail. If you are poor, it's a quick job. You are almost known to be guilty, else you would not be there. Why should anyone be in the criminal court if he were not guilty? He would not be there if he could be anywhere else. The officials have no time to look after all these cases. The people who are on the outside, who are running banks and building churches and making jails, they have no time to examine 600 or 700 prisoners each year to see whether they are guilty or innocent. If the courts were organized to promote justice the people would elect somebody to defend all these criminals, somebody as smart as the prosecutor—and give him as many detectives and as many assistants to help, and pay as much money to defend you as to prosecute you. We have a very able man for state's attorney, and he has many assistants, detectives and policemen without end, and judges to hear the cases—everything handy.

Most all of our criminal code consists in offenses against property. People are sent to jail because they have committed a crime against property. It is of very little consequence whether one hundred people more or less go to jail who ought not to go—you must protect property, because in this world property is of more importance than anything else.

How is it done? These people who have property fix it so they can protect what they have. When somebody commits a crime it does not follow that he has done something that is morally wrong. The man on the outside who has committed no crime may have done something. For instance: to take all the coal in the United States and raise the price two dollars or three dollars when there is no need of it, and thus kill thousands of babies and send thousands of people to the poorhouse and tens of thousands to jail, as is done every year in the United States—this is a greater crime than all the people in our jails ever committed; but the law does not punish it. Why? Because the fellows who control the earth make the laws. If you and I had the making of the laws, the first thing we would do would be to punish the fellow who gets control of the earth. Nature put this coal in the ground for me as well as for them and nature made the prairies up here to raise wheat for me as well as for them, and then the great railroad companies came along and fenced it up.

Most all of the crimes for which we are punished are property crimes. There are a few personal crimes, like murder—but they are very few. The crimes committed are mostly those against property. If this punishment is right the criminals must have a lot of property. How much money is there in this crowd? And yet you are all here for crimes against property. The people up and down the Lake Shore have not committed crime; still they have so much property they don't know what to do with it. It is perfectly plain why these people have not committed crimes against property; they make the laws and therefore do not need to break them. And in order for you to get some property you are obliged to break the rules of the game. I don't know but what some of you may have had a very nice chance to get rich by carrying a hod for one dollar a day, twelve hours. Instead of taking that nice, easy profession, you are a burglar. If you had had been given a chance to be a banker you would rather follow that. Some of you may have had a chance to work as a switchman on a railroad where you know, according to statistics, that you cannot live and keep all your limbs more than seven years, and you can get fifty dollars or seventy-five dollars a month for taking your lives in your hands; and instead of taking that lucrative position you chose to be a sneak thief, or something like that. Some of you made that sort of choice. I don't know which I would take if I was reduced to this choice. I have an easier choice.

I will guarantee to take from this jail, or any jail in the world, five hundred men who have been the worst criminals and law-breakers who ever got into jail, and I will go down to our lowest streets and take five hundred of the most abandoned prostitutes, and go out somewhere where there is plenty of land, and will give them a chance to make a living, and they will be as good people as the average in the community.

There is a remedy for the sort of condition we see here. The world never finds it out, or when it does find it out it does not enforce it. You may pass a law punishing every person with death for burglary, and it will make no difference. Men will commit it just the same. In England there was a time when one hundred different offenses were punishable with death, and it made no difference. The English people strangely found out that so fast as they repealed the severe penalties and so fast as they did away with punishing men by death, crime decreased instead of increased; that the smaller the penalty the fewer the crimes.

Hanging men in our county jails does not prevent murder. It makes murderers.

And this has been the history of the world. It's easy to see how to do away with what we call crime. It is not so easy to do it. I will tell you how to do it. It can be done by giving the people a chance to live—by destroying special privileges. So long as big criminals can get the coal fields, so long as the big criminals have control of the city council and get the public streets for streetcars and gas rights—this is bound to send thousands of poor people to jail. So long as men are allowed to monopolize all the earth, and compel others to live on such terms as these men see fit to make, then you are bound to get into jail.

The only way in the world to abolish crime and criminals is to abolish the big ones and the little ones together. Make fair conditions of life. Give men a chance to live. Abolish the right of private ownership of land, abolish monopoly, make the world partners in production, partners in the good things of life. Nobody would steal if he could get something of his own some easier way. Nobody will commit burglary when he has a house full. No girl will go out on the streets when she has a comfortable place at home. The man who owns a sweatshop or a department store may not be to blame himself for the condition of his girls, but when he pays them five dollars, three dollars, and two dollars a week, I wonder where he thinks they will get the rest of their money to live. The only way to cure these conditions is by equality. There should be no jails. They do not accomplish what they pretend to accomplish. If you would wipe them out there would be no more criminals than now. They terrorize nobody. They are a blot upon any civilization, and a jail is an evidence of the lack of charity of the people on the outside who make the jails and fill them with the victims of their greed.

Jane Addams
(1860–1935)

JANE ADDAMS was born in Cedarville, Illinois, and was graduated from Rockford College in 1881. Eight years later, she, along with Ellen Gates, opened Hull House in Chicago—one of the first social settlements in the United States. The remainder of Addams' life was devoted to social welfare (especially the improvement of slum life), and in 1931, as a result of her concern for international peace, she was named a co-winner of the Nobel Peace prize. Her major works are *Democracy and Social Ethics* (1902), *Newer Ideals of Peace* (1907), *Twenty Years at Hull House* (1910), and *The Second Twenty Years at Hull House* (1930).

"Survivals of Militarism in Civil Government" is the second chapter of *Newer Ideals of Peace*.

SURVIVALS OF MILITARISM
IN CIVIL GOVERNMENT

We are accustomed to say that the machinery of government incorporated in the charters of the early American cities, as in the Federal and State constitutions was worked out by men who were strongly under the influence of the historians and doctrinaires of the eighteenth century. The most significant representative of these men is Thomas Jefferson, and their most telling phrase, the familiar opening that "all men are created free and equal."

We are only now beginning to suspect that the present admitted failure in municipal administration, the so-called "shame of American cities," may be largely due to the inadequacy of those eighteenth-century ideals, with the breakdown of the machinery which they provided. We recognize the weakness inherent in the historic and doctrinaire method when it attempts to deal with growing and human institutions. While these men were strongly under the influence of peace ideals which were earnestly advocated, both in France and in America, even in the midst of their revolutionary periods, and while they read the burning poets and philosophers of their remarkable century, their idealism, after all, was largely founded upon theories concerning "the natural man," a creature of their sympathetic imaginations.

Because their idealism was of the type that is afraid of experience, these founders refused to look at the difficulties and blunders which a self-governing people were sure to encounter, and insisted that, if only the people had freedom, they would walk continuously in the paths of justice and righteousness. It was inevitable, therefore, that they should have remained quite untouched by that worldly wisdom which counsels us to know life as it is, and by that very modern belief that if the world is ever to go right at all, it must go right in its own way.

A man of this generation easily discerns the crudeness of "that eighteenth-century conception of essentially unprogressive human nature in all the empty dignity of its 'inborn rights.' "[1] Because he has grown familiar with a more passionate human creed, with the modern evolutionary conception of the slowly advancing race whose rights are not "inalienable," but hard-won in the tragic process of experience, he realizes that these painfully acquired rights must be carefully cherished or they may at any moment slip out of our hands. We know better in America than anywhere else that civilization is not a broad road, with mile-stones indicating how far each nation has proceeded upon it, but a complex struggle forward, each race and nation contributing its quota; that the variety and continuity of this commingled life afford its charm and value. We would not, if we could, conform them to one standard. But this modern attitude, which may even now easily subside into negative tolerance, did not exist among the founders of the Republic, who, with all their fine talk of the "natural man" and what he would accomplish when he obtained freedom and equality, did not really trust the people after all.

They timidly took the English law as their prototype, "whose very root is in the relation between sovereign and subject, between lawmaker and those whom the law restrains," which has traditionally concerned itself more with the guarding of prerogative and with the rights of property than with the spontaneous life of the people. They serenely incorporated laws and survivals which registered the successful struggle of the barons against the aggressions of the sovereign, although the new country lacked both nobles and kings. Misled by the name of government, they founded their new government by an involuntary reference to a lower social state than that which they actually saw about them. They depended upon penalties, coercion, compulsion, remnants of military codes, to hold the community together; and it may be possible to trace much of the maladministration of our cities to these survivals, to the fact that our early democracy was a moral romanticism, rather than a well-grounded belief in social capacity and in the efficiency of the popular will.

It has further happened that as the machinery, groaning under the pressure of new social demands put upon it, has broken down that from time to time, we have mended it by giving more power to administrative officers, because we still distrusted the will of the people. We are willing to cut off the dislocated part or to tighten the gearing, but are afraid to substitute a machine of newer invention and greater capacity. In the hour of danger we revert to the military and legal type although they become less and less appropriate to city life in proportion as the city grows more

1. Josiah Royce, *The Spirit of Modern Philosophy*, p. 275.—*Author*.

complex, more varied in resource and more highly organized, and is, therefore, in greater need of a more diffused local autonomy.

A little examination will easily show that in spite of the fine phrases of the founders, the Government became an entity by itself away from the daily life of the people. There was no intention to ignore them nor to oppress them. But simply because its machinery was so largely copied from the traditional European Governments which did distrust the people, the founders failed to provide the vehicle for a vital and genuinely organized expression of the popular will. The founders carefully defined what was germane to government and what was quite outside its realm, whereas the very crux of local self-government, as has been well said, is involved in the "right to locally determine the scope of the local government," in response to the needs as they arise.

They were anxious to keep the reins of government in the hands of the good and professedly public-spirited, because, having staked so much upon the people whom they really knew so little, they became eager that they should appear well, and should not be given enough power to enable them really to betray their weaknesses. This was done in the same spirit in which a kind lady permits herself to give a tramp five cents, believing that, although he may spend it for drink, he cannot get very drunk upon so small a sum. In spite of a vague desire to trust the people, the founders meant to fall back in every crisis upon the old restraints which government has traditionally enlisted in its behalf, and were, perhaps, inevitably influenced by the experiences of the Revolutionary War. Having looked to the sword for independence from oppressive governmental control, they came to regard the sword as an essential part of the government they had succeeded in establishing.

Regarded from the traditional standpoint, government has always needed this force of arms. The king, attempting to control the growing power of the barons as they wrested one privilege after another from him, was obliged to use it constantly; the barons later successfully established themselves in power only to be encroached upon by the growing strength and capital of the merchant class. These are now, in turn, calling upon the troops and militia for aid, as they are shorn of a pittance here and there by the rising power of the proletariat. The imperial, the feudal, the capitalistic forms of society each created by revolt against oppression from above, preserved their own forms of government only by carefully guarding their hardly won charters and constitutions. But in the very countries where these successive social forms have developed, full of survivals of the past, some beneficent and some detrimental, governments are becoming modified more rapidly than in this democracy where we ostensibly threw off traditional governmental oppression only to encase ourselves in a theory of virtuous revolt against oppressive government, which in many instances has proved more binding than the actual oppression itself.

Did the founders cling too hard to that which they had won through persecution, hardship, and finally through a war of revolution? Did these doctrines seem so precious to them that they were determined to tie men up to them as long as possible, and allow them no chance to go on to new devices of government, lest they slight these that had been so hardly won? Did they estimate, not too highly, but by too exclusive a valuation, that which they had secured through the shedding of blood?

Man has ever overestimated the spoils of war, and tended to lose his sense of proportion in regard to their value. He has ever surrounded them with a glamour beyond their deserts. This is quite harmless when the booty is an enemy's sword hung over a household fire, or a battered flag decorating a city hall, but when the spoil of war is an idea which is bound on the forehead of the victor until it cramps his growth, a theory which he cherishes in his bosom until it grows so large and near that it afflicts its possessor with a sort of disease of responsibility for its preservation, it may easily overshadow the very people for whose cause the warrior issued forth.

Was this overestimation of the founders the cause of our subsequent failures? or rather did not the fault lie with their successors, and does it not now rest with us, that we have wrapped our inheritance in a napkin and refused to add thereto? The founders fearlessly took the noblest word of their century and incorporated it into a public document. They ventured their fortunes and the future of their children upon its truth. We, with the belief of a progressive, developing human life, apparently accomplish less than they with their insistence upon rights and liberties which they so vigorously opposed to mediaeval restrictions and obligations. We are in that first period of conversion when we hold a creed which forecasts newer and larger possibilities for governmental development, without in the least understanding its spiritual implications. Although we have scrupulously extended the franchise to the varied immigrants among us, we have not yet admitted them into real political followship.

It is easy to demonstrate that we consider our social and political problems almost wholly in the light of one wise group whom we call native Americans, legislating for the members of humbler groups whom we call immigrants. The first embodies the attitude of contempt or, at best, the patronage of the successful towards those who have as yet failed to succeed. We may consider the so-called immigration situation as an illustration of our failure to treat our growing Republic in the spirit of a progressive and developing democracy.

The statement is made many times that we, as a nation, are rapidly reaching the limit of our powers of assimilation, that we receive further

masses of immigrants at the risk of blurring those traits and characteristics which we are pleased to call American, with its corollary that the
national standard of living is in danger of permanent debasement. Were
we not in the midst of a certain intellectual dearth and apathy, of a
skepticism in regard to the ideals of self-government which have ceased
to charm men, we would see that we are testing our national life by a
tradition too provincial and limited to meet its present motley and cosmopolitan character; that we lack mental energy, adequate knowledge, and
a sense of the youth of the earth. The constant cry that American institutions are in danger betrays a spiritual waste, not due to our infidelity to
national ideals, but arising from the fact that we fail to enlarge those
ideals in accord with our faithful experience of life. Our political machinery devised for quite other conditions, has not been readjusted and
adapted to the successive changes resulting from our development. The
clamor for the town meeting, for the colonial and early century ideals of
government is in itself significant, for we are apt to cling to the past
through a very paucity of ideas.

   In a sense the enormous and unprecedented moving about over the
face of the earth on the part of all nations is in itself the result of philo-
sophic dogma of the eighteenth century—of the creed of individual liberty.
The modern system of industry and commerce presupposes freedom of
occupation, of travel, and residence; even more, it unhappily rests in a
large measure upon the assumption of a body of the unemployed and the
unskilled, ready to be absorbed or dropped according to the demands of
production: but back of that, or certainly preceding its later developments,
lies "the eternal rights" doctrine of the eighteenth century. Even so late
as 1892 an official treaty of the United States referred to the "inalienable
rights of man to change his residence and religion." This dogma of the
schoolmen, dramatized in France and penetrating under a thousand forms
into the most backward European States, is still operating as an obscure
force in sending emigrants to America and in our receiving them here.
But in the second century of its existence it has become too barren and
chilly to induce any really zealous or beneficent activity on behalf of the
immigrants after they arrive. On the other hand those things which we
do believe—the convictions which might be formulated to the immeasurable benefit of the immigrants, and to the everlasting good of our national
life, have not yet been satisfactorily stated, nor apparently apprehended
by us, in relation to this field. We have no method by which to discover
men, to spiritualize, to understand, to hold intercourse with aliens and to
receive of what they bring. A century-old abstraction breaks down before
this vigorous test of concrete cases and their demand for sympathetic interpretation. When we are confronted by the Italian lazzaroni, the peasants
from the Carpathian foothills, and the proscribed traders from Galatia,

we have no national ideality founded upon realism and tested by our growing experience with which to meet them, but only the platitudes of our crudest youth. The philosophers and statesmen of the eighteenth century believed that the universal franchise would cure all ills; that liberty and equality rested only upon constitutional rights and privileges; that to obtain these two and to throw off all governmental oppression constituted the full duty of the progressive patriot. We still keep to this formalization because the philosophers of this generation give us nothing newer. We ignore the fact that world-wide problems can no longer be solved by a political constitution assuring us against opposition, but that we must frankly face the proposition that the whole situation is more industrial than political. Did we apprehend this, we might then realize that the officers of the Government who are dealing with naturalization papers and testing the knowledge of the immigrants concerning the Constitution of the United States, are only playing with counters representing the beliefs of a century ago, while the real issues are being settled by the great industrial and commercial interests which are at once the products and the masters of our contemporary life. As children who are allowed to amuse themselves with poker chips pay no attention to the real game which their elders play with the genuine cards in their hands, so we shut our eyes to the exploitation and industrial debasement of the immigrant, and say, with placid contentment, that he has been given the rights of an American citizen, and that, therefore, all our obligations have been fulfilled. It is as if we should undertake to cure the contemporary political corruption founded upon a disregard of the Inter-State Commerce Acts, by requiring the recreant citizens to repeat the Constitution of the United States.

As yet no vigorous effort is made to discover how far our present system of naturalization, largely resting upon laws enacted in 1802, is inadequate, although it *may have* met the requirements of "the fathers." These processes were devised to test new citizens who had immigrated to the United States from political rather than from economic pressure, although these two have always been in a certain sense coextensive. Yet the early Irish came to America to seek an opportunity for self-government, denied them at home; the Germans and Italians started to come in largest numbers after the absorption of their smaller States into the larger nations; and the immigrants from Russia are the conquered Poles, Lithuanians, Finns, and Jews. On some such obscure notion the processes of naturalization were worked out, and, with a certain degree of logic, the first immigrants were presented with the Constitution of the United States as a type and epitome of that which they had come to seek. So far as they now come in search of political liberty, as many of them do every day, the test is still valid, but, in the meantime, we cannot ignore those significant figures which show emigration to rise with periods of depression in given countries, and immigration to be checked by periods of depression in America, and we refuse to see how largely the question has become an economic one.

At the present moment, as we know, the actual importing of immigrants is left largely to the energy of steamship companies and to those agents for contract labor who are keen enough to avoid the restrictive laws. The business man is here again in the saddle, as he so largely is in American affairs. From the time that the immigrants first make the acquaintance of the steamship agent in their own villages, at least until a grandchild is born on the new soil, they are subjected to various processes of exploitation from purely commercial and self-seeking interests. It begins with the representatives of the transatlantic lines and their allies, who convert the peasant holdings into money, and provide the prospective emigrants with needless supplies, such as cartridge belts and bowie knives. The brokers, in manufactured passports, send their clients by successive stages for a thousand miles to a port suiting their purposes. On the way the emigrants' eyes are treated that they may pass the physical test; they are taught to read sufficiently well to meet the literacy test; they are lent enough money to escape the pauper test, and by the time they have reached America, they are so hopelessly in debt that it requires months of work to repay all they have received. During this time they are completely under the control of the last broker in the line, who has his dingy office in an American city. The exploitation continues under the employment agency whose operations verge into those of the politician, through the naturalization henchman, the petty lawyers who foment their quarrels and grievances by the statement that in a free country everybody "goes to law," by the liquor dealers who stimulate a lively trade among them, and, finally, by the lodging-house keepers and the landlords who are not obliged to give them the housing which the American tenant demands. It is a long dreary road, and the immigrant is successfully exploited at each turn. At moments one looking on is driven to quote the Titanic plaint of Walt Whitman: "As I stand aloof and look, there is to me something profoundly affecting in large masses of men following the lead of those who do not believe in men."

The sinister aspect of this exploitation lies in the fact that it is carried on by agents whose stock in trade are the counters and terms of citizenship. It is said that at the present moment there are more of these agents in Palermo than perhaps in any other European port, and that those politicians who have found it impossible to stay even in that corrupt city are engaged in the brokerage of naturalization papers in the United States. Certainly one effect of the stringent contract labor laws has been to make the padrones more powerful because "smuggled alien labor" has become more valuable to American corporations, and also to make simpler the delivery of immigrant votes according to the dictates of commercial interests. It becomes a veritable system of poisoning the notions of decent government; but because the entire process is carried on in political terms, because the poker chips are colored, red, white, and blue, we are childishly indifferent to it. An elaborate avoidance of restrictions quickly adapts itself to changes either in legislation here or at the points of departure, because none of the legislation is founded upon a real analysis of the situation. For instance, a new type of broker in Russia during the Russian-Japanese War made use of the situation in the interests of young Russian Jews. If one of these men leaves the country ordinarily, his family is obliged to pay three hundred rubles to the Government, but if he first joins the army, his family is free from this obligation for he has passed into the keeping of his sergeant. Out of four hundred Russian Jews who, during three months, were drafted into the army at a given recruiting station, only ten reported, the rest having escaped through immigration. Of course the entire undertaking is much more hazardous, because the man is a deserter from the army in addition to his other disabilities; but the brokers merely put up the price of their services and continue their undertakings.

All these evasions of immigration laws and regulations are simply possible because the governmental tests do not belong to the current situation, and because our political ideas are inherited from governmental conditions not our own. In our refusal to face the situation, we have persistently ignored the political ideals of the Celtics, Germanic, Latin, and Slavic immigrants who have successively come to us; and in our overwhelming ambition to remain Anglo-Saxon, we have fallen into the Anglo-Saxon temptation of governing all peoples by one standard. We have failed to work out a democratic government which should include the experiences and hopes of all the varied peoples among us. We justify the situation by some such process as that employed by each English elector who casts a vote for seventy-five subjects besides himself. He indirectly determines—although he may be a narrow-minded tradesman or a country squire interested only in his hounds and horses—the colonial policy, which shall in turn control the destinies of the Egyptian child toiling in the cotton factory in Alexandria, and of the half-starved Parsee working the opium fields of North India. Yet he cannot, in the nature of the case, be informed of the needs of these far-away people and he would venture to attempt it only in regard to people whom he considered "inferior."

Pending a recent election, a Chicago reformer begged his hearers to throw away all selfish thoughts of themselves when they went to the polls and to vote in behalf of the poor and ignorant foreigners of the city. It would be difficult to suggest anything which would result in a more serious confusion than to have each man, without personal knowledge and experiences, consider the interests of the newly arrived immigrant. The voter would have to give himself over to a veritable dabauch of altruism in order to persuade himself that his vote would be of the least value to those men of whom he knew so little, and whom he considered so remote and alien to himself. In truth the attitude of the advising reformer was in reality so contemptuous that he had never considered the immigrants really partakers and molders of the political life of his country.

This attitude of contempt, of provincialism, this survival of the spirit of the conqueror toward an inferior people has many manifestations, but none so harmful as when it becomes absorbed and imitated and is finally evinced by the children of the foreigners toward their own parents.

We are constantly told of the increase of criminals in the second generation of immigrants, and, day after day, one sees lads of twelve and fourteen throwing off the restraint of family life and striking out for themselves. The break has come thus early, partly from the forced development of the child under city conditions, partly because the parents have had no chance of following, even remotely, this development, but largely because the Americanized child has copied the contemptuous attitude towards the foreigner which he sees all about him. The revolt has in it something of the city impatience of country standards, but much more of America against Poland or Italy. It is all wretchedly sordid with bitterness on the part of the parents, and hardhearted indifference and recklessness on the part of the boy. Only occasionally can the latter be appealed to by filial affection after the first break has once been thoroughly made; and yet, sometimes, even these lads see the pathos of the situation. A probation officer from Hull-House one day surprised three truants who were sitting by a bonfire which they had built near the river. Sheltered by an empty freight car, the officer was able to listen to their conversation. The Pole, the Italian, and the Bohemian boys who had broken the law by staying away from school, by building a fire in dangerous proximity to freight cars, and by "swiping" the potatoes which they were roasting, seemed to have settled down into an almost halcyon moment of gentleness and reminiscence. The Italian boy commiserated his parents because they hated the cold and the snow and "couldn't seem to get used to it"; the Pole said that his father missed seeing folks that he knew and was "sore on this country"; the Bohemian lad really grew quite tender about this old grandmother and the "stacks of relations" who came to see her every Sunday in the old country, where, in contrast to her loneliness here, she evidently had been a person of consequence. All of them felt the pathos of the situation, but the predominant note was the cheap contempt of the new American for foreigners, even though they are of his own blood. The weakneing of the tie which connects one generation with another may be called the domestic results of the contemptuous attitude. But the social results of the contemptuous attitude are even more serious and nowhere so grave as in the modern city.

Men are there brought together by multitudes in response to the concentration of industry and commerce without bringing with them the natural social and family ties or the guild relationships which distinguished the mediaeval cities and held even so late as the eighteenth century, when the country people came to town in response to the normal and slowly formed ties of domestic service, family affection, and apprenticeship. Men who come to a modern city by immigration break all these older ties and the national bond in addition. There is all the more necessity to develop that cosmopolitan bond which forms their substitute. The immigrants will be ready to adapt themselves to a new and vigorous civic life founded upon the recognition of their needs if the Government which is at present administered in our cities, will only admit that these needs are germane to its functions. The framers of the carefully prepared charters, upon which the cities are founded, did not foresee that after the universal franchise had once been granted, social needs and ideals were bound to enter in as legitimate objects of political action. Neither did these framers realize, on the other hand, that the only people in a democracy who can legitimately become the objects of repressive government, are those people who are too undeveloped to use their liberty or those who have forfeited their right to full citizenship. We have, therefore, a municipal administration in America which concerns itself only grudgingly with the social needs of the people, and is largely reduced to the administration of restrictive measures. The people who come most directly in contact with the executive officials, who are the legitimate objects of their control, are the vicious, who need to be repressed; and the semi-dependent poor, who appeal to them in their dire need; or, for quite the reverse reason, those who are trying to avoid an undue taxation, resenting the fact that they should be made to support a government which, from the nature of the case, is too barren to excite their real enthusiasm.

The instinctive protest against this mechanical method of civic control, with the lack of adjustment between the natural democratic impulse and the fixed external condition, inevitably produces the indifferent citizen, and the so-called "professional politician." The first, because he is not vicious, feels that the real processes of government do not concern him and wishes only to be let alone. The latter easily adapts himself to an illegal avoidance of the external fixed conditions by assuming that these conditions have been settled by doctrinaires who did not in the least understand the people, while he, the politician, makes his appeal beyond the conditions to the real desires of the people themselves. He is thus not only "the people's friend," but their interpreter. It is interesting to note how often simple people refer to "them," meaning the good and great who govern but do not understand, and to "him," meaning the alderman, who represents them in these incomprehensible halls of State, as an ambassador to a foreign country to whose borders they themselves could not possibly penetrate, and whose language they do not speak.

In addition to this difficulty inherent in the difference between the traditional and actual situation, there is another, which constantly arises on the purely administrative side. The traditional governments which the founders had copied, in proceeding by fixed standards to separate the vicious from the good, and then to legislate against the vicious, had enforced these restrictive measures by trained officials, usually with a military background. In a democracy, however, the officers entrusted with the enforcement of this restrictive legislation, if not actually elected by the people themselves, are still the appointments of those thus elected and are, therefore, good-natured men who have made friends by their kindness and social qualities. This is only decreasingly true even in those cities where appointments are made by civil service examinations. The carrying out of repressive legislation, the remnant of a military state of society, in a democracy is at last put into the hands of men who have attained office because of political pull. The repressive measures must be enforced by those sympathizing with the people and belonging to those against whom the measures operate. This anomalous situation produces almost inevitably one result: that the police authorities themselves are turned into allies of vice and crime. This may be illustrated from almost any of the large American cities in the relation existing between the police force and the gambling and other illicit life. The officers are often flatly told that the enforcement of an ordinance which the better element of the city has insisted upon passing, is impossible; that they are expected to control only the robbery and crime that so often associate themselves with vice. As Mr. Wilcox[2] has recently pointed out, public sentiment itself assumes a certain hypocrisy, and in the end we have "the abnormal conditions which are created when vice is protected by the authorities," and in the very worst cases there develops a sort of municipal blackmail in which the administration itself profits by the violation of law. The very governmental agencies which were designed to protect the citizen from vice, foster and protect him in its pursuance because everybody involved is thoroughly confused by the human element in the situation. Further than this, the officer's very kindness and human understanding is that which leads to his downfall, for he is forced to uphold the remnant of a military discipline in a self-governing community. It is not remarkable, perhaps, that the police department, the most vigorous survival of militarism to be

2. Delos F. Wilcox, *The American City*, p. 200.—*Author.*

found in American cities, has always been responsible for the most exaggerated types of civic corruption. It is sad, however, that this corruption has largely been due to the kindliness of the officers and to their lack of military training. There is no doubt that the reasonableness of keeping the saloons in lower New York open on Sunday was apparent to the policemen of the East Side force long before it dawned upon the reform administration; and yet, that the policemen allowed themselves to connive at law-breaking, was the beginning of their disgraceful downfall. Because kindness to an enemy may mean death or the annihilation of the army which he guards, all kindness is illicit on the part of the military sentinel on duty; but to bring that code over bodily into a peaceful social state is to break down the morals of both sides, of the enforcer of the ill-adapted law, as well as of those against whom it is so maladroitly directed.

In order to meet this situation, there is almost inevitably developed a politician of the corrupt type so familiar in American cities, the politician who has become successful because he has made friends with the vicious. The semi-criminal, who are constantly brought in contact with administrative government are naturally much interested in its operations. Having much at stake, as a matter of course, they attend the primaries and all the other election processes which so quickly tire the good citizens whose interest in the government is a self-imposed duty. To illustrate: it is a matter of much moment to a gambler whether there is to be a "wide-open town" or not; it means the success or failure of his business; it involves, not only the pleasure, but the livelihood, of all his friends. He naturally attends to the election of the alderman, to the appointment and retention of the policeman. He is found at the caucus "every time," and would be much amused if he were praised for the performance of his civic duty; but, because he and the others who are concerned in semi-illicit business do attend the primaries, the corrupt politician is nominated over and over again.

As this type of politician is successful from his alliance with crime, there also inevitably arises from time to time a so-called reformer who is shocked to discover the state of affairs, the easy partnership between vice and administrative government. He dramatically uncovers the situation and arouses great indignation against it on the part of good citizens. If this indignation is enough, he creates a political fervor which is translated into a claim upon public gratitude. In portraying the evil he is fighting, he does not recognize, or at least does not make clear, all the human kindness upon which it has grown. In his speeches he inevitably offends a popular audience, who know that the evil or corruption exists in all degrees and forms of human weakness, but who also know that these evils are by no means always hideous, and sometimes even are lovable. They resent his over-drawn pictures of vice and of the life of the vicious; their sense of fair play, their deep-rooted desire for charity and justice, are all outraged.

To illustrate from a personal experience: Some years ago a famous New York reformer came to Chicago to tell us of his phenomenal success, his trenchant methods of dealing with the city "gambling-hells," as he chose to call them. He proceeded to describe the criminals of lower New York in terms and phrases which struck at least one of his auditors as sheer blasphemy against our common human nature. I thought of the criminals whom I knew, of the gambler for whom each Saturday I regularly collected his weekly wage of $24.00, keeping $18.00 for his wife and children and giving him $6.00 on Monday morning. His despairing statement, "the thing is growing on me, and I can never give it up," was certainly not the cry of a man living in hell, but of him who, through much tribulation had at least kept the loyal intention. I remembered the three girls who had come to me with a paltry sum of money collected from the pawn and sale of their tawdry finery in order that one of their number might be spared a death in the almshouse and that she might have the wretched comfort during the closing weeks of her life of knowing that, although she was an outcast, she was not a pauper. I recalled the first murderer whom I had ever known, a young man who was singing his baby to sleep and stopped to lay it in its cradle before he rushed downstairs into his father's saloon to scatter the gang of boys who were teasing the old man by giving him English orders. The old man could not understand English and the boys were refusing to pay for the drinks they had consumed, but technically had not ordered.

For one short moment I saw the situation from the point of view of humbler people, who sin often through weakness and passion, but seldom through hardness of heart, and I felt that in a democratic community such sweeping condemnations and conclusions as the speaker was pouring forth could never be accounted for righteousness.

As the policeman who makes terms with vice, and almost inevitably slides into making gain from vice, merely represents the type of politician who is living off the weakness of his fellows, so the over-zealous reformer who exaggerates vice until the public is scared and awestruck, represents the type of politician who is living off the timidity of his fellows. With the lack of civic machinery for simple democratic expression, for a direct dealing with human nature as it is, we seem doomed to one type or the other—corruptionists or anti-crime committees.

And one sort or the other we will continue to have so long as we distrust the very energy of existence, the craving for enjoyment, the pushing of vital forces, the very right of every citizen to be what he is without pretense or assumption of virtue. Too often he does not really admire these virtues, but he imagines them somewhere as a standard adopted by the virtuous whom he does not know. That old Frankenstein, the ideal man of the eighteenth century, is still haunting us, although he never existed save in the brain of the doctrinaire.

This dramatic and feverish triumph of the self-seeker, see-sawing with that of the interested reformer, does more than anything else, perhaps, to keep the American citizen away from the ideals of genuine evolutionary democracy. Whereas repressive government, from the nature of the case, has to do with the wicked who are happily always in a minority in the community, a normal democratic government would naturally have to do with the great majority of the population in their normal relations to each other.

After all, the so-called "slum politician" ventures his success upon an appeal to human sentiment and generosity. This venture often results in an alliance between the popular politician and the humblest citizens, quite as naturally as the reformer who stands for honest business administration usually becomes allied with the type of business man whose chief concern it is to guard his treasure and to prevent a rise in taxation. The community is again insensibly divided into two camps, the repressed, who is dimly conscious that he has no adequate outlet for his normal life and the repressive, represented by the cautious, careful citizen holding fast to his own, —once more the conqueror and his humble people.

III.
Divided America
(1917–1960)

America's entrance into World War I in 1917 marked our country's full-scale emergence as an international power. America's role as a world power now displaced the perhaps nostalgic ideal of isolationism, but along with this displacement there emerged a division of priorities. The United States was caught in the dilemma of fighting several wars abroad, while it neglected, or minimized, the rights of the disfranchised at home. With the inevitable emphasis on militarization to protect our world role, the government's concern with the needs of many of its citizens decreased. Indeed, with the rise of America as a world power one notes a corresponding lessening of interest in implementing and safeguarding the ideals of the Declaration of Independence and the Constitution. H. L. Mencken notices, for example, democracy's "curious distrust of itself—its apparently ineradicable tendency to abandon its whole philosophy at the first sign of strain"; and Randolph Bourne observes this tendency in many intellectuals, who "in a time of danger and disaster . . . jump for some dogma to cling to." But it is Dwight Macdonald, commenting on the conclusion to World War II, who summarizes the cruel division between democracy's world image and its questionable practice:

It seems fitting that The Bomb was not developed by any of the totalitarian powers, where the political atmosphere might at first glance seem to be more suited to it, but by the two "democracies," the last major powers to continue to pay at least ideological respect to the humanitarian-democratic tradition.

While the first four selections in this section deal essentially with America's dilemmas as a world power, it is Mary McCarthy who provides the transition to the dividedness *within* our country: "as the richest nation in the world, we have developed the psychology of rich people: we are afraid of poverty, of 'agitators,' of any jarring notes in the national harmony." The last three essays in this section—all by black authors—confront the principal jarring note of national harmony, which is, of course, racism.

H. L. Mencken
(1880–1956)

MENCKEN was born in Baltimore, where he became an important journalist and social critic. Together with G. J. Nathan, he co-edited the *Smart Set* (1914–1923) and later the same two men established *The American Mercury* (1924), which Mencken edited for nine years. Mencken's major collection of essays, *Prejudices*, was published in six volumes (1919–1927), and he is also the author of *The American Language* (1919) and numerous other works.

"Coda" is Section IV of Mencken's book *Notes on Democracy*, published in 1926.

CODA

The Future of Democracy

Whether or not democracy is destined to survive in the world until the corruptible puts on incorruption and the immemorial Christian dead leap out of their graves, their faces shining and their yells resounding—this is something, I confess, that I don't know, nor is it necessary, for the purposes of the present inquiry, that I venture upon the hazard of a guess. My business is not prognosis, but diagnosis. I am not engaged in therapeutics, but in pathology. That simple statement of fact, I daresay, will be accepted as a confession, condemning me out of hand as unfit for my task, and even throwing a certain doubt upon my *bona fides*. For it is one of the peculiar intellectual accompaniments of democracy that the concept of the insoluble becomes unfashionable—nay, almost infamous. To lack a remedy is to lack the very license to discuss disease. The causes of this are to be sought, without question, in the nature of democracy itself. It came into the world as a cure-all, and it remains primarily a cure-all to this day. Any boil upon the body politic, however vast and raging, may be relieved by taking a vote; any flux of blood may be stopped by passing a law. The aim of government is to repeal the laws of nature, and re-enact them with moral amendments. War becomes simply a device to end war. The state, a mystical emanation from the mob, takes on a transcendental potency, and acquires the power to make over the father which begat it. Nothing remains inscrutable and beyond remedy, not even the way of a man with a maid. It was not so under the ancient and accursed systems of despotism, now happily purged out of the world. They, too, I grant you, had certain pretensions of an homeric gaudiness, but they at least refrained from attempts to abolish sin, poverty, stupidity, cowardice, and other such immutable realities. Mediaeval Christianity, which was a theological and

186

philosophical *apologia* for those systems, actually erected belief in that immutability into a cardinal article of faith. The evils of the world were incurable: one put off the quest for a perfect moral order until one got to heaven, *post mortem*. There arose, in consequence, a scheme of checks and balances that was consummate and completely satisfactory, for it could not be put to a test, and the logical holes in it were chinked with miracles. But no more. To-day the Holy Saints are deposed. Now each and every human problem swings into the range of practical politics. The worst and oldest of them may be solved facilely by travelling bands of lady Ph.D.'s each bearing the mandate of a Legislature of kept men, all unfaithful to their protectors.

Democracy becomes a substitute for the old religion, and the antithesis of it: the Ku Kluxers, though their reasoning may be faulty, are not far off the facts in their conclusion that Holy Church is its enemy. It shows all the magical potency of the great systems of faith. It has the power to enchant and disarm; it is not vulnerable to logical attack. I point for proof to the appalling gyrations and contortions of its chief exponents. Read, for example, the late James Bryce's "Modern Democracies." Observe how he amasses incontrovertible evidence that democracy doesn't work— and then concludes with a stout declaration that it does. Or, if his two fat volumes are too much for you, turn to some school reader and give a judicious perusal to Lincoln's Gettysburg Address, with its argument that the North fought the Civil War to save self-government to the world!—a thesis echoed in falsetto, and by feebler men, fifty years later. It is im- possible, by any device known to philosophers, to meet doctrines of that sort; they obviously lie outside the range of logical ideas. There is, in the human mind, a natural taste for such hocus-pocus. It greatly simplifies the process of ratiocination, which is unbearably painful to the great ma- jority of men. What dulls and baffles the teeth may be got down con- veniently by an heroic gulp. No doubt there is an explanation here of the long-continued popularity of the dogma of the Trinity, which remains unstated in plain terms after two thousand years. And no doubt the dogma of Transubstantiation came under fire in the Reformation because it had grown too simple and comprehensible—because even the Scholastic philos- ophy had been unable to convert its plain propositions into something that could be believed without being understood. Democracy is shot through with this delight in the incredible, this banal mysticism. One can- not discuss it without colliding with preposterous postulates, all of them cherished like authentic hairs from the whiskers of Moses himself. I have alluded to its touching acceptance of the faith that progress is illimitable and ordained by God—that every human problem, in the very nature of things, may be solved. There are corollaries that are even more naïve. One, for example, is to the general effect that optimism is a virtue in itself—

that there is a mysterious merit in being hopeful and of glad heart, even in the presence of adverse and immovable facts. This curious notion turns the glittering wheels of Rotary, and is the motive power of the political New Thoughters called Liberals. Certainly the attitude of the average American Liberal toward the so-called League of Nations offered superb clinical material to the student of democratic psychopathology. He began by arguing that the League would save the world. Confronted by proofs of its fraudulence, he switched to the doctrine that believing in it would save the world. So, later on, with the Washington Disarmament Conference. The man who hopes absurdly, it appears, is in some fantastic and gaseous manner a better citizen than the man who detects and exposes the truth. Bear this sweet democratic axiom clearly in mind. It is, fundamentally, what is the matter with the United States.

As I say, my present mandate does not oblige me to conjure up a system that will surpass and shame democracy as democracy surpasses and shames the polity of the Andaman Islanders or the Great Khan—a system full-blown and perfect, like Prohibition, and ready to be put into effect by the simple adoption of an amendment to the Constitution. Such a system, for all I know, may lie outside the farthest soarings of the human mind, though that mind can weigh the stars and know God. Until the end of the chapter the ants and bees may flutter their sardonic antennae at us in that department, as they do in others: the last joke upon man may be that he never learned how to govern himself in a rational and competent manner, as the last joke upon woman may be that she never had a baby without wishing that the Day of Judgment were a week past. I am not even undertaking to prove here that democracy is too full of evils to be further borne. On the contrary, I am convinced that it has some valuable merits, not often described, and I shall refer to a few of them presently. All I argue is that its manifest defects, if they are ever to be got rid of at all, must be got rid of by examining them realistically—that they will never cease to afflict all the more puissant and exemplary nations so long as discussing them is impeded by concepts borrowed from theology. As for me, I have never encountered any actual evidence, convincing to an ordinary jury, that *vox populi* is actually *vox Dei*. The proofs, indeed, run the other way. The life of the inferior man is one long protest against the obstacles that God interposes to the attainment of his dreams, and democracy, if it is anything at all, is simply one way of getting 'round those obstacles. Thus it represents, not a jingling echo of what seems to be divine will, but a raucous defiance of it. To that extent, perhaps, it is truly civilized, for civilization, as I have argued elsewhere, is best described as an effort to remedy the blunders and check the cruel humours of the Cosmic Kaiser. But what is defiant is surely not official, and what is not official is open to examination.

For all I know, democracy may be a self-limiting disease, as civilization itself seems to be. There are obvious paradoxes in its philosophy, and some of them have a suicidal smack. It offers John Doe a means to rise above his place beside Richard Roe, and then, by making Roe his equal, it takes away the chief usufructs of the rising. I here attempt no pretty logical gymnastics: the history of democratic states is a history of disingenuous efforts to get rid of the second half of that dilemma. There is not only the natural yearning of Doe to use and enjoy the superiority that he has won; there is also the natural tendency of Roe, as an inferior man, to acknowledge it. Democracy, in fact, is always inventing class distinctions, despite its theoretical abhorrence of them. The baron has departed, but in his place stand the grand goblin, the supreme worthy archon, the sovereign grand commander. Democratic man, as I have remarked, is quite unable to think of himself as a free individual; he must belong to a group, or shake with fear and loneliness—and the group, of course, must have its leaders. It would be hard to find a country in which such brummagem serene highnesses are revered with more passionate devotion than they get in the United States. The distinction that goes with mere office runs far ahead of the distinction that goes with actual achievement. A Harding is regarded as genuinely superior to a Halsted,[1] no doubt because his doings are better understood. But there is a form of human striving that is understood by democratic man even better than Harding's, and that is the striving for money. Thus the plutocracy, in a democratic state, tends to take the place of the missing aristocracy, and even to be mistaken for it. It is, of course, something quite different. It lacks all the essential characters of a true aristocracy: a clean tradition, culture, public spirit, honesty, honour, courage—above all, courage. It stands under no bond of obligation to the state; it has no public duty; it is transient and lacks a goal. Its most puissant dignitaries of to-day came out of the mob only yesterday—and from the mob they bring all its peculiar ignobilities. As practically encountered, the plutocracy stands quite as far from the *honnête homme* as it stands from the Holy Saints. Its main character is its incurable timorousness; it is for ever grasping at the straws held out by demagogues. Half a dozen gabby Jewish youths, meeting in a back room to plan a revolution—in other words, half a dozen kittens preparing to upset the Matterhorn—are enough to scare it half to death. Its dreams are of banshees, hobgoblins, bugaboos. The honest, untroubled snores of a Percy or a Hohenstaufen are quite beyond it.

The plutocracy, as I say, is comprehensible to the mob because its aspira-

1. The first reference is to Warren G. Harding, twenty-ninth President of the United States (1921–1923), whose administration became known for its ineffectuality and corruption. William Stewart Halsted, professor of surgery at Johns Hopkins University, was one of America's leading surgeons.—*Editor.*

tions are essentially those of inferior men: it is not by accident that Christianity, a mob religion, paves heaven with gold and precious stones, *i.e.*, with money. There are, of course, reactions against this ignoble ideal among men of more civilized tastes, even in democratic states, and sometimes they arouse the mob to a transient distrust of certain of the plutocratic pretensions. But that distrust seldom arises above mere envy, and the polemic which engenders it is seldom sound in logic or impeccable in motive. What it lacks is aristocratic disinterestedness, born of aristocratic security. There is no body of opinion behind it that is, in the strictest sense, a free opinion. Its chief exponents, by some divine irony, are pedagogues of one sort or another—which is to say, men chiefly marked by their haunting fear of losing their jobs. Living under such terrors, with the plutocracy policing them harshly on one side and the mob congenitally suspicious of them on the other, it is no wonder that their revolt usually peters out in metaphysics, and that they tend to abandon it as their families grow up, and the costs of heresy become prohibitive. The pedagogue, in the long run, shows the virtues of the Congressman, the newspaper editorial writer or the butler, not those of the aristocrat. When, by any chance, he persists in contumacy beyond thirty, it is only too commonly a sign, not that he is heroic, but simply that he is pathological. So with most of his brethren of the Utopian Fife and Drum Corps, whether they issue out of his own seminary or out of the wilderness. They are fanatics; not statesmen. Thus politics, under democracy, resolves itself into impossible alternatives. Whatever the label on the parties, or the war cries issuing from the demagogues who lead them, the practical choice is between the plutocracy on the one side and a rabble of preposterous impossibilists on the other. One must either follow the *New York Times*, or one must be prepared to swallow Bryan[2] and the Bolsheviki. It is a pity that this is so. For what democracy needs most of all is a party that will separate the good that is in it theoretically from the evils that beset it practically, and then try to erect that good into a workable system. What it needs beyond everything is a party of liberty. It produces, true enough, occasional libertarians, just as despotism produces occasional regicides, but it treats them in the same drum-head way. It will never have a party of them until it invents and installs a genuine aristocracy, to breed them and secure them.

Last Words

I have alluded somewhat vaguely to the merits of democracy. One of them is quite obvious: it is, perhaps, the most charming form of government ever devised by man. The reason is not far to seek. It is based upon

2. William Jennings Bryan was a noted speaker, political leader, and advocate of religious fundamentalism.—*Editor.*

propositions that are palpably not true—and what is not true, as everyone knows, is always immensely more fascinating and satisfying to the vast majority of men than what is true. Truth has a harshness that alarms them, and an air of finality that collides with their incurable romanticism. They turn, in all the great emergencies of life, to the ancient promises, transparently false but immensely comforting, and of all those ancient promises there is none more comforting than the one to the effect that the lowly shall inherit the earth. It is at the bottom of the dominant religious system of the modern world, and it is at the bottom of the dominant political system. The latter, which is democracy, gives it an even higher credit and authority than the former, which is Christianity. More, democracy gives it a certain appearance of objective and demonstrable truth. The mob man, functioning as citizen, gets a feeling that he is really important to the world—that he is genuinely running things. Out of his maudlin herding after rogues and mountebanks there comes to him a sense of vast and mysterious power —which is what makes archbishops, police sergeants, the grand goblins of the Ku Klux and other magnificoes happy. And out of it there comes, too, a conviction that he is somehow wise, that his views are taken seriously by his betters—which is what makes United States Senators, fortune-tellers and Young Intellectuals happy. Finally, there comes out of it a glowing consciousness of a high duty triumphantly done—which is what makes hangmen and husbands happy.

All these forms of happiness, of course, are illusory. They don't last. The democrat, leaping into the air to flap his wings and praise God, is forever coming down with a thump. The seeds of his disaster, as I have shown, lie in his own stupidity: he can never get rid of the naïve delusion— so beautifully Christian!—that happiness is something to be got by taking it away from the other fellow. But there are seeds, too, in the very nature of things: a promise, after all, is only a promise, even when it is supported by divine revelation, and the chances against its fulfilment may be put into a depressing mathematical formula. Here the irony that lies under all human aspiration shows itself: the quest for happiness, as always, brings only *un*happiness in the end. But saying that is merely saying that the true charm of democracy is not for the democrat but for the spectator. That spectator, it seems to me, is favoured with a show of the first cut and calibre. Try to imagine anything more heroically absurd! What grotesque false pretences! What a parade of obvious imbecilities! What a welter of fraud! But is fraud unamusing? Then I retire forthwith as a psychologist. The fraud of democracy, I contend, is more amusing than any other—more amusing even, and by miles, than the fraud of religion. Go into your praying-chamber and give sober thought to any of the more characteristic democratic inventions: say, Law Enforcement. Or to any of the typical democratic prophets: say, the late Archangel Bryan. If you don't come out paled and palsied by mirth then you will not laugh on the Last Day itself, when Presbyterians step out of the grave like chicks from the egg, and wings blossom from their scapulae, and leap into interstellar space with roars of joy.

I have spoken hitherto of the possibility that democracy may be a self-limiting disease, like measles. It is, perhaps, something more: it is self-devouring. One cannot observe it objectively without being impressed by its curious distrust of itself—its apparently ineradicable tendency to abandon its whole philosophy at the first sign of strain. I need not point to what happens invariably in democratic states when the national safety is menaced. All the great tribunes of democracy, on such occasions, convert themselves, by a process as simple as taking a deep breath, into despots of an almost fabulous ferocity. Lincoln, Roosevelt and Wilson come instantly to mind: Jackson and Cleveland are in the background, waiting to be recalled. Nor is this process continued to times of alarm and terror: it is going on day in and day out. Democracy always seems bent upon killing the thing it theoretically loves. I have rehearsed some of its operations against liberty, the very cornerstone of its political metaphysic. It not only wars upon the thing itself; it even wars upon mere academic advocacy of it. I offer the spectacle of Americans jailed for reading the Bill of Rights as perhaps the most gaudily humorous ever witnessed in the modern world. Try to imagine monarchy jailing subjects for maintaining the divine right of Kings! Or Christianity damning a believer for arguing that Jesus Christ was the Son of God! This last, perhaps, has been done: anything is possible in that direction. But under democracy the remotest and most fantastic possibility is a commonplace of every day. All the axioms resolve themselves into thundering paradoxes, many amounting to downright contradictions in terms. The mob is competent to rule the rest of us—but it must be rigorously policed itself. There is a government, not of men, but of laws—but men are set upon benches to decide finally what the law is and may be. The highest function of the citizen is to serve the state—but the first assumption that meets him, when he essays to discharge it, is an assumption of his disingenuousness and dishonour. Is that assumption commonly sound? Then the farce only grows the more glorious.

I confess, for my part, that it greatly delights me. I enjoy democracy immensely. It is incomparably idiotic, and hence incomparably amusing. Does it exalt dunderheads, cowards, trimmers, frauds, cads? Then the pain of seeing them go up is balanced and obliterated by the joy of seeing them come down. Is it inordinately wasteful, extravagant, dishonest? Then so is every other form of government: all alike are enemies to laborious and virtuous men. Is rascality at the very heart of it? Well, we have borne that rascality since 1776, and continue to survive. In the long run, it may turn out that rascality is necessary to human government, and even to civilization itself—that civilization, at bottom, is nothing but a colossal swindle. I do not know: I report only that when the suckers are running well the spectacle is infinitely exhilarating. But I am, it may be, a somewhat malicious man: my sympathies, when it comes to suckers, tend to be coy. What I can't make out is how any man can believe in democracy who feels for and with them, and is pained when they are debauched and made a show of. How can any man be a democrat who is sincerely a democrat?

Randolph Bourne
(1886–1918)

RANDOLPH BOURNE was born in Bloomfield, New Jersey, and was graduated from Columbia University in 1913. A superb essayist, Bourne became an important social and political critic. His major collections of essays, *Untimely Papers* (1919) and *The History of a Literary Radical* (1920), were published posthumously.

"The War and the Intellectuals" first appeared in *The Seven Arts* (June 1917).

THE WAR AND
THE INTELLECTUALS*

To those of us who still retain an irreconcilable animus against war, it has been a bitter experience to see the unanimity with which the American intellectuals have thrown their support to the use of war-technique in the crisis in which America found herself. Socialists, college professors, publicists, new-republicans, practitioners of literature, have vied with each other in confirming with their intellectual faith the collapse of neutrality and the riveting of the war-mind on a hundred million more of the world's people. And the intellectuals are not content with confirming our belligerent gesture. They are now complacently asserting that it was they who effectively willed it, against the hesitation and dim perceptions of the American democratic masses. A war made deliberately by the intellectuals! A calm moral verdict, arrived at after a penetrating study of inexorable facts! Sluggish masses, too remote from the world-conflict to be stirred, too lacking in intellect to perceive their danger! An alert intellectual class, saving the people in spite of themselves, biding their time with Fabian strategy until the nation could be moved into war without serious resistance! An intellectual class, gently guiding a nation through sheer force of ideas into what the other nations entered only through predatory craft or popular hysteria or militarist madness! A war free from any taint of self-seeking, a war that will secure the triumph of democracy and internationalize the world! This is the picture which the more self-conscious intellectuals have formed of themselves, and which they are slowly impressing upon a population which is being led no man knows whither

* The United States did not enter World War I (1914–1918) until April 6, 1917. "Making the world safe for democracy" was a popular slogan used to justify America's entrance into the War. The Treaty of Versailles (1919) formally ended World War I. —*Editor.*

by an indubitably intellectualized President. And they are right, in that the war certainly did not spring from either the ideals or the prejudices, from the national ambitions or hysterias, of the American people, however acquiescent the masses prove to be, and however clearly the intellectuals prove their putative intuition.

Those intellectuals who have felt themselves totally out of sympathy with this drag toward war will seek some explanation for this joyful leadership. They will want to understand this willingness of the American intellect to open the sluices and flood us with the sewage of the war spirit. We cannot forget the virtuous horror and stupefaction which filled our college professors when they read the famous manifesto of their ninety-three German colleagues in defence of their war. To the American academic mind of 1914 defence of war was inconceivable. From Bernhardi[1] it recoiled as from a blasphemy, little dreaming that two years later would find it creating its own cleanly reasons for imposing military service on the country and for talking of the rough rude currents of health and regeneration that war would send through the American body politic. They would have thought anyone mad who talked of shipping American men by the hundreds of thousands—conscripts—to die on the fields of France. Such a spiritual change seems catastrophic when we shoot our minds back to those days when neutrality was a proud thing. But the intellectual progress has been so gradual that the country retains little sense of the irony. The war sentiment, begun so gradually but so perseveringly by the preparedness advocates who came from the ranks of big business, caught hold of one after another of the intellectual groups. With the aid of Roosevelt, the murmurs became a monotonous chant, and finally a chorus so mighty that to be out of it was at first to be disreputable and finally almost obscene. And slowly a strident rant was worked up against Germany which compared very creditably with the German fulminations against the greedy power of England. The nerve of the war-feeling centered, of course, in the richer and older classes of the Atlantic seaboard, and was keenest where there were French or English business and particularly social connections. The sentiment then spread over the country as a class-phenomenon, touching everywhere those upper-class elements in each section who identified themselves with this Eastern ruling group. It must never be forgotten that in every community it was the least liberal and least democratic elements among whom the preparedness and later the war sentiment was found. The farmers were apathetic, the small business men and workingmen are still apathetic towards the war. The election was a vote of confidence of these latter classes in a President who would

1. Friedrich Von Bernhardi was a German general and military historian whose book, *Germany and the Next War* (1912), advocated Germany's use of war.—*Editor.*

keep the faith of neutrality.[2] The intellectuals, in other words, have identified themselves with the least democratic forces in American life. They
have assumed the leadership for war of those very classes whom the
American democracy has been immemorially fighting. Only in a world
where irony was dead could an intellectual class enter war at the head of
such illiberal cohorts in the avowed cause of world-liberalism and world-
democracy. No one is left to point out the undemocratic nature of this
war-liberalism. In a time of faith, skepticism is the most intolerable of
all insults.

Our intellectual class might have been occupied, during the last two
years of the war, in studying and clarifying the ideals and aspirations of
the American democracy, in discovering a true Americanism which would
not have been merely nebulous but might have federated the different
ethnic groups and traditions. They might have spent the time in endeavoring to clear the public mind of the cant of war, to get rid of old mystical
notions that clog our thinking. We might have used the time for a great
wave of education, for setting our house in spiritual order. We could at
least have set the problem before ourselves. If our intellectuals were going
to lead the administration, they might conceivably have tried to find some
way of securing peace by making neutrality effective. They might have
turned their intellectual energy not to the problem of jockeying the nation
into war, but to the problem of using our vast neutral power to attain
democratic ends for the rest of the world and ourselves without the use
of the malevolent technique of war. They might have failed. The point is
that they scarcely tried. The time was spent not in clarification and education but in a mulling over of nebulous ideals of democracy and liberalism
and civilization which had never meant anything fruitful to those ruling
classes who now so glibly used them, and in giving free rein to the elementary instinct of self-defence. The whole era has been spiritually wasted.
The outstanding feature has been not its Americanism but its intense
colonialism. The offence of our intellectuals was not so much that they
were colonial—for what could we expect of a nation composed of so many
national elements?—but that it was so one-sidedly and partisanly colonial.
The official, reputable expression of the intellectual class has been that of
the English colonial. Certain portions of it have been even more loyalist
than the King, more British even than Australia. Other colonial attitudes
have been vulgar. The colonialism of the other American stocks was denied
a hearing from the start. America might have been made a meeting-ground
for the different national attitudes. An intellectual class, cultural colonists
of the different European nations, might have threshed out the issues

2. In the 1916 campaign Woodrow Wilson pledged himself to non-intervention in the
European war.—*Editor.*

here as they could not be threshed out in Europe. Instead of this, the English colonials in university and press took command at the start, and we became an intellectual Hungary where thought was subject to an effective process of Magyarization. The reputable opinion of the American intellectuals became more and more either what could be read pleasantly in London, or what was written in an earnest effort to put Englishmen straight on their war-aims and war-technique. This Magyarization of thought produced as a counter-reaction a peculiarly offensive and inept German apologetic, and the two partisans divided the field between them. The great masses, the other ethnic groups, were inarticulate. American public opinion was almost as little prepared for war in 1917 as it was in 1914.

The sterile results of such an intellectual policy are inevitable. During the war the American intellectual class has produced almost nothing in the way of original and illuminating interpretation. Veblen's "Imperial Germany"; Patten's "Culture and War," and addresses; Dewey's "German Philosophy and Politics"; a chapter or two in Weyl's "American Foreign Policies";—is there much else of creative value in the intellectual repercussion of the war? It is true that the shock of war put the American intellectual to an unusual strain. He had to sit idle and think as spectator not as actor. There was no government to which he could docilely and loyally tender his mind as did the Oxford professors to justify England in her own eyes. The American's training was such as to make the fact of war almost incredible. Both in his reading of history and in his lack of economic perspective he was badly prepared for it. He had to explain to himself something which was too colossal for the modern mind, which outran any language or terms which we had to interpret it in. He had to expand his sympathies to the breaking-point, while pulling the past and present into some sort of interpretative order. The intellectuals in the fighting countries had only to rationalize and justify what their country was already doing. Their task was easy. A neutral, however, had really to search out the truth. Perhaps perspective was too much to ask of any mind. Certainly the older colonials among our college professors let their prejudices at once dictate their thought. They have been comfortable ever since. The war has taught them nothing and will teach them nothing. And they have had the satisfaction, under the rigor of events, of seeing prejudice submerge the intellects of their younger colleagues. And they have lived to see almost their entire class, pacifists and democrats too, join them as apologists for the "gigantic irrelevance" of war.

We have had to watch, therefore, in this country the same process which so shocked us abroad,—the coalescence of the intellectual classes in support of the military programme. In this country, indeed, the socialist intellectuals did not even have the grace of their German brothers and wait for the declaration of war before they broke for cover. And when they declared for war they showed how thin was the intellectual veneer of their socialism. For they called us in terms that might have emanated from any bourgeois journal to defend democracy and civilization, just as if it was not exactly against these very bourgeois democracies and capitalist civilizations that socialists had been fighting for decades. But so subtle is the spiritual chemistry of the "inside" that all this intellectual cohesion— herd-instinct becomes herd-intellect—which seemed abroad so hysterical and so servile, comes to us here in highly rational terms. We go to war to save the world from subjugation! But the German intellectuals went to war to save their culture from barbarization! And the French went to war to save their beautiful France! And the English to save international honor! And Russia, most altruistic and self-sacrificing of all, to save a small State from destruction! Whence is our miraculous intuition of our moral spotlessness? Whence our confidence that history will not unravel huge economic and imperialist forces upon which our rationalizations float like bubbles. The Jew often marvels that his race alone should have been chosen as the true people of the cosmic God. Are not our intellectuals equally fatuous when they tell us that our war of all wars is stainless and thrillingly achieving for good?

An intellectual class that was wholly rational would have called insistently for peace and not for war. For months the crying need has been for a negotiated peace, in order to avoid the ruin of deadlock. Would not the same amount of resolute statesmanship thrown into intervention have secured a peace that would have been a subjugation for neither side? Was the terrific bargaining power of a great neutral ever really used? Our war followed, as all wars follow, a monstrous failure of diplomacy. Shamefacedness should now be our intellectuals' attitude, because the American play for peace was made so little more than a polite play. The intellectuals have still to explain why, willing as they now are to use force to continue the war to absolute exhaustion, they were not willing to use force to coerce the world to a speedy peace.

Their forward vision is no more convincing than their past rationality. We go to war now to internationalize the world! But surely their League to Enforce Peace is only a palpable apocalyptic myth, like the syndicalists' myth of the "general strike." It is not a rational programme so much as a glowing symbol for the purpose of focusing belief, of setting enthusiasm on fire for international order. As far as it does this it has pragmatic value, but as far as it provides a certain radiant mirage of idealism for this war and for a world order founded on mutual fear, it is dangerous and obnoxious. Idealism should be kept for what is ideal. It is depressing to think that the prospect of a world so strong that none dare challenge it should be the immediate ideal of the American intellectual. If the League is only a makeshift, a coalition into which we enter to restore order, then it is only a description of existing fact, and the idea should be treated as such. But if it is an actually prospective outcome of the settlement, the keystone of American policy, it is neither realizable nor desirable. For the programme of such a League contains no provision for dynamic national growth or for international economic justice. In a world which requires recognition of economic internationalism far more than of political internationalism, an idea is reactionary which proposes to petrify and federate the nations as political and economic units. Such a scheme for international order is a dubious justification for American policy. And if American policy had been sincere in its belief that our participation would achieve international beatitude, would we not have made our entrance into the war conditional upon a solemn general agreement to respect in the final settlement these principles of international order? Could we have afforded, if our war was to end war by the establishment of a league of honor, to risk the defeat of our vision and our betrayal in the settlement? Yet we are in the war, and no such solemn agreement was made, nor has it even been suggested.

The case of the intellectuals seems, therefore, only very speciously rational. They could have used their energy to force a just peace or at least to devise other means than war for carrying through American policy. They could have used their intellectual energy to ensure that our participation in the war meant the international order which they wish. Intellect was not so used. It was used to lead an apathetic nation into an irresponsible war, without guarantees from those belligerents whose cause we were saving. The American intellectual, therefore, has been rational neither in his hindsight nor his foresight. To explain him we must look beneath the intellectual reasons to the emotional disposition. It is not so much what they thought as how they felt that explains our intellectual class. Allowing for colonial sympathy, there was still the personal shock in a world-war which outraged all our preconceived notions of the way the world was tending. It reduced to rubbish most of the humanitarian internationalism and democratic nationalism which had been the emotional thread of our intellectuals' life. We had suddenly to make a new orientation. There were mental conflicts. Our latent colonialism strove with our longing for American unity. Our desire for peace strove with our desire for national responsibility in the world. That first lofty and remote and not altogether unsound feeling of our spiritual isolation from the conflict could not last. There was the itch to be in the great experience which the rest of the world was having. Numbers of intelligent people who had never been stirred by the horrors of capitalistic peace at home were shaken out of their slumber by the horrors of war in Belgium. Never having felt responsibility for labor wars and oppressed masses and excluded races at home, they had a large fund of idle emotional capital to invest in the oppressed nationalities and ravaged villages of Europe. Hearts that had felt only ugly contempt for democratic strivings at home beat in tune with the struggle for freedom abroad. All this was natural, but it tended to over-emphasize our responsibility. And it threw our thinking out of gear. The task of making our own country detailedly fit for peace was abandoned in favor of a feverish concern for the management of the war, advice to the fighting governments on all matters, military, social and political, and a gradual working up of the conviction that we were ordained as a nation to lead all erring brothers towards the light of liberty and democracy. The failure of the American intellectual class to erect a creative attitude toward the war can be explained by these sterile mental conflicts which the shock to our ideals sent raging through us.

Mental conflicts end either in a new and higher synthesis or adjustment, or else in a reversion to more primitive ideas which have been outgrown but to which we drop when jolted out of our attained position. The war caused in America a recrudescence of nebulous ideals which a younger generation was fast outgrowing because it had passed the wistful stage and was discovering concrete ways of getting them incarnated in actual institutions. The shock of the war threw us back from this pragmatic work into an emotional bath of these old ideals. There was even a somewhat rarefied revival of our primitive Yankee boastfulness, the reversion of senility to that republican childhood when we expected the whole world to copy our republican institutions. We amusingly ignored the fact that it was just that Imperial German regime, to whom we are to teach the art of self-government, which our own Federal structure, with its executive irresponsibility in foreign policy and with its absence of parliamentary control, most resembles. And we are missing the exquisite irony of the unaffected homage paid by the American democratic intellectuals to the the last and most detested of Britain's tory premiers as the representative of a "liberal" ally, as well as the irony of the selection of the best hated of America's bourbon "old guard" as the missionary of American democracy to Russia.[3]

The intellectual state that could produce such things is one where reversion has taken place to more primitive ways of thinking. Simple syllogisms are substituted for analysis, things are known by their labels, our heart's desire dictates what we shall see. The American intellectual class, having failed to make the higher syntheses, regresses to ideas that can issue in quick, simplified action. Thought becomes an easy rationalization of what is actually going on or what is to happen inevitably tomorrow. It is true that certain groups did rationalize their colonialism and attach the doctrine

3. Bourne is here referring to Lord Balfour, British Foreign Secretary and former prime minister, and Elihu Root, who headed an Ameican mission to Russia.—*Editor.*

of the inviolability of British seapower to the doctrine of a League of Peace. But this agile resolution of the mental conflict did not become a higher synthesis, to be creatively developed. It gradually merged into a justification for our going to war. It petrified into a dogma to be propagated. Criticism flagged and emotional propaganda began. Most of the socialists, the college professors and the practitioners of literature, however, have not even reached this high-water mark of synthesis. Their mental conflicts have been resolved much more simply. War in the interests of democracy! This was almost the sum of their philosophy. The primitive idea to which they regressed became almost insensibly translated into a craving for action. War was seen as the crowning relief of their indecision. At last action, irresponsibility, the end of anxious and torturing attempts to reconcile peace-ideals with the drag of the world towards Hell. An end to the pain of trying to adjust the facts to what they ought to be! Let us consecrate the facts as ideal! Let us join the greased slide towards war! The momentum increased. Hesitations, ironies, consciences, considerations,—all were drowned in the elemental blare of doing something aggressive, colossal. The new-found Sabbath "peacefulness of being at war"! The thankfulness with which so many intellectuals lay down and floated with the current betrays the hesitation and suspense through which they had been. The American university is a brisk and happy place these days. Simple, unquestioning action has superseded the knots of thought. The thinker dances with reality.

With how many of the acceptors of war has it been mostly a dread of intellectual suspense? It is a mistake to suppose that intellectuality necessarily makes for suspended judgments. The intellect craves certitude. It takes effort to keep it supple and pliable. In a time of danger and disaster we jump desperately for some dogma to cling to. The time comes, if we try to hold out, when our nerves are sick with fatigue, and we seize in a great healing wave of release some doctrine that can be immediately translated into action. Neutrality meant suspense, and so it became the object of loathing to frayed nerves. The vital myth of the League of Peace provides a dogma to jump to. With war the world becomes motor again and speculation is brushed aside like cobwebs. The blessed emotion of self-defense intervenes too, which focused millions in Europe. A few keep up a critical pose after war is begun, but since they usually advise action which is in one-to-one correspondence with what the mass is already doing, their criticism is little more than a rationalization of the common emotional drive.

The results of war on the intellectual class are already apparent. Their thought becomes little more than a description and justification of what is going on. They turn upon any rash one who continues idly to speculate. Once the war is on, the conviction spreads that individual thought is helpless, that the only way one can count is as a cog in the great wheel. There is no good holding back. We are told to dry our unnoticed and ineffective tears and plunge into the great work. Not only is everyone forced into line, but the new certitude becomes idealized. It is a noble realism which opposes itself to futile obstruction and the cowardly refusal to face facts. This realistic boast is so loud and sonorous that one wonders whether realism is always a stern and intelligent grappling with realities. May it not be sometimes a mere surrender to the actual, an abdication of the ideal through a sheer fatigue from intellectual suspense? The pacifist is roundly scolded for refusing to face the facts, and for retiring into his own world of sentimental desire. But is the realist, who refuses to challenge or criticise facts, entitled to any more credit than that which comes from following the line of least resistance? The realist thinks he at least can control events by linking himself to the forces that are moving. Perhaps he can. But if it is a question of controlling war, it is difficult to see how the child on the back of a mad elephant is to be any more effective in stopping the beast than is the child who tries to stop him from the ground. The ex-humanitarian, turned realist, sneers at the snobbish neutrality, colossal conceit, crooked thinking, dazed sensibilities, of those who are still unable to find any balm of consolation for this war. We manufacture consolations here in America while there are probably not a dozen men fighting in Europe who did not long ago give up every reason for their being there except that nobody knew how to get them away.

But the intellectuals whom the crisis has crystallized into an acceptance of war have put themselves into a terrifyingly strategic position. It is only on the craft, in the stream, they say, that one has any chance of controlling the current forces for liberal purposes. If we obstruct, we surrender all power for influence. If we responsibly approve, we then retain our power for guiding. We will be listened to as responsible thinkers, while those who obstructed the coming of war have committed intellectual suicide and shall be cast into outer darkness. Criticism by the ruling powers will only be accepted from those intellectuals who are in sympathy with the general tendency of the war. Well, it is true that they may guide, but if their stream leads to disaster and the frustration of national life, is their guiding any more than a preference whether they shall go over the right-hand or the left-hand side of the precipice? Meanwhile, however, there is comfort on board. Be with us, they call, or be negligible, irrelevant. Dissenters are already excommunicated. Irreconcilable radicals, wringing their hands among the debris, become the most despicable and impotent of men. There seems no choice for the intellectual but to join the mass of acceptance. But again the terrible dilemma arises, either support what is going on, in which case you count for nothing because you are swallowed in the mass and great incalculable forces bear you on; or remain aloof, passively resistant, in which case you count for nothing because you are outside the machinery of reality.

Is there no place left, then, for the intellectual who cannot yet crystallize, who does not dread suspense, and is not yet drugged with fatigue? The American intellectuals, in their preoccupation with reality, seem to have forgotten that the real enemy is War rather than imperial Germany. There is work to be done to prevent this war of ours from passing into popular mythology as a holy crusade. What shall we do with leaders who tell us that we go to war in moral spotlessness, or who make "democracy" synonymous with a republican form of government? There is work to be done in still shouting that all the revolutionary by-products will not justify the war, or make war anything else than the most noxious complex of all the evils that afflict men. There must be some to find no consolation whatever, and some to sneer at those who buy the cheap emotion of sacrifice. There must be some irreconcilables left who will not even accept the war with walrus tears. There must be some to call unceasingly for peace, and some to insist that the terms of settlement shall be not only liberal but democratic. There must be some intellectuals who are not willing to use the old discredited counters again and to support a peace which would leave all the old inflammable materials of armament lying about the world. There must still be opposition to any contemplated "liberal" world-order founded on military coalitions. The "irreconcilable" need not be disloyal. He need not even be "impossibilist." His apathy towards war should take the form of a heightened energy and enthusiasm for the education, the art, the interpretation that make for life in the midst of the world of death. The intellectual who retains his animus against war will push out more boldly than ever to make his case solid against it. The old ideals crumble; new ideals must be forged. His mind will continue to roam widely and ceaselessly. The thing he will fear most is premature crystallization. If the American intellectual class rivets itself to a "liberal" philosophy that perpetuates the old errors, there will then be need for "democrats" whose task will be to divide, confuse, disturb, keep the intellectual waters constantly in motion to prevent any such ice from ever forming.

W. E. B. Du Bois
(1868–1963)

DU BOIS was born in Great Barrington, Massachusetts. He was graduated from Fisk University in 1888 and later took his Ph.D. degree at Harvard University. Combining a career of teaching, writing, and social protest, Du Bois became a prominent Negro historian and sociologist. Among his many activities, he taught at Atlanta University, edited *Crises* (1910–1932), and helped found the National Association for the Advancement of Colored People (1909), an organization he subsequently left in 1948. Four of his major works are *The Souls of Black Folk* (1903), *Darkwater* (1920), *Dusk of Dawn* (1940), and *The Autobiography of W. E. B. Du Bois* (1968).

"The Souls of White Folk" is Chapter Two of Du Bois' book *Darkwater*.

THE SOULS
OF WHITE FOLK

High in the tower, where I sit above the loud complaining of the human sea, I know many souls that toss and whirl and pass, but none there are that intrigue me more than the Souls of White Folk.

Of them I am singularly clairvoyant. I see in and through them. I view them from unusual points of vantage. Not as a foreigner do I come, for I am native, not foreign, bone of their thought and flesh of their language. Mine is not the knowledge of the traveler or the colonial composite of dear memories, words and wonder. Nor yet is my knowledge that which servants have of masters, or mass of class, or capitalist of artisan. Rather I see these souls undressed and from the back and side. I see the working of their entrails. I know their thoughts and they know that I know. This knowledge makes them now embarrassed, now furious! They deny my right to live and be and call me misbirth! My word is to them mere bitterness and my soul, pessimism. And yet as they preach and strut and shout and threaten, crouching as they clutch at rags of facts and fancies to hide their nakedness, they go twisting, flying by my tired eyes and I see them ever stripped,—ugly, human.

The discovery of personal whiteness among the world's peoples is a very modern thing,—a nineteenth and twentieth century matter, indeed. The ancient world would have laughed at such a distinction. The Middle Age regarded skin color with mild curiosity; and even up into the eighteenth century we were hammering our national manikins into one, great, Universal Man, with fine frenzy which ignored color and race even more than birth. Today we have changed all that, and the world in a sudden, emotional conversion has discovered that it is white and by that token, wonderful!

This assumption that of all the hues of God whiteness alone is inherently and obviously better than brownness or tan leads to curious acts; even the sweeter souls of the dominant world as they discourse with me on weather, weal, and woe are continually playing above their actual word an obligato of tune and tone, saying:

"My poor, un-white thing! Weep not nor rage. I know, too well, that the curse of God lies heavy on you. Why? That is not for me to say, but be brave! Do your work in your lowly sphere, praying the good Lord that into heaven above, where all is love, you may, one day, be born— white!?"

I do not laugh. I am quite straight-faced as I ask soberly:

"But what on earth is whiteness that one should so desire it?" Then always, somehow, some way, silently but clearly, I am given to understand that whiteness is the ownership of the earth forever and ever, Amen!

Now what is the effect on a man or a nation when it comes passionately to believe such an extraordinary dictum as this? That nations are coming to believe it is manifest daily. Wave on wave, each with increasing virulence, is dashing this new religion of whiteness on the shores of our time. Its first effects are funny: the strut of the Southerner, the arrogance of the Englishman amuck, the whoop of the hoodlum who vicariously leads your mob. Next it appears dampening generous enthusiasm in what we once counted glorious, to free the slave is discovered to be tolerable only in so far as it freed his master! Do we sense somnolent writhings in black Africa or angry groans in India or triumphant banzais in Japan? "To your tents, O Israel!" These nations are not white!

After the more comic manifestations, and the chilling of generous enthusiasm come subtler, darker deeds. Everything considered, the title to the universe claimed by White Folk is faulty. It ought, at least, to look plausible. How easy, then, by emphasis and omission to make children believe that every great soul the world ever saw was a white man's soul; that every great thought the world ever knew was a white man's thought; that every great deed the world ever did was a white man's deed; that every great dream the world ever sang was a white man's dream. In fine, that if from the world were dropped everything that could not fairly be attributed to White Folk, the world would, if anything, be even greater, truer, better than now. And if all this be a lie, is it not a lie in a great cause?

Here it is that the comedy verges to tragedy. The first minor note is struck, all unconsciously, by those worthy souls in whom consciousness of high descent brings burning desire to spread the gift abroad,—the obligation of nobility to the ignoble. Such sense of duty assumes two things: a real possession of the heritage and its frank appreciation by the humble-born. So long, then, as humble black folk, voluble with thanks, receive barrels of old clothes from lordly and generous whites, there is much mental peace and moral satisfaction. But when the black man begins to dispute the white man's title to certain alleged bequests of the Fathers in wage and position, authority and training; and when his attitude toward charity is sullen anger rather than humble jollity; when he insists on his human right to swagger and swear and waste,—then the spell is suddenly broken and the philanthropist is ready to believe that Negroes are impudent, that the South is right, and that Japan wants to fight America.

After this the descent to Hell is easy. On the pale, white faces which the great billows whirl upward to my tower I see again and again, often and still more often, a writing of human hatred, a deep and passionate hatred, vast by the very vagueness of its expressions. Down through the green waters, on the bottom of the world, where men move to and fro, I have seen a man—an educated gentleman—grow livid with anger because a little, silent, black woman was sitting by herself in a Pullman car. He was a white man. I have seen a great, grown man curse a little child, who had wandered into the wrong waiting-room, searching for its mother: "Here, you damned black—" He was white. In Central Park I have seen the upper lip of a quiet, peaceful man curl back in a tigerish snarl of rage because black folk rode by in a motor car. He was a white man. We have seen, you and I, city after city drunk and furious with ungovernable lust of blood; mad with murder, destroying, killing, and cursing; torturing human victims because somebody accused of crime happened to be of the same color as the mob's innocent victims and because that color was not white! We have seen,—Merciful God! in these wild days and in the name of Civilization, Justice, and Motherhood,—what have we not seen, right here in America, of orgy, cruelty, barbarism, and murder done to men and women of Negro descent.

Up through the foam of green and weltering waters wells this great mass of hatred, in wilder, fiercer violence, until I look down and know that today to the millions of my people no misfortune could happen,—of death and pestilence, failure and defeat—that would not make the hearts of millions of their fellows beat with fierce, vindictive joy! Do you doubt it? Ask your own soul what it would say if the next census were to report that half of black America was dead and the other half dying.

Unfortunate? Unfortunate. But where is the misfortune? Mine? Am I, in my blackness, the sole sufferer? I suffer. And yet, somehow, above the suffering, above the shackled anger that beats the bars, above the hurt that crazes there surges in me a vast pity,—pity for a people imprisoned and enthralled, hampered and made miserable for such a cause, for such a phantasy!

Conceive this nation, of all human peoples, engaged in a crusade to make the "World Safe for Democracy"! Can you imagine the United States protesting against Turkish atrocities in Armenia, while the Turks are silent about mobs in Chicago and St. Louis; what is Louvain compared with Memphis, Waco, Washington, Dyersburg, and Estill Springs? In short, what is the black man but America's Belgium, and how could America condemn in Germany that which she commits, just as brutally, within her own borders?

A true and worthy ideal frees and uplifts a people; a false ideal imprisons and lowers. Say to men, earnestly and repeatedly: "Honesty is best, knowledge is power; do unto others as you would be done by." Say this and act it and the nation must move toward it, if not to it. But say to a people: "The one virtue is to be white," and the people rush to the inevitable conclusion, "Kill the 'nigger'!"

Is not this the record of present America? Is not this its headlong progress? Are we not coming more and more, day by day, to making the statement "I am white," the one fundamental tenet of our practical morality? Only when this basic, iron rule is involved is our defense of right nation-wide and prompt. Murder may swagger, theft may rule and prostitution may flourish and the nation gives but spasmodic, intermittent and lukewarm attention. But let the murderer be black or the thief brown or the violator of womanhood have a drop of Negro blood, and the righteousness of the indignation sweeps the world. Nor would this fact make the indignation less justifiable did not we all know that it was blackness that was condemned and not crime.

In the awful cataclysm of World War, where from beating, slandering, and murdering us the white world turned temporarily aside to kill each other, we of the Darker Peoples looked on in mild amaze.

Among some of us, I doubt not, this sudden descent of Europe into hell brought unbounded surprise; to others, over wide area, it brought the *Schaden Freude* of the bitterly hurt; but most of us, I judge, looked on silently and sorrowfully, in sober thought, seeing sadly the prophecy of our own souls.

Here is a civilization that has boasted much. Neither Roman nor Arab, Greek nor Egyptian, Persian nor Mongol ever took himself and his own perfectness with such disconcerting seriousness as the modern white man. We whose shame, humiliation, and deep insult his aggrandizement so often involved were never deceived. We looked at him clearly, with world-old eyes, and saw simply a human thing, weak and pitiable and cruel, even as we are and were.

These super-men and world-mastering demi-gods listened, however, to no low tongues of ours, even when we pointed silently to their feet of clay. Perhaps we, as folk of simpler soul and more primitive type, have been most struck in the welter of recent years by the utter failure of white religion. We have curled our lips in something like contempt as we have witnessed glib apology and weary explanation. Nothing of the sort deceived us. A nation's religion is its life, and as such white Christianity is a miserable failure.

Nor would we be unfair in this criticism: We know that we, too, have failed, as you have, and have rejected many a Buddha, even as you have denied Christ; but we acknowledge our human frailty, while you, claiming super-humanity, scoff endlessly at our shortcomings.

The number of white individuals who are practising with even reasonable approximation the democracy and unselfishness of Jesus Christ is so small and unimportant as to be fit subject for jest in Sunday supplements and in *Punch, Life, Le Rire,* and *Fliegende Blätter.* In her foreign mission work the extraordinary self-deception of white religion is epitomized: solemnly the white world sends five million dollars worth of missionary propaganda to Africa each year and in the same twelve months adds twenty-five million dollars worth of the vilest gin manufactured. Peace to the augurs of Rome!

We may, however, grant without argument that religious ideals have always far outrun their very human devotees. Let us, then, turn to more mundane matters of honor and fairness. The world today is trade. The world has turned shopkeeper; history is economic history; living is earning a living. Is it necessary to ask how much of high emprise and honorable conduct has been found here? Something, to be sure. The establishment of world credit systems is built on splendid and realizable faith in fellowmen. But it is, after all, so low and elementary a step that sometimes it looks merely like honor among thieves, for the revelations of highway robbery and low cheating in the business world and in all its great modern centers have raised in the hearts of all true men in our day an exceeding great cry for revolution in our basic methods and conceptions of industry and commerce.

We do not, for a moment, forget the robbery of other times and races when trade was a most uncertain gamble; but was there not a certain honesty and frankness in the evil that argued a saner morality? There are more merchants today, surer deliveries, and wider well-being, but are there not, also, bigger thieves, deeper injustice, and more calloused selfishness in well-being? Be that as it may,—certainly the nicer sense of honor that has risen ever and again in groups of forward-thinking men has been curiously and broadly blunted. Consider our chiefest industry,—fighting. Laboriously the Middle Ages built its rules of fairness—equal armament, equal notice, equal conditions. What do we see today? Machine-guns against assegais; conquest sugared with religion; mutilation and rape masquerading as culture,—all this, with vast applause at the superiority of white over black soldiers!

War is horrible! This the dark world knows to its awful cost. But has it just become horrible, in these last days, when under essentially equal conditions, equal armament, and equal waste of wealth white men are fighting white men, with surgeons and nurses hovering near?

Think of the wars through which we have lived in the last decade: in German Africa, in British Nigeria, in French and Spanish Morocco, in China, in Persia, in the Balkans, in Tripoli, in Mexico, and in a dozen lesser places—were not these horrible, too? Mind you, there were for most of these wars no Red Cross funds.

Behold little Belgium and her pitiable plight, but has the world forgotten Congo? What Belgium now suffers is not half, not even a tenth, of what she has done to black Congo since Stanley's great dream of 1880. Down the dark forests of inmost Africa sailed this modern Sir Galahad, in the name of "the noble-minded men of several nations," to introduce commerce and civilization. What came of it? "Rubber and murder, slavery in its worst form," wrote Glave in 1895.

Harris declares that King Leopold's régime meant the death of twelve million natives, "but what we who were behind the scenes felt most keenly was the fact that the real catastrophe in the Congo was desolation and murder in the larger sense. The invasion of family life, the ruthless destruction of every social barrier, the shattering of every tribal law, the introduction of criminal practices which struck the chiefs of the people dumb with horror—in a word, a veritable avalanche of filth and immorality overwhelmed the Congo tribes."

Yet the fields of Belgium laughed, the cities were gay, art and science flourished; the groans that helped to nourish this civilization fell on deaf ears because the world round about was doing the same sort of thing elsewhere on its own account.

As we saw the dead dimly through rifts of battlesmoke and heard faintly the cursings and accusations of blood brothers, we darker men said: This is not Europe gone mad; this is not aberration nor insanity; this is Europe; this seeming Terrible is the real soul of white culture—back of all culture,—stripped and visible today. This is where the world has arrived,—these dark and awful depths and not the shining and ineffable heights of which it boasted. Here is whither the might and energy of modern humanity has really gone.

But may not the world cry back at us and ask: "What better thing have you to show? What have you done or would do better than this if you had today the world rule? Paint with all riot of hateful colors the thin skin of European culture,—is it not better than any culture that arose in Africa or Asia?"

It is. Of this there is no doubt and never has been; but why is it better? Is it better because Europeans are better, nobler, greater, and more gifted than other folk? It is not. Europe has never produced and never will in our day bring forth a single human soul who cannot be matched and overmatched in every line of human endeavor by Asia and Africa. Run the gamut, if you will, and let us have the Europeans who in sober truth overmatch Nefertari, Mohammed, Rameses and Askia, Confucius, Buddha, and Jesus Christ. If we could scan the calendar of thousands of lesser men, in like comparison, the result would be the same; but we cannot do this because of the deliberately educated ignorance of white schools by which they remember Napoleon and forget Sonni Ali.

The greatness of Europe has lain in the width of the stage on which she has played her part, the strength of the foundation on which she has builded, and a natural, human ability no whit greater (if as great) than that of other days and races. In other words, the deeper reasons for the triumph of European civilization lie quite outside and beyond Europe,—back in the universal struggles of all mankind.

Why, then, is Europe great? Because of the foundations which the mighty past have furnished her to build upon: the iron trade of ancient, black Africa, the religion and empire-building of yellow Asia, the art and science of the "dago" Mediterranean shore, east, south, and west, as well as north. And where she has builded securely upon this great past and learned from it she has gone forward to greater and more splendid human triumph; but where she has ignored this past and forgotten and sneered at it, she has shown the cloven hoof of poor, crucified humanity,—she has played, like other empires gone, the world fool!

If, then, European triumphs in culture have been greater, so, too, may her failures have been greater. How great a failure and a failure in what does the World War betoken? Was it national jealousy of the sort of the seventeenth century? But Europe has done more to break down national barriers than any preceding culture. Was it fear of the balance of power in Europe? Hardly, save in the half-Asiatic problems of the Balkans. What, then, does Hauptmann mean when he says: "Our jealous enemies forged an iron ring about our breasts and we know our breasts had to expand,—that we had to split asunder this ring or else we had to cease breathing. But Germany will not cease to breathe and so it came to pass that the iron ring was forced apart."

Whither is this expansion? What is that breath of life, thought to be so indispensable to a great European nation? Manifestly it is expansion overseas; it is colonial aggrandizement which explains, and alone adequately explains, the World War. How many of us today fully realize the current theory of colonial expansion, of the relation of Europe which is white, to the world which is black and brown and yellow? Bluntly put, that theory is this: It is the duty of white Europe to divide up the darker world and administer it for Europe's good.

This Europe has largely done. The European world is using black and brown men for all the uses which men know. Slowly but surely white culture is evolving the theory that "darkies" are born beasts of burden for white folk. It were silly to think otherwise, cries the cultured world, with stronger and shriller accord. The supporting arguments grow and twist themselves in the mouths of merchant, scientist, soldier, traveler, writer, and missionary: Darker peoples are dark in mind as well as in body; of dark, uncertain, and imperfect descent; of frailer, cheaper stuff; they are cowards in the face of mausers and maxims; they have no feelings, aspirations, and loves; they are fools, illogical idiots,—"half-devil and half-child."

Such as they are civilization must, naturally, raise them, but soberly and in limited ways. They are not simply dark white men. They are not "men" in the sense that Europeans are men. To the very limited extent of their shallow capacities lift them to be useful to whites, to raise cotton, gather rubber, fetch ivory, dig diamonds,—and let them be paid what men think they are worth—white men who know them to be well-nigh worthless.

Such degrading of men by men is as old as mankind and the invention of no one race or people. Ever have men striven to conceive of their victims as different from the victors, endlessly different, in soul and blood, strength and cunning, race and lineage. It has been left, however, to Europe and to modern days to discover the eternal world-wide mark of meanness,—color!

Such is the silent revolution that has gripped modern European culture in the later nineteenth and twentieth centuries. Its zenith came in Boxer times: White supremacy was all but world-wide, Africa was dead, India conquered, Japan isolated, and China prostrate, while white America whetted her sword for mongrel Mexico and mulatto South America, lynching her own Negroes the while. Temporary halt in this program was made by little Japan and the white world immediately sensed the peril of such "yellow" presumption! What sort of a world would this be if yellow men must be treated "white"? Immediately the eventual overthrow of Japan became a subject of deep thought and intrigue, from St. Petersburg to San Francisco, from the Key of Heaven to the Little Brother of the Poor.

The using of men for the benefit of masters is no new invention of modern Europe. It is quite as old as the world. But Europe proposed to apply it on a scale and with an elaborateness of detail of which no former world ever dreamed. The imperial width of the thing,—the heaven-defying audacity—makes its modern newness.

The scheme of Europe was no sudden invention, but a way out of long-pressing difficulties. It is plain to modern white civilization that the subjection of the white working classes cannot much longer be maintained. Education, political power, and increased knowledge of the technique and meaning of the industrial process are destined to make a more and more equitable distribution of wealth in the near future. The day of the very rich is drawing to a close, so far as individual white nations are concerned. But there is a loophole. There is a chance for exploitation on an immense scale for inordinate profit, not simply to the very rich, but to the middle class and to the laborers. This chance lies in the exploitation of darker peoples. It is here that the golden hand beckons. Here are no labor unions or votes or questioning onlookers or inconvenient consequences. These men may be used down to the very bone, and shot and maimed in "punitive" expeditions when they revolt. In these dark lands "industrial development" may repeat in exaggerated form every horror of the industrial history of Europe, from slavery and rape to disease and maiming, with only one test of success,—dividends!

This theory of human culture and its aims has worked itself through warp and woof of our daily thought with a thoroughness that few realize. Everything great, good, efficient, fair, and honorable is "white"; everything mean, bad, blundering, cheating, and dishonorable is "yellow"; a bad taste is "brown"; and the devil is "black." The changes of this theme are continually rung in picture and story, in newspaper heading and moving-picture, in sermon and school book, until, of course, the King can do no wrong,—a White Man is always right and a Black Man has no rights which a white man is bound to respect.

There must come the necessary despisings and hatreds of these savage half-men, this unclean *canaille* of the world—these dogs of men. All through the world this gospel is preaching. It has its literature, it has its priests, it has its secret propaganda and above all—it pays!

There's the rub,—it pays. Rubber, ivory, and palm-oil, coffee, and cocoa; bananas, oranges, and other fruit; cotton, gold, and copper—they, and a hundred other things which dark and sweating bodies hand up to the white world from their pits of slime, pay and pay well, but of all that the world gets the black world gets only the pittance that the white world throws it disdainfully.

Small wonder, then, that in the practical world of things-that-be there is jealousy and strife for the possession of the labor of dark millions, for the right to bleed and exploit the colonies of the world where this golden stream may be had, not always for the asking, but surely for the whipping and shooting. It was this competition for the labor of yellow, brown, and black folks that was the cause of the World War. Other causes have been glibly given and other contributing causes there doubtless were, but they were subsidiary and subordinate to this vast quest of the dark world's wealth and toil.

Colonies, we call them, these places where "niggers" are cheap and the

earth is rich; they are those outlands where like a swarm of hungry
locusts white masters may settle to be served as kings, wield the lash of
slave-drivers, rape girls and wives, grow as rich as Croesus and send
homeward a golden stream. They belt the earth, these places, but they
cluster in the tropics, with its darkened peoples: in Hong Kong and Anam,
in Borneo and Rhodesia, in Sierra Leone and Nigeria, in Panama and
Havana—these are the El Dorados toward which the world powers stretch
itching palms.

Germany, at last one and united and secure on land, looked across the
seas and seeing England with sources of wealth insuring a luxury and
power which Germany could not hope to rival by the slower processes
of exploiting her own peasants and working-men, especially with these
workers half in revolt, immediately built her navy and entered into a desperate competition for possession of colonies of darker peoples. To South
America, to China, to Africa, to Asia Minor, she turned like a hound
quivering on the leash, impatient, suspicious, irritable, with blood-shot
eyes and dripping fangs, ready for the awful word. England and France
crouched watchfully over their bones, growling and wary, but gnawing
industriously, while the blood of the dark world whetted their greedy
appetites. In the background, shut out from the highway to the seven
seas, sat Russia and Austria, snarling and snapping at each other and at
the last Mediterranean gate to the El Dorado, where the Sick Man enjoyed
bad health, and where millions of serfs in the Balkans, Russia, and Asia
offered a feast to greed well-nigh as great as Africa.

The fateful day came. It had to come. The cause of war is preparation
for war; and of all that Europe has done in a century there is nothing
that has equaled in energy, thought, and time her preparation for wholesale
murder. The only adequate cause of this preparation was conquest and
conquest, not in Europe, but primarily among the darker peoples of Asia
and Africa; conquest, not for assimilation and uplift, but for commerce
and degradation. For this, and this mainly, did Europe gird herself at
frightful cost for war.

The red day dawned when the tinder was lighted in the Balkans and
Austro-Hungary seized a bit which brought her a step nearer to the world's
highway; she seized one bit and poised herself for another. Then came
that curious chorus of challenges, those leaping suspicions, raking all
causes for distrust and rivalry and hatred, but saying little of the real and
greatest cause.

Each nation felt its deep interests involved. But how? Not, surely, in
the death of Ferdinand the Warlike; not, surely, in the old, half-forgotten
revanche for Alsace-Lorraine; not even in the neutrality of Belgium. No!
But in the possession of land overseas, in the right to colonies, the chance

to levy endless tribute on the darker world,—on coolies in China, on starving peasants in India, on black savages in Africa, on dying South Sea Islanders, on Indians of the Amazon—all this and nothing more.

Even the broken reed on which we had rested high hopes of eternal peace,—the guild of the laborers—the front of that very important movement for human justice on which we had builded most, even this flew like a straw before the breath of king and kaiser. Indeed, the flying had been foreshadowed when in Germany and America "international" Socialists had all but read yellow and black men out of the kingdom of industrial justice. Subtly had they been bribed, but effectively: Were they not lordly whites and should they not share in the spoils of rape? High wages in the United States and England might be the skilfully manipulated result of slavery in Africa and of peonage in Asia.

With the dog-in-the-manger theory of trade, with the determination to reap inordinate profits and to exploit the weakest to the umost there came a new imperialism,—the rage for one's own nation to own the earth or, at least, a large enough portion of it to insure as big profits as the next nation. Where sections could not be owned by one dominant nation there came a policy of "open door," but the "door" was open to "white people only." As to the darkest and weakest of peoples there was but one unanimity in Europe,—that which Herr Dernberg of the German Colonial Office called the agreement with England to maintain white "prestige" in Africa,—the doctrine of the divine right of white people to steal.

Thus the world market most wildly and desperately sought today is the market where labor is cheapest and most helpless and profit is most abundant. This labor is kept cheap and helpless because the white world despises "darkies." If one has the temerity to suggest that these workingmen may walk the way of white workingmen and climb by votes and self-assertion and education to the rank of men, he is howled out of court. They cannot do it and if they could, they shall not, for they are the enemies of the white race and the whites shall rule forever and forever and everywhere. Thus the hatred and despising of human beings from whom Europe wishes to extort her luxuries has led to such jealousy and bickering between European nations that they have fallen afoul of each other and have fought like crazed beasts. Such is the fruit of human hatred.

But what of the darker world that watches? Most men belong to this world. With Negro and Negroid, East Indian, Chinese, and Japanese they form two-thirds of the population of the world. A belief in humanity is a belief in colored men. If the uplift of mankind must be done by men, then the destinies of this world will rest ultimately in the hands of darker nations.

What, then, is this dark world thinking? It is thinking that as wild and awful as this shameful war was, *it is nothing to compare with that fight for freedom which black and brown and yellow men must and will make unless their oppression and humiliation and insult at the hands of the White World cease. The Dark World is going to submit to its present treatment just as long as it must and not one moment longer.*

Let me say this again and emphasize it and leave no room for mistaken meaning: The World War was primarily the jealous and avaricious struggle for the largest share in exploiting darker races. As such it is and must be but the prelude to the armed and indignant protest of these despised and raped peoples. Today Japan is hammering on the door of justice, China is raising her half-manacled hands to knock next, India is writhing for the freedom to knock, Egypt is sullenly muttering, the Negroes of South and West Africa, or the West Indies, and of the United States are just awakening to their shameful slavery. Is, then, this war the end of wars? Can it be the end, so long as sits enthroned, even in the souls of those who cry peace, the despising and robbing of darker peoples? If Europe hugs this delusion, then this is not the end of world war,—it is but the beginning!

We see Europe's greatest sin precisely where we found Africa's and Asia's,—in human hatred, the despising of men; with this difference, however: Europe has the awful lesson of the past before her, has the splendid results of widened areas of tolerance, sympathy, and love among men, and she faces a greater, an infinitely greater, world of men than any preceding civilization ever faced.

It is curious to see America, the United States, looking on herself, first, as a sort of natural peace-maker, then as a moral protagonist in this terrible time. No nation is less fitted for this role. For two or more centuries America has marched proudly in the van of human hatred,—making bonfires of human flesh and laughing at them hideously, and making the insulting of millions more than a matter of dislike,—rather a great religion, a world war-cry: Up white, down black; to your tents, O white folk, and world war with black and parti-colored mongrel beasts!

Instead of standing as a great example of the success of democracy and the possibility of human brotherhood America has taken her place as an awful example of its pitfalls and failures, so far as black and brown and yellow peoples are concerned. And this, too, in spite of the fact that there has been no actual failure; the Indian is not dying out, the Japanese and Chinese have not menaced the land, and the experiment of Negro suffrage has resulted in the uplift of twelve million people at a rate probably unparalleled in history. But what of this? America, Land of Democracy, wanted to believe in the failure of democracy so far as darker peoples were concerned. Absolutely without excuse she established a caste system, rushed into preparation for war, and conquered tropical colonies. She stands today shoulder to shoulder with Europe in Europe's worst sin against civilization. She aspires to sit among the great nations who arbitrate the fate of "lesser breeds without the law" and she is at times heartily ashamed even of the large number of "new" white people whom her democracy had admitted to place and power. Against this surging forward of Irish and Germany, of Russian Jew, Slav and "dago" her social bars have not availed, but against Negroes she can and does take her unflinching and immovable stand, backed by this new public policy of Europe. She trains her immigrants to this despising of "niggers" from the day of their landing, and they carry and send the news back to the submerged classes in the fatherlands.

All this I see and hear up in my tower, above the thunder of the seven seas. From my narrowed windows I stare into the night that looms beneath the cloud-swept stars. Eastward and westward storms are breaking,—great, ugly whirlwinds of hatred and blood and cruelty. I will not believe them inevitable. I will not believe that all that was must be, that all the shameful drama of the past must be done again today before the sunlight sweeps the silver seas.

If I cry amid this roar of elemental forces, must my cry be in vain, because it is but a cry,—a small and human cry amid Promethean gloom?

Back beyond the world and swept by these wild, white faces of the awful dead, why will this Soul of White Folk,—this modern Prometheus,—hang bound by his own binding, tethered by a fable of the past? I hear his mighty cry reverberating through the world, "I am white!" Well and good, O Prometheus, divine thief! Is not the world wide enough for two colors, for many little shinings of the sun? Why, then, devour your own vitals if I answer even as proudly, "I am black!"

Dwight Macdonald
(1906–   )

MACDONALD was born in New York City and went to Phillips Exeter Academy and Yale University. He has written for *Fortune*, the *Partisan Review*, *Politics* (which he founded and he edited and wrote for from 1944 to 1949), *Esquire*, the *New Yorker*, and *Encounter*. His two most recent books are *Memoirs of a Revolutionist* (1957) and *Against the American Grain* (1962).

"The Bomb" first appeared in the journal *Politics* (September 1945).

THE BOMB

1

At 9:15 on the morning of August 6, 1945, an American plane dropped a single bomb on the Japanese city of Hiroshima. Exploding with the force of 20,000 tons of TNT, The Bomb destroyed in a twinkling two-thirds of the city, including, presumably, most of the 343,000 human beings who lived there. No warning was given. This atrocious action places "us," the defender of civilization, on a moral level with "them," the beasts of Maidanek. And "we," the American people are just as much and as little responsible for this horror as "they," the German people.

So much is obvious. But more must be said. For the atomic bomb renders anticlimatical even the ending of the greatest war in history. (1) *The concepts, "war" and "progress," are now obsolete.* Both suggest human aspirations, emotions, aims, consciousness. "The greatest achievement of organized science in history," said President Truman after the Hiroshima catastrophe—which it probably was, and so much the worse for organized science. (2) *The futility of modern warfare should now be clear.* Must we not now conclude, with Simone Weil, that the technical aspect of war today is the evil, regardless of political factors? Can one imagine that the Bomb could ever be used "in a good cause"? Do not such means instantly, of themselves, corrupt any cause? (3) *The Bomb is the natural product of the kind of society we have created.* It is as easy, normal and unforced an expression of the American Way of Life as electric iceboxes, banana splits, and hydromatic-drive automobiles. We do not dream of a world in which atomic fission will be "harnessed to constructive ends." The new energy will be at the service of the rulers; it will change their strength but not their aims. The underlying populations

should regard this new source of energy with lively interest—the interest
of victims. (4) *Those who wield destructive power are outcasts from
humanity.* They may be gods, they may be brutes, but they are not men.
(5) *We must "get" the national State before it "gets" us.* Every individual
who wants to have his humanity—and indeed his skin—had better begin
thinking "dangerous thoughts" about sabotage, resistance, rebellion, and
the fraternity of all men everywhere. The mental attitude known as "negativism" is a good start.

2

What first appalled us was its blast. "TNT is barely twice as strong as black
powder was six centuries ago. World WAR II developed explosives up to
60% more powerful than TNT. The atomic bomb is more than 12,000
times as strong as the best improvement in TNT. One hundred and twenty-
three planes, each bearing a single atomic bomb, would carry as much
destructive power as all the bombs (2,453,595 tons) dropped by the
Allies on Europe during the war." (*Time*, August 20, 1945)

It has slowly become evident, however, that the real horror of The Bomb
is not blast but radioactivity. Splitting the atom sets free all kinds of radioactive substances, whose power is suggested by the fact that at the Hanford
bomb plant, the water used for cooling the "pile" (the structure of uranium
and other substances whose atomic interaction produces the explosive)
carried off enough radiation to "heat the Columbia River appreciably."
Time added: "Even the wind blowing over the chemical plant picked up
another load of peril, for the stacks gave off a radioactive gas." And
Smyth notes: "The fission products produced in one day's run of a
100,000–kilowatt chain-reacting pile of uranium might be sufficient to
make a large area uninhabitable."

There is thus no question as to the potential horror of The Bomb's
radioactivity. The two bombs actually used were apparently designed as
explosive and not gas bombs, perhaps from humanitarian considerations,
perhaps to protect the American troops who will later have to occupy
Japan. But intentions are one thing, results another. So feared was radioactivity at Hanford that the most elaborate precautions were taken in the
way of shields, clothes, etc. No such precautions were taken, obviously,
on behalf of the inhabitants of Hiroshima; the plane dropped its cargo of
half-understood poisons and sped away. What happened? The very sensitivity of the army and the scientists on the subject is ominous. When one
of the lesser experts who had worked on the bomb, a Dr. Harold Jacobson
of New York, stated publicly that Hiroshima would be "uninhabitable"
for seventy years, he was at once questioned by FBI agents, after which,

"ill and upset," he issued another statement emphasizing that this was merely his own personal opinion, and that his colleagues disagreed with him.

The point is that none of those who produced and employed this monstrosity really knew just how deadly or prolonged these radioactive poisons would be. Which did not prevent them from completing their assignment, nor the army from dropping the bombs. Perhaps only among men like soldiers and scientists, trained to think "objectively"—i.e., in terms of means, not ends—could such irresponsibility and moral callousness be found. In any case, it was undoubtedly the most magnificent scientific experiment in history, with cities as the laboratories and people as the guinea pigs.

The official platitude about Atomic Fission is that it can be a Force for Good (production) or a Force for Evil (war), and that the problem is simply how to use its Good rather than its Bad potentialities. This is "just common sense." But, as Engels once remarked, Common Sense has some very strange adventures when it leaves its cozy bourgeois fireside and ventures out into the real world. For, given our present institutions—and the official apologists, from Max Lerner to President Conant of Harvard, envisage at most only a little face-lifting on these—how can The Bomb be "controlled," how can it be "internationalized"? Already the great imperialisms are jockeying for position in World War III. How can we expect them to give up the enormous advantage offered by The Bomb? May we hope that the destructive possibilities are so staggering that, for simple self-preservation, they will agree to "outlaw" The Bomb? Or that they will foreswear war itself because an "atomic" war would probably mean the mutual ruin of all contestants? The same reasons were advanced before World War I to demonstrate its "impossibility"; also before World War II. The devastation of these wars was as terrible as had been predicted—yet they took place. Like all the great advances in technology of the past century, Atomic Fission is something in which Good and Evil are so closely intertwined that it is hard to see how the Good can be extracted and the Evil thrown away. A century of effort has failed to separate the Good of capitalism (more production) from the Evil (exploitation, wars, cultural barbarism). *This* atom has never been split, and perhaps never will be.

The Marxian socialists, both revolutionary and reformist, also accept the potentialities-for-Good-or-for-Evil platitude, since this platitude is based on a faith in Science and Progress which is shared by Marxists as well as conservatives, and is indeed still the basic assumption of Western thought. (In this respect, Marxism appears to be simply the most profound and consistent intellectual expression of this faith.) Since the Marxists make as a precondition of the beneficial use of Atomic Fission a basic change in present institutions, their position is not open to the objections noted just above. But if one looks deeper than the political level, the Marxist version of the platitude seems at the very least inadequate. It blunts our reaction to the present horror by reducing it to an episode in an historical schema which will "come out all right" in the end, and thus makes us morally callous (with resulting ineffectuality in our actions against the *present* horror) and too optimistic about the problem of evil; and it ignores the fact that such atrocities as The Bomb and the Nazi death camps are *right now* brutalizing, warping, deadening the human beings who are expected to change the world for the better; that modern technology has its own anti-human dynamics which has proved so far much more powerful than the liberating effects the Marxist schema expects from it.

The bomb produced two widespread and, from the stand-point of The Authorities, undesirable emotional reactions in this country: a feeling of guilt at "our" having done this to "them," and anxiety lest some future "they" do this to "us." Both feelings were heightened by the superhuman *scale* of The Bomb. The Authorities have therefore made valiant attempts to reduce the thing to a human context, where such concepts as Justice, Reason, Progress could be employed. Such moral defenses are offered as: the war was shortened and many lives, Japanese as well as American, saved; "we" had to invent and use The Bomb against "them" lest "they" invent and use it against "us"; the Japanese deserve it because they started the war, treated prisoners barbarously, etc., or because they refused to surrender. The flimsiness of these justifications is apparent; *any* atrocious action, absolutely *any* one, could be excused on such grounds. For there is really only one possible answer to the problem posed by Dostoievski's Grand Inquisitor: if all mankind could realize eternal and complete happiness by torturing to death a single child, would this act be morally justified?

Somewhat subtler is the strategy by which The Authorities—by which term I mean not only the political leaders but also the scientists, intellectuals, trade-unionists and businessmen who function on the top levels of our society—tried to ease the deep fears aroused in everyone by The Bomb. From President Truman down, they emphasized that The Bomb has been produced in the normal, orderly course of scientific experiment, that it is thus simply the latest step in man's long struggle to control the forces of nature, in a word that it is Progress. But this is a knife that cuts both ways: the effect on me, at least, was to intensify some growing doubts about the "Scientific Progress" which had whelped this monstrosity. Last April, I noted that in our movies "the white coat of the scientist is as blood-chilling a sight as Dracula's black cape. . . . If the scientist's laboratory has acquired in Popular Culture a ghastly atmosphere, is this not perhaps one of those deep intuitions of the masses? From Frankenstein's laboratory to Maidanek [or, now, to Hanford and Oak Ridge] is not a long journey. Was there a popular suspicion, perhaps only half conscious, that the 19th century trust in science was mistaken . . . ?"

These questions seem more and more relevant. I doubt if we shall get satisfactory answers from the scientists (who, indeed, seem professionally incapable even of asking, let alone answering, them). The greatest of them all, who in 1905 constructed the equation which provided the theoretical basis for Atomic Fission, could think of nothing better to tell us after the bombings than: "No one in the world should have any fear or apprehension about atomic energy being a supernatural product. In developing atomic energy, science merely imitated the reaction of the sun's rays. ["Merely" is good!—DM] Atomic power is no more unnatural than when I sail my boat on Saranac Lake." Thus, Albert Einstein. As though it were not precisely the natural, the perfectly rational and scientifically demonstrable that is now chilling our blood! How human, intimate, friendly by comparison are ghosts, witches, spells, werewolves and poltergeists! Indeed, all of us except a few specialists know as much about witches as we do about atom-splitting; and all of us with no exceptions are even less able to defend ourselves against The Bomb than against witchcraft. No silver bullet, no crossed sticks will help us there. As though to demonstrate this, Einstein himself, when asked about the unknown radioactive poisons which were beginning to alarm even editorial writers, replied "emphatically": "I will not discuss that." Such emphasis is not reassuring.

Nor was President Truman reassuring when he pointed out: "This development, which was carried forward by the many thousand participants with the utmost energy and the very highest sense of national duty . . . probably represents the greatest achievement of the combined efforts of science, industry, labor and the military in all history." Nor Professor Smyth: "The weapon has been created not by the devilish inspiration of some warped genius but by the arduous labor of thousands of normal men and women working for the safety of their country." Again, the effort to "humanize" The Bomb by showing how it fits into our normal, everyday life also cuts the other way: it reveals how inhuman our normal life has become.

The pulp writers could imagine things like the atomic bomb; in fact, life is becoming more and more like a Science Fiction story, and the arrival on earth of a few six-legged Martians with Death Rays would hardly make the front page. But the pulp writers' imaginations were limited; *their* atom bombs were created by "devilish" and "warped" geniuses, not by "thousands of normal men and women"—including some of the most eminent scientists of our time, the labor movement (the army "warmly" thanked the AFL and the CIO for achieving "what at times seemed impossible provision of adequate manpower"), various great corporations (DuPont, Eastman, Union Carbon & Carbide), and the president of Harvard University.

Only a handful, of course, knew what they were creating. None of the 125,000 construction and factory workers knew. Only three of the plane crew that dropped the first bomb knew what they were letting loose. It hardly needs to be stressed that there is something askew with a society in which vast numbers of citizens can be organized to create a horror like The Bomb without even knowing they are doing it. What real content, in such a case, can be assigned to notions like "democracy" and "government of, by and for the people"? The good Professor Smyth expresses the opinion that "the people of this country" should decide for themselves about the future development of The Bomb. To be sure, no vote was taken on the creation and employment of the weapon. However, says the Professor reassuringly, these questions "have been seriously considered by all concerned [i.e., by the handful of citizens who were permitted to know what was going on] and vigorously debated among the scientists, and the conclusions reached have been passed along to the highest authorities.

"These questions are not technical questions; they are political and social questions, and the answers given to them may affect all mankind for generations. In thinking about them, the men on the project have been thinking as citizens of the United States vitally interested in the welfare of the human race. It has been their duty and that of the responsible high Government officials who were informed to look beyond the limits of the present war and its weapons to the ultimate implications of these discoveries. This was a heavy responsibility.

"In a free country like ours, such questions should be debated by the people and decisions must be made by the people through their representatives."

It would be unkind to subject the above to critical analysis beyond noting that every statement of what-is contradicts every statement of what-should-be.

Atomic fission makes me sympathize, for the first time, with the old Greek notion of *Hubris*, that lack of restraint in success which invited the punishment of the gods. Some scientist remarked the other day that it was fortunate that the only atom we as yet know how to split is that of uranium, a rare substance; for if we should learn how to split the atom of iron or some other common ore, the chain reaction might flash through vast areas and the molten interior of the globe come flooding out to put an end to us and our Progress. It is *Hubris* when President Truman declares: "The force from which the sun draws its power has been loosed against those who brought war to the Far East." Or when the *Times* editorialist echoes: "The American answer to Japan's contemptuous rejection of the Allied surrender ultimatum of July 26 has now been delivered upon Japanese soil in the shape of a new weapon which unleashes against it the forces of the universe." Invoking the Forces of the Universe to back up the ultimatum of July 26 is rather like getting in God to tidy up the living room.

It seems fitting that The Bomb was not developed by any of the totalitarian powers, where the political atmosphere might at first glance seem to be more suited to it, but by the two "democracies," the last major powers to continue to pay at least ideological respect to the humanitarian-democratic tradition. It also seems fitting that the heads of these governments, by the time The Bomb exploded, were not Roosevelt and Churchill, figures of a certain historical and personal stature, but Attlee and Truman, both colorless mediocrities, Average Men elevated to their positions by the mechanics of the system. All this emphasizes that perfect automatism, that absolute lack of human consciousness or aims which our society is rapidly achieving. As a uranium "pile," once the elements have been brought together, inexorably runs through a series of "chain reactions" until the final explosion takes place, so the elements of our society act and react, regardless of ideologies or personalities, until The Bomb explodes over Hiroshima. The more commonplace the personalities and senseless the institutions, the more grandiose the destruction. It is *Götterdämmerung* without the gods.

The scientists themselves whose brain-work produced The Bomb appear not as creators but as raw material, to be hauled about and exploited like uranium ore. Thus, Dr. Otto Hahn, the German scientist who in 1939 first split the uranium atom and who did his best to present Hitler with an atom bomb, has been brought over to this country to pool his knowledge with our own atomic "team" (which includes several Jewish refugees who were kicked out of Germany by Hitler). Thus Professor Kaputza, Russia's leading experimenter with uranium, was decoyed from Cambridge University in the thirties back to his native land, and, once there, refused permission to return. Thus a recent report from Yugoslavia tells of some eminent native atom-splitter being high-jacked by the Red Army (just like a valuable machine tool) and rushed by plane to Moscow.

Insofar as there is any moral responsibility assignable for The Bomb, it rests with those scientists who developed it and those political and military leaders who employed it. Since the rest of us Americans did not even know what was being done in our name—let alone have the slightest possibility of stopping it—The Bomb becomes the most dramatic illustration to date of the fallacy of "The Responsibility of Peoples."

Yet how can even those immediately concerned be held responsible? A general's function is to win wars, a president's or prime minister's to defend the interests of the ruling class he represents, a scientist's to extend the frontiers of knowledge; how can any of them, then, draw the line at the atom bomb, or indeed anywhere, regardless of their "personal feelings"? The dilemma is absolute, when posed in these terms. The social order is an impersonal mechanism, the war is an impersonal process, and they grind along automatically; if some of the human parts rebel at their function, they will be replaced by more amenable ones; and their rebellion will mean that they are simply thrust aside, without changing anything. The Marxists say this must be so until there is a revolutionary change; but such a change never seemed farther away. What, then, can a man do *now?* How can he escape playing his part in the ghastly process?

Quite simply by not playing it. Many eminent scientists, for example, worked on The Bomb: Fermi of Italy, Bohr of Denmark, Chadwick of England, Oppenheimer, Urey and Compton of USA. It is fair to expect such men, of great knowledge and intelligence, to be aware of the consequences of their actions. And they seem to have been so. Dr. Smyth observes: "Initially, many scientists could and did hope that some principle would emerge which would prove that atomic bombs were inherently impossible. The hope has faded gradually. . . ." Yet they all accepted the "assignment," and produced The Bomb. Why? Because they thought of themselves as specialists, technicians, and not as complete men. Specialists in the sense that the process of scientific discovery is considered to be morally neutral, so that the scientist may deplore the uses to which his discoveries are put by the generals and politicians but may not refuse to make them for that reason; and specialists also in that they reacted to the war as partisans of one side, whose function was the narrow one of defeating the Axis governments even if it meant sacrificing their broader responsibilities as human beings.

But, fortunately for the honor of science, a number of scientists refused to take part in the project. I have heard of several individual cases over here, and Sir James Chadwick has revealed "that some of his colleagues refused to work on the atomic bomb for fear they might be creating a planet-destroying monster." These scientists reacted as whole men, not as special-ists or part-isans. Today the tendency is to think of peoples as responsible and individuals as irresponsible. The reversal of both these conceptions is the first condition of escaping the present decline to barbarism. The more each individual thinks and behaves as a whole Man (hence responsibly) rather than as a specialized part of some nation or profession (hence irresponsibly), the better hope for the future. To insist on acting as a responsible individual in a society which reduces the individual to impotence may be foolish, reckless, and ineffectual; or it may be wise, prudent and effective. But whichever it is, only thus is there a chance of changing our present tragic destiny. All honor then to the as yet anonymous British and American scientists—Men I would rather say —who were so wisely foolish as to refuse their cooperation on The Bomb! This is "resistance," this is "negativism," and in it lies our best hope.

Mary McCarthy
(1912–   )

MARY McCARTHY was born in Seattle, Washington, and graduated from Vassar College in 1933. She has been a drama critic, has edited the *Partisan Review* (1937–1938), and has taught at Bard College and Sarah Lawrence. She is well known for such works as *The Groves of Academe* (1952), *The Group* (1963), and a recent volume of articles about her trip to Hanoi.

"The Contagion of Ideas" was a speech delivered to a group of teachers in the summer of 1952. It was reprinted in McCarthy's book *On the Contrary* (1961).

THE CONTAGION
OF IDEAS*

The Declaration of Independence speaks of certain unalienable rights given to Man by God—the rights to life, liberty, and the pursuit of happiness. Yet nothing is clearer than that these rights are far from unalienable. They can be taken from a man by other men; they can be surrendered by a whole people to the state; if they are to be preserved at all, the state, presumably, must secure them. In the days of the Founding Fathers, these rights had a certain sacred character that flowed from a belief in God; they were hallowed in the individual by the supposed intention of the Creator and were hardly to be distinguished from the sacredness of life itself. God meant man to be free, paradoxically, to obey his conscience; indeed, man's freedom imposed on him the *duty* of obeying the inner voice, in defiance, if necessary, of law and common opinion.

Today, in a secular society that no longer believes in God, we retain a lip-belief in the doctrine of inherent rights without knowing what we mean by them or where they are supposed to come from. In practice, we look to the state as the source of rights and the patenter of new rights that have suddenly come to light—the right to teach, the right to a government job, and so on, though it is evident that no one has the right to teach inherent in him as a human being. But when we look to the state as the source of rights, these rights lose their sacred character and become mere privileges which the state can withdraw at any time from individuals or groups that displease it. This is the situation of the Communists in the

* Generally, Mary McCarthy's essay is written in response to Senator Joseph McCarthy's unsupported allegations that communists had infiltrated the highest levels of the U.S. government. It was Senator McCarthy who gave wide currency to the phrase the "Red Menace," a phrase which was "legitimized" by the passage of the McCarran Act (1951). —*Editor*.

United States today; their liberty is looked upon by the public as a privilege accorded them by the government that they have misused and that therefore ought to be taken away from them. Liberty, as it is conceived by current opinion, has nothing inherent about it; it is a sort of gift or trust bestowed on the individual by the state pending *good behavior*. We see this notion applied not only to Communists but to racketeers like Frank Costello and Erickson, who are deprived of their freedom to remain silent before Congressional committees; their Constitutional rights are suspended, as long as they remain uncooperative. Thus a Communist is free to testify to his party-associations; Costello is free to testify to his illegal gambling transactions; but neither is free to be silent. In the same way, other, more parvenu rights fade overnight into privileges —the right to strike, for example, or the right to teach in the public schools turns out to depend on the teacher's or the trade union's "good behavior," i.e., on political criteria. In short, these so-called rights are not, realistically speaking, rights at all but resemble, rather, licenses, like hunting licenses, licenses to carry firearms, or driving licenses, which keep having to be renewed and are subject to all sorts of restrictions and limitations. This is very clear in the case of a passport: nobody, it is claimed, has a right to a passport inherent in him as a citizen, and if this right does not exist, then a passport becomes simply a travel permit which can be canceled for infractions of discipline, exactly like a license to drive.

Once the state is looked upon as the *source* of rights, rather than their bound protector, freedom becomes conditional on the pleasure of the state. You may say that in practice this has always been true and always will be: the state has always decided how much freedom shall be had and by whom. Yet the difference between a democracy and a tyranny or despotism is that in theory the citizen of a democracy possesses inherent rights, and this theory becomes the working hypothesis, i.e., the practice of a democratic state. However, without a belief in a Creator as the divine provider of rights, the theory tends to shift and to be stood, even, on its head, i.e., to turn into a doctrine of privileges vested in the state and dealt out by it to citizens who can prove their worthiness to enjoy them. That is what is happening today; rights and privileges have become so confused that to talk of rights at all is to invite a demonstration that there are none, for every right can be shown to be contingent and not absolute. If you argue today's vexed cases in terms of rights, you will lose the argument every time, strangely enough, to advocates of "freedom." Nobody, they will tell you, has a right to a Hollywood swimming pool, nobody has a right to perform on television or the radio, nobody has a right to a government job, nobody has a right to a passport, nobody has a right to teach in a public school, nobody has a right to conspire against government. Conversely, a Hollywood screen-producer has a right to fire whom he chooses, radio and television companies have a right to be responsible to their advertisers, and the advertisers have a right to be responsible to the public, and the public has a right to complain of Communist performers on the air; a school board has the right to refuse to allow subversives to teach the children in its care; the government has the right to keep Communists out of its service, to refuse passports to citizens according to its own judgment, to revoke visas of entry, and in general to withhold the rights of citizenship from those who would take them from others. Agreed, but what exactly are these "rights" we are speaking of? Closely examined, they seem to be not rights but powers. What is meant is that nobody has the power to keep the government from denying a passport or to keep an employer from firing a Communist, to prevent a school board from screening the teachers it selects for its children; and, conversely, no schoolteacher or radio-performer has, in himself, the power to retain his job. Powers, once they have been weakened, cease to be thought of as rights, or a right, on the defensive, is an enfeebled power. Take the right of an employer to hire and fire; this right, once universally recognized and seemingly, almost, a "natural" right, now exists chiefly in small business and in households, where no union power is massed to limit it; similarly, the "right to work," which a few years ago meant the right to a job, now has shifted to mean the right of a worker *not* to belong to a union and is really the old employer's right to hire and fire presented in a proletarian disguise. Rights which appear natural and unquestioned take on a highly unnatural look when the power that bred them wanes. I might like to assert the right of a Communist to perform on the radio, but I lack the power to implement it, a power that could only be created by a *demand* for Communists on the air. Since there is not likely soon to be a demand for Communists, on the air, or in the schools, or in the government service, it becomes rather futile to urge their "right" to be employed in these fields. In default of a real demand, can a synthetic one be improvised, in the interests of pluralism? Is a university president with liberal ideas obligated by his principles to hire a token Communist on his faculty—in fairness to minorities? Should a breakfast-food company be obliged to keep a Communist artiste on its payroll, to show that it does not discriminate? No. Communism is not a commodity that we can force entrepreneurs to stock. When the argument is put in this way, scarcely anyone today would defend the right of a Communist, qua Communist, to a job in entertainment or education. Where the problem really presents itself is not in terms of general propositions but in specific cases. For example, should Paul Robeson be allowed to sing on the radio? Here it is easy for the liberal to answer yes, the more so since there is a real demand for Robeson as a singer. And the question for the university president is not whether he should hire new Communists in order to prove himself a liberal, but whether he should get rid of the ones he already has on his staff. Here again, the answer is not difficult. Most liberal college presidents would object to firing a teacher simply because he was a Communist, though few would be likely to insist, in public, on the college's "right" to keep him. The usual course is to deny that the teacher concerned is a Communist, thus avoiding the whole question of the "right to teach," since this right, openly invoked, will be disputed and the college will probably lose its right, i.e., its power, to harbor him.

To my mind, this situation would be greatly clarified if we thought, not just in terms of rights, but of goods, if we endeavored to treat individuals not in terms of what was owing to them by society or the state, but in terms of what an open society owed to its own image. If we thought of liberty not only as a right but as a good, we would be more hesitant to deprive people of it than we are when we think of it as a privilege or license within the bestowal of the state. If liberty is a good, a primary, axiomatic good, then the more that can be had of it, the better, and we should tend, even in situations of danger, to think of maximums rather than minimums. When weighing such questions as that of the right to a passport or of the right to Communists to teach or even of Frank Costello not to testify, we would ask ourselves how much liberty our free society ought to extend, if it is to live up to its name, rather than how much liberty was owing to this or that individual. Advocates of the curtailment of liberties tend to reason in broad scholastic syllogisms; they seldom feel it necessary to show, concretely, how the exercise of a given liberty will endanger the body politic. The Communist conspiracy, in theory, menaces the internal security of the United States; therefore, it is reasoned, every Communist is a dangerous conspirator, potentially, and must be treated as though he were one in fact. The case of Dr. Fuchs, a *secret* Communist sympathizer, who transmitted atomic information, is used as an argument for jailing *open* Communists, who would never, in any case, be employed on an atomic energy project. Or it is maintained that though the Communists are not an internal danger now, they would be duty-bound, in wartime, to disrupt the armed services and sabotage defense industries; what is overlooked in this chain of reasoning is that we *are* at war with Communist forces in Korea, and yet Harry Bridges' powerful West Coast maritime union, admittedly Communist-dominated, has been unable to halt a single shipment of war materials to the battlefront.

To argue these questions on theoretical grounds is to lose sight of common sense—the common sense which, after all, is the rationale of a democracy; a belief in common sense is the informing spirit of all democratic institutions, from the jury system to universal suffrage. No emergency can justify the national suspension of common sense, yet just that is being urged on us as a necessary measure to cope with Communism. We are told, for instance, that Communists' minds are not free and that therefore they are not "fit" to be teachers, but no attempt is made to show this on a common-sense level or to indicate, in contrast, for that matter, what minds are free. The same argument could be used against permitting Catholics to teach. I myself would think it a poor idea to have our schools staffed by large numbers of Communists, but nobody is proposing that. The question is whether, in our energetically anti-Communist society, it is worthwhile to construct a whole apparatus of repression to stamp out the few Communist teachers who have managed to survive in our school systems. Those who would say yes would pretend that the infection of a single school child's mind ought to be avoided, for moral reasons, at the cost of a whole society. But this is the purest scholasticism. In the thirties, when the Communists were a genuine power in the intellectual world, we liberals thought it our duty to expose them in the schools and colleges where they pontificated. I do not think we were wrong, but I think we are wrong today if we fail to acknowledge that the situation has changed and that the student today, far from being in danger of being indoctrinated by Communism, is in danger of being stupefied by the complacent propaganda for democracy that accompanies him to school, follows him through school, goes home with him, speaks to him in the movies and on television, and purrs him to sleep from the radio. The strange thing is that this current indoctrination for democracy has very much the same tone—pious, priggish, groupy—that we objected to in the Stanlinism of the popular-front period.

Advocates of "realism" (as opposed to "idealism") in the treatment of Communists seem bent on ignoring the realities of the current situation. Those who, like Sidney Hook, advocate the refusal of teaching jobs to avowed Communists while insisting that mere fellow-travelers should have the right to teach, are courting the very result they deprecate—the growth of an underground Communism that does not acknowledge its name. Clearly, it would be more sensible to ban fellow-travelers from the schools while allowing avowed Communists, under that label, to have their representative say. In my academic experience, the fellow-traveler is far more insidious to deal with than the Party member, for the fellow-traveler invariably calls himself a "liberal" and points to some small difference he maintains with official Marxism to certify his claim to that title; students are frequently taken in by him, to the point where they became fellow-travelers themselves while imagining that they are liberals or else conceive a lasting repulsion for what they suppose to be liberal attitudes. When a science instructor recently left her job at a woman's college, the housekeeper found her Party card in her bedroom safe; no one had ever suspected her of Communism because she had never expressed any political views, though there were a number of vocal fellow-travelers on the faculty, which was considered very "pink." Now a policy that would guard students from this woman's influence while permitting fellow-travelers to teach has only one merit: that of bureaucratic simplicity. It is easier, from an administrative point of view, to clean out "card-carrying" Communists, whose names are known to the FBI, than to draw a line between a fellow-traveler and a liberal. And it might be easier, then, to fire all liberals, to avoid making mistakes. Easiest of all, finally, would be to use machines to teach —a solution not so remote as it sounds.

There is a great deal of talk today about the "dilemma" confronting the liberal. He must choose, it is said, between his traditional notions of freedom and the survival of the free world. This dilemma is totally spurious— the invention of illiberal people. If there were a strong Communist Party in America, allied to the Soviet Union, the choice for the liberal might be painful, as it might have been had there been a strong Fascist Party allied to the Nazis during the last war. As it is, the liberal's only problem is to avoid succumbing to the illusion of "having to choose."

To heighten this illusion, which common sense rejects, the strength of the Communists is claimed to lie not in their numbers but somewhere else, somewhere less evident to the ordinary, uninitiated person. The uninitiated anti-Communists subscribe to a doctrine that one might call Gresham's Law as transferred to the field of ideas—the notion that bad ideas drive out good. According to this notion, Communism is an idea that is peculiarly contagious. The Communists may be few in number, but their ideas are felt to have a mysterious potency that other ideas do not possess. Nobody contends, for instance, that Communist teachers constitute a majority or even a considerable minority in our schools. Nor does anybody point to a single primary school child who has been indoctrinated with Communism or suggest how, even in theory, such indoctrination might be accomplished. No; it is enough to show that a primary school teacher belongs or has belonged to a subversive organization; from this, I quote, arises "the danger of infection," as if Communism were a sort of airborne virus that could be wafted from a teacher to her pupils, without anybody's seeing it and even though the whole hygiene of school and family and civic life today was such, one would think, as to sterilize the child against such "germs."

Everyone who has had any experience of teaching knows how difficult it is to indoctrinate a pupil with anything—with the use of algebraic symbols, the rules of punctuation, the dates of American history; yet a Communist teacher, presumably, can "infect" *her* pupils with Marxism-Leninism-Stalinism by, to quote one writer, "the tone of her voice." She is able, moreover, to cite another popular image, to "plant the seeds" of Communism, undetected by parents or school superintendents or principals or fellow-teachers; she does it "by suggestion." The inference is that a single Communist teacher has more persuasion in her little finger than a school system consisting of ninety-nine others has in its whole organized body, more persuasion than all the forces of radio, movies, television, and comic books combined.

Yet no one, as I say, has produced (so far as I know) a single case history of a primary school child in the United States who has been indoctrinated with Communism. "Tragic cases," however, are often alluded to of somewhat older young people whose lives have been ruined by being exposed to a Communist teacher or professor. There may have been a few such cases in the thirties, tragic or not, yet we do not hear that such well-known figures as Hiss or Chambers or Remington or Elizabeth Bentley "got that way" because of a teacher. The most Elizabeth Bentley can say, in her autobiography, is that at Vassar she was exposed to godless and atheistic influences that softened her up for Communism. But to save the soul of one Elizabeth Bentley, or a dozen, should all non-believing teachers be eliminated from our colleges? The direct "causation" of Communism cannot be established, but surely a large number of Communists, present and ex-, would claim that they became so in reaction against their conservative parents and teachers; the revolutionary as rebel against authority is a familiar psychological cliché. Then should conservative teachers be eliminated?

The truth is that most young people who became Communists in the United States in the thirties and early forties did so either in response to the misery of the depression or in response to the threat of fascism as exemplified by Hitler. The few in this country who become Communists today probably do so in the mistaken hope that Communism offers protection against a third world catastrophe: war. It is not a question, really, of the contagion of ideas but of a relation that is felt to exist beween certain ideas and an actual situation, to which the ideas seem applicable. When an anti-Communist argues that Communist ideas are highly contagious and that mere contact with a Communist is therefore dangerous for a school child or student, he is making an implicit confession. He is admitting to the fear that Communist ideas are catching, not just because they are "bad" and tend to drive out "good" ideas, but because they have a more evident correspondence with the realities of social inequity than he suspects his own ideas have. If Communist ideas are contagious or, rather, if we feel uneasily that they are, is not this precisely because they contain a "germ" of truth? We can laugh at Soviet "equality," Soviet "justice," Soviet "economic democracy," but only in the Soviet context; in France, Italy, China, Indonesia, the American South, these words have the power to shame us. We are afraid of export Communism, though not of the Soviet domestic article, because our own export, democracy, is competing under the same labels, and we know that our own capitalist society to a

Chinese peasant or a Sicilian peasant or even an American Negro might appear even more unjust and unequal than the Soviet product.

The fear and hatred of Communism expressed in America today is not just a revulsion from the crimes of Stalin, from the deportation camps and forced labor and frame-up trials; it is also a fear and hatred of the original ideals of Communism. In a certain sense, the crimes of Stalin come as welcome news to America: they are taken as proof that socialism does not "work." In equality, we would like to believe, is a law of nature, and by "we" I do not mean only wealthy businessmen or blackguards like Senator McCarthy or Southern racists. As the richest nation in the world, we have developed the psychology of rich people: we are afraid of poverty, of "agitators," of any jarring notes in the national harmony. The behavior of our local Communists outrages our sense of majesty, while abroad, all over the globe, our Congressmen are filling satchels with instances of foreign ingratitude. Like all rich people, we feel we are not appreciated, and we suffer from ideas of reference; if anybody speaks about "privilege" or "exploitation," we think they must mean us; if we see a film in which the poor are good and the rich are bad, we wonder whether it is not Communist-inspired. We do not like to hear attacks on segregation, on the use of the atomic bomb, on NATO, unless we are sure that the person talking is "on our side."

It is this guilty fear of criticism, at bottom, this sense of being sur-rounded by an unappreciative world, that is the source of our demands for loyalty, from teachers, from public performers, from veterans getting subsidized housing, from all those, in short, whom we regard as our pen-sioners. Certainly, the administration of loyalty oaths, like a mass vac-cination against Communism, does not make any practical sense. And if we are particularly sensitive about our schools, it is because we fear that children, with their natural lack of bias, their detached and innocent faculty of observation, will be all too ready to prick up their ears if they hear our society criticized, even implicitly, in the "tone" of a teacher's voice. Our children, we feel, may listen to *her* more than they will listen to us, because they have already noticed the injustices of our society and want to know the why of it, instead of being told that "God made it that way." People with bad consciences always fear the judgment of children.

We did not behave this way toward fascists and fascist sympathizers during the war. We did not make a national effort to root them out of our schools and colleges or demand that they take loyalty oaths; on the whole, we did nothing to disturb them or to prevent the spread of their ideas. This was not because we found their doctrines more tolerable than we find the doctrines of Communism. On the contrary. Their ideas seemed to us so crazy and disgusting that we could not imagine anybody's being taken in by them, though in fact some people were. But this was, as we used to call it, the "lunatic fringe." The proof that we do not regard Communists as lunatics is precisely this fear we have that their ideas may be catching, this fear, as I say, of the "germ" of truth. And this germ phobia will be with us as long as we ourselves try to sell the white lie of democracy abroad, to the starving nations who in fact are the "children"— the ignorant and uneducated—whose allegiance we question, rightly, and whose judgment of us we, rightly, dread.

Ralph Ellison
(1914–   )

ELLISON was born in Oklahoma City and studied music at Tuskegee Institute. He gained literary prominence with the publication of his novel, *Invisible Man* (1952), which won the National Book Award. Since that time, he has lectured at New York University, Columbia University, Fisk, Antioch, Princeton, Bennington and Bard College. *Shadow and Act* (1964), a collection of essays, is his latest book.

"Twentieth-Century Fiction and the Black Mask of Humanity" was written in 1946 and published in the December 1953 issue of *Confluence*. The essay has been reprinted in *Shadow and Act*.

TWENTIETH-CENTURY
FICTION AND THE BLACK
MASK OF HUMANITY

Perhaps the most insidious and least understood form of segregation is that of the word. And by this I mean the word in all its complex formulations, from the proverb to the novel and stage play, the word with all its subtle power to suggest and foreshadow overt action while magically disguising the moral consequences of that action and providing it with symbolic and psychological justification. For if the word has the potency to revive and make us free, it has also the power to blind, imprison and destroy.

The essence of the word is its ambivalence, and in fiction it is never so effective and revealing as when both potentials are operating simultaneously, as when it mirrors both good and bad, as when it blows both hot and cold in the same breath. Thus it is unfortunate for the Negro that the most powerful formulations of modern American fictional words have been so slanted against him that when he approaches for a glimpse of himself he discovers an image drained of humanity.

Obviously the experiences of Negroes—slavery, the grueling and continuing fight for full citizenship since Emancipation, the stigma of color, the enforced alienation which constantly knifes into our natural identification with our country—have not been that of white Americans. And though as passionate believers in democracy Negroes identify themselves with the broader American ideals, their sense of reality springs, in part, from an American experience which most white men not only have not had, but one with which they are reluctant to identify themselves even when presented in forms of the imagination. Thus when the white American, holding up most twentieth-century fiction, says, "This is American reality," the Negro tends to answer (not at all concerned that Americans tend generally to fight against any but the most flattering imaginative depictions of their lives), "Perhaps, but you've left out this, and this, and this. And most of all, what you'd have the world accept as me isn't even human."

Nor does he refer only to second-rate works but to those of our most representative authors. Either like Hemingway and Steinbeck (in whose joint works I recall not more than five American Negroes) they tend to ignore them, or like the earlier Faulkner, who distorted Negro humanity to fit his personal versions of Southern myth, they seldom conceive Negro characters possessing the full, complex ambiguity of the human. Too often what is presented as the American Negro (a most complex example of Western man) emerges an oversimplified clown, a beast or an angel. Seldom is he drawn as that sensitively focused process of opposites, of good and evil, of instinct and intellect, of passion and spirituality, which literary art has projected as the image of man. Naturally, the attitude of Negroes toward this writing is one of great reservation. Which, indeed, bears out Richard Wright's remarks that there is in progress between black and white Americans a struggle over the nature of reality.

Historically this is but a part of that larger conflict between older, dominant groups of white Americans, especially the Anglo-Saxons, on the one hand, and the newer white and non-white groups on the other, over the major group's attempt to impose its ideals upon the rest, insisting that its exclusive image be accepted as the image of the American. This conflict should not, however, be misunderstood. For despite the impact of the American idea upon the world, the "American" himself has not (fortunately for the United States, its minorities, and perhaps for the world) been finally defined. So that far from being socially undesirable this struggle between Americans as to what the American is to be is part of that democratic process through which the nation works to achieve itself. Out of this conflict the ideal American character—a type truly great enough to possess the greatness of the land, a delicately poised unity of divergencies—is slowly being born.

But we are concerned here with fiction, not history. How is it then that our naturalistic prose—one of the most vital bodies of twentieth-century fiction, perhaps the brightest instrument for recording sociological fact, physical action, the nuance of speech, yet achieved—becomes suddenly dull when confronting the Negro?

Obviously there is more in this than the mere verbal counterpart of lynching or segregation. Indeed, it represents a projection of processes lying at the very root of American culture and certainly at the central core of its twentieth-century literary forms, a matter having less to do with the mere "reflection" of white racial theories than with processes molding the attitudes, the habits of mind, the cultural atmosphere and the artistic and intellectual traditions that condition men dedicated to democracy to practice, accept and, most crucial of all, often blind themselves to the essentially undemocratic treatment of their fellow citizens.

It should be noted here that the moment criticism approaches Negro-white relationships it is plunged into problems of psychology and symbolic ritual. Psychology, because the distance between Americans, Negroes and whites, is not so much spatial as psychological; while they might dress and often look alike, seldom on deeper levels do they think alike. Ritual, because the Negroes of fiction are so consistently false to human life that we must question just what they truly represent, both in the literary work and in the inner world of the white American.[1]

Despite their billings as images of reality, these Negroes of fiction are counterfeits. They are projected aspects of an internal symbolic process through which, like a primitive tribesman dancing himself into the group frenzy necessary for battle, the white American prepares himself emotionally to perform a social role. These fictive Negroes are not, as sometimes interpreted, simple racial clichés introduced into society by a ruling class to control political and economic realities. For although they are manipulated to that end, such an externally one-sided interpretation relieves the individual of personal responsibility for the health of democracy. Not only does it forget that a democracy is a collectivity of individuals, but it never suspects that the tenacity of the stereotype springs exactly from the fact that its function is no less personal than political. Color prejudice springs not from the stereotype alone, but from an internal psychological state; not from misinformation alone, but from an inner need to believe. It thrives not only on the obscene witch-doctoring of men like Jimmy Byrnes and Malan, but upon an inner craving for symbolic magic. The prejudiced individual creates his own stereotypes, very often unconsciously, by reading into situations involving Negroes those stock meanings which justify his emotional and economic needs.

Hence whatever else the Negro stereotype might be as a social instrumentality, it is also a key figure in a magic rite by which the white

---

1. Perhaps the ideal approach to the work of literature would be one allowing for insight into the deepest psychological motives of the writer at the same time that it examined all external sociological factors operating within a given milieu. For while objectively a social reality, the work of art is, in its genesis, a projection of a deeply personal process, and any approach that ignores the personal at the expense of the social is necessarily incomplete. Thus when we approach contemporary writing from the perspective of segregation, as is commonly done by sociology-minded thinkers, we automatically limit ourselves to one external aspect of a complex whole, which leaves us little to say concerning its personal, internal elements. On the other hand, American writing has been one of the most important twentieth-century literatures, and though negative as a social force it is technically brilliant and emotionally powerful. Hence were we to examine it for its embodiment of these positive values, there would be other more admiring things to be said.—*Author.*

American seeks to resolve the dilemma arising between his democratic beliefs and certain antidemocratic practices, between his acceptance of the sacred democratic belief that all men are created equal and his treatment of every tenth man as though he were not.

Thus on the moral level I propose that we view the whole of American life as a drama acted out upon the body of a Negro giant, who, lying trussed up like Gulliver, forms the stage and the scene upon which and within which the action unfolds. If we examine the beginning of the Colonies, the application of this view is not, in its economic connotations at least, too far-fetched or too difficult to see. For then the Negro's body was exploited as amorally as the soil and climate. It was later, when white men drew up a plan for a democratic way of life, that the Negro began slowly to exert an influence upon America's moral consciousness. Gradually he was recognized as the human factor placed outside the democratic master plan, a human "natural" resource who, so that white men could become more human, was elected to undergo a process of institutionalized dehumanization.

Until the Korean War this moral role had become obscured within the staggering growth of contemporary science and industry, but during the nineteenth century it flared nakedly in the American consciousness, only to be repressed after the Reconstruction. During periods of national crises, when the United States rounds a sudden curve on the pitch-black road of history, this moral awareness surges in the white American's conscience like a raging river revealed at his feet by a lightning flash. Only then is the veil of anti-Negro myths, symbols, stereotypes and taboos drawn somewhat aside. And when we look closely at our literature it is to be seen operating even when the Negro seems most patently the little man who isn't there.

I see no value either in presenting a catalogue of Negro characters appearing in twentieth-century fiction or in charting the racial attitudes of white writers. We are interested not in quantities but in qualities. And since it is impossible here to discuss the entire body of this writing, the next best thing is to select a framework in which the relationships with which we are concerned may be clearly seen. For brevity let us take three representative writers: Mark Twain, Hemingway and Faulkner. Twain for historical perspective and as an example of how a great nineteenth-century writer handled the Negro; Hemingway as the prime example of the artist who ignored the dramatic and symbolic possibilities presented by this theme; and Faulkner as an example of a writer who has confronted Negroes with such mixed motives that he has presented them in terms of both the "good nigger" and the "bad nigger" stereotypes, and who yet has explored perhaps more successfully than anyone else, either white or black, certain forms of Negro humanity.

For perspective let us begin with Mark Twain's great classic, *Huckleberry Finn*. Recall that Huckleberry has run away from his father, Miss Watson and the Widow Douglas (indeed the whole community, in relation to which he is a young outcast) and has with him as companion on the raft upon which they are sailing down the Mississippi the Widow Watson's runaway Negro slave, Jim. Recall, too, that Jim, during the critical moment of the novel, is stolen by two scoundrels and sold to another master, presenting Huck with the problem of freeing Jim once more. Two ways are open, he can rely upon his own ingenuity and "steal" Jim into freedom or he might write the Widow Watson and request reward money to have Jim returned to her. But there is a danger in this course, remember, since the angry widow might sell the slave down the river into a harsher slavery. It is this course which Huck starts to take, but as he composes the letter he wavers.

"It was a close place." [he tells us] "I took it [the letter] up, and held it in my hand. I was trembling, because I'd got to decide, forever, 'twixt two things, and I knowed it. I studied a minute, sort of holding my breath, and then says to myself:

" 'Alright, then, I'll *go* to hell'—and tore it up, . . . It was awful thoughts and awful words, but they was said . . . And I let them stay said, and never thought no more about reforming. I shoved the whole thing out of my head and said I would take up wickedness again, which was in my line, being brung up to it, and the other warn't. And for a starter I would . . . steal Jim out of slavery again. . . ."

And a little later, in defending his decision to Tom Sawyer, Huck comments, "I know you'll say it's dirty, low-down business but *I'm* low-down. And I'm going to steal him. . . ."

We have arrived at a key point of the novel and, by an ironic reversal, of American fiction, a pivotal moment announcing a change of direction in the plot, a reversal as well as a recognition scene (like that in which Oedipus discovers his true identity) wherein a new definition of necessity is being formulated. Huck Finn has struggled with the problem poised by the clash between property rights and human rights, between what the community considered to be the proper attitude toward an escaped slave and his knowledge of Jim's humanity, gained through their adventures as fugitives together. He has made his decision on the side of humanity. In this passage Twain has stated the basic moral issue centering around Negroes and the white American's democratic ethics. It dramatizes as well the highest point of tension generated by the clash between the direct, human relationships of the frontier and the abstract, inhuman, market-dominated relationships fostered by the rising middle class—which in Twain's day was already compromising dangerously with the most inhuman aspects of the defeated slave system. And just as politically these forces reached their sharpest tension in the outbreak of the Civil War, in *Huckleberry Finn* (both the boy and the novel) their human implications come to sharpest focus around the figure of the Negro.

Huckleberry Finn knew, as did Mark Twain, that Jim was not only a slave but a human being, a man who in some ways was to be envied, and who expressed his essential humanity in his desire for freedom, his will to possess his own labor, in his loyalty and capacity for friendship and in his love for his wife and child. Yet Twain, though guilty of the sentimentality common to humorists, does not idealize the slave. Jim is drawn in all his ignorance and superstition, with his good traits and his bad. He, like all men, is ambiguous, limited in circumstance but not in possibility. And it will be noted that when Huck makes his decision he identifies himself with Jim and accepts the judgment of his superego—that internalized representative of the community—that his action is evil. Like Prometheus, who for mankind stole fire from the gods, he embraces the evil implicit in his act in order to affirm his belief in humanity. Jim, therefore, is not simply a slave, he is a symbol of humanity, and in freeing Jim, Huck makes a bid to free himself of the conventionalized evil taken for civilization by the town.

This conception of the Negro as a symbol of Man—the reversal of what he represents in most contemporary thought—was organic to nineteenth-century literature. It occurs not only in Twain but in Emerson, Thoreau, Whitman and Melville (whose symbol of evil, incidentally was white), all of whom were men publicly involved in various forms of deeply personal rebellion. And while the Negro and the color black were associated with the concept of evil and ugliness far back in the Christian era, the Negro's emergence as a symbol of value came, I believe, with Rationalism and the rise of the romantic individual of the eighteenth century. This, perhaps, because the romantic was in revolt against the old moral authority, and if he suffered a sense of guilt, his passion for personal freedom was such that he was willing to accept evil (a tragic attitude) even to identifying himself with the "noble slave"—who symbolized the darker, unknown potential side of his personality, that underground side, turgid with possibility, which might, if given a chance, toss a fistful of mud into the sky and create a "shining star."

Even that prototype of the bourgeois, Robinson Crusoe, stopped to speculate as to his slave's humanity. And the rising American industrialists of the late nineteenth-century were to rediscover what their European counterparts had learned a century before: that the good man Friday was as sound an investment for Crusoe morally as he was economically, for not only did Friday allow Crusoe to achieve himself by working for him, but by functioning as a living scapegoat to contain Crusoe's guilt over breaking with the institutions and authority of the past, he made it possible to exploit even his guilt economically. The man was one of the first missionaries.

Mark Twain was alive to this irony and refused such an easy (and dangerous) way out. Huck Finn's acceptance of the evil implicit in his "emancipation" of Jim represents Twain's acceptance of his personal responsibility in the condition of society. This was the tragic face behind his comic mask.

But by the twentieth century this attitude of tragic responsibility had disappeared from our literature along with that broad conception of democracy which vitalized the work of our greatest writers. After Twain's compelling image of black and white fraternity the Negro generally disappears from fiction as a rounded human being. And if already in Twain's time a novel which was optimistic concerning a democracy which would include all men could not escape being banned from public libraries, by our day his great drama of interracial fraternity had become, for most Americans at least, an amusing boy's story and nothing more. But, while a boy, Huck Finn has become by the sommersault motion of what William Empson terms "pastoral," an embodiment of the heroic, and an exponent of humanism. Indeed, the historical and artistic justification for his adolescence lies in the fact that Twain was depicting a transitional period of American life; its artistic justification is that adolescence is the time of the "great confusion" during which both individuals and nations flounder between accepting and rejecting the responsibilities of adulthood. Accordingly, Huck's relationship to Jim, the river, and all they symbolize, is that of a humanist; in his relation to the community he is an individualist. He embodies the two major conflicting drives operating in nineteenth-century America. And if humanism is man's basic attitude toward a social order which he accepts, and individualism his basic attitude toward one he rejects, one might say that Twain, by allowing these two attitudes to argue dialectically in his work of art, was as highly moral an artist as he was a believer in democracy, and vice versa.

History, however, was to bring an ironic reversal to the direction which Huckleberry Finn chose, and by our day the divided ethic of the community had won out. In contrast with Twain's humanism, individualism was thought to be the only tenable attitude for the artist.

Thus we come to Ernest Hemingway, one of the two writers whose art is based most solidly upon Mark Twain's language, and one who perhaps has done most to extend Twain's technical influence upon our fiction. It was Hemingway who pointed out that all modern American writing springs from *Huckleberry Finn*. (One might add here that equally as much of it derives from Hemingway himself.) But by the twenties the element of rejection implicit in Twain had become so dominant an attitude of the

American writer that Hemingway goes on to warn us to "stop where the Nigger Jim is stolen from the boys. That is the real end. The rest is just cheating."

So thoroughly had the Negro, both as man and as a symbol of man, been pushed into the underground of the American conscience that Hemingway missed completely the structural, symbolic and moral necessity for that part of the plot in which the boys rescue Jim. Yet it is precisely this part which gives the novel its significance. Without it, except as a boy's tale, the novel is meaningless. Yet Hemingway, a great artist in his own right, speaks as a victim of that culture of which he is himself so critical, for by his time that growing rift in the ethical fabric pointed out by Twain had become completely sundered—snagged upon the irrepressible moral reality of the Negro. Instead of the single democratic ethic for every man, there now existed two: one, the idealized ethic of the Constitution and the Declaration of Independence, reserved for white men; and the other, the pragmatic ethic designed for Negroes and other minorities, which took the form of discrimination. Twain had dramatized the conflict leading to this division in its earlier historical form, but what was new here was that such a moral division, always a threat to the sensitive man, was ignored by the artist in the most general terms, as when Hemingway rails against the rhetoric of the First World War.

Hemingway's blindness to the moral values of *Huckleberry Finn* despite his sensitivity to its technical aspects duplicated the one-sided vision of the twenties. Where Twain, seeking for what Melville called "the common continent of man," drew upon the rich folklore of the frontier (not omitting the Negro's) in order to "Americanize" his idiom, thus broadening his stylistic appeal, Hemingway was alert only to Twain's technical discoveries—the flexible colloquial language, the sharp naturalism, the thematic potentialities of adolescence. Thus what for Train was a means to a moral end became for Hemingway an end in itself. And just as the trends toward technique for the sake of technique and production for the sake of the market lead to the neglect of the human need out of which they spring, so do they lead in literature to a marvelous technical virtuosity won at the expense of a gross insensitivity to fraternal values.

It is not accidental that the disappearance of the human Negro from our fiction coincides with the disappearance of deep-probing doubt and a sense of evil. Not that doubt in some form was not always present, as the works of the lost generation, the muckrakers and the proletarian writers make very clear. But it is a shallow doubt, which seldom turns inward upon the writer's own values; almost always it focuses outward, upon some scapegoat with which he is seldom able to identify himself as Huck Finn identified himself with the scoundrels who stole Jim and with Jim himself. This particular naturalism explored everything except the nature of man.

And when the artist would no longer conjure with the major moral problem in American life, he was defeated as a manipulator of profound social passions. In the United States, as in Europe, the triumph of industrialism had repelled the artist with the blatant hypocrisy between its ideals and its acts. But while in Europe the writer became the most profound critic of these matters, in our country he either turned away or was at best half-hearted in his opposition—perhaps because any profound probing of human values, both within himself and within society, would have brought him face to face with the rigidly tabooed subject of the Negro. And now the tradition of avoiding the moral struggle had led not only to the artistic segregation of the Negro but to the segregation of real fraternal, i.e., democraic, values.

The hard-boiled school represented by Hemingway, for instance, is usually spoken of as a product of World War I disillusionment, yet it was as much the product of a tradition which arose even before the Civil War—that tradition of intellectual evasion for which Thoreau criticized Emerson in regard to the Fugitive Slave Law, and which had been growing swiftly since the failure of the ideals in whose name the Civil War was fought. The failure to resolve the problem symbolized by the Negro has contributed indirectly to the dispossession of the artist in several ways. By excluding our largest minority from the democratic process, the United States weakened all national symbols and rendered sweeping public rituals which would dramatize the American dream impossible; it robbed the artist of a body of unassailable public beliefs upon which he could base his art; it deprived him of a personal faith in the ideals upon which society supposedly rested; and it provided him with no tragic mood indigenous to his society upon which he could erect a tragic art. The result was that he responded with an attitude of rejection, which he expressed as artistic individualism. But too often both his rejection and individualism were narrow; seldom was he able to transcend the limitations of pragmatic reality, and the quality of moral imagination—the fountainhead of great art—was atrophied within him.

Malraux has observed that contemporary American writing is the only important literature not created by intellectuals, and that the creators possess "neither the relative historical culture, nor the love of ideas (a prerogative of professors in the United States)" of comparable Europeans. And is there not a connection between the non-intellectual aspects of this writing (though many of the writers are far more intellectual than they admit or than Malraux would suspect) and its creators' rejection of broad social responsibility, between its non-concern with ideas and its failure to project characters who grasp the broad sweep of American life, or who even attempt to state its fundamental problems? And has not this affected the types of heroes of his fiction, is it not a partial explanation of why it has created no characters possessing broad insight into their situations or the emotional, psychological and intellectual complexity which would allow them to possess and articulate a truly democratic world view?

It is instructive that Hemingway, born into a civilization characterized by violence, should seize upon the ritualized violence of the culturally distant Spanish bullfight as a laboratory for developing his style, For it was, for Americans, an amoral violence (though not for the Spaniards) which he was seeking. Otherwise he might have studied that ritual of violence closer to home, that ritual in which the sacrifice is that of a human scapegoat, the lynching bee. Certainly this rite is not confined to the rope as agency, nor to the South as scene, nor even to the Negro as victim.

But let us not confuse the conscious goals of twentieth-century fiction with those of the nineteenth century, let us take it on its own terms. Artists such as Hemingway were seeking a technical perfection rather than moral insight. (Or should we say that theirs was a morality of technique?) They desired a style stripped of unessentials, one that would appeal without resorting to what was considered worn-out rhetoric, or best of all without any rhetoric whatsoever. It was felt that through the default of the powers that ruled society the artist had as his major task the "pictorial presentation of the evaluation of a personal problem." Instead of recreating and extending the national myth as he did this, the writer now restricted himself to elaborating his personal myth. And although naturalist in his general style, he was not interested, like Balzac, in depicting a society, or even, like Mark Twain, in portraying the moral situation of a nation. Rather he was engaged in working out a personal problem through the evocative, emotion-charged images and ritual-therapy available through the manipulation of art forms. And while art was still an instrument of freedom, it was now mainly the instrument of a questionable personal freedom for the artist, which too often served to enforce the "unfreedom" of the reader.

This because it is not within the province of the artist to determine whether his work is social or not. Art by its nature is social. And while the artist can determine within a certain narrow scope the type of social effect he wishes his art to create, here his will is definitely limited. Once introduced into society, the work of art begins to pulsate with those meanings, emotions, ideas brought to it by its audience and over which the artist has but limited control. The irony of the "lost generation" writers is that while disavowing a social role it was the fate of their works to perform a social function which re-enforced those very social values which they most violently opposed. How could this be? Because in its genesis the work of art, like the stereotype, is personal; psychologically it represents the socialization of some profoundly personal problem involving

guilt (often symbolic murder—parricide, fratricide—incest, homosexual-
ity, all problems at the base of personality) from which by expressing them
along with other elements (images, memories, emotions, ideas) he seeks
transcendence. To be effective as personal fulfillment, if it is to be more
than dream, the work of art must simultaneously evoke images of reality
and give them formal organization. And it must, since the individual's
emotions are formed in society, shape them into socially meaningful pat-
terns (even Surrealism and Dadaism depended upon their initiates). Nor,
as we can see by comparing literature with reportage, is this all. The work
of literature differs basically from reportage not merely in its presentation
of a pattern of events, nor in its concern with emotion (for a report might
well be an account of highly emotional events), but in the deep personal
necessity which cries fullthroated in the work of art and which seeks transcendence in the form of ritual.

Malcolm Cowley, on the basis of the rites which he believes to be the
secret dynamic of Hemingway's work, has identified him with Poe, Haw-
thorne and Melville, "the haunted and nocturnal writers," he calls them,
"the men who dealt with images that were symbols of an inner world." In
Hemingway's works, he writes, "we can recognize rites of animal sacrifice
. . . of sexual union . . . of conversion . . . and of symbolic death and
rebirth." I do not believe, however, that the presence of these rites in
writers like Hemingway is as important as the fact that here, beneath the
dead-pan prose, the cadences of understatement, the anti-intellectualism,
the concern with every "fundamental" of man except that which distinguishes him from the animal—that here is the twentieth-century form of
that magical rite which during periods of great art has been to a large
extent public and explicit. Here is the literary form by which the personal
guilt of the pulverized individual of our rugged era is expatiated: not
through his identification with the guilty acts of an Oedipus, a Macbeth or
a Medea, by suffering their agony and loading his sins upon their "strong
and passionate shoulders," but by being gored with a bull, hooked with
a fish, impaled with a grasshopper on a fishhook; not by identifying himself with human heroes, but with those who are indeed defeated.

On the social level this writing performs a function similar to that of
the stereotypes: it conditions the reader to accept the less worthy values
of society, and it serves to justify and absolve our sins of social irresponsibility. With unconscious irony it advises stoic acceptance of those conditions of life which it so accurately describes and which it pretends to
reject. And when I read the early Hemignway I seem to be in the presence
of Huckleberry Finn who, instead of identifying himself with humanity
and attempting to steal Jim free, chose to write the letter which sent him
back into slavery. So that now he is a Huck full of regret and nostalgia,

suffering a sense of guilt that fills even his noondays with nightmares, and against which, like a terrified child avoiding the cracks in the sidewalk, he seeks protection through the compulsive minor rituals of his prose.

The major difference between nineteenth- and twentieth-century writers is not in the latter's lack of personal rituals—a property of all fiction worthy of being termed literature—but in the social effect aroused within their respective readers. Melville's ritual (and his rhetoric) was based upon materials that were more easily available, say, than Hemingway's. They represented a blending of his personal myth with universal myths as traditional as any used by Shakespeare or the Bible, while until *For Whom the Bell Tolls* Hemingway's was weighted on the personal side. The difference in terms of perspective of belief is that Melville's belief could still find a public object. Whatever else his works were "about" they also managed to be about democracy. But by our day the democratic dream had become too shaky a structure to support the furious pressures of the artist's doubt. And as always when the belief which nurtures a great social myth declines, large sections of society become prey to superstition. For man without myth is Othello with Desdemona gone: chaos descends, faith vanishes and superstitions prowl in the mind.

Hard-boiled writing is said to appeal through its presentation of sheer fact, rather than through rhetoric. The writer puts nothing down but what he pragmatically "knows." But actually one "fact" itself—which in literature must be presented simultaneously as image and as event—became a rhetorical unit. And the symbolic ritual which has set off the "fact"—that is, the fact unorganized by vital social myths (which might incorporate the findings of science and still contain elements of mystery)—is the rite of superstition. The superstitious individual responds to the capricious event, the fact that seems to explode in his face through blind fatality. For it is the creative function of myth to protect the individual from the irrational, and since it is here in the realm of the irrational that, impervious to science, the stereotype grows, we see that the Negro stereotype is really an image of the unorganized, irrational forces of American life, forces through which, by projecting them in forms of images of an easily dominated minority, the white individual seeks to be at home in the vast unknown world of America. Perhaps the object of the stereotype is not so much to crush the Negro as to console the white man.

Certainly there is justification for this view when we consider the work of William Faulkner. In Faulkner most of the relationships which we have pointed out between the Negro and contemporary writing come to focus: the social and the personal, the moral and the technical, the nineteenth-century emphasis upon morality and the modern accent upon the personal myth. And on the strictly literary level he is prolific and complex enough to speak for those Southern writers who are aggressively anti-Negro and for those younger writers who appear most sincerely interested in depicting the Negro as a rounded human being. What is more, he is the greatest artist the South has produced. While too complex to be given more than a glance in these notes, even a glance is more revealing of what lies back of the distortion of the Negro in modern writing than any attempt at a group survey might be.

Faulkner's attitude is mixed. Taking his cue from the Southern mentality in which the Negro is often dissociated into a malignant stereotype (the bad nigger) on the one hand and a benign stereotype (the good nigger) on the other, most often Faulkner presents characters embodying both. The dual function of this dissociation seems to be that of avoiding moral pain and thus to justify the South's racial code. But since such a social order harms whites no less than blacks, the sensitive Southerner, the artist, is apt to feel its effects acutely—and within the deepest levels of his personality. For not only is the social division forced upon the Negro by the ritualized ethic of discrimination, but upon the white man by the strictly enforced set of anti-Negro taboos. The conflict is always with him. Indeed, so rigidly has the recognition of Negro humanity been tabooed that the white Southerner is apt to associate any form of personal rebellion with the Negro. So that for the Southern artist the Negro becomes a symbol of his personal rebellion, his guilt and his repression of it. The Negro is thus a compelling object of fascination, and this we see very clearly in Faulkner.

Sometimes in Faulkner the Negro is simply a villain, but by an unconsciously ironic transvaluation his villainy consists, as with Loosh in *The Unvanquished*, of desiring his freedom. Or again the Negro appears benign, as with Ringo, of the same novel, who uses his talent not to seek personal freedom but to remain the loyal and resourceful retainer. Not that I criticize loyalty in itself, but that loyalty given where one's humanity is unrecognized seems a bit obscene. And yet in Faulkner's story, "The Bear," he brings us as close to the moral implication of the Negro as Twain or Melville. In the famous "difficult" fourth section, which Malcolm Cowley advises us to skip very much as Hemingway would have us skip the end of *Huckleberry Finn*, we find an argument in progress in which one voice (that of a Southern abolitionist) seeks to define Negro humanity against the other's enumeration of those stereotypes which many Southerners believe to be the Negro's basic traits. Significantly the mentor of the young hero of this story, a man of great moral stature, is socially a Negro.

Indeed, through his many novels and short stories, Faulkner fights out the moral problem which was repressed after the nineteenth century, and it was shocking for some to discover that for all his concern with the South, Faulkner was actually seeking out the nature of man. Thus we must turn to him for that continuity of moral purpose which made for the greatness of our classics. As for the Negro minority, he has been more willing perhaps than any other artist to start with the stereotype, accept it as true, and then seek out the human truth which it hides. Perhaps his is the example for our writers to follow, for in his work technique has been put once more to the task of creating value.

Which leaves these final things to be said. First, that this is meant as no plea for white writers to define Negro humanity, but to recognize the broader aspects of their own. Secondly, Negro writers and those of the other minorities have their own task of contributing to the total image of the American by depicting the experience of their own groups. Certainly theirs is the task of defining Negro humanity, as this can no more be accomplished by others than freedom, which must be won again and again each day, can be conferred upon another. A people must define itself, and minorities have the responsibility of having their ideals and images recognized as part of the composite image which is that of the still forming American people.

The other thing to be said is that while it is unlikely that American writing will ever retrace the way to the nineteenth century, it might be worthwhile to point out that for all its technical experimentation it is nevertheless an ethical instrument, and as such it might well exercise some choice in the kind of ethic it prefers to support. The artist is no freer than the society in which he lives, and in the United States the writers who stereotype or ignore the Negro and other minorities in the final analysis stereotype and distort their own humanity. Mark Twain knew that in *his* America humanity masked its face with blackness.

Richard Wright
(1908–1960)

WRIGHT was born near Natchez, Mississippi. He wrote for *New Masses* and *The Daily Worker* before he moved to Paris in 1946. His major works are *Uncle Tom's Children* (1938), *Native Son* (1940), *Black Boy* (1945), and *White Man, Listen!* (1957).

"The Ethics of Living Jim Crow," an autobiographical essay, is the opening section of *Uncle Tom's Children*.

THE ETHICS OF LIVING JIM CROW
An Autobiographical Sketch

1

My first lesson in how to live as a Negro came when I was quite small. We were living in Arkansas. Our house stood behind the railroad tracks. Its skimpy yard was paved with black cinders. Nothing green ever grew in that yard. The only touch of green we could see was far away, beyond the tracks, over where the white folks lived. But cinders were good enough for me and I never missed the green growing things. And anyhow cinders were fine weapons. You could always have a nice hot war with huge black cinders. All you had to do was crouch behind the brick pillars of a house with your hands full of gritty ammunition. And the first woolly black head you saw pop out from behind another row of pillars was your target. You tried your very best to knock it off. It was great fun.

I never fully realized the appalling disadvantages of a cinder environment till one day the gang to which I belonged found itself engaged in a war with the white boys who lived beyond the tracks. As usual we laid down our cinder barrage thinking that this would wipe the white boys out. But they replied with a steady bombardment of broken bottles. We doubled our cinder barrage, but they hid behind trees, hedges, and the sloping embankments of their lawns. Having no such fortifications, we retreated to the brick pillars of our homes. During the retreat a broken milk bottle caught me behind the ear, opening a deep gash which bled profusely. The sight of blood pouring over my face completely demoralized our ranks. My fellow-combatants left me standing paralyzed in the center of the yard, and scurried for their homes. A kind neighbor saw me and rushed me to a doctor, who took three stitches in my neck.

I sat brooding on my front steps, nursing my wound and waiting for my mother to come from work. I felt that a grave injustice had been done me. It was all right to throw cinders. The greatest harm a cinder could do was leave a bruise. But broken bottles were dangerous; they left you cut, bleeding, and helpless.

When night fell, my mother came from the white folks' kitchen. I raced down the street to meet her. I could just feel in my bones that she would understand. I knew she would tell me exactly what to do next time. I grabbed her hand and babbled out the whole story. She examined my wound, then slapped me.

"How come yuh didn't hide?" she asked me. "How come yuh awways fightin'?"

I was outraged, and bawled. Between sobs I told her that I didn't have any trees or hedges to hid behind. There wasn't a thing I could have used as a trench. And you couldn't throw very far when you were hiding behind the brick pillars of a house. She grabbed a barrel stave, dragged me home, stripped me naked, and beat me till I had a fever of one hundred and two. She would smack my rump with the stave, and, while the skin was still smarting, impart to me gems of Jim Crow wisdom. I was never to throw cinders any more. I was never to fight any more wars. I was never, never, under any conditions, to fight *white* folks again. And they were absolutely right in clouting me with the broken milk bottle. Didn't I know she was working hard every day in the hot kitchens of the white folks to make money to take care of me? When was I ever going to learn to be a good boy? She couldn't be bothered with my fights. She finished by telling me that I ought to be thankful to God as long as I lived that they didn't kill me.

All that night I was delirious and could not sleep. Each time I closed my eyes I saw monstrous white faces suspended from the ceiling, leering at me.

From that time on, the charm of my cinder yard was gone. The green trees, the trimmed hedges, the cropped lawns grew very meaningful, became a symbol. Even today when I think of white folks, the hard, sharp outlines of white houses surrounded by trees, lawns, and hedges are present somewhere in the background of my mind. Through the years they grew into an overreaching symbol of fear.

It was a long time before I came in close contact with white folks again. We moved from Arkansas to Mississippi. Here we had the good fortune not to live behind the railroad tracks, or close to white neighborhoods. We lived in the very heart of the local Black Belt. There were black churches and black preachers; there were black schools and black teachers; black groceries and black clerks. In fact, everything was so solidly black that for a long time I did not even think of white folks, save in remote and vague terms. But this could not last forever. As one grows older one eats more. One's clothing costs more. When I finished grammar school I had to go to work. My mother could no longer feed and clothe me on her cooking job.

There is but one place where a black boy who knows no trade can get a job, and that's where the houses and faces are white, where the trees, lawns, and hedges are green. My first job was with an optical company in Jackson, Mississippi. The morning I applied I stood straight and neat before the boss, answering all his questions with sharp yessirs and nosirs. I was very careful to pronounce my *sirs* distinctly, in order that he might know that I was polite, that I knew where I was, and that I knew he was a *white* man. I wanted that job badly.

He looked me over as though he were examining a prize poodle. He questioned me closely about my schooling, being particularly insistent about how much mathematics I had had. He seemed very pleased when I told him I had had two years of algebra.

"Boy, how would you like to try to learn something around here?" he asked me.

"I'd like it fine, sir," I said, happy. I had visions of "working my way up." Even Negroes have those visions.

"All right," he said. "Come on."

I followed him to the small factory.

"Pease," he said to a white man of about thirty-five, "this is Richard. He's going to work for us."

Pease looked at me and nodded.

I was then taken to a white boy of about seventeen.

"Morrie, this is Richard, who's going to work for us."

"Whut yuh sayin' there, boy!" Morrie boomed at me.

"Fine!" I answered.

The boss instructed these two to help me, teach me, give me jobs to do, and let me learn what I could in my spare time.

My wages were five dollars a week.

I worked hard, trying to please. For the first month I got along O.K. Both Pease and Morrie seemed to like me. But one thing was missing. And I kept thinking about it. I was not learning anything and nobody was volunteering to help me. Thinking they had forgotten that I was to learn something about the mechanics of grinding lenses, I asked Morrie one day to tell me about the work. He grew red.

"Whut yuh tryin' t' do, nigger, get smart?" he asked.

"Naw; I ain' tryin' t' git smart," I said.

"Well, don't if yuh know what's good for yuh!"

I was puzzled. Maybe he just doesn't want to help me, I thought. I went to Pease.

"Say, are yuh crazy, you black bastard?" Pease asked me, his gray eyes growing hard.

I spoke out, reminding him that the boss had said I was to be given a chance to learn something.

"Nigger, you think you're *white*, don't you?"

"Naw, sir!"

"Well, you're acting mighty like it!"

"But, Mr. Pease, the boss said . . ."

Pease shook his fist in my face.

"This is a *white* man's work around here, and you better watch yourself!"

From then on they changed toward me. They said good-morning no more. When I was just a bit slow in performing some duty, I was called a lazy black son-of-a-bitch.

Once I thought of reporting all this to the boss. But the mere idea of what would happen to me if Pease and Morrie should learn that I had "snitched" stopped me. And after all the boss was a white man, too. What was the use?

The climax came at noon one summer day. Pease called me to his workbench. To get to him I had to go between two narrow benches and stand with my back against a wall.

"Yes, sir," I said.

"Richard, I want to ask you something," Pease began pleasantly, not looking up from his work.

"Yes, sir," I said again.

Morrie came over, blocking the narrow passage between the benches. He folded his arms, staring at me solemnly.

I looked from one to the other, sensing that something was coming.

Pease looked up and spoke very slowly.

"Richard, *Mr.* Morrie here tells me you called me *Pease*."

I stiffened. A void seemed to open up in me. I knew this was the showdown.

He meant that I had failed to call him Mr. Pease. I looked at Morrie. He was gripping a steel bar in his hands. I opened my mouth to speak, to protest, to assure Pease that I had never called him simply *Pease*, and that I had never had any intentions of doing so, when Morrie grabbed me by the collar, ramming my head against the wall.

"Now, be careful, nigger!" snarled Morrie, baring his teeth. "I heard yuh call 'im *Pease!* 'N' if yuh say yuh didn't yuh're callin' me a *lie*, see?" He waved the steel bar threateningly.

If I had said: No, sir, Mr. Pease, I never called you *Pease*, I would have been automatically calling Morrie a liar. And if I had said: Yes, sir, Mr. Pease, I called you *Pease*, I would have been pleading guilty to having uttered the worst insult that a Negro can utter to a southern white man. I stood hesitating, trying to frame a neutral reply.

"Richard, I asked you a question!" said Pease. Anger was creeping into his voice.

"I don't remember calling you *Pease*, Mr. Pease," I said cautiously. "And if I did, I sure didn't mean . . ."

"You black son-of-a-bitch! You called me *Pease*, then!" he spat, slapping me till I bent sideways over a bench. Morrie was on top of me, demanding:

"Didn't yuh call 'im *Pease?* If yuh say yuh didn't, I'll rip yo' gut string loose with this bar, yuh black granny dodger! Yuh can't call a white man a lie 'n' get erway with it, you black son-of-a-bitch!"

I wilted. I begged them not to bother me. I knew what they wanted. They wanted me to leave.

"I'll leave," I promised. "I'll leave right *now*."

They gave me a minute to get out of the factory. I was warned not to show up again, or tell the boss.

I went.

When I told the folks at home what had happened, they called me a fool. They told me that I must never again attempt to exceed my boundaries. When you are working for white folks, they said, you got to "stay in your place" if you want to keep working.

2

My Jim Crow education continued on my next job, which was portering in a clothing store. One morning, while polishing brass out front, the boss and his twenty-year old son got out of their car and half dragged and half kicked a Negro woman into the store. A policeman standing at the corner looked on, twirling his night-stick. I watched out of the corner of my eye, never slackening the strokes of my chamois upon the brass. After a few minutes, I heard shrill screams coming from the rear of the store. Later the woman stumbled out, bleeding, crying, and holding her stomach. When she reached the end of the block, the policeman grabbed her and accused her of being drunk. Silently, I watched him throw her into a patrol wagon.

When I went to the rear of the store, the boss and his son were washing their hands at the sink. They were chuckling. The floor was bloody and strewn with wisps of hair and clothing. No doubt I must have appeared pretty shocked, for the boss slapped me reassuringly on the back.

"Boy, that's what we do to niggers when they don't want to pay their bills," he said, laughing.

His son looked at me and grinned.

"Here, hava cigarette," he said.

Not knowing what to do, I took it. He lit his and held the match for me. This was a gesture of kindness, indicating that even if they had beaten the poor old woman, they would not beat me if I knew enough to keep my mouth shut.

"Yes, sir," I said, and asked no questions.

After they had gone, I sat on the edge of a packing box and stared at the bloody floor till the cigarette went out.

That day at noon, while eating in a hamburger joint, I told my fellow Negro porters what had happened. No one seemed surprised. One fellow, after swallowing a huge bite, turned to me and asked:

"Huh! Is tha' all they did t' her?"

"Yeah. Wasn't tha' enough?" I asked.

"Shucks! Man, she's a lucky bitch!" he said, burying his lips deep into a juicy hamburger. "Hell, it's a wonder they didn't lay her when they got through."

3

I was learning fast, but not quite fast enough. One day, while I was delivering packages in the suburbs, my bicycle tire was punctured. I walked along the hot, dusty road, sweating and leading my bicycle by the handle-bars.

A car slowed at my side.

"What's the matter, boy?" a white man called.

I told him my bicycle was broken and I was walking back to town.

"That's too bad," he said. "Hop on the running board."

He stopped the car. I clutched hard at my bicycle with one hand and clung to the side of the car with the other.

"All set?"

"Yes, sir," I answered. The car started.

It was full of young white men. They were drinking. I watched the flask pass from mouth to mouth.

"Wanna drink, boy?" one asked.

I laughed as the wind whipped my face. Instinctively obeying the freshly planted precepts of my mother, I said:

"Oh, no!"

The words were hardly out of my mouth before I felt something hard and cold smash me between the eyes. It was an empty whisky bottle. I saw stars, and fell backwards from the speeding car into the dust of the road, my feet becoming entangled in the steel spokes of my bicycle. The white men piled out and stood over me.

"Nigger, ain't yuh learned no better sense'n tha' yet?" asked the man who hit me. "Ain' yuh learned t' say *sir* t' a white man yet?"

Dazed, I pulled to my feet. My elbows and legs were bleeding. Fists doubled, the white man advanced, kicking my bicycle out of the way.

"Aw, leave the bastard alone. He's got enough," said one.

They stood looking at me. I rubbed my shins, trying to stop the flow of blood. No doubt they felt a sort of contemptuous pity, for one asked: "Yuh wanna ride t' town now, nigger? Yuh reckon yuh know enough t' ride now?"

"I wanna walk," I said, simply.

Maybe it sounded funny. They laughed.

"Well, walk, yuh black son-of-a-bitch!"

When they left they comforted me with:

"Nigger, yuh sho better be damn glad it wuz us yuh talked t' tha' way. Yuh're a lucky bastard, 'cause if you'd said tha' t' somebody else, yuh might've been a dead nigger now."

4

Negroes who have lived South know the dread of being caught alone upon the streets in white neighborhoods after the sun has set. In such a simple situation as this the plight of the Negro in America is graphically symbolized. While white strangers may be in these neighborhoods trying to get home, they can pass unmolested. But the color of a Negro's skin makes him easily recognizable, makes him suspect, converts him into a defenseless target.

Late one Saturday night I made some deliveries in a white neighborhood. I was pedaling my bicycle back to the store as fast as I could, when a police car, swerving toward me, jammed me into the curbing.

"Get down and put up your hands!" the policemen ordered.

I did. They climbed out of the car, guns drawn, faces set, and advanced slowly.

"Keep still!" they ordered.

I reached my hands higher. They searched my pockets and packages. They seemed dissatisfied when they could find nothing incriminating. Finally, one of them said:

"Boy, tell your boss not to send you out in white neighborhoods after sundown."

As usual, I said:

"Yes, sir."

5

My next job was a hall-boy in a hotel. Here my Jim Crow education broadened and deepened. When the bell-boys were busy, I was often called to assist them. As many of the rooms in the hotel were occupied by prostitutes, I was constantly called to carry them liquor and cigarettes. These women were nude most of the time. They did not bother about clothing, even for bell-boys. When you went into their rooms, you were supposed to take their nakedness for granted, as though it startled you no more than a blue vase or a red rug. Your presence awoke in them no sense of shame, for you were not regarded as human. If they were alone, you could steal sidelong glimpses at them. But if they were receiving men, not a flicker of your eyelids could show. I remember one incident vividly. A new woman, a huge, snowy-skinned blonde, took a room on my floor. I was sent to wait upon her. She was in bed with a thick-set man; both were nude and uncovered. She said she wanted some liquor and slid out of bed and waddled across the floor to get her money from a dresser drawer. I watched her.

"Nigger, what in hell you looking at?" the white man asked me, raising himself upon his elbows.

"Nothing," I answered, looking miles deep into the blank wall of the room.

"Keep your eyes where they belong, if you want to be healthy!" he said.

"Yes, sir."

6

One of the bell-boys I knew in this hotel was keeping steady company with one of the Negro maids. Out of a clear sky the police descended upon his home and arrested him, accusing him of bastardy. The poor boy swore he had had no intimate relations with the girl. Nevertheless, they forced him to marry her. When the child arrived, it was found to be much lighter in complexion than either of the two supposedly legal parents. The white men around the hotel made a great joke of it. They spread the rumor that some white cow must have scared the poor girl while she was carrying the baby. If you were in their presence when this explanation was offered, you were supposed to laugh.

7

One of the bell-boys was caught in bed with a white prostitute. He was castrated and run out of town. Immediately after this all bell-boys and hall-boys were called together and warned. We were given to understand that the boy who had been castrated was a "mighty, mighty lucky bastard." We were impressed with the fact that next time the management of the hotel would not be responsible for the lives of "trouble-makin' niggers." We were silent.

8

One night, just as I was about to go home, I met one of the Negro maids. She lived in my direction, and we fell in to walk part of the way home together. As we passed the white night-watchman, he slapped the maid on her buttock. I turned around, amazed. The watchman looked at me with a long, hard, fixed-under stare. Suddenly he pulled his gun and asked:

"Nigger, don't yuh like it?"

I hesitated.

"I asked yuh don't yuh like it?" he asked again, stepping forward.

"Yes, sir," I mumbled.

"Talk like it, then!"

"Oh, yes, sir!" I said with as much heartiness as I could muster.

Outside, I walked ahead of the girl, ashamed to face her. She caught up with me and said:

"Don't be a fool! Yuh couldn't help it!"

This watchman boasted of having killed two Negroes in self-defense.

Yet, in spite of all this, the life of the hotel ran with an amazing smoothness. It would have been impossible for a stranger to detect anything. The maids, the hall-boys, and the bell-boys were all smiles. They had to be.

9

I had learned my Jim Crow lessons so thoroughly that I kept the hotel job till I left Jackson for Memphis. It so happened that while in Memphis I applied for a job at a branch of the optical company. I was hired. And for some reason, as long as I worked there, they never brought my past against me.

Here my Jim Crow education assumed quite a different form. It was no longer brutally cruel, but subtly cruel. Here I learned to lie, to steal, to dissemble. I learned to play that dual role which every Negro must play if he wants to eat and live.

For example, it was almost impossible to get a book to read. It was assumed that after a Negro had imbibed what scanty schooling the state furnished he had no further need for books. I was always borrowing books from men on the job. One day I mustered enough courage to ask one of the men to let me get books from the library in his name. Surprisingly, he consented. I cannot help but think that he consented because he was a Roman Catholic and felt a vague sympathy for Negroes, being himself an object of hatred. Armed with a library card, I obtained books in the following manner: I would write a note to the librarian, saying: "Please let this nigger boy have the following books." I would then sign it with the white man's name.

When I went to the library, I would stand at the desk, hat in hand, looking as unbookish as possible. When I received the books desired I would take them home. If the books listed in the note happened to be out, I would sneak into the lobby and forge a new one. I never took any chances guessing with the white librarian about what the fictitious white man would want to read. No doubt if any of the white patrons had suspected that some of the volumes they enjoyed had been in the home of a Negro, they would not have tolerated it for an instant.

The factory force of the optical company in Memphis was much larger than that in Jackson, and more urbanized. At least they liked to talk, and would engage the Negro help in conversation whenever possible. By this means I found that many subjects were taboo from the white man's point of view. Among the topics they did not like to discuss with Negroes were the following: American white women; the Ku Klux Klan; France, and how Negro soldiers fared while there; French women; Jack Johnson; the entire northern part of the United States; the Civil War; Abraham Lincoln; U. S. Grant; General Sherman; Catholics; the Pope; Jews; the Republican Party; slavery; social equality; Communism; Socialism; the 13th and 14th Amendments to the Constitution; or any topic calling for positive knowledge or manly self-assertion on the part of the Negro. The most accepted topics were sex and religion.

There were many times when I had to exercise a great deal of ingenuity to keep out of trouble. It is a southern custom that all men must take off their hats when they enter an elevator. And especially did this apply to us blacks with rigid force. One day I stepped into an elevator with my arms full of packages. I was forced to ride with my hat on. Two white men stared at me coldly. Then one of them very kindly lifted my hat and placed it upon my armful of packages. Now the most accepted response for a Negro to make under such circumstances is to look at the white men out of the corner of his eye and grin. To have said: "Thank you!" would have made the white man *think* that you *thought* you were receiving from him a personal service. For such an act I have seen Negroes take a blow in the mouth. Finding the first alternative distasteful, and the second dangerous, I hit upon an acceptable course of action which fell safely between these two poles. I immediately—no sooner than my hat was lifted —pretended that my packages were about to spill, and appeared deeply distressed with keeping them in my arms. In this fashion I evaded having to acknowledge his service, and in spite of adverse circumstances, salvaged a slender shred of personal pride.

How do Negroes feel about the way they have to live? How do they discuss it when alone among themselves? I think this question can be answered in a single sentence. A friend of mine who ran an elevator once told me:

"Lawd, man! Ef it wuzn't fer them polices 'n' them ol' lynch-mobs, there wouldn't be nothin' but uproar down here!"

James Baldwin
(1924–   )

JAMES BALDWIN was born and grew up in New York City. He lived in Paris for several years. He has won numerous awards and fellowships and is the author of, among other works, *Go Tell It on the Mountain* (1953), *Notes of A Native Son* (1955), *Nobody Knows My Name* (1960), and *The Fire Next Time* (1963).

The essay "Notes of a Native Son" first appeared in *Harper's Magazine* (November 1955) and is reprinted in the book *Notes of a Native Son*.

NOTES OF A NATIVE SON

On the 29th of July, in 1943, my father died. On the same day, a few hours later, his last child was born. Over a month before this, while all our energies were concentrated in waiting for these events, there had been, in Detroit, one of the bloodiest race riots of the century. A few hours after my father's funeral, while he lay in state in the undertaker's chapel, a race riot broke out in Harlem. On the morning of the 3rd of August, we drove my father to the graveyard through a wilderness of smashed plate glass.

The day of my father's funeral had also been my nineteenth birthday. As we drove him to the graveyard, the spoils of injustice, anarchy, discontent, and hatred were all around us. It seemed to me that God himself had devised, to mark my father's end, the most sustained and brutally dissonant of codas. And it seemed to me, too, that the violence which rose all about us as my father left the world had been devised as a corrective for the pride of his eldest son. I had declined to believe in that apocalypse which had been central to my father's vision; very well, life seemed to be saying, here is something that will certaintly pass for an apocalypse until the real thing comes along. I had inclined to be contemptuous of my father for the conditions of his life, for the conditions of our lives. When his life had ended I began to wonder about that life and also, in a new way, to be apprehensive about my own.

I had not known my father very well. We had got on badly, partly because we shared, in our different fashions, the vice of stubborn pride. When he was dead I realized that I had hardly ever spoken to him. When he had been dead a long time I began to wish I had. It seems to be typical of life in America, where opportunities, real and fancied, are thicker than anywhere else on the globe, that the second generation has no time to talk to the first. No one, including my father, seems to have known exactly how old he was, but his mother had been born during slavery. He was of the first generation of free men. He, along with thousands of other Negroes, came North after 1919 and I was part of that generation which had never seen the landscape of what Negroes sometimes call the Old Country.

He had been born in New Orleans and had been a quite young man there during the time that Louis Armstrong, a boy, was running errands for the dives and honky-tonks of what was always presented to me as one of the most wicked of cities—to this day, whenever I think of New Orleans, I also helplessly think of Sodom and Gomorrah. My father never mentioned Louis Armstrong, except to forbid us to play his records; but there was a picture of him on our wall for a long time. One of my father's strongwilled female relatives had placed it there and forbade my father to take it down. He never did, but he eventually maneuvered her out of the house and when, some years later, she was in trouble and near death, he refused to do anything to help her.

He was, I think, very handsome. I gather this from photographs and from my own memories of him, dressed in his Sunday best and on his way to preach a sermon somewhere, when I was little. Handsome, proud, and ingrown, "like a toe-nail," somebody said. But he looked to me, as I grew older, like pictures I had seen of African tribal chieftains: he really should have been naked, with warpaint on and barbaric mementos, standing among spears. He could be chilling in the pulpit and indescribably cruel in his personal life and he was certainly the most bitter man I have ever met; yet it must be said that there was something else in him, buried in him, which lent him his tremendous power and, even, a rather crushing charm. It had something to do with his blackness, I think—he was very black—with his blackness and his beauty, and with the fact that he knew that he was black but did not know that he was beautiful. He claimed to be proud of his blackness but it had also been the cause of much humiliation and it had fixed bleak boundaries to his life. He was not a young man when we were growing up and he had already suffered many kinds of ruin; in his outrageously demanding and protective way he loved his children, who were black like him and menaced, like him; and all these things sometimes showed in his face when he tried, never to my knowledge with any success, to establish contact with any of us. When he took one of his children on his knee to play, the child always became fretful and began to cry; when he tried to help one of us with our homework the absolutely unabating tension which emanated from him caused our minds and our tongues to become paralyzed, so that he, scarcely knowing why, flew into a rage and the child, not knowing why, was punished. If it ever entered his head to bring a surprise home for his children, it was, almost unfailingly, the wrong surprise and even the big watermelons he often brought home on his back in the summertime led to the most appalling scenes. I do not remember, in all those years, that one of his children was ever glad to see him come home. From what I was able to gather of his early life, it seemed that this inability to establish contact with other people had always marked him and had been one of the things which had driven him out of New Orleans. There was something in him, therefore, groping and tentative, which was never expressed and which was buried with him. One saw it most clearly when he was facing new people and hoping to impress them. But he never did, not for long. We went from church to smaller and more improbable church, he found himself in less and less demand as a minister, and by the time he died none of his friends had come to see him for a long time. He had lived and died in an intolerable bitterness of spirit and it frightened me, as we drove him to the graveyard through those unquiet, ruined streets, to see how powerful and overflowing this bitterness could be and to realize that this bitterness now was mine.

When he died I had been away from home for a little over a year. In that year I had had time to become aware of the meaning of all my father's bitter warnings, had discovered the secret of his proudly pursed lips and rigid carriage: I had discovered the weight of white people in the world. I saw that this had been for my ancestors and now would be for me an awful thing to live with and that the bitterness which had helped to kill my father could also kill me.

He had been ill a long time—in the mind, as we now realized, reliving instances of his fantastic intransigence in the new light of his affliction and endeavoring to feel a sorrow for him which never, quite, came true. We had not known that he was being eaten up by paranoia, and the discovery that his cruelty, to our bodies and our minds, had been one of the symptoms of his illness was not, then, enough to enable us to forgive him. The younger children felt, quite simply, relief that he would not be coming home anymore. My mother's observation that it was he, after all, who had kept them alive all these years meant nothing because the problems of keeping children alive are not real for children. The older children felt, with my father gone, that they could invite their friends to the house without fear that their friends would be insulted or, as had sometimes happened with me, being told that their friends were in league with the devil and intended to rob our family of everything we owned. (I didn't fail to wonder, and it made me hate him, what on earth we owned that anybody else would want.)

His illness was beyond all hope of healing before anyone realized that he was ill. He had always been so strange and had lived, like a prophet, in such unimaginably close communion with the Lord that his long silences which were punctuated by moans and hallelujahs and snatches of old songs while he sat at the living-room window never seemed odd to us. It was not until he refused to eat because, he said, his family was trying to poison him that my mother was forced to accept as a fact what had, until then, been only an unwilling suspicion. When he was committed, it was discovered that he had tuberculosis and, as it turned out, the disease of his mind allowed the disease of his body to destroy him. For the doctors could not force him to eat, either, and, though he was fed intravenously, it was clear from the beginning that there was no hope for him.

In my mind's eye I could see him, sitting at the window, locked up in his terrors; hating and fearing every living soul including his children who had betrayed him, too, by reaching towards the world which had despised him. There were nine of us. I began to wonder what it could have felt like for such a man to have had nine children whom he could barely feed. He used to make little jokes about our poverty, which never, of course, seemed very funny to us; they could not have seemed very funny to him, either, or else our all too feeble response to them would never have caused such rages. He spent great energy and achieved, to our chagrin, no small amount of success in keeping us away from the people who surrounded us, people who had all-night rent parties to which we listened when we should have been sleeping, people who cursed and drank and flashed razor blades on Lenox Avenue. He could not understand why, if they had so much energy to spare, they could not use it to make their lives better. He treated almost everybody on our block with a most uncharitable asperity and neither they, nor, of course, their children were slow to reciprocate.

The only white people who came to our house were welfare workers and bill collectors. It was almost always my mother who dealt with them, for my father's temper, which was at the mercy of his pride, was never to be trusted. It was clear that he felt their very presence in his home to be a violation: this was conveyed by his carriage, almost ludicrously stiff, and by his voice, harsh and vindictively polite. When I was around nine or ten I wrote a play which was directed by a young, white schoolteacher, a woman, who then took an interest in me, and gave me books to read and, in order to corroborate my theatrical bent, decided to take me to see what she somewhat tactlessly referred to as "real" plays. Theatergoing was forbidden in our house, but, with the really cruel intuitiveness of a child, I suspected that the color of this woman's skin would carry the day for me. When, at school, she suggested taking me to the theater, I did not, as I might have done if she had been a Negro, find a way of discouraging her, but agreed that she should pick me up at my house one evening. I then, very cleverly, left all the rest to my mother, who suggested to my father, as I knew she would, that it would not be very nice to let such a kind woman make the trip for nothing. Also, since it was a schoolteacher, I imagine that my mother countered the idea of sin with the idea of "education," which word, even with my father, carried a kind of bitter weight. Before the teacher came my father took me aside to ask *why* she was coming, what *interest* she could possibly have in our house, in a boy like me. I said I didn't know but I, too, suggested that it had something to do with education. And I understood that my father was waiting for me to say something—I didn't quite know what; perhaps that I wanted his protection against this teacher and her "education." I said none of these things and the teacher came and we went out. It was clear, during the brief interview in our living room, that my father was agreeing very much against his will and that he would have refused permission if he had dared. The fact that he did not dare caused me to despise him: I had no way of knowing that he was facing in that living room a wholly unprecedented and frightening situation.

Later, when my father had been laid off from his job, this woman became very important to us. She was really a very sweet and generous woman and went to a great deal of trouble to be of help to us, particularly during one awful winter. My mother called her by the highest name she knew: she said she was a "christian." My father could scarcely disagree but during the four or five years of our relatively close association he never trusted her and was always trying to surprise in her open, Midwestern face the genuine, cunningly hidden, and hideous motivation. In later years, particularly when it began to be clear that this "education" of mine was going to lead me to perdition, he became more explicit and warned me that my white friends in high school were not really my friends and that I would see, when I was older, how white people would do anything to keep a Negro down. Some of them could be nice, he admitted, but none of them were to be trusted and most of them were not even nice. The best thing was to have as little to do with them as possible. I did not feel this way and I was certain, in my innocence, that I never would.

But the year which preceded my father's death had made a great change in my life. I had been living in New Jersey, working in defense plants, working and living among southerners, white and black. I knew about the south, of course, and about how southerners treated Negroes and how they expected them to behave, but it had never entered my mind that anyone would look at me and expect *me* to behave that way. I learned in New Jersey that to be a Negro meant, precisely, that one was never looked at but was simply at the mercy of the reflexes the color of one's skin caused in other people. I acted in New Jersey as I had always acted, that is as though I thought a great deal of myself—I had to *act* that way— with results that were, simply, unbelievable. I had scarcely arrived before I had earned the enmity, which was extraordinarily ingenious, of all my superiors and nearly all my co-workers. In the beginning, to make matters worse, I simply did not know what was happening. I did not know what

I had done, and I shortly began to wonder what *anyone* could possibly do, to bring about such unanimous, active, and unbearably vocal hostility. I knew about jim-crow but I had never experienced it. I went to the same self-service restaurant three times and stood with all the Princeton boys before the counter, waiting for a hamburger and coffee; it was always an extraordinarily long time before anything was set before me; but it was not until the fourth visit that I learned that, in fact, nothing had ever been set before me: I had simply picked something up. Negroes were not served there, I was told, and they had been waiting for me to realize that I was always the only Negro present. Once I was told this, I determined to go there all the time. But now they were ready for me and, though some dreadful scenes were subsequently enacted in that restaurant, I never ate there again.

It was the same story all over New Jersey, in bars, bowling alleys, diners, places to live. I was always being forced to leave, silently, or with mutual imprecations. I very shortly became notorious and children giggled behind me when I passed and their elders whispered or shouted—they really believed that I was mad. And it did begin to work on my mind, of course; I began to be afraid to go anywhere and to compensate for this I went places to which I really should not have gone and where, God knows, I had no desire to be. My reputation in town naturally enhanced my reputation at work and my working day became one long series of acrobatics designed to keep me out of trouble. I cannot say that these acrobatics succeeded. It began to seem that the machinery of the organization I worked for was turning over, day and night, with but one aim: to eject me. I was fired once, and contrived, with the aid of a friend from New York, to get back on the payroll; was fired again, and bounced back again. It took a while to fire me for the third time, but the third time took. There were no loopholes anywhere. There was not even any way of getting back inside the gates.

That year in New Jersey lives in my mind as though it were the year during which, having an unsuspected predilection for it, I first contracted some dread, chronic disease, the unfailing symptom of which is a kind of blind fever, a pounding in the skull and fire in the bowels. Once this disease is contracted, one can never be really carefree again, for the fever, without an instant's warning, can recur at any moment. It can wreck more important things than race relations. There is not a Negro alive who does not have this rage in his blood—one has the choice, merely, of living with it consciously or surrendering to it. As for me, this fever has recurred in me, and does, and will until the day I die.

My last night in New Jersey, a white friend from New York took me to the nearest big town, Trenton, to go to the movies and have a few drinks. As it turned out, he also saved me from, at the very least, a violent whipping. Almost every detail of that night stands out very clearly in my memory. I even remember the name of the movie we saw because its title impressed me as being so patly ironical. It was a movie about the German occupation of France, starring Maureen O'Hara and Charles Laughton and called *This Land Is Mine*. I remember the name of the diner we walked into when the movie ended: it was the "American Diner." When we walked in the counterman asked what we wanted and I remember answering with the casual sharpness which had become my habit: "We want a hamburger and a cup of coffee, what do you think we want?" I do not know why, after a year of such rebuffs, I so completely failed to anticipate his answer, which was, of course, "We don't serve Negroes here." This reply failed to discompose me, at least for the moment. I made some sardonic comment about the name of the diner and we walked out into the streets.

This was the time of what was called the "brown-out," when the lights in all American cities were very dim. When we re-entered the streets something happened to me which had the force of an optical illusion, or a nightmare. The streets were very crowded and I was facing north. People were moving in every direction but it seemed to me, in that instant, that all of the people I could see, and many more than that, were moving toward me, against me, and that everyone was white. I remember how their faces gleamed. And I felt, like a physical sensation, a *click* at the nape of my neck as though some interior string connecting my head to my body had been cut. I began to walk. I heard my friend call after me, but I ignored him. Heaven only knows what was going on in his mind, but he had the good sense not to touch me—I don't know what would have happened if he had—and to keep me in sight. I don't know what was going on in my mind, either; I certainly had no conscious plan. I wanted to do something to crush these white faces, which were crushing me. I walked for perhaps a block or two until I came to an enormous, glittering, and fashionable restaurant in which I knew not even the intercession of the Virgin would cause me to be served. I pushed through the doors and took the first vacant seat I saw, at a table for two, and waited.

I do not know how long I waited and I rather wonder, until today, what I could possibly have looked like. Whatever I looked like, I frightened the waitress who shortly appeared, and the moment she appeared all of my fury flowed towards her. I hated her for her white face, and for her great, astonished, frightened eyes. I felt that if she found a black man so frightening I would make her fright worthwhile.

She did not ask me what I wanted, but repeated, as though she had learned it somewhere, "We don't serve Negroes here." She did not say it with the blunt, derisive hostility to which I had grown so accustomed, but, rather, with a note of apology in her voice, and fear. This made me colder and more murderous than ever. I felt I had to do something with my hands. I wanted her to come close enough for me to get her neck between my hands.

So I pretended not to have understood her, hoping to draw her closer. And she did step a very short step closer, with her pencil poised incongruously over her pad, and repeated the formula: ". . . don't serve Negroes here."

Somehow, with the repetition of that phrase, which was already ringing in my head like a thousand bells of a nightmare, I realized that she would never come any closer and that I would have to strike from a distance. There was nothing on the table but an ordinary watermug half full of water, and I picked this up and hurled it with all my strength at her. She ducked and it missed her and shattered against the mirror behind the bar. And, with that sound, my frozen blood abruptly thawed, I returned from wherever I had been, I *saw*, for the first time, the restaurant, the people with their mouths open, already, as it seemed to me, rising as one man, and I realized what I had done, and where I was, and I was frightened. I rose and began running for the door. A round, potbellied man grabbed me by the nape of the neck just as I reached the doors and began to beat me about the face. I kicked him and got loose and ran into the streets. My friend whispered, *"Run!"* and I ran.

My friend stayed outside the restaurant long enough to misdirect my pursuers and the police, who arrived, he told me, at once. I do not know what I said to him when he came to my room that night. I could not have said much. I felt, in the oddest, most awful way, that I had somehow betrayed him. I lived it over and over and over again, the way one relives an automobile accident after it has happened and one finds oneself alone and safe. I could not get over two facts, both equally difficult for the imagination to grasp, and one was that I could have been murdered. But the other was that I had been ready to commit murder. I saw nothing very clearly but I did see this: that my life, my *real* life, was in danger, and not from anything other people might do but from the hatred I carried in my own heart.

2

I had returned home around the second week in June—in great haste because it seemed that my father's death and my mother's confinement were both but a matter of hours. In the case of my mother, it soon became clear that she had simply made a miscalculation. This had always been her tendency and I don't believe that a single one of us arrived in the world, or has since arrived anywhere else, on time. But none of us dawdled so intolerably about the business of being born as did my baby sister. We sometimes amused ourselves, during those endless, stifling weeks, by picturing the baby sitting within in the safe, warm dark, bitterly regretting the necessity of becoming a part of our chaos and stubbornly putting it off as long as possible. I understood her perfectly and congratulated her on showing such good sense so soon. Death, however, sat as purposefully at my father's bedside as life stirred within my mother's womb and it was harder to understand why he so lingered in that long shadow. It seemed that he had bent, and for a long time, too, all of his energies towards dying. Now death was ready for him but my father held back.

All of Harlem, indeed, seemed to be infected by waiting. I had never before known it to be so violently still. Racial tensions throughout this country were exacerbated during the early years of the war, partly because the labor market brought together hundreds of thousands of ill-prepared people and partly because Negro soldiers, regardless of where they were born, received their military training in the south. What happened in defense plants and army camps had repercussions, naturally, in every Negro ghetto. The situation in Harlem had grown bad enough for clergymen, policemen, educators, politicians, and social workers to assert in one breath that there was no "crime wave" and to offer, in the very breath, suggestions as to how to combat it. These suggestions always seemed to involve playgrounds, despite the fact that racial skirmishes were occurring in the playgrounds, too. Playground or not, crime wave or not, the Harlem police force had been augmented in March, and the unrest grew—perhaps, in fact, partly as a result of the ghetto's instinctive hatred of policemen. Perhaps the most revealing news item, out of the steady parade of reports of muggings, stabbings, shootings, assualts, gang wars, and accusations of police brutality, is the item concerning six Negro girls who set upon a white girl in the subway because, as they all too accurately put it, she was stepping on their toes. Indeed she was, all over the nation.

I had never before been so aware of policemen, on foot, on horseback, on corners, everywhere, always two by two. Nor had I ever been so aware of small knots of people. They were on stoops and on corners and in doorways, and what was striking about them, I think, was that they did not seem to be talking. Never, when I passed these groups did the usual sound of a curse or a laugh ring out and neither did there seem to be any hum of gossip. There was certainly, on the other hand, occurring between them communication extraordinarily intense. Another thing that was striking was the unexpected diversity of the prepared people who made up these groups. Usually, for example, one would see a group of sharpies standing on the street corner, jiving the passing chicks; or a group of older men, usually for some reason, in the vicinity of a barber shop, discussing baseball scores, or the numbers, or making rather chilling observations about women they had known. Women, in a general way, tended to be seen less often together—unless they were church women, or very young girls, or prostitutes met together for an unprofessional instant. But that summer I saw the strangest combinations: large, respectable, churchly matrons standing on the stoops or the corners with their hair tied up, together with a girl in sleazy satin whose face bore the marks of gin and the razor, or heavy-set, abrupt, no-nonsense older men, in company with the most disreputable and fanatical "race" men, or these same "race" men with the sharpies, or these sharpies with the churchly women. Seventh Day Adventists and Methodists and Spiritualists seemed to be hobnobbing with Holyrollers and they were all, alike, entangled with the most flagrant disbelievers; something heavy in their stance seemed to indicate that they had all, incredibly, seen a common vision, and on each face there seemed to be the same strange, bitter shadow.

The churchly women and the matter-of-fact, no-nonsense men had children in the Army. The sleazy girls they talked to had lovers there, the sharpies and the "race" men had friends and brothers there. It would have demanded an unquestioning patriotism, happily as uncommon in this country as it is undesirable, for these people not to have been disturbed by the bitter letters they received, by the newspaper stories they read, not to have been enraged by the posters, then to be found all over New York, which described the Japanese as "yellow-bellied Japs." It was only the "race" men, to be sure, who spoke ceaselessly of being revenged—how this vengeance was to be exacted was not clear—for the indignities and dangers suffered by Negro boys in uniform; but everybody felt a directionless, hopeless bitterness, as well as that panic which can scarcely be suppressed when one knows that a human being one loves is beyond one's reach, and in danger. This helplessness and this gnawing uneasiness does something, at length, to even the toughest mind. Perhaps the best way to sum all this up is to say that the people I knew felt, mainly, a peculiar kind of relief when they knew that their boys were being shipped out of the south, to do battle overseas. It was, perhaps, like feeling that the most dangerous part of a dangerous journey had been passed and that now, even if death should come, it would come with honor and without the complicity of their countrymen. Such a death would be, in short, a fact with which one could hope to live.

It was on the 28th of July, which I believe was a Wednesday, that I visited my father for the first time during his illness and for the last time in his life. The moment I saw him I knew why I had put off this visit so long. I had told my mother that I did not want to see him because I hated him. But this was not true. It was only that I *had* hated him and I wanted to hold on to this hatred. I did not want to look on him as a ruin: it was not a ruin I had hated. I imagine that one of the reasons people cling to their hates so stubbornly is because they sense, once hate is gone, that they will be forced to deal with pain.

We traveled out to him, his older sister and myself, to what seemed to be the very end of a very Long Island. It was hot and dusty and we wrangled, my aunt and I, all the way out, over the fact that I had recently begun to smoke and, as she said, to give myself airs. But I knew that she wrangled with me because she could not bear to face the fact of her brother's dying. Neither could I endure the reality of her despair, her un-stated bafflement as to what had happened to her brother's life, and her own. So we wrangled and I smoked and from time to time she fell into a heavy reverie. Covertly, I watched her face, which was the face of an old woman; it had fallen in, the eyes were sunken and lightless; soon she would be dying, too.

In my childhood—it had not been so long ago—I had thought her beau-tiful. She had been quick-witted and quick-moving and very generous with all the children and each of her visits had been an event. At one time one of my brothers and myself had thought of running away to live with her. Now she could no longer produce out of her handbag some unexpected and yet familiar delight. She made me feel pity and revulsion and fear. It was awful to realize that she no longer caused me to feel affection. The closer we came to the hospital the more querulous she became and at the same time, naturally, grew more dependent on me. Between pity and guilt and fear I began to feel that there was another me trapped in my skull like a jack-in-the box who might escape my control at any moment and fill the air with screaming.

She began to cry the moment we entered the room and she saw him lying there, all shriveled and still, like a little black monkey. The great, gleaming apparatus which fed him and would have compelled him to be still even if he had been able to move brought to mind, not beneficence, but torture; the tubes entering his arm made me think of pictures I had seen when a child, of Gulliver, tied down by the pygmies on that island. My aunt wept and wept, there was a whistling sound in my father's throat; nothing was said; he could not speak. I wanted to take his hand, to say something. But I do not know what I could have said, even if he could have heard me. He was not really in that room with us, he had at last really embarked on his journey; and though my aunt told me that he said he was going to meet Jesus, I did not hear anything except that whistling in his throat. The doctor came back and we left, into that unbearable train again, and home. In the morning came the telegram saying that he was dead. Then the house was suddenly full of relatives, friends, hysteria, and confusion and I quickly left my mother and the children to the care of those impressive women, who, in Negro comunities at least, automatically appear at times of bereavement armed with lotions, proverbs, and patience, and an ability to cook. I went downtown. By the time I returned, later the same day, my mother had been carried to the hospital and the baby had been born.

3

For my father's funeral I had nothing black to wear and this posed a nagging problem all day long. It was one of those problems, simple, or impossible of solution, to which the mind insanely clings in order to avoid the mind's real trouble. I spent most of that day at the downtown apartment of a girl I knew, celebrating my birthday with whiskey and wondering what to wear that night. When planning a birthday celebration one naturally does not expect that it will be up against competition from a funeral and this girl had anticipated taking me out that night, for a big dinner and a night club afterwards. Sometime during the course of that long day we decided that we would go out anyway, when my father's funeral service was over. I imagine *I* decided it, since, as the funeral hour approached, it became clearer and clearer to me that I would not know what to do with myself when it was over. The girl, stifling her very lively concern as to the possible effects of the whiskey on one of my father's chief mourners, concentrated on being conciliatory and practically helpful. She found a black shirt for me somewhere and ironed it and, dressed in the darkest pants and jacket I owned, and slightly drunk, I made my way to my father's funeral.

The chapel was full, but not packed, and very quiet. There were, mainly, my father's relatives, and his children, and here and there I saw faces I had not seen since childhood, the faces of my father's one-time friends. They were very dark and solemn now, seeming somehow to suggest that they had known all along that something like this would happen. Chief among the mourners was my aunt, who had quarreled with my father all his life; by which I do not mean to suggest that her mourning was insincere or that she had not loved him. I suppose that she was one of the few people in the world who had, and their incessant quarreling proved precisely the strength of the tie that bound them. The only other person in the world, as far as I knew, whose relationship to my father rivaled my aunt's in depth was my mother, who was not there.

It seemed to me, of course, that it was a very long funeral. But it was, if anything, a rather shorter funeral than most, nor, since there were no overwhelming, uncontrollable expressions of grief, could it be called—if I dare to use the word—successful. The minister who preached my father's funeral sermon was one of the few my father had still been seeing as he neared his end. He presented to us in his sermon a man whom none of us had ever seen—a man thoughtful, patient, and forbearing, a Christian inspiration to all who knew him, and a model for his children. And no doubt the children, in their disturbed and guilty state, were almost ready to believe this; he had been remote enough to be anything and, anyway, the shock of the incontrovertible, that it was really our father lying up there in that casket, prepared the mind for anything. His sister moaned and this grief-stricken moaning was taken as corroboration. The other faces held a dark, non-committal thoughtfulness. This was not the man they had known, but they had scarcely expected to be confronted with *him*; this was, in a sense deeper than questions of fact, the man they had not known, and the man they had not known may have been the real one. The real man, whoever he had been, had suffered and now he was dead: this was all that was sure and all that mattered now. Every man in the chapel hoped that when his hour came he, too, would be eulogized, which is to say forgiven, and that all of his lapses, greeds, errors, and strayings from the truth would be invested with coherence and looked upon with charity. This was perhaps the last thing human beings could give each other and it was what they demanded, after all, of the Lord. Only the Lord saw the midnight tears, only He was present when one of His children, moaning and wringing hands, paced up and down the room. When one slapped one's child in anger the recoil in the heart reverberated through heaven and became part of the pain of the universe. And when the children were hungry and sullen and distrustful and one watched them, daily, growing wilder, and further away, and running head-long into danger, it was the Lord who knew what the charged heart endured as the strap was laid to the backside; the Lord alone who knew what one *would* have said if one had had, like the Lord, the gift of the living word. It was the Lord who knew of the impossibility every parent in that room faced: how to prepare the child for the day when the child would be despised and how to *create* in the child—by what means?—a stronger antidote to this poison than one had found for oneself. The avenues, side streets, bars, billiard halls, hospitals, police stations, and even the playgrounds of Harlem—not to mention the houses of correction, the jails, and the morgue—testified to the potency of the poison while remaining silent as to the efficacy of whatever antidote, irresistibly raising the question of whether or not such an antidote existed; raising, which was worse, the question of whether or not an antidote was desirable; perhaps poison should be fought with poison. With these several schisms in the mind and with more terrors in the heart than could be named, it was better not to judge the man who had gone down under an impossible burden. It was better to remember: *Thou knowest this man's fall; but thou knowest not his wrassling.*

While the preacher talked and I watched the children—years of changing their diapers, scrubbing them, slapping them, taking them to school, and scolding them had had the perhaps inevitable result of making me love them, though I am not sure I knew this then—my mind was busily breaking out with a rash of disconnected impressions. Snatches of popular songs, indecent jokes, bits of books I had read, movie sequences, faces, voices, political issues—I thought I was going mad; all these impressions suspended, as it were, in the solution of the faint nausea produced in me by the heat and liquor. For a moment I had the impression that my alcoholic breath, inefficiently disguised with chewing gum, filled the entire chapel. Then someone began singing one of my father's favorite songs and, abruptly, I was with him, sitting on his knee, in the hot, enormous, crowded church which was the first church we attended. It was the Abyssinia Baptist Church on 138th Street. We had not gone there long. With this image, a host of others came. I had forgotten, in the rage of my growing up, how proud my father had been of me when I was little. Apparently, I had had a voice and my father had liked to show me off before the members of the church. I had forgotten what he had looked like when he was pleased but now I remembered that he had always been grinning with pleasure when my solos ended. I even remembered certain expressions on his face when he teased my mother—had he loved her? I would never know. And when had it all begun to change? For now it seemed that he had not always been cruel. I remembered being taken for a haircut and scraping my knee on the footrest of the barber's chair and I remembered my father's face as he soothed my crying and applied the stinging iodine. Then I remembered our fights, fights which had been of the worst possible kind because my technique had been silence.

I remembered the one time in all our life together when we had really spoken to each other.

It was on a Sunday and it must have been shortly before I left home. We were walking, just the two of us, in our usual silence, to or from church. I was in high school and had been doing a lot of writing and I was, at about this time, the editor of the high school magazine. But I had also been a Young Minister and had been preaching from the pulpit. Lately, I had been taking fewer engagements and preached as rarely as possible. It was said in the church, quite truthfully, that I was "cooling off."

My father asked me abruptly, "You'd rather write than preach, wouldn't you?"

I was astonished at his question—because it was a real question. I answered, "Yes."

That was all we said. It was awful to remember that that was all we had *ever* said.

The casket now was opened and the mourners were being led up the aisle to look for the last time on the deceased. The assumption was that the family was too overcome with grief to be allowed to make this journey alone and I watched while my aunt was led to the casket and, muffled in black, and shaking, led back to her seat. I disapproved of forcing the children to look on their dead father, considering that the shock of his death, or, more truthfully, the shock of death as a reality, was already a little more than a child could bear, but my judgment in this matter had been overruled and there they were, bewildered and frightened and very small, being led, one by one, to the casket. But there is also something very gallant about children at such moments. It has something to do with their silence and gravity and with the fact that one cannot help them. Their legs, somehow, seem *exposed*, so that it is at once incredible and terribly clear that their legs are all they have to hold them up.

I had not wanted to go to the casket myself and I certainly had not wished to be led there, but there was no way of avoiding either of these forms. One of the deacons led me up and I looked on my father's face. I cannot say that it looked like him at all. His blackness had been equivocated by powder and there was no suggestion in that casket of what his power had or could have been. He was simply an old man dead, and it was hard to believe that he had ever given anyone either joy or pain. Yet, his life filled that room. Further up the avenue his wife was holding his newborn child. Life and death so close together, and love and hatred, and right and wrong, said something to me which I did not want to hear concerning man, concerning the life of man.

After the funeral, while I was downtown desperately celebrating my birthday, a Negro soldier, in the lobby of the Hotel Braddock, got into a fight with a white policeman over a Negro girl. Negro girls, white policemen, in or out of uniform, and Negro males—in or out of uniform—were part of the furniture of the lobby of the Hotel Braddock and this was certainly not the first time such an incident had occurred. It was destined, however, to receive an unprecedented publicity, for the fight between the policeman and the soldier ended with the shooting of the soldier. Rumor, flowing immediately to the streets outside, stated that the soldier had been shot in the back, an instantaneous and revealing invention, and that the soldier had died protecting a Negro woman. The facts were somewhat different—for example, the soldier had not been shot in the back, and was not dead, and the girl seems to have been as dubious a symbol of womanhood as her white counterpart in Georgia usually is, but no one was interested in the facts. They preferred the invention because this invention expressed and corroborated their hates and fears so perfectly. It is just as well to remember that people are always doing this. Perhaps many of those legends, including Christianity, to which the world clings began their conquest of the world with just some such concerted surrender to distortion. The effect, in Harlem, of this particular legend was like the effect of a lit match in a tin of gasoline. The mob gathered before the doors of the Hotel Braddock simply began to swell and to spread in every direction, and Harlem exploded.

The mob did not cross the ghetto lines. It would have been easy, for example, to have gone over Morningside Park on the west side or to have crossed the Grand Central railroad tracks at 125th Street on the east side, to wreak havoc in white neighborhoods. The mob seems to have been mainly interested in something more potent and real than the white face, that is, in white power, and the principal damage done during the riot of the summer of 1943 was to white business establishments in Harlem. It might have been a far bloodier story, of course, if, at the hour the riot began, these establishments had still been open. From the Hotel Braddock the mob fanned out, east and west along 125th Street, and for the entire length of Lenox, Seventh, and Eighth avenues. Along each of these avenues, and along each major side street—116th, 125th, 135th, and so on—bars, stores, pawnshops, restaurants, even little luncheonettes had been smashed open and entered and looted—looted, it might be added, with more haste than efficiency. The shelves really looked as though a bomb had struck them. Cans of beans and soup and dog food, along with toilet paper, corn flakes, sardines, and milk tumbled every which way, and abandoned cash registers and cases of beer leaned crazily out of the splintered windows and were strewn along the avenues. Sheets, blankets, and clothing of every description formed a kind of path, as though people had dropped them while running. I truly had not realized that Harlem *had* so many stores until I saw them all smashed open; the first time the word *wealth* ever entered my mind in relation to Harlem was when I saw it scattered in the streets. But one's first, incongruous impression of plenty was countered immediately by an impression of waste. None of this was doing anybody any good. It would have been better to have left the plate glass as it had been and the goods lying in the stores.

It would have been better, but it would also have been intolerable, for Harlem had needed something to smash. To smash something is the ghetto's chronic need. Most of the time it is the members of the ghetto who smash each other, and themselves. But as long as the ghetto walls are standing there will always come a moment when these outlets do not work. That summer, for example, it was not enough to get into a fight on Lenox Avenue, or curse out one's cronies in the barber shops. If ever, indeed, the violence which fills Harlem's churches, pool halls, and bars erupts outward in a more direct fashion, Harlem and its citizens are likely to vanish in an apocalyptic flood. That this is not likely to happen is due to a great many reasons, most hidden and powerful among them the Negro's real relation to the white American. This relation prohibits, simply, anything as uncomplicated and satisfactory as pure hatred. In order really to hate white people, one has to blot so much out of the mind—and the heart—that this hatred itself becomes an exhausting and self-destructive pose. But this does not mean, on the other hand, that love comes easily: the white world is too powerful, too complacent, too ready with gratuitous humiliation, and, above all, too ignorant and too innocent for that. One is absolutely forced to make perpetual qualifications and one's own reactions are always canceling each other out. It is this, really, which has driven so many people mad, both white and black. One is always in the position of having to decide between amputation and gangrene. Amputation is swift but time may prove that the amputation was not necessary—or one may delay the amputation too long. Gangrene is slow, but it is impossible to be sure that one is reading one's symptoms right. The idea of going through life as a cripple is more than one can bear, and equally unbearable is the risk of swelling up slowly, in agony, with poison. And the trouble, finally, is that the risks are real even if the choices do not exist.

"But as for me and my house," my father had said, "we will serve the Lord." I wondered, as we drove him to his resting place, what this line had meant for him. I had heard him preach it many times. I had preached it once myself, proudly giving it an interpretation different from my father's. Now the whole thing came back to me, as though my father and I were on our way to Sunday school and I were memorizing the golden text: *And if it seem evil unto you to serve the Lord, choose you this day whom you will serve; whether the gods which your fathers served that were on the other side of the flood, or the gods of the Amorites, in whose land ye dwell: but as for me and my house, we will serve the Lord.* I suspected in these familiar lines a meaning which had never been there for me before. All of my father's texts and songs, which I had decided were meaningless, were arranged before me at his death like empty bottles, waiting to hold the meaning which life would give them for me. This was his legacy: nothing is ever escaped. That bleakly memorable morning I hated the unbelievable streets and the Negroes and whites who had, equally, made them that way. But I knew that it was folly, as my father would have said, this bitterness was folly. It was necessary to hold on to the things that mattered. The dead man mattered, the new life mattered; blackness and whiteness did not matter; to believe that they did was to acquiesce in one's own destruction. Hatred, which could destroy so much, never failed to destroy the man who hated and this was an immutable law.

It began to seem that one would have to hold in the mind forever two ideas which seemed to be in opposition. The first idea was acceptance, the acceptance, totally without rancor, of life as it is, and men as they are: in the light of this idea, it goes without saying that injustice is a commonplace. But this did not mean that one could be complacent, for the second idea was of equal power: that one must never, in one's own life, accept these injustices as commonplace but must fight them with all one's strength. This fight begins, however, in the heart and it now had been laid to my charge to keep my own heart free of hatred and despair. This intimation made my heart heavy and, now that my father was irrecoverable, I wished that he had been beside me so that I could have searched his face for the answers which only the future would give me now.

IV.
Confrontation
(1960–1970)

It would be presumptuous to try to sum up the bewildering variety of events of the 1960s. This much, however, may be said: it has been a decade of confrontation, a revolutionary decade nourished, to a great extent, by the seeds of the American Revolution. In their varying ways, all the authors in this section are affirming the self-evident truths of the Declaration of Independence—that "all men are created equal, that they are endowed by their creator with certain unalienable rights, that among these are life, liberty and the pursuit of happiness."

These were some of the voices we heard in the sixties. Norman Mailer on the alienation of man from responsibility:

The average experience today is to meet few people who are authentic. Our minds belong to one cause, our hands manipulate a machine which works against our cause. . . . This plague appears to us as a sickening of our substance, an electrification of our nerves, a deterioration of desire, an apathy about the future, a detestation of the present, an amnesia of the past.

Michael Harrington on poverty in America:

To be impoverished is to be an internal alien.

LeRoi Jones on tokenism and American Liberals:

They, liberals, are people with extremely heavy consciences and almost non-existent courage. Too little is always enough. And it is always the *symbol* that appeals to them most.

287

Martin Luther King, Jr., on freedom and the black man in America:

We know through painful experience that freedom is never voluntarily given by the oppressor; it must be demanded by the oppressed.

Eric Norden on the war in Vietnam:

To many critics of the war this 'new breed of Americans' bears a disquieting resemblance to an old breed of Germans.

And Truman Nelson on the rights and duties of American citizenship:

It was just as plainly understood by the founding fathers that all government is a contract, and if it gives no rights, or even diminished rights, you owe it no duties.

Norman Mailer
(1923–   )

NORMAN MAILER was born in Long Branch, New Jersey, and was graduated from Harvard University in 1943. He has contributed articles to numerous magazines and is the author of, among other works, *The Naked and the Dead* (1948), *Barbary Shore* (1951), *The Deer Park* (1955), *The Presidential Papers* (1963), and *Why Are We in Viet Nam?* (1967). Mailer recently ran, unsuccessfully, for Mayor of New York.

Mailer's half of a debate with William Buckley was first published as "The Role of the Right Wing in America Today" in the January 1963 issue of *Playboy*. The essay, retitled "The Real Meaning of the Right Wing in America," has been reprinted as the Eighth Presidential Paper in Mailer's book *The Presidential Papers* (1963).

THE REAL MEANING OF
THE RIGHT WING
IN AMERICA

Would you care to hear a story Robert Welch likes to tell?[1]
"The minister has preached a superb sermon. It has moved his congregation to lead nobler and more righteous lives. Then the minister says, 'That, of course, was the Lord's side. For the next half hour, to be fair, I'll give equal time to the Devil.'"

Well, ladies and gentlemen, upon me has fallen the unhappy task of following Mr. Buckley.[2] Mr. Buckley was so convincing in his speech that if I had not been forewarned that the Devil cannot know how far he has fallen from Paradise, I would most certainly have decided Mr. Buckley was an angel. A dishonest angel, perhaps, but then which noble speaker is not?

I did not come here, however, to give Mr. Buckley compliments. I appear, presumably, to discuss the real meaning of the Right Wing in America, a phenomenon which is not necessarily real in its meaning, for the Right Wing covers a spectrum of opinion as wide as the perculiarities one encounters on the Left. If we of the Left are a family of anarchists and Communists, socialists, pacifists, nihilists, beatniks, international spies, terrorists, hipsters and Bowery bums, secret agents, dope addicts, sex maniacs and scholarly professors, what indeed is one to make of the Right, which includes the president of a corporation or the Anglican headmaster of a preparatory school, intellectually attired in the fine ideas of

---

1. Robert Welch is the chief spokesman for the John Birch Society, a contemporary version of the Know-Nothings (see footnote, p. 150). He is the author of *The Politician*, a notoriously pro-Joseph McCarthy and anti-Dwight Eisenhower book.—*Editor*.
2. William Buckley is the editor of the *National Review* and a notable political conservative. He is the author of such books as *God and Man at Yale* and *Up From Liberalism*. Like Norman Mailer, he ran for Mayor of New York City and lost.—*Editor*.

Edmund Burke, down the road to the Eisenhower-is-a-Communist set of arguments, all the way down the road to an American Nazi like George Lincoln Rockwell, or to the sort of conservatives who attack property with bombs in California. On a vastly more modest and civilized scale, Mr. Buckley may commit a mild mayhem on the American sense of reality when he says McCarthy inaugurated no reign of terror. Perhaps, I say, it was someone else.

But it is easy to mock the Right Wing. I would rather put the best face one can on it. I think there are any number of interesting adolescents and young men and women going to school now who find themselves drawn to the Right. Secretly drawn. Some are drawn to conservatism today much as they might have been attracted to the Left 30 years ago. They are the ones who are curious for freedom, the freedom not only to make money but the freedom to discover their own nature, to discover good and to discover—dare I say it?—evil. At bottom they are ready to go to war with a ready-made world which they feel is stifling them.

I hope it is evident that I do not see the people in the Right Wing as a simple group of fanatics, but rather as a contradictory stew of reactionaries and individualists, fascists and libertarians, libertarians like John Dos Passos for example.[3] It could be said that most Right Wingers don't really know what they want. I would not include Mr. Buckley in this category, but I think it can be said the politics of the Right in America reflects an emotion more than an insight.

I think of a story told me by a Southerner about his aunt. She lived in a small town in South Carolina. She was a spinster. She came from one of the better families in town. Not surprisingly, the house where she lived had been in the family for a long time. She loved the trees on the walk which bordered each side of the street which ran by her house. They were very old trees.

The City Council passed a bill to cut down those trees. The street had to be widened. A bypass from the highway was being constructed around the old bypass of the business district. The reason for the new bypass was to create a new business district: a supermarket, a superpharmacy, a superservice station, a chromium-plated diner, a new cemetery with plastic tombstones, a new armory for the Army Reserve, an auto supply store, a farm implements shop, a store for Venetian blinds, a laundromat and an information booth for tourists who would miss the town on the new bypass but could read about it in the Chamber of Commerce's literature as they drove on to Florida.

3. An established American writer, John Dos Passos has written novels, essays, and has worked as a newspaper correspondent. During the twenties and thirties he participated in many left-wing activities, but in recent years he has adopted a conservative viewpoint.—*Editor.*

Well, the old lady fought the bypass. To her, it was sacrilege that these trees be cut down. She felt that if there were any value to some older notions of grace and courtesy, courage under duress, and gallantry to ladies, of faith in God and the structure of His ways, that if there were any value at all to chivalry, tradition and manners, the children of the new generations could come to find it more naturally by walking down an avenue of old homes and trees than by reading the *National Review* in front of the picture window under the metal awning of the brand-new town library.

Secretly the old lady had some radical notions. She seemed to think that the old street and the trees on this old street were the property of everyone in the town, because everyone in the town could have the pleasure of walking down that street. At her gloomiest she even used to think that a new generation of Negroes growing up in the town, strong, hostile, too smart, and just loaded with Northern ideas, would hate the South forever and never forgive the past once the past was destroyed. If they grew up on the edge of brand-new bypasses in cement-brick homes with asbestos roofs and squatty hothouse bushes in the artificial fertilizer of the front yard, why then, how could they ever come to understand that not everyone in the old South was altogether evil and that there had been many whites who learned much from the Negro and loved him, that it was Negro slaves who had first planted these trees, and that it was Negro love of all that grew well which had set the trunks of these trees growing in so straight a route right into the air. So the old lady fought the execution of these old trees. She went to see the Mayor, she talked to everyone on the City Council, she circulated a petition among her neighbors, she proceeded to be so active in the defense of these old trees that many people in town began to think she was just naturally showing her age. Finally, her nephew took her aside. It was impossible to stop the bypass, he explained to her, because there was a man in town who had his heart set on it, and no one in town was powerful enough to stop this man. Not on a matter so special as these trees.

Who was this powerful and villainous man? Who would destroy the beauty of a fine old street? she wanted to know. Was it a Communist? No. Was it the leader for the National Association for the Advancement of Colored People? No. Was it perhaps a Freedom Rider? No. Was it a beatnik or a drug addict? No. Wasn't it one of those New York agitators? No, no, it wasn't even a Cuban. The sad fact of the matter was that the powerful and villainous man was married to the richest woman in the country, came himself from an excellently good family, owned half the real estate around, and was president of the biggest local corporation, which was a large company for making plastic luncheon plates. He was a man who had been received often in the old lady's house. He had even talked to her about joining his organization. He was the leader of the local council of the John Birch Society.

Mr. Buckley may say I am being unfair. The man who puts the new bypass through does not have to be the local leader of the John Birch Society. He can also be a Republican, or a Democratic mayor, a white liberal Southerner, or—and here Mr. Buckley might tell my story with pleasure—he could be a Federal man. The bypass might be part of a national superhighway. The villain might even be a Federal man who is under scrutiny by the Senate Investigating Committee, the House Un-American Affairs Committee, the FBI, and the CIA. It seems not to matter —a man can be a fellow-traveler or a reactionary—either way those trees get chopped down, and the past is unreasonably destroyed.

The moral well may be that certain distinctions have begun to disappear. The average experience today is to meet few people who are authentic. Our minds belong to one cause, our hands manipulate a machine which works against our cause. We are not our own masters. We work against ourselves. We suffer from a disease. It is a disease which afflicts almost all of us by now, so prevalent, insidious and indefinable that I choose to call it a plague.

I think somewhere, at some debatable point in history, it is possible man caught some unspeakable illness of the psyche, that he betrayed some secret of his being and so betrayed the future of his species. I could not begin to trace the beginning of this plague, but whether it began early or late, I think it is accelerating now at the most incredible speed, and I would go so far as to think that many of the men and women who belong to the Right Wing are more sensitive to this disease than virtually any other people in this country. I think it is precisely this sensitivity which gives power to the Right Wing's passions.

Now this plague appears to us as a sickening of our substance, an electrification of our nerves, a deterioration of desire, an apathy about the future, a detestation of the present, and amnesia of the past. Its forms are many, its flavor is unforgettable: It is the disease which destroys flavor. Its symptoms appear everywhere: in architecture, medicine, in the deteriorated quality of labor, the insubstantiality of money, the ravishment of nature, the impoverishment of food, the manipulation of emotion, the emptiness of faith, the displacement of sex, the deterioration of language, the reduction of philosophy, and the alienation of man from the product of his work and the results of his acts.

What a modest list! What a happy century. One could speak for hours on each of the categories of this plague. But we are here tonight to talk about other matters. So I will try to do no more than list the symptoms of this plague.

Even 25 years ago architecture, for example, still told one something about a building and what went on within it. Today, who can tell the difference between a modern school and a modern hospital, between a modern hospital and a modern prison, or a prison and a housing project? The airports look like luxury hotels, the luxury hotels are indistinguishable from a modern corporation's home office, and the home office looks like an air-conditioned underground city on the moon.

In medicine, not so long ago, just before the war, there still used to be diseases. Diptheria, smallpox, German measles, scarlet fever. Today there are allergies, viruses, neuroses, incurable diseases. Surgery may have made some mechanical advances, but sickness is more mysterious than ever. No one knows quite what a virus is, nor an allergy, nor how to begin to comprehend an incurable disease. We have had an avalanche of antibiotics, and now we have a rampage of small epidemics with no distinctive set of symptoms.

Nature is wounded in her fisheries, her forests. Airplanes spray insecticides. Species of insects are removed from the chain of life. Crops are poisoned just slightly. We grow enormous tomatoes which have no taste. Food is raised in artificial circumstances, with artificial nutrients, full of alien chemicals and foreign bodies.

Our emotions are turned like television dials by men in motivational research. Goods are not advertised to speak to our needs but to our secret itch. Our secondary schools have a curriculum as interesting as the wax paper on breakfast food. Our educational system teaches us not to think, but to know the answer. Faith is half-empty. Until the churches can offer an explanation for Buchenwald or Siberia or Hiroshima, they are only giving solace to the unimaginative. They are neglecting the modern crisis. For all of us live today as divided men. Our hope for the future must be shared with the terror that we may go exploding into the heavens at the same instant 10,000,000 other souls are being exploded beside us. Not surprising, then, if many people no longer look to sex as an act whose final purpose is to continue the race.

Language is drowning in jargons of mud. Philosophy is in danger of becoming obsolescent. Metaphysics disappears, logical positivism arises. The mass of men begin to have respect not for those simple ideas which are mysteries, but on the contrary for those simple ideas which are certitudes. Soon a discussion of death will be considered a betrayal of philosophy.

Finally, there is a vast alienation of man from responsibility. One hundred years ago Marx was writing about the alienation of man from his tools and the product of his work. Today that alienation has gone deeper. Today we are alienated from our acts. A writer I know interviewed Dr. Teller, "the father of the hydrogen bomb." There was going to be a new test of that bomb soon. "Are you going to see it?" asked the reporter. "Who is interested in that?" asked Teller. "That is just a big bang." Face to face with a danger they cannot name, there are still many people on the Right Wing who sense that there seems to be some almost palpable conspiracy to tear life away from its roots. There is a biological rage at the heart of much Right Wing polemic. They feel as if somebody, or some group—in New York no doubt—are trying to poison the very earth, air and water of their existence. In their mind, this plague is associated with collectivism, and I am not so certain they are wrong. The essence of biology seems to be challenge and response, risk and survival, war and the lessons of war. It may be biologically true that life cannot have beauty without its companion—danger. Collectivism promises security. It spreads security the way a knife spreads margarine. Collectivism may well choke the pores of life.

But there is a contradiction here. Not all of the Right Wing, after all, is individual and strong. Far from it. The Right Wing knows better than I would know how many of them are collectivists in their own hearts, how many detest questions and want answers, loathe paradox, and live with a void inside themselves, a void of fear, a void of fear for the future and for what is unexpected, which fastens upon Communists as equal, one to one, with the Devil. The Right Wing often speaks of freedom when what it desires is iron law, when what it really desires is collectivism managed by itself. If the Right Wing is reacting to the plague, all too many of the powerful people on the Right—the presidents of more than a few corporations in California, for example—are helping to disseminate the plague. I do not know if this applies to Senator Goldwater who may be an honorable and upright man, but I think it can do no harm to take a little time to study the application of his ideas.

As a thoroughgoing conservative, the Senator believes in increasing personal liberty by enlarging economic liberty. He is well known for his views. He would reduce the cost of public welfare and diminish the present power of the unions, he would lower the income tax, dispense with subsidies to the farmer, decentralize the Federal Government and give states' rights back to the states, he would limit the Government's spending, and he would discourage any interference by Washington in the education of the young. It is a complete, comprehensive program. One may agree with it or disagree. But no doubt it is a working program. The reasonableness of this program is attractive. It might even reduce the depredations of the plague. There is just one trouble with it. It does not stop here. Senator Goldwater takes one further step. He would carry the cold war to the Soviet Union, he would withdraw diplomatic recognition, he would recognize, I quote, that:

. . . If our objective is victory over communism, we must achieve superiority in all of the weapons—military, as well as political and economic—that may be useful in reaching that goal. Such a program costs money, but so long as the money is spent wisely and efficiently, I would spend it. I am not in favor of economizing on the nation's safety.

It is the sort of statement which inspires a novelist's imagination long enough to wonder what might happen to the Senator's program if he were elected President. For we may be certain he is sincere in his desire to achieve superiority in all the weapons, including such ideological weapons as arriving first on the moon. But what of the cost? There is one simple and unforgettable figure. More than 60 cents out of every dollar spent by the Government is spent on military security already. Near to two thirds of every dollar. And our national budget in 1963 will be in the neighborhood of $90,000,000,000. If we add what will be spent on foreign aid, the figure will come to more than 75 cents in every dollar.

Yet these expenditures have not given us a clear superiority to the Soviet Union. On the contrary, Senator Goldwater points out that we must still *achieve* superiority. Presumably, he would increase the amount of money spent on defense. This, I suppose, would not hinder him from reducing the income tax, nor would it force him to borrow further funds. He could regain any moneys lost in this reduction by taking the money from welfare and education, that is he could if he didn't increase our defense efforts by more than 10 percent, for if he did that, we would be spending more already than the money we now spend on welfare. And of course that part of the population which would be most affected by the cessation of welfare, that is, so to speak, the impoverished part of the population, might not be happy. And it is not considered wise to have a portion of the populace unhappy when one is expanding one's ability to go to war, unless one wishes to put them in uniform. Perhaps Goldwater might not reduce the expenditures on welfare during this period. He might conceivably increase them a little in order to show that over the short period, during the crisis, during the arms buildup while we achieve superiority over the Russians, a conservative can take just as good care of the masses as a liberal. Especially since we may assume the Russians would be trying to achieve superiority over us at the same time we are trying to achieve superiority over them, so that an arms and munitions competition would be taking place and there would be enough money spent for everyone.

But let me move on to education where the problem is more simple. To achieve superiority over the Russians there, we simply need more technicians, engineers and scientists. We also have to build the laboratories in which to teach them. Perhaps, most reluctantly, just for the duration of the crisis, which is to say for the duration of his period in office, President Goldwater might have to increase the Federal budget for education. That would be contrary to his principles. But perhaps he could recover some of those expenditures by asking the farmer to dispense with subsidies. The farmer would not mind if additional Government funds were allocated to education and welfare, and he was not included. The farmer would not mind if the larger corporations of America, General Dynamics and General Motors, General Electric, United States Steel and A.T.&T. were engaged in rather large new defense contracts. No, the farmer would not mind relinquishing his subsidy. Not at all. Still, to keep him as happy as everyone else Goldwater might increase his subsidy. Just for the duration of the crisis. Just for the duration of enlightened conservatism in office. It would not matter about the higher income tax, the increased farm subsidies, the enlarged appropriation for welfare, the new magnified role of the Federal Government in education, President Goldwater could still give the states back their rights. He would not have to integrate the schools down South. He could drive the Russians out of the Congo, while the White Councils were closing the white colleges in order not to let a black man in. Yes, he could. For the length of a 20-minute speech in Phoenix, Arizona, he could. But you know and I know and he knows what he would do—he would do what President Eisenhower did. He would send troops in to integrate the schools of the South. He would do that if he wanted to keep the Russians out of the Congo.

Poor President Goldwater. At least he could cut down on the power of the unions. He could pass a Right-To-Work act. Indeed he could. He could carry the war to the Russians, he could achieve superiority, while the unions of America were giving up their power and agreeing not to strike. Yes. Yes. Of course he could. Poor President Goldwater. He might have to end by passing a law which would make it illegal ever to pass a Right-To-Work law. Under Goldwater, the American people would never have to be afraid of creeping socialism. They would just have state conservatism, creeping state conservatism. Yes, there are conservatives like the old lady who wished to save the trees and there are conservatives who talk of saving trees in order to get the power to cut down the trees.

So long as there is a cold war, there cannot be a conservative administration in America. There cannot for the simplest reason. Conservatism depends upon a huge reduction in the power and the budget of the central Government. Indeed, so long as there is a cold war, there are no politics of consequence in America. It matters less each year which party holds the power. Before the enormity of defense expenditures, there is no alternative to an ever-increasing welfare state. It can be an interesting welfare state like the present one, or a dull welfare state like President Eisenhower's. It can even be a totally repressive welfare state like President Goldwater's well might be. But the conservatives might recognize that greater economic liberty is not possible so long as one is building a greater war machine. To pretend that both can be real is hypocritical beyond belief. The conservatives are then merely mouthing impractical ideas which they presume may bring them power. They are sufficiently experienced to know that only liberalism can lead America into total war without popular violence, or an active underground.

There is an alternative. Perhaps it is ill-founded. Perhaps it is impractical. I do not know enough to say. I fear there is no one in this country who knows enough to say. Yet I think the time may be approaching for a great debate on this alternative. I say that at least this alternative is no more evil and no more visionary than Barry Goldwater's promise of a conservative America with superiority in all the weapons. So I say—in modesty and in doubt, I say—the alternative may be to end the cold war. The cold war has been an instrument of megalomaniacal delusion to this country. It is the poison of the Right Wing. It is the poison they feed themselves and it is the poison they feed the nation. Communism may be evil incarnate, but it is a most complex evil which seems less intolerable today than it did under Stalin. I for one do not understand an absolute evil which is able to ameliorate its own evil. I say an evil which has captured the elements of the good is complex. To insist communism is a simple phenomenon can only brutalize the minds of the American people. Already, it has given this country over to the power of every huge corporation and organization in America. It has helped to create an America run by committees. It has stricken us with secret waste and hatred. It has held back the emergence of an America more alive and more fantastic than any America yet created.

So I say: End the cold war. Pull back our boundaries to what we can defend and to what wishes to be defended. There is one dread advantage to atomic war. It enables one powerful nation to be the equal of many nations. We do not have to hold every loose piece of real estate on earth to have security. Let communism come to those countries it will come to. Let us not use up our substance trying to hold onto nations which are poor, underdeveloped, and bound to us only by the depths of their hatred for us. We cannot equal the effort the Communists make in such places. We are not dedicated in that direction. We were not born to do that. We have had our frontier already. We cannot be excited to our core, our historic core, by the efforts of new underdeveloped nations to expand their frontiers. No, we are better engaged in another place, we are engaged in making the destiny of Western man, a destiny which seeks now to explore out beyond the moon and in back into the depths of the soul. With some small fraction of the money we spend now on defense we can truly defend ourselves and Western Europe, we can develop, we can become extraordinary, we can go a little further toward completing the heroic vision of Western man. Let the Communists flounder in the countries they acquire. The more countries they hold, the less supportable will become the contradiction of their ideology, the more bitter will grow the divisions in their internal interest, and the more enormous their desire to avoid a war which could only destroy the economies they will have developed at such vast labor and such vast waste. Let it be their waste, not ours. Our mission may be not to raise the level of minimum subsistence in the world so much as it may be to show the first features and promise of that incalculable renaissance men may someday enter. So let the true war begin. It is not a war between West and East, between capitalism and communism, or democracy and totalitarianism; it is rather the deep war which has gone on for six centuries in the nature of Western man, it is the war between the conservative and the rebel, between authority and instinct, between the two views of God which collide in the mind of the West, the ceremonious conservative view which believes that if God allows one man to be born wealthy and another poor, we must not tamper unduly with this conception of place, this form of society created by God, for it is possible the poor man is more fortunate than the rich, since he may be judged less severely on his return to eternity. That is the conservative view and it is not a mean nor easy view to deny.

The rebel or the revolutionary might argue, however, that the form of society is not God's creation, but a result of the war between God and the Devil, that this form is no more than the line of the battlefield upon which the Devil distributes wealth against God's best intention. So man must serve as God's agent, seeking to shift the wealth of our universe in such a way that the talent, creativity and strength of the future, dying now by dim dull deaths in every poor man alive, will come to take its first breath, will show us what a mighty renaissance is locked in the unconscious of the dumb. It is the argument which claims that no conservative can ever be certain those imbued with the value of tradition did not give more devotion to their garden, their stable, their kennel, the livery of their servant and the oratorical style of their clergyman than God intended. Which conservative indeed can be certain that if his class once embodied some desire of the Divine Will, that it has not also now incurred God's displeasure after all these centuries of organized Christianity and enormous Christian greed? Which conservative can swear that it was not his class who gave the world a demonstration of greed so complete, an expropriation and spoilation of backward lands and simple people so avid, so vicious, so insane, a class which finally gave such suck to the Devil, that the most backward primitive in the darkest jungle would sell the grave and soul of his dearest ancestor for a machine with which to fight back? That is the war which has meaning, that great and mortal debate between rebel and conservative where each would argue the other is an agent of the Devil. That is the war we can welcome, the war we can expect if the cold war will end. It is the war which will take life and power from the statistical congelations of the Center and give it over to Left and to Right, it is the war which will teach us our meaning, where we will discover ourselves and whether we are good and where we are not, so it is the war which will give the West what is great within it, the war which gives birth to art and furnishes strength to fight the plague. Art, free inquiry and the liberty to speak may be the only cure against the plague.

But first, I say, first there is another debate America must have. Do we become totalitarian or do we end the cold war? Do we accept the progressive collectivization of our lives which eternal cold war must bring, or do we gamble on the chance that we have argument enough already to be secure and to be free, and do we seek therefore to discover ourselves, and Nature willing, discover the conservative or rebellious temper of these tortured times? And when we are done, will we know truly who has spoken within us, the Lord, or the Fallen Prince?

LeRoi Jones
(1934-)

LEROI JONES was born in Newark, New Jersey. He took his B.A. from Howard University (1954) and has been a member of the New School for Social Research. Jones has won several fellowships and is the author of such diverse works as *Blues People* (1963), *The Dead Lecturer* (1964), *The System of Dante's Hell* (1965), and *Home* (1966).

"Tokenism: 300 Years for Five Cents" was first published in *Kulchur*. It is reprinted in *Home*.

TOKENISM: 300 YEARS
FOR FIVE CENTS

1

In Marietta, Georgia, the Lockheed Airplane people maintain a plant that employs more than 10,000 people, only a few of whom are black people. As is customary in the South, all the black people who work in that Lockheed plant work at menial jobs such as porters, messengers, haulers, etc. Recently, however, the national office of the NAACP and the Federal Government have been chiding the Lockheed people to hire Negroes in capacities other than the traditional porter-messenger syndrome. And I suppose it is a credit to those organizations that they finally did get Lockheed to concur with their wishes; in fact, the Marietta plant promoted one of their Negro porters to a clerical position. This move was hailed by the Federal Government, the NAACP, and similar secret societies as "a huge step forward in race relations" (to quote from *The New York Times*). The Negro who received the promotion, thus becoming "a symbol of American determination to rid itself of the stigma of racial discrimination" (op. cit.), was shown smiling broadly (without his broom) and looking generally symbolic. *The Times* added that his promotion and this symbolic move toward "racial understanding" also gives the ex-porter a five-cents-an-hour increase, or two dollars more a week. This means that instead of forty-five dollars a week (if, indeed, the porter made that much) this blazing symbol of social progress now makes forty-seven dollars a week.

There are almost 20,000,000 Negroes in the United States. One of these 20 million has been given a two-dollar raise and promoted to a clerical job that my two-year-old daughter could probably work out without too much trouble. And we are told that this act is *symbolic* of the "gigantic strides the Negro has taken since slavery."

In 1954, the Supreme Court ruled that segregated schools were illegal, and that, indeed, segregation in public schools should be wiped out "with all deliberate speed." Since 1954, this ruling has affected about 6.9 per cent of the nearly 4,000,000 Negro students in Southern segregated schools, and there are four states, Mississippi, South Carolina, Georgia, and Alabama, who have ignored the ruling entirely. And yet, here again, we are asked to accept the ruling itself (with its hypocritical double-talk —what is "all deliberate speed"?) as yet another example of "the gigantic strides," etc. The fact that the ruling affects only 6.9 per cent of 4,000,000 Negro students in the South (and this percentage stands greatly boosted by the inclusion of figures from the "liberal" border states such as Maryland, Missouri, and the District of Columbia—in fact Maryland and the District account for *more than half* of the total percentage) apparently does not matter to the liberals and other eager humanists who claim huge victories in their "ceaseless war on inequality."

Negroes have been in this country since the early part of the seventeenth century. And they have only "legally" been free human beings since the middle of the nineteenth. So we have two hundred years of complete slavery and now for the last one hundred years a "legal" freedom that has so many ands, ifs, or buts that I, for one, cannot accept it as freedom at all but see it as a legal fiction that has been perpetuated to assuage the occasional loud rumbles of moral conscience that must at times smite all American white men.

These last hundred years, according to our official social chiropractors, have been for American Negroes years of progress and advancement. As *Time* magazine said, "Never has the Negro been able to purchase so much and never has he owned so much, free and clear." That is, everything but his own soul. It is not "progress" that the majority of Negroes want, but Freedom. And I apologize if that word, Freedom, sounds a little too unsophisticated or a little too much like 1930's social renascence for some people; the fact remains that it is the one thing that has been most consistently denied the Negro in America (as well as black men all over the world).

Self-determination is the term used when referring to some would-be nation's desire for freedom. The right to choose one's own path. The right to become exactly what one thinks himself capable of. And it strikes me as monstrous that a nation or, for that matter, a civilization like our Western civilization, reared for the last five hundred years exclusively in the humanistic bombast of the Renaissance, should find it almost impossible to understand the strivings of enslaved peoples to free themselves. It is this kind of paradox that has caused the word "Nationalism" to be despised and/or feared in the West, or shrugged off in official circles as "just another Communist plot." Even here in the United States the relatively mild attempts at "integration" in the South are met by accusations of being Communist-inspired. (And I would add as, say, a note of warning to the various Southern congressmen whose sole qualification for office is that they are more vociferous in their disparagement of Negroes than their opponents, that if they persist in crediting the Communists with every attempt at delivering the black American out of his real and constant bondage, someone's going to believe them . . . namely the new or aspirant nations of Asia, Latin America, and Africa.)

2

Actual slavery in the United States was supposed to have been brought to an end by the Civil War. There is rather bitter insistence in the point that it was *Americans* who were supposedly being freed; the African slaves had long since become American slaves. But it is by now almost a truism to point out that there was much more at stake in that war than the emancipation of the slaves. The Civil War, or at least the result of the Civil War, was undoubtedly the triumph of the Northern industrial classes over the Southern agricultural classes. As so many writers have termed it, "the triumph of American capitalism." The small oligarchy of American industrial capital had overcome its last great enemy, the rich Southern planter, and was now more or less free to bring the very processes of American government under its control.

But on the surface the Civil War looked like a great moral struggle out of which the side of right and justice had emerged victorious. The emancipation of Negroes, the passage, by the Republican Congress, of the 13th, 14th and 15th amendments (to give a "legal basis" for black citizenship), and the setting up of the Reconstruction governments in the South, all gave promise that a new era had arrived for Negroes. And in fact it had, but was of a complexion which was not immediately apparent, and was certainly not the new era most Negroes would have looked forward to.

The Reconstruction governments fell because the Northern industrialists joined with the planter classes of the South to disfranchise the Negro once again, frightened that a "coalition" of the poor and disfranchised Southern whites—the agrarian interests—and the newly freed Negroes might prove too strong a threat to their designs of absolute political and economic control of the South. As E. Franklin Frazier points out in *Black Bourgeosie*, "When agrarian unrest among the 'poor whites' of the South joined forces with the Populist movement, which represented the general unrest among American farmers, the question of race was used to defeat the co-operation of 'poor whites' and Negroes. It was then that the demagogues assumed leadership of the 'poor whites' and provided a solution of the class conflict among whites that offered no challenge to the political power and economic privileges of the industrialists and the planter class. The program, which made the Negro the scapegoat, contained the following provisions: (1) The Negro was completely disfranchised by all sorts of legal subterfuges, with the threat of force in the background; (2) the funds which are appropriated on a per capita basis for Negro school children were diverted to white schools; and (3) a legal system of segregation in all phases of public life was instituted. In order to justify this program, the demagogues, who were supported by the white propertied classes, engaged for twenty-five years in a campaign to prove that the Negro was subhuman, morally de-generate and intellectually incapable of being educated."

3

Tokenism, or what I define as the setting up of social stalemates or the extension of meager privilege to some few "selected" Negroes in order that a semblance of compromise or "progress," or a lessening in racial repression might seem to be achieved, while actually helping to maintain the status quo just as rigidly, could not, of course, really come into being until after the emancipation. Before that, there was no real need to extend even a few tokens to the slave. There was, indeed, no reason why anyone had to create the illusion for the slave that he was "making progress," or governing himself, or any other such untruth. In a sense, however, the extension of "special privileges" to Negro house servants ("house niggers") did early help to create a new class of Negro, within the slave system. The "house nigger" not only assimilated "massa's" ideas and attitudes at a rapid rate, but his children were sometimes allowed to learn trades and become artisans and craftsmen. And it was these artisans and craftsmen who made up the bulk of the 500,000 black "freedmen" extant at the beginning of the Civil War.

The Reconstruction governments are the first actual example of the kind of crumb-dropping that was to characterize the Federal Government's attitude regarding the status of the "free" Negro. The Reconstruction governments were nothing but symbols, since no real lands were ever given to the Negroes, and even any political influence which had come to the ex-slaves as part of the Reconstruction was nullified by 1876 (the so-called redemption of the South).

Another aspect of tokenism is the setting apart or appointing of "leaders" among Negroes who in effect glorify whatever petty symbol the white ruling classes think is necessary for Negroes to have at that particular time. So, at the fall of the Reconstruction governments, the industrialist-financier-planter oligarchy found an able "leader" in Booker T. Washington, a Negro through whom these interests could make their wishes known to the great masses of Negroes. After the North had more or less washed its hands of the whole "Southern mess," and it was a generally accepted idea that the Negroes had ruined the Reconstruction simply because they were incapable of governing themselves, Booker T. Washington came into great prominence and influence as a Negro leader because he accepted the idea of segregation as a "solution" to the race problem, and also because he advocated that Negroes learn trades rather than go into any of the ambitious professions.

"Coming from Booker T. Washington, who enjoyed entré into the society of Standard Oil executives, railroad magnates, and Andrew Carnegie, the strategy was persuasive. Washington avowed his loyalty to laissez faire, took his stand in the South as a southerner, and accepted social inequality for the foreseeable future. Blocked by the power of the whites and told by their own spokesman that 'white leadership is preferable,' most Negroes followed . . ." (from *The Contours of American History*, W. A. Williams).

The wealth and influence of the great industrialists backed the Washington solution and as Williams points out, "Washington's position was made almost impregnable through the generosity of northern white philanthropists who liked his ideology (which included a code of labor quietism and even strikebreaking)." Negro intellectuals like W. E. B. DuBois who attacked Washington's position had little chance to shake it, opposed by such formidable opponents as the monied interests and the philanthropists, who replaced the "radical republican" idea of actually redistributing land to the freed Negroes with ineffective philanthropies such as Howard University or Tuskeegee (which was Booker T.'s pet—a college for Negroes that taught trades, e.g., carpentry, masonry). And of course, as it was intended, the tokens did very little to improve the general conditions of Negroes anywhere. The Sumner-Stevens plan of redistributing land among the freedmen, in fact even breaking up the large plantations and making small farms for both white and black would have changed the entire history of this country had it been implemented in good faith. But such an idea definitely proved a threat to the hold of the planters and industrialists over the politics and economy of the South. So it was defeated.

4

Radicals like DuBois (who left Atlanta University so he would not embarrass them with his opinions) helped set up the National Association for the Advancement of Colored People in 1909. At that time the organization was considered extremely radical, and it was merely asking —but for the first time—for "complete equality." Most of the financiers and philanthropists who made a sometime hobby out of extending stale crumbs to Negroes denounced the organization. Also, most of the so-called Negro middle class could not abide by the radicalism of the organization's program, and some of them (the Negro educators in particular, who depended on the philanthropists for their bread, butter, and prestige) brought as much pressure as they could on the fledgling NAACP to modify its policies. (And I think it is not too violent a digression to ask just what kind of men or what kind of desperation would have to be inflicted upon a man's soul in order for him to say that giving him equal rights in his own country is "to radical"? E. Franklin Frazier does a very good job in *Black Bourgeosie* of describing the type of man who would be capable of such social pathology.) But radicalism or no, when the First World War ended and the great exodus of Negroes from the South began, membership in the NAACP grew tremendously. Yet despite the great support the NAACP received from the Negro masses in its incunabula, the organization was more and more influenced by its white liberal supporters and gradually modified its program and position to that of the white middle class, thereby swiftly limiting its appeal to the middle-class Negro. Today, the NAACP is almost completely out of touch with the great masses of blacks and bases its programs on a "liberal" middle-class line, which affects only a very tiny portion of the 20,000,000 Negroes living in the Uinted States. It has, in fact, become little more than a token itself.

5

A rich man told me recently that a liberal is a man who tells other people what to do with their money. I told him that was right from the side of the telescope he looked through, but that as far as I was concerned a liberal was a man who told other people what to do with their poverty.

I mention this peculiarly American phenomenon, i.e., American Liberalism, because it is just this group of amateur social theorists, American Liberals, who have done most throughout American history to insure the success of tokenism. Whoever has proposed whatever particular social evasion or dilution—to whatever ignominious end—it is usually the liberal who gives that lie the greatest lip service. They, liberals, are people with extremely heavy consciences and almost nonexistent courage. Too little is always enough. And it is always the *symbol* that appeals to them most. The single futile housing project in the jungle of slums and disease eases the liberals' conscience, so they are loudest in praising it—even though it might not solve any problems at all. The single black student in the Southern university, the promoted porter in Marietta, Georgia—all ease the liberals' conscience like a benevolent but highly addictive drug. And, for them, "moderation" is a kind of religious catch phrase that they are wont to mumble on street corners even alone late at night.

Is it an excess for a man to ask to be free? To declare, even vehemently, that no man has the right to dictate the life of another man? Is it so radical and untoward for nations to claim the right of self-determination? Freedom *now!* has become the cry of a great many American Negroes and colonial nations. Not freedom "when you get ready to give it," as some spurious privilege or shabby act of charity; but *now!* The liberal says, "You are a radical." So be it.

Liberals, as good post-Renaissance men, believe wholeheartedly in *progress.* There are even those people who speak knowingly about "progress in the arts." But progress is not, and never has been the question as far as the enslaving of men is concerned. Africans never asked to be escorted to the New World. They never had any idea that learning "good English" and wearing shoes had anything to do with the validity of their lives on earth. Slavery was not anything but an unnecessarily cruel and repressive method of making money for the Western white man. Colonialism was a more subtle, but equally repressive method of accomplishing the same end. The liberal is in a strange position because his conscience, unlike the conscience of his richer or less intelligent brothers, has always bothered him about these acts, but never sufficiently to move him to any concrete action except the setting up of palliatives and symbols to remind him of his own good faith. In fact, even though the slave trade, for instance, was entered into for purely commercial reasons, after a few years the more liberal-minded Americans began to try to justify it as a method of converting heathens to Christianity. (And, again, you can see how perfect Christianity was for the slave then; a great number of slave uprisings were dictated by the African's gods or the new slaves' desire to return to the land of their gods. As I put it in a recent essay on the sociological development of blues: "You can see how necessary, how perfect, it was that Christianity came first, that the African was given something 'to take his mind off Africa,' that he was forced, if he still wished to escape the filthy paternalism and cruelty of slavery, to wait at least until he died, when he could be transported peacefully and majestically to 'the promised land.' " I'm certain the first Negro spirituals must have soothed a lot of consciences as well as enabling a little more relaxation among the overseers. It almost tempts me toward another essay tentatively titled *Christianity as a Deterrent to Slave Uprisings.* More tokens.

A Negro who is told that the "desegregation" of a bus terminal in Georgia somehow represents "progress" is definitely being lied to. Progress to where? The bare minimum of intelligent life is what any man wants. This was true in 1600 when the first slaves were hauled off the boats, and it has not changed. Perhaps the trappings and the external manifestations that time and the lessons of history have proposed make some things seem different or changed in the world, but the basic necessities of useful life are the same. If a tractor has replaced a mule, the need to have the field produce has not changed. And if a black man can speak English now, or read a newspaper, whereas (ask any liberal) he could not in 18 so-and-so, he is no better off now than he was then if he still cannot receive the basic privileges of manhood. In fact, he is perhaps worse off than in 18 so-and-so since he is now being constantly persuaded that he is receiving these basic privileges (or, at least, he is told that he soon will, e.g., R. Kennedy's high comic avowal that perhaps in forty years a Negro might be president).

But, for me, the idea of "progress" is a huge fallacy. An absurd Western egoism that has been foisted on the rest of the world as an excuse for slavery and colonialism. An excuse for making money. Because this progress the Western slavemaster is always talking about means simply the mass acquisition of all the dubious fruits of the industrial revolution. And the acquisition of material wealth has, in my mind, only very slightly to do with self-determination or freedom. Somehow, and most especially in the United States, the fact that more Negroes can buy new Fords this year than they could in 1931 is supposed to represent some great stride *forward*. To where? How many new Fords will Negroes have to own before police in Mississippi stop using police dogs on them. How many television sets and refrigerators will these same Negroes have to own before they are allowed to vote without being made to live in tents, or their children allowed decent educations? And even if a bus station in Anniston, Alabama, is "integrated," how much does this help reduce the 25 per cent unemployment figure that besets Negroes in Harlem.

If, right this minute, I were, in some strange fit of irrationality, to declare that "I am a free man and have the right of complete self-determination," chances are that I would be dead or in jail by nightfall. But being an American Negro, I am supposed to be conditioned to certain "unfortunate" aspects of American democracy. And all my reactions are supposedly based on this conditioning, which is, in effect, that even as a native born American, etc., etc., there are certain things I cannot do because I have a black skin. Tokenism is that philosophy (of psychological exploitation) which is supposed to assuage my natural inclinations toward complete freedom. For the middle-class Negro this assuagement can take the form it takes in the mainstream of American life, i.e., material acquisition, or the elevating of one "select" coon to some position that seems heaped in "prestige," e.g., Special Delegate to the United Nations, Director of Public Housing, Assistant Press Secretary to the President of the United States, Vice President In Charge of Personnel for Chock Full 'O Nuts, Borough President of Manhattan, etc. The "Speaking of People" column in *Ebony* magazine is the banal chronicler of such "advances," e.g., the first Negro sheriff of Banwood, Utah, or the first Negro Asst. Film Editor for BRRR films. But the lower class Negro cannot use this kind of token-ism, so he is pretty much left in the lurch. But so effective is this kind of crumb-dropping among the *soi-disant* black middle class that these people become the actual tokens themselves, or worse. Thus when an issue like the treacherous relief cuts in Newburgh, New York, presents itself, the black middle class is actually likely to side with reactionaries, even though, as in the Newburgh case, such a situation harms a great many poorer Negroes. This kind of process reaches perhaps its most absurd, albeit horrible, manifestation when a man like George Schuyler, in the Negro paper *The Pittsburgh Courier*, can write editorials *defending the Portuguese* in Angola, even after the United States Government itself had been pressured into censuring this NATO ally. It is also a man like Schuy-ler who is willing to support one of the great aphorisms of tokenism (this one begun by the worst elements of racist neo-colonialism) that somehow a man, usually a black man, must "make progress to freedom." That some-how, a man must show he is *"ready* for independence or self-determina-tion." A man is either free or he is not. There cannot be any apprentice-ship for freedom. My God, what makes a black man, in America or Africa, or any of the other oppressed colonial peoples of the world, less ready for freedom than the average *Daily News* reading American white man?

But again, while it is true that there is a gulf of tokens seemingly sepa-rating the middle-class Negro from the great masses of Negroes (just as there is seemingly a great gulf of tokens separating the "select cadre" of a great many colonial countries from their oppressed people), I insist that it is only an artificial separation, and that the black bourgeosie (and their foreign cousins) are no better off than the poorest Negro in this country. But how to tell the *first* Negro Asst. Film Editor of BRRR films that he is just as bad off as the poorest and most oppressed of his black brothers? Tokenism is no abstract philosophy; it was put into action by hardheaded realists.

But realists or no, there is in the world now among most of its op-pressed peoples, a growing disaffection with meaningless platitudes, and a reluctance to be had by the same shallow phrases that have character-ized the hypocritical attitude of the West toward the plight of the Amer-ican black man and all colonial peoples. There will be fewer and fewer tragedies like the murder of Patrice Lumumba.[1] The new nations will no longer allow themselves to be sucked in by these same hackneyed sirens of tokenism or malevolent liberalism. The world, my friends, is definitely changing.

1. Patrice Lumumba was the prime Minister of the Democratic Republic of the Congo until General Joseph Mobutu seized power on September 13, 1960. On December 2, 1960, Lumumba was arrested and later sent to the secessionist province of Katanga where he was murdered.—*Editor.*

Michael Harrington
(1928–   )

MICHAEL HARRINGTON was born in St. Louis. He took his B.A. from Holy Cross College (1947), an M.A. from the University of Chicago (1949), and has studied at Yale Law School. He has been an editor, a political organizer, and the author of two important books, *The Other America* (1963) and *The Accidental Century* (1965).

"The Invisible Land" is the opening chapter of *The Other America*.

THE INVISIBLE LAND

There is a familiar America. It is celebrated in speeches and advertised on television and in the magazines. It has the highest mass standard of living the world has ever known.

In the 1950's this America worried about itself, yet even its anxieties were products of abundance. The title of a brilliant book was widely misinterpreted, and the familiar America began to call itself "the affluent society." There was introspection about Madison Avenue and tail fins; there was discussion of the emotional suffering taking place in the suburbs. In all this, there was an implicit assumption that the basic grinding economic problems had been solved in the United States. In this theory the nation's problems were no longer a matter of basic human needs, of food, shelter, and clothing. Now they were seen as qualitative, a question of learning to live decently amid luxury.

While this discussion was carried on, there existed another America. In it dwelt somewhere between 40,000,000 and 50,000,000 citizens of this land. They were poor. They still are.

To be sure, the other America is not impoverished in the same sense as those poor nations where millions cling to hunger as a defense against starvation. This country has escaped such extremes. That does not change the fact that tens of millions of Americans are, at this very moment, maimed in body and spirit, existing at levels beneath those necessary for human decency. If these people are not starving, they are hungry, and sometimes fat with hunger, for that is what cheap foods do. They are without adequate housing and education and medical care.

The Government has documented what this means to the bodies of the poor, and the figures will be cited throughout this book. But even more basic, this poverty twists and deforms the spirit. The American poor are pessimistic and defeated, and they are victimized by mental suffering to a degree unknown in Suburbia.

This book is a description of the world in which these people live; it is about the other America. Here are the unskilled workers, the migrant farm workers, the aged, the minorities, and all the others who live in the economic underworld of American life. In all this, there will be statistics, and that offers the opportunity for disagreement among honest and sincere men. I would ask the reader to respond critically to every assertion, but not to allow statistical quibbling to obscure the huge, enormous, and intolerable fact of poverty in America. For, when all is said and done, that fact is unmistakable, whatever its exact dimensions, and the truly human reaction can only be outrage. As W. H. Auden wrote:

> Hunger allows no choice
> To the citizen or the police;
> We must love one another or die.

1

The millions who are poor in the United States tend to become increasingly invisible. Here is a great mass of people, yet it takes an effort of the intellect and will even to see them.

I discovered this personally in a curious way. After I wrote my first article on poverty in America, I had all the statistics down on paper. I had proved to my satisfaction that there were around 50,000,000 poor in this country. Yet, I realized I did not believe my own figures. The poor existed in the Government reports; they were percentages and numbers in long, close columns, but they were not part of my experience. I could prove that the other America existed, but I had never been there.

My response was not accidental. It was typical of what is happening to an entire society, and it reflects profound social changes in this nation. The other America, the America of poverty, is hidden today in a way that it never was before. Its millions are socially invisible to the rest of us. No wonder that so many misinterpreted Galbraith's title and assumed that "the affluent society" meant that everyone had a decent standard of life. The misinterpretation was true as far as the actual day-to-day lives of two-thirds of the nation were concerned. Thus, one must begin a description of the other America by understanding why we do not see it.

There are perennial reasons that make the other America an invisible land.

Poverty is often off the beaten track. It always has been. The ordinary tourist never left the main highway, and today he rides interstate turnpikes. He does not go into the valleys of Pennsylvania where the towns look like movie sets of Wales in the thirties. He does not see the company houses in rows, the rutted roads (the poor always have bad roads whether they live in the city, in towns, or on farms), and everything is black and dirty. And even if he were to pass through such a place by accident, the tourist would not meet the unemployed men in the bar or the women coming home from a runaway sweatshop.

Then, too, beauty and myths are perennial masks of poverty. The traveler comes to the Appalachians in the lovely season. He sees the hills, the streams, the foliage—but not the poor. Or perhaps he looks at a run-down mountain house and, remembering Rousseau rather than seeing with his eyes, decides that "those people" are truly fortunate to be living the way they are and that they are lucky to be exempt from the strains and tensions of the middle class. The only problem is that "those people," the quaint inhabitants of those hills, are undereducated, underprivileged, lack medical care, and are in the process of being forced from the land into a life in the cities, where they are misfits.

These are normal and obvious causes of the invisibility of the poor. They operated a generation ago; they will be functioning a generation hence. It is more important to understand that the very development of American society is creating a new kind of blindness about poverty. The poor are increasingly slipping out of the very experience and consciousness of the nation.

If the middle class never did like ugliness and poverty, it was at least aware of them. "Across the tracks" was not a very long way to go. There were forays into the slums at Christmas time; there were charitable organizations that brought contact with the poor. Occasionally, almost everyone passed through the Negro ghetto or the blocks of tenements, if only to get downtown to work or to entertainment.

Now the American city has been transformed. The poor still inhabit the miserable housing in the central area, but they are increasingly isolated from contact with, or sight of, anybody else. Middle-class women coming in from Suburbia on a rare trip may catch the merest glimpse of the other America on the way to an evening at the theater, but their children are segregated in suburban schools. The business or professional man may drive along the fringes of slums in a car or bus, but it is not an important experience to him. The failures, the unskilled, the disabled, the aged, and the minorities are right there, across the tracks, where they have always been. But hardly anyone else is.

In short, the very development of the American city has removed poverty from the living, emotional experience of millions upon millions of middle-class Americans. Living out in the suburbs, it is easy to assume that ours is indeed, an affluent society.

This new segregation of poverty is compounded by a well-meaning ignorance. A good many concerned and sympathetic Americans are aware that there is much discussion of urban renewal. Suddenly, driving through the city, they notice that a familiar slum has been torn down and that there are towering, modern buildings where once there had been tenements or hovels. There is a warm feeling of satisfaction, of pride in the way things are working out; the poor, it is obvious, are being taken of.

The irony in this (as the chapter on housing will document) is that the truth is nearly the exact opposite to the impression. The total impact of the various housing programs in postwar America has been to squeeze more and more people into existing slums. More often than not, the modern apartment in a towering building rents at $40 a room or more. For, during the past decade and a half, there has been more subsidization of middle- and upper-income housing than there has been of housing for the poor.

Clothes make the poor invisible too: America has the best-dressed poverty the world has ever known. For a variety of reasons, the benefits of mass production have been spread much more evenly in this area than in many others. It is much easier in the United States to be decently dressed than it is to be decently housed, fed, or doctored. Even people with terribly depressed incomes can look prosperous.

This is an extremely important factor in defining our emotional and existential ignorance of poverty. In Detroit the existence of social classes became much more difficult to discern the day the companies put lockers in the plants. From that moment on, one did not see men in work clothes on the way to the factory, but citizens in slacks and white shirts. This process has been magnified with the poor throughout the country. There are tens of thousands of Americans in the big cities who are wearing shoes, perhaps even a stylishly cut suit or dress, and yet are hungry. It is not a matter of planning, though it almost seems as if the affluent society had given out costumes to the poor so that they would not offend the rest of society with the sight of rags.

Then, many of the poor are the wrong age to be seen. A good number of them (over 8,000,000) are sixty-five years of age or better; an even larger number are under eighteen. The aged members of the other America are often sick, and they cannot move. Another group of them live out their lives in loneliness and frustration: they sit in rented rooms, or else they stay close to a house in a neighborhood that has completely changed from the old days. Indeed, one of the worst aspects of poverty among the aged is that these people are out of sight and out of mind, and alone.

The young are somewhat more visible, yet they too stay close to their neighborhoods. Sometimes they advertise their poverty through a lurid tabloid story about a gang killing. But generally they do not disturb the quiet streets of the middle class.

And finally, the poor are politically invisible. It is one of the cruelest ironies of social life in advanced countries that the dispossessed at the bottom of society are unable to speak for themselves. The people of the other America do not, by far and large, belong to unions, to fraternal organizations, or to political parties. They are without lobbies of their own; they put forward no legislative program. As a group, they are atomized. They have no face; they have no voice.

Thus, there is not even a cynical political motive for caring about the poor, as in the old days. Because the slums are no longer centers of powerful political organizations, the politicians need not really care about their inhabitants. The slums are no longer visible to the middle class, so much of the idealistic urge to fight for those who need help is gone. Only the social agencies have a really direct involvement with the other America, and they are without any great political power.

To the extent that the poor have a spokesman in American life, that role is played by the labor movement. The unions have their own particular idealism, an ideology of concern. More than that, they realize that the existence of a reservoir of cheap, unorganized labor is a menace to wages and working conditions throughout the entire economy. Thus, many union legislative proposals—to extend the coverage of minimum wage and social security, to organize migrant farm laborers—articulate the needs of the poor.

That the poor are invisible is one of the most important things about them. They are not simply neglected and forgotten as in the old rhetoric of reform; what is much worse, they are not seen.

One might take a remark from George Eliot's *Felix Holt* as a basic statement of what this book is about:

> . . . there is no private life which has not been determined by a wider public life, from the time when the primeval milkmaid had to wander with the wanderings of her clan, because the cow she milked was one of a herd which had made the pasture bare. Even in the conservatory existence where the fair Camellia is sighed for by the noble young Pineapple, neither of them needing to care about the frost or rain outside, there is a nether apparatus of hot-water pipes liable to cool down on a strike of the gardeners or a scarcity of coal.
>
> And the lives we are about to look back upon do not belong to those conservatory species; they are rooted in the common earth, having to endure all the ordinary chances of past and present weather.

Forty to 50,000,000 people are becoming increasingly invisible. That is a shocking fact. But there is a second basic irony of poverty that is equally important: if one is to make the mistake of being born poor, he should choose a time when the majority of the people are miserable too.

J. K. Galbraith develops this idea in *The Affluent Society*, and in doing so defines the "newness" of the kind of poverty in contemporary America. The old poverty, Galbraith notes, was general. It was the condition of life of an entire society, or at least of that huge majority who were without special skills or the luck of birth. When the entire economy advanced, a good many of these people gained higher standards of living. Unlike the poor today, the majority poor of a generation ago were an immediate (if cynical) concern of political leaders. The old slums of the immigrants had the votes; they provided the basis for labor organizations; their very numbers could be a powerful force in political conflict. At the same time the new technology required higher skills, more education, and stimulated an upward movement for millions.

Perhaps the most dramatic case of the power of the majority poor took place in the 1930's. The Congress of Industrial Organizations literally organized millions in a matter of years. A labor movement that had been declining and confined to a thin stratum of the highly skilled suddenly embraced masses of men and women in basic industry. At the same time this acted as a pressure upon the Government, and the New Deal codified some of the social gains in law like the Wagner Act. The result was not a basic transformation of the American system, but it did transform the lives of an entire section of the population.

In the thirties one of the reasons for these advances was that misery was general. There was no need then to write books about unemployment and poverty. That was the decisive social experience of the entire society, and the apple sellers even invaded Wall Street. There was political sympathy from middle-class reformers; there were an élan and spirit that grew out of a deep crisis.

Some of those who advanced in the thirties did so because they had unique and individual personal talents. But for the great mass, it was a question of being at the right point in the economy at the right time in history, and utilizing that position for common struggle. Some of those who failed did so because they did not have the will to take advantage of new opportunities. But for the most part the poor who were left behind had been at the wrong place in the economy at the wrong moment in history.

These were the people in the unorganizable jobs, in the South, in the minority groups, in the fly-by-night factories that were low on capital and high on labor. When some of them did break into the economic mainstream—when, for instance, the CIO opened up the way for some Negroes to find good industrial jobs—they proved to be as resourceful as anyone else. As a group, the other Americans who stayed behind were not originally composed primarily of individual failures. Rather, they were victims of an impersonal process that selected some for progress and discriminated against others.

Out of the thirties came the welfare state. Its creation had been stimulated by mass impoverishment and misery, yet it helped the poor least of all. Laws like unemployment compensation, the Wagner Act, the various farm programs, all these were designed for the middle third in the cities, for the organized workers, and for the upper third in the country, for the big market farmers. If a man works in an extremely low-paying job, he may not even be covered by social security or other welfare programs. If he receives unemployment compensation, the payment is scaled down according to his low earnings.

One of the major laws that was designed to cover everyone, rich and poor, was social security. But even here the other Americans suffered discrimination. Over the years social security payments have not even provided a subsistence level of life. The middle third have been able to supplement the Federal pension through private plans negotiated by unions, through joining medical insurance schemes like Blue Cross, and so on. The poor have not been able to do so. They lead a bitter life, and then have to pay for that fact in old age.

Indeed, the paradox that the welfare state benefits those least who need help most is but a single instance of a persistent irony in the other America. Even when the money finally trickles down, even when a school is built in a poor neighborhood, for instance, the poor are still deprived. Their entire environment, their life, their values, do not prepare them to take advantage of the new opportunity. The parents are anxious for the children to go to work; the pupils are pent up, waiting for the moment when their education has complied with the law.

Today's poor, in short, missed the political and social gains of the thirties. They are, as Galbraith rightly points out, the first minority poor in history, the first poor not to be seen, the first poor whom the politicians could leave alone.

The first step toward the new poverty was taken when millions of people proved immune to progress. When that happened, the failure was not individual and personal, but a social product. But once the historic accident takes place, it begins to become a personal fate.

The new part of the other America saw the rest of society move ahead. They went on living in depressed areas, and often they tended to become depressed human beings. In some of the West Virginia towns, for instance, an entire community will become shabby and defeated. The young and the adventurous go to the city, leaving behind those who cannot move and those who lack the will to do so. The entire area becomes permeated with failure, and that is one more reason the big corporations shy away.

Indeed, one of the most important things about the new poverty is that it cannot be defined in simple, statistical terms. Throughout this book a crucial term is used: aspiration. If a group has internal vitality, a will—if it has aspiration—it may live in dilapidated housing, it may eat an inadequate diet, and it may suffer poverty, but it is not impoverished. So it was in those ethnic slums of the immigrants that played such a dramatic role in the unfolding of the American dream. The people found themselves in slums, but they were not slum dwellers.

But the new poverty is constructed so as to destroy aspiration; it is a system designed to be impervious to hope. The other America does not contain the adventurous seeking a new life and land. It is populated by the failures, by those driven from the land and bewildered by the city, by old people suddenly confronted with the torments of loneliness and poverty, and by minorities facing a wall of prejudice.

In the past, when poverty was general in the unskilled and semi-skilled work force, the poor were all mixed together. The bright and the dull, those who were going to escape into the great society and those who were to stay behind, all of them lived on the same street. When the middle third rose, this community was destroyed. And the entire invisible land of the other Americans became a ghetto, a modern poor farm for the rejects of society and of the economy.

It is a blow to reform and the political hopes of the poor that the middle class no longer understands that poverty exists. But, perhaps more important, the poor are losing their links with the great world. If statistics and sociology can measure a feeling as delicate as loneliness (and some of the attempts to do so will be cited later on), the other America is becoming increasingly populated by those who do not belong to anybody or anything. They are no longer participants in an ethnic culture from the old country; they are less and less religious; they do not belong to unions or clubs. They are not seen, and because of that they themselves cannot see. Their horizon has become more and more restricted; they see one another, and that means they see little reason to hope.

Galbraith was one of the first writers to begin to describe the newness of contemporary poverty, and that is to his credit. Yet because even he underestimates the problem, it is important to put his definition into perspective.

For Galbraith, there are two main components of the new poverty: case poverty and insular poverty. Case poverty is the plight of those who suffer from some physical or mental disability that is personal and individual and excludes them from the general advance. Insular poverty exists in areas like the Appalachians or the West Virginia coal fields, where an entire section of the country becomes economically obsolete.

Physical and mental disabilities are, to be sure, an important part of poverty in America. The poor are sick in body and in spirit. But this is not an isolated fact about them, an individual "case," a stroke of bad luck. Disease, alcoholism, low IQ's, these express a whole way of life. They are, in the main, the effects of an environment, not the biographies of unlucky individuals. Because of this, the new poverty is something that cannot be dealt with by first aid. If there is to be a lasting assault on the shame of the other America, it must seek to root out of this society an entire environment, and not just the relief of individuals.

But perhaps the idea of "insular" poverty is even more dangerous. To speak of "islands" of the poor (or, in the more popular term, of "pockets of poverty") is to imply that one is confronted by a serious, but relatively minor, problem. This is hardly a description of a misery that extends to 40,000,000 or 50,000,000 people in the United States. They have remained impoverished in spite of increasing productivity and the creation of a welfare state. That fact alone should suggest the dimensions of a serious and basic situation.

And yet, even given these disagreements with Galbraith, his achievement is considerable. He was one of the first to understand that there are enough poor people in the United States to constitute a subculture of misery, but not enough of them to challenge the conscience and the imagination of the nation.

Finally, one might summarize the newness of contemporary poverty by saying: These are the people who are immune to progress. But then the facts are even more cruel. The other Americans are the victims of the very inventions and machines that have provided a higher living standard for the rest of the society. They are upside-down in the economy, and for them greater productivity often means worse jobs; agricultural advance becomes hunger.

In the optimistic theory, technology is an undisguised blessing. A general increase in productivity, the argument goes, generates a higher standard of living for the whole people. And indeed, this has been true for the middle and upper thirds of American society, the people who made such striking gains in the last two decades. It tends to overstate the automatic character of the process, to omit the role of human struggle. (The CIO was organized by men in conflict, not by economic trends.) Yet it states a certain truth—for those who are lucky enough to participate in it.

But the poor, if they were given to theory, might argue the exact opposite. They might say: Progress is misery.

As the society became more technological, more skilled, those who learn to work the machines, who get the expanding education, move up. Those who miss out at the very start find themselves at a new disadvantage. A generation ago in American life, the majority of the working people did not have high-school educations. But at that time industry was organized on a lower level of skill and competence. And there was a sort of continuum in the shop: the young who left school at sixteen could begin as a laborer, and gradually pick up skill as he went along.

Today the situation is quite different. The good jobs require much more academic preparation, much more skill from the very outset. Those who lack a high-school education tend to be condemned to the economic underworld—to low-paying service industries, to backward factories, to sweeping and janitorial duties. If the fathers and mothers of the contemporary poor were penalized a generation ago for their lack of schooling, their children will suffer all the more. The very rise in productivity that created more money and better working conditions for the rest of the society can be a menace to the poor.

But then this technological revolution might have an even more disastrous consequence: it could increase the ranks of the poor as well as intensify the disabilities of poverty. At this point it is too early to make any final judgment, yet there are obvious danger signals. There are millions of Americans who live just the other side of poverty. When a recession comes, they are pushed onto the relief rolls. (Welfare payments in New York respond almost immediately to any economic decline.) If automation continues to inflict more and more penalties on the unskilled and the semiskilled, it could have the impact of permanently increasing the population of the other America.

Even more explosive is the possibility that people who participated in the gains of the thirties and the forties will be pulled back down into poverty. Today the mass production industries where unionization made such a difference are contracting. Jobs are being destroyed. In the process, workers who had achieved a certain level of wages, who had won working conditions in the shop, are suddenly confronted with impoverishment. This is particularly true for anyone over forty years of age and for members of minority groups. Once their job is abolished, their chances of ever getting similar work are very slim.

It is too early to say whether or not this phenomenon is temporary, or whether it represents a massive retrogression that will swell the numbers of the poor. To a large extent, the answer to this question will be determined by the political response of the United States in the sixties. If serious and massive action is not undertaken, it may be necessary for statisticians to add some old-fashioned, pre-welfare-state poverty to the misery of the other America.

Poverty in the 1960's is invisible and it is new, and both those factors make it more tenacious. It is more isolated and politically powerless than ever before. It is laced with ironies, not the least of which is that many of the poor view progress upside-down, as a menace and a threat to their lives. And if the nation does not measure up to the challenge of automation, poverty in the 1960's might be on the increase.

2

There are mighty historical and economic forces that keep the poor down; and there are human beings who help out in this grim business, many of them unwittingly. There are sociological and political reasons why poverty is not seen; and there are misconceptions and prejudices that literally blind the eyes. The latter must be understood if anyone is to make the necessary act of intellect and will so that the poor can be noticed.

Here is the most familiar version of social blindness: "The poor are that way because they are afraid of work. And anyway they will have big cars. If they were like me (or my father or my grandfather), they could pay their own way. But they prefer to live on the dole and cheat the taxpayer."

This theory, usually thought of as a virtuous and moral statement, is one of the means of making it impossible for the poor ever to pay their way. There are, one must assume, citizens of the other America who choose impoverishment out of fear of work (though, writing it down, I really do not believe it). But the real explanation of why the poor are where they are is that they made the mistake of being born to the wrong parents, in the wrong section of the country, in the wrong industry, or in the wrong racial or ethnic group. Once that mistake has been made, they could have been paragons of will and morality, but most of them would never even have had a chance to get out of the other America.

There are two important ways of saying this: The poor are caught in a vicious circle; or, The poor live in a culture of poverty.

In a sense, one might define the contemporary poor in the United States as those who, for reasons beyond their control, cannot help themselves. All the most decisive factors making for opportunity and advance are against them. They are born going downward, and most of them stay down. They are victims whose lives are endlessly blown round and round the other America.

Here is one of the most familiar forms of the vicious circle of poverty. The poor get sick more than anyone else in the society. That is because they live in slums, jammed together under unhygienic conditions; they have inadequate diets, and cannot get decent medical care. When they become sick, they are sick longer than any other group in the society. Because they are sick more often and longer than anyone else, they lose wages and work, and find it difficult to hold a steady job. And because of this, they cannot pay for good housing, for a nutritious diet, for doctors. At any given point in the circle, particularly when there is a major illness, their prospect is to move to an even lower level and to begin the circle, round and round, toward even more suffering.

This is only one example of the vicious circle. Each group in the other America has its own particular version of the experience, and these will be detailed throughout this book. But the pattern, whatever its variations, is basic to the other America.

The individual cannot usually break out of this vicious circle. Neither can the group, for it lacks the social energy and political strength to turn its misery into a cause. Only the larger society, with its help and resources, can really make it possible for these people to help themselves. Yet those who could make the difference too often refuse to act because of their ignorant, smug moralisms. They view the effects of poverty— above all, the warping of the will and spirit that is a consequence of being poor—as choices. Understanding the vicious circle is an important step in breaking down this prejudice.

There is an even richer way of describing this same, general idea: Poverty in the United States is a culture, an institution, a way of life.

There is a famous anecdote about Ernest Hemingway and F. Scott Fitzgerald. Fitzgerald is reported to have remarked to Hemingway, "The rich are different." And Hemingway replied, "Yes, they have money." Fitzgerald had much the better of the exchange. He understood that being rich was not a simple fact, like a large bank account, but a way of looking at reality, a series of attitudes, a special type of life. If this is true of the rich, it is ten times truer of the poor. Everything about them, from the condition of their teeth to the way in which they love, is suffused and permeated by the fact of their poverty. And this is sometimes a hard idea for a Hemingway-like middle-class America to comprehend.

The family structure of the poor, for instance, is different from that of the rest of the society. There are more homes without a father, there is less marriage, more early pregnancy and, if Kinsey's statistical findings can be used, markedly different attitudes toward sex. As a result of this, to take but one consequence of the fact, hundreds of thousands, and perhaps millions, of children in the other America never know stability and "normal" affection.

Or perhaps the policeman is an even better example. For the middle class, the police protect property, give directions, and help old ladies. For the urban poor, the police are those who arrest you. In almost any slum there is a vast conspiracy against the forces of law and order. If someone approaches asking for a person, no one there will have heard of him, even if he lives next door. The outsider is "cop," bill collector, investigator (and, in the Negro ghetto, most dramatically, he is "the Man").

While writing this book, I was arrested for participation in a civil-rights demonstration. A brief experience of a night in a cell made an abstraction personal and immediate: the city jail is one of the basic institutions of the other America. Almost everyone whom I encountered in the "tank" was poor: skid-row whites, Negroes, Puerto Ricans. Their poverty was an incitement to arrest in the first place. (A policeman will be much more careful with a well-dressed, obviously educated man who might have political connections than he will with someone who is poor.) They did not have money for bail or for lawyers. And, perhaps most important, they waited their arraignment with stolidity, in a mood of passive acceptance. They expected the worst, and they probably got it.

There is, in short, a language of the poor, a psychology of the poor, a world view of the poor. To be impoverished is to be an internal alien, to grow up in a culture that is radically different from the one that dominates the society. The poor can be described statistically; they can be analyzed as a group. But they need a novelist as well as a sociologist if we are to see them. They need an American Dickens to record the smell and texture and quality of their lives. The cycles and trends, the massive forces, must be seen as affecting persons who talk and think differently.

I am not that novelist. Yet in this book I have attempted to describe the faces behind the statistics, to tell a little of the "thickness" of personal life in the other America. Of necessity, I have begun with large groups: the dispossessed workers, the minorities, the farm poor, and the aged. Then, there are three cases of less massive types of poverty, including the only single humorous component in the other America. And finally, there are the slums, and the psychology of the poor.

Throughout, I work on an assumption that cannot be proved by Government figures or even documented by impressions of the other America. It is an ethical proposition, and it can be simply stated: In a nation with a technology that could provide every citizen with a decent life, it is an outrage and a scandal that there should be such social misery. Only if one begins with this assumption is it possible to pierce through the invisibility of 40,000,000 to 50,000,000 human beings and to see the other America. We must perceive passionately, if this blindness is to be lifted from us. A fact can be rationalized and explained away; an indignity cannot.

What shall we tell the American poor, once we have seen them? Shall we say to them that they are better off than the Indian poor, the Italian poor, the Russian poor? That is one answer, but it is heartless. I should put it another way. I want to tell every well-fed and optimistic American that it is intolerable that so many millions should be maimed in body and in spirit when it is not necessary that they should be. My standard of comparison is not how much worse things used to be. It is how much better they could be if only we were stirred.

Martin Luther King, Jr.
(1929–1968)

KING was born in Atlanta, Georgia. He took an A.B. from Morehouse College (1948), a B.D. from Crozer Theological Seminary (1951), and a Ph.D. (1955) and D.D. (1959) from Boston University. He was the president of the Southern Christian Leadership Conference and won the Nobel Peace Prize in 1964. Among his many writings are *Stride Toward Freedom* (1958), *Why We Can't Wait* (1963), *Where Do We Go From Here: Chaos or Community?* (1967). He was assassinated April 4, 1968, in Memphis, Tennessee.

The "Letter from Birmingham Jail" appears in King's book *Why We Can't Wait*. The author explains the circumstances under which it was written thus: "This response to a published statement by eight fellow clergymen from Alabama (Bishop C. C. J. Carpenter, Bishop Joseph A. Durick, Rabbi Hilton L. Grafman, Bishop Paul Hardin, Bishop Holan B. Harmon, the Reverend George M. Murray, the Reverend Edward V. Ramage and the Reverend Earl Stalings) was composed under somewhat constricting circumstances. Begun on the margins of the newspaper in which the statement appeared while I was in jail, the letter was continued on scraps of writing paper supplied by a friendly Negro trusty, and concluded on a pad my attorneys were eventually permitted to leave me. Although the text remains in substance unaltered, I have indulged in the author's prerogative of polishing it for publication."

LETTER FROM
BIRMINGHAM JAIL

April 16, 1963

My Dear Fellow Clergymen:

While confined here in the Birmingham city jail, I came across your recent statement calling my present activities "unwise and untimely." Seldom do I pause to answer criticism of my work and ideas. If I sought to answer all the criticisms that cross my desk, my secretaries would have little time for anything other than such correspondence in the course of the day, and I would have no time for constructive work. But since I feel that you are men of genuine good will and that your criticisms are sincerely set forth, I want to try to answer your statement in what I hope will be patient and reasonable terms.

I think I should indicate why I am here in Birmingham, since you have been influenced by the view which argues against "outsiders coming in." I have the honor of serving as president of the Southern Christian Leadership Conference, an organization operating in every southern state, with headquarters in Atlanta, Georgia. We have some eighty-five affiliated organizations across the South, and one of them is the Alabama Christian Movement for Human Rights. Frequently we share staff, educational and financial resources with our affiliates. Several months ago the affiliate here in Birmingham asked us to be on call to engage in a nonviolent direct-action program if such were deemed necessary. We readily consented, and when the hour came we lived up to our promise. So I, along with several members of my staff, am here because I was invited here. I am here because I have organizational ties here.

But more basically, I am in Birmingham because injustice is here. Just as the prophets of the eighth century B.C. left their villages and carried their "thus saith the Lord" far beyond the boundaries of their home towns, and just as the Apostle Paul left his village of Tarsus and carried the gospel of Jesus Christ to the far corners of the Greco-Roman world, so am I compelled to carry the gospel of freedom beyond my own home town. Like Paul, I must constantly respond to the Macedonian call for aid.

Moreover, I am cognizant of the interrelatedness of all communities and states. I cannot sit idly by in Atlanta and not be concerned about what happens in Birmingham. Injustice anywhere is a threat to justice everywhere. We are caught in an inescapable network of mutuality, tied in a single garment of destiny. Whatever affects one directly, affects all indirectly. Never again can we afford to live with the narrow, provincial "outside agitator" idea. Anyone who lives inside the United States can never be considered an outsider anywhere within its bounds.

You deplore the demonstrations taking place in Birmingham. But your statement, I am sorry to say, fails to express a similar concern for the conditions that brought about the demonstrations. I am sure that none of you would want to rest content with the superficial kind of social analysis that deals merely with effects and does not grapple with underlying causes. It is unfortunate that demonstrations are taking place in Birmingham, but it is even more unfortunate that the city's white power structure left the Negro community with no alternative.

In any nonviolent campaign there are four basic steps: collection of the facts to determine whether injustices exist; negotiation; self-purification; and direct action. We have gone through all these steps in Birmingham. There can be no gainsaying the fact that racial injustice engulfs this community. Birmingham is probably the most thoroughly segregated city in the United States. Its ugly record of brutality is widely known. Negroes have experienced grossly unjust treatment in the courts. There have been more unsolved bombings of Negro homes and churches in Birmingham than in any other city in the nation. These are the hard, brutal facts of the case. On the basis of these conditions, Negro leaders sought to negotiate with the city fathers. But the latter consistently refused to engage in good-faith negotiation.

Then, last September, came the opportunity to talk with leaders of Birmingham's economic community. In the course of the negotiations, certain promises were made by the merchants—for example, to remove the stores' humiliating racial signs. On the basis of these promises, the Reverend Fred Shuttlesworth and the leaders of the Alabama Christian Movement for Human Rights agreed to a moratorium on all demonstrations. As the weeks and months went by, we realized that we were the victims of a broken promise. A few signs, briefly removed, returned; the others remained.

As in so many past experiences, our hopes had been blasted, and the shadow of deep disappointment settled upon us. We had no alternative except to prepare for direct action, whereby we would present our very bodies as a means of laying our case before the conscience of the local and the national community. Mindful of the difficulties involved, we decided to undertake a process of self-purification. We began a series of workshops on non-violence, and we repeatedly asked ourselves: "Are you able to accept blows without retaliating?" "Are you able to endure the ordeal of jail?" We decided to schedule our direct-action program for the Easter season, realizing that except for Christmas, this is the main shopping period of the year. Knowing that a strong economic-withdrawal program would be the by-product of direct action, we felt that this would be the best time to bring pressure to bear on the merchants for the needed change.

Then it occurred to us that Birmingham's mayoralty election was coming up in March, and we speedily decided to postpone action until after election day. When we discovered that the Commissioner of Public Safety, Eugene "Bull" Connor, had piled up enough votes to be in the run-off, we decided again to postpone action until the day after the run-off so that the demonstrations could not be used to cloud the issues. Like many others, we waited to see Mr. Connor defeated, and to this end we endured postponement after postponement. Having aided in this community need, we felt that our direct-action program could be delayed no longer.

You may well ask: "Why direct action? Why sit-ins, marches and so forth? Isn't negotiation a better path?" You are quite right in calling for negotiation. Indeed, this is the very purpose of direct action. Non-violent direct action seeks to create such a crisis and foster such a tension that a community which has constantly refused to negotiate is forced to confront the issue. It seeks so to dramatize the issue that it can no longer be ignored. My citing the creation of tension as part of the work of the nonviolent resister may sound rather shocking. But I must confess that I am not afraid of the word "tension." I have earnestly opposed violent tension, but there is a type of constructive, nonviolent tension which is necessary for growth. Just as Socrates felt that it was necessary to create a tension in the mind so that individuals could rise from the bondage of myths and half-truths to the unfettered realm of creative analysis and objective appraisal, so must we see the need for nonviolent gadflies to create the kind of tension in society that will help men rise from the dark depths of prejudice and racism to the majestic heights of understanding and brotherhood.

The purpose of our direct-action program is to create a situation so crisis-packed that it will inevitably open the door to negotiation. I therefore concur with you in your call for negotiation. Too long has our beloved Southland been bogged down in a tragic effort to live in monologue rather than dialogue.

One of the basic points in your statement is that the action that I and my associates have taken in Birmingham is untimely. Some have asked: "Why didn't you give the new city administration time to act?" The only answer that I can give to this query is that the new Birmingham administration must be prodded about as much as the outgoing one before it will act. We are sadly mistaken if we feel that the election of Albert Boutwell as mayor will bring the millennium to Birmingham. While Mr. Boutwell is a much more gentle person than Mr. Connor, they are both segregationists, dedicated to maintenance of the status quo. I have hope that Mr. Boutwell will be reasonable enough to see the futility of massive resistance to desegregation. But he will not see this without pressure from devotees of civil rights. My friends, I must say to you that we have not made a single gain in civil rights without determined legal and nonviolent pressure. Lamentably, it is an historical fact that privileged groups seldom give up their privileges voluntarily. Individuals may see the moral light and voluntarily give up their unjust posture; but, as Reinhold Niebuhr has reminded us, groups tend to be more immoral than individuals.

We know through painful experience that freedom is never voluntarily given by the oppressor; it must be demanded by the oppressed. Frankly, I have yet to engage in a direct-action campaign that was "well timed" in the view of those who have not suffered unduly from the disease of segregation. For years now I have heard the word "Wait!" It rings in the ear of every Negro with piercing familiarity. This "Wait" has almost always meant "Never." We must come to see, with one of our distinguished jurists, that "justice too long delayed is justice denied."

We have waited for more than 340 years for our constitutional and God-given rights. The nations of Asia and Africa are moving with jetlike speed toward gaining political independence, but we still creep at horse-and-buggy pace toward gaining a cup of coffee at a lunch counter. Perhaps it is easy for those who have never felt the stinging darts of segregation to say, "Wait." But when you have seen vicious mobs lynch your mothers and fathers at will and drown your sisters and brothers at whim; when you have seen hate-filled policemen curse, kick and even kill your black brothers and sisters; when you see the vast majority of your twenty million Negro brothers smothering in an airtight cage of poverty in the midst of an affluent society; when you suddenly find yor tongue twisted and your speech stammering as you seek to explain to your six-year-old daughter why she can't go to the public amusement park that has just been advertised on television, and see tears welling up in her eyes when she is told that Funtown is closed to colored children, and see ominous clouds of inferiority beginning to form in her little mental sky, and see her beginning to distort her personality by developing an unconscious bitterness toward white people; when you have to concoct an answer for a five-year-old son who is asking: "Daddy, why do white people treat colored people so mean?"; when you take a cross-country drive and find it necessary to sleep night after night in the uncomfortable corners of your automobile because no motel will accept you; when you are humiliated day in and day out by nagging signs reading "white" and "colored"; when your first name becomes "nigger," your middle name becomes "boy" (however old you are) and your last name becomes "John," and your wife and mother are never given the respected title "Mrs."; when you are harried by day and haunted by night by the fact that you are a Negro, living constantly at tiptoe stance, never quite knowing what to expect next, and are plagued with inner fears and outer resentments; when you are forever fighting a degenerating sense of "nobodiness"—then you will understand why we find it difficult to wait. There comes a time when the cup of endurance runs over, and men are no longer willing to be plunged into the abyss of despair. I hope, sirs, you can understand our legitimate and unavoidable impatience.

You express a great deal of anxiety over our willingness to break laws. This is certainly a legitimate concern. Since we so diligently urge people to obey the Supreme Court's decision of 1943 outlawing segregation in the public schools, at first glance it may seem rather paradoxical for us consciously to break laws. One may well ask: "How can you advocate breaking some laws and obeying others?" The answer lies in the fact that there are two types of laws: just and unjust. I would be the first to advocate obeying just laws. One has not only a legal but a moral responsibility to obey just laws. Conversely, one has a moral responsibility to disobey unjust laws. I would agree with St. Augustine that "an unjust law is no law at all."

Now, what is the difference between the two? How does one determine whether a law is just or unjust? A just law is a man-made code that squares with the moral law or the law of God. An unjust law is a code that is out of harmony with the moral law. To put it in the terms of St. Thomas Aquinas: An unjust law is a human law that is not rooted in eternal law and natural law. Any law that uplifts human personality is just. Any law that degrades human personality is unjust. All segregation statutes are unjust because segregation distorts the soul and damages the personality. It gives the segregator a false sense of superiority and the segregated a false sense of inferiority. Segregation, to use the terminology of the Jewish philosopher Martin Buber, substitutes an "I-it" relationship for an "I-thou" relationship and ends up relegating persons to the status of things. Hence segregation is not only politically, economically and sociologically unsound, it is morally wrong and sinful. Paul Tillich has said that sin is separation. Is not segregation an existential expression of man's tragic separation, his awful estrangement, his terrible sinfulness? Thus it is that I can urge men to obey the 1954 decision of the Supreme Court, for it is morally right; and I can urge them to disobey segregation ordinances, for they are morally wrong.

Let us consider a more concrete example of just and unjust laws. An unjust law is a code that a numerical or power majority group compels a minority group to obey but does not make binding on itself. This is *difference* made legal. By the same token, a just law is a code that a majority compels a minority to follow and that it is willing to follow itself. This is *sameness* made legal.

Let me give another explanation. A law is unjust if it is inflicted on a minority that, as a result of being denied the right to vote, had no part in enacting or devising the law. Who can say that the legislature of Alabama which set up that State's segregation laws was democratically elected? Throughout Alabama all sorts of devious methods are used to prevent Negroes from becoming registered voters, and there are some counties in which, even though Negroes constitute a majority of the population, not a single Negro is registered. Can any law enacted under such circumstances be considered democratically structured?

Sometimes a law is just on its face and unjust in its application. For instance, I have been arrested on a charge of parading without a permit. Now, there is nothing wrong in having an ordinance which requires a permit for a parade. But such an ordinance becomes unjust when it is used to maintain segregation and to deny citizens the First-Amendment privilege of peaceful assembly and protest.

I hope you are able to see the distinction I am trying to point out. In no sense do I advocate evading or defying the law, as would the rabid segregationist. That would lead to anarchy. One who breaks an unjust law must do so openly, lovingly, and with a willingness to accept the penalty. I submit that an individual who breaks a law that conscience tells him is unjust, and who willingly accepts the penalty of imprisonment in order to arouse the conscience of the community over its injustice, is in reality expressing the highest respect for law.

Of course, there is nothing new about this kind of civil disobedience. It was evidenced sublimely in the refusal of Shadrach, Meshach and Abednego to obey the laws of Nebuchadnezzar, on the ground that a higher moral law was at stake. It was practiced superbly by the early Christians, who were willing to face hungry lions and the excruciating pain of chopping blocks rather than submit to certain unjust laws of the Roman Empire. To a degree, academic freedom is a reality today because Socrates practiced civil disobedience. In our own nation, the Boston Tea Party represented a massive act of civil disobedience.

We should never forget that everything Adolf Hitler did in Germany was "legal" and everything the Hungarian freedom fighters did in Hungary was "illegal." It was "illegal" to aid and comfort a Jew in Hitler's Germany. Even so, I am sure that, had I lived in Germany at the time, I would have aided and comforted my Jewish brothers. If today I lived in a Communist country where certain principles dear to the Christian faith are suppressed, I would openly advocate disobeying that country's anti-religious laws.

I must make two honest confessions to you, my Christian and Jewish brothers. First, I must confess that over the past few years I have been gravely disappointed with the white moderate. I have almost reached the regrettable conclusion that the Negro's great stumbling block in his stride toward freedom is not the White Citizen's Counciler or the Ku Klux Klanner, but the white moderate, who is more devoted to "order" than to justice; who prefers a negative peace which is the absence of tension to a positive peace which is the presence of justice; who constantly says: "I agree with you in the goal you seek, but I cannot agree with your methods of direct action"; who paternalistically believes he can set the timetable for another man's freedom; who lives by a mythical concept of time and who constantly advises the Negro to wait for a "more convenient season." Shallow understanding from people of good will is more frustrating than absolute misunderstanding from people of ill will. Lukewarm acceptance is much more bewildering than outright rejection.

I had hoped that the white moderate would understand that law and order exist for the purpose of establishing justice and that when they fail in this purpose they became the dangerously structured dams that block the flow of social progress. I had hoped that the white moderate would understand that the present tension in the South is a necessary phase of the transition from an obnoxious negative peace, in which the Negro passively accepted his unjust plight, to a substantive and positive peace, in which all men will respect the dignity and worth of human personality. Actually, we who engage in nonviolent direct action are not the creators of tension. We merely bring to the surface the hidden tension that is already alive. We bring it out in the open, where it can be seen and dealt with. Like a boil that can never be cured so long as it is covered up but must be opened with all its ugliness to the natural medicines of air and light, injustice must be exposed, with all the tension its exposure creates, to the light of human conscience and the air of national opinion before it can be cured.

In your statement you assert that our actions, even though peaceful, must be condemned because they precipitate violence. But is this a logical assertion? Isn't this like condemning a robbed man because his possession of money precipitated the evil act of robbery? Isn't this like condemning

Socrates because his unswerving commitment to truth and his philosophical inquiries precipitated the act by the misguided populace in which they made him drink hemlock. Isn't this like condemning Jesus because his unique God-consciousness and never-ceasing devotion to God's will precipitated the evil act of crucifixion? We must come to see that, as the federal courts have consistently affirmed, it is wrong to urge an individual to cease his efforts to gain his basic constitutional rights because the quest may precipitate violence. Society must protect the robbed and punish the robber.

I had also hoped that the white moderate would reject the myth concerning time in relation to the struggle for freedom. I have just received a letter from a white brother in Texas. He writes: "All Christians know that the colored people will receive equal rights eventually, but it is possible that you are in too great a religious hurry. It has taken Christianity almost two thousand years to accomplish what it has. The teachings of Christ take time to come to earth." Such an attitude stems from a tragic misconception of time, from the strangely irrational notion that there is something in the very flow of time that will inevitably cure all ills. Actually, time itself is neutral; it can be used either destructively or constructively. More and more I feel that the people of ill will have used time much more effectively than have the people of good will. We will have to repent in this generation not merely for the hateful words and actions of the bad people but for the appalling silence of the good people. Human progress never rolls in on wheels of inevitability; it comes through the tireless efforts of men willing to be co-workers with God, and without this hard work, time itself becomes an ally of the forces of social stagnation. We must use time creatively, in the knowledge that the time is always ripe to do right. Now is the time to make real the promise of democracy and transform our pending national elegy into a creative psalm of brotherhood. Now is the time to lift our national policy from the quicksand of racial injustice to the solid rock of human dignity.

You speak of our activity in Birmingham as extreme. At first I was rather disappointed that fellow clergymen would see my nonviolent efforts as those of an extremist. I began thinking about the fact that I stand in the middle of two opposing forces in the Negro community. One is a force of complacency, made up in part of Negroes who, as a result of long years of oppression, are so drained of self-respect and a sense of "somebodiness" that they have adjusted to segregation; and in part of a few middle-class Negroes who, because of a degree of academic and economic security and because in some ways they profit by segregation, have become insensitive to the problems of the masses. The other force is one of bitterness and hatred, and it comes perilously close to advocating violence. It is expressed in the various black nationalist groups that are springing up across the nation, the largest and best-known being Elijah Muhammad's Muslim movement. Nourished by the Negro's frustration over the continued existence of racial discrimination, this movement is made up of people who have lost faith in America, who have absolutely repudiated Christianity, and who have concluded that the white man is an incorrigible "devil."

I have tried to stand between these two forces, saying that we need emulate neither the "do-nothingism" of the complacent nor the hatred and despair of the black nationalist. For there is the more excellent way of love and nonviolent protest. I am grateful to God that, through the influence of the Negro church, the way of nonviolence became an integral part of our struggle.

If this philosophy had not emerged, by now many streets of the South would, I am convinced, be flowing with blood. And I am further convinced that if our white brothers dismiss as "rabble-rousers" and "outside agitators" those of us who employ nonviolent direct action, and if they refuse to support our nonviolent efforts, millions of Negroes will, out of frustration and despair, seek solace and security in black-nationalist ideologies—a development that would inevitably lead to a frightening racial nightmare.

Oppressed people cannot remain oppressed forever. The yearning for freedom eventually manifests itself, and that is what has happened to the American Negro. Something within has reminded him of his birthright of freedom, and something without has reminded him that it can be gained. Consciously or unconsciously, he has been caught up by the *Zeitgeist*, and with his black brothers of Africa and his brown and yellow brothers of Asia, South America and the Caribbean, the United States Negro is moving with a sense of great urgency toward the promised land of racial justice. If one recognizes this vital urge that has engulfed the Negro community, one should readily understand why public demonstrations are taking place. The Negro has many pent-up resentments and latent frustrations, and he must release them. So let him march; let him make prayer pilgrimages to the city hall; let him go on freedom rides— and try to understand why he must do so. If his repressed emotions are not released in nonviolent ways, they will seek expression through violence; this is not a threat but a fact of history. So I have not said to my people: "Get rid of your discontent." Rather, I have tried to say that this normal and healthy discontent can be channeled into the creative outlet of nonviolent direct action. And now this approach is being termed extremist.

But though I was initially disappointed at being categorized as an extremist, as I continued to think about the matter I gradually gained a measure of satisfaction from the label. Was not Jesus an extremist for love: "Love your enemies, bless them that curse you, do good to them that hate you, and pray for them which despitefully use you, and persecute you."

Was not Amos an extremist for justice: "Let justice roll down like waters and righteousness like an ever-flowing stream." Was not Paul an extremist for the Christian gospel: "I bear in my body the marks of the Lord Jesus." Was not Martin Luther an extremist: "Here I stand; I cannot do otherwise, so help me God." And John Bunyan: "I will stay in jail to the end of my days before I make a butchery of my conscience." And Abraham Lincoln: "This nation cannot survive half slave and half free." And Thomas Jefferson: "We hold these truths to be self-evident, that all men are created equal. . . ." So the question is not whether we will be extremists, but what kind of extremists we will be. Will we be extremists for hate or for love? Will we be extremists for the preservation of injustice or for the extension of justice? In that dramatic scene on Calvary's hill three men were crucified. We must never forget that all three were crucified for the same crime—the crime of extremism. Two were extremists for immorality, and thus fell below their environment. The other, Jesus Christ, was an extremist for love, truth and goodness, and thereby rose above his environment. Perhaps the South, the nation and the world are in dire need of creative extremists.

I had hoped that the white moderate would see this need. Perhaps I was too optimistic; perhaps I expected too much. I suppose I should have realized that few members of the oppressor race can understand the deep groans and passionate yearnings of the oppressed race, and still fewer have the vision to see that injustice must be rooted out by strong, persistent and determined action. I am thankful, however, that some of our white brothers in the South have grasped the meaning of this social revolution and committed themselves to it. They are still all too few in quantity, but they are big in quality. Some—such as Ralph McGill, Lillian Smith, Harry Golden, James McBride Dabbs, Ann Braden and Sarah Patton Boyle—have written about our struggle in eloquent and prophetic terms. Others have marched with us down nameless streets of the South. They have languished in filthy, roach-infested jails, suffering the abuse and brutality of policemen who view them as "dirty nigger-lovers." Unlike so many of their moderate brothers and sisters, they have recognized the urgency of the moment and sensed the need for powerful "action" antidotes to combat the disease of segregation.

Let me take note of my other major disappointment. I have been so greatly disappointed with the white church and its leadership. Of course, there are some notable exceptions. I am not unmindful of the fact that each of you has taken some significant stands on this issue. I commend you, Reverend Stallings, for your Christian stand on this past Sunday, in welcoming Negroes to your worship service on a nonsegregated basis. I commend the Catholic leaders of this state for integrating Spring Hill College several years ago.

But despite these notable exceptions, I must honestly reiterate that I have been disappointed with the church. I do not say this as one of those negative critics who can always find something wrong with the church. I say this as a minister of the gospel, who loves the church; who was nurtured in its bosom; who has been sustained by its spiritual blessings and who will remain true to it as long as the cord of life shall lengthen.

When I was suddenly catapulted into the leadership of the bus protest in Montgomery, Alabama, a few years ago, I felt we would be supported by the white church. I felt that the white ministers, priests and rabbis of the South would be among our strongest allies. Instead, some have been outright opponents, refusing to understand the freedom movement and misrepresenting its leaders; all too many others have been more cautious than courageous and have remained silent behind the anesthetizing security of stained-glass windows.

In spite of my shattered dreams, I came to Birmingham with the hope that the white religious leadership of this community would see the justice of our cause and, with deep moral concern, would serve as the channel through which our just grievances would reach the power structure. I had hoped that each of you would understand. But again I have been disappointed.

I have heard numerous southern religious leaders admonish their worshipers to comply with a desegregation decision because it is the law, but I have longed to hear white ministers declare: "Follow this decree because integration is morally right and because the Negro is your brother." In the midst of blatant injustices inflicted upon the Negro, I have watched white churchmen stand on the sideline and mouth pious irrelevancies and sanctimonious trivialities. In the midst of a mighty struggle to rid our nation of racial and economic injustice, I have heard many ministers say: "Those are social issues, with which the gospel has no real concern." And I have watched many churches commit themselves to a completely otherworldly religion which makes a strange, un-Biblical distinction between body and soul, between the sacred and the secular.

I have traveled the length and breadth of Alabama, Mississippi and all the other southern states. On sweltering summer days and crisp autumn mornings I have looked at the South's beautiful churches with their lofty spires pointing heavenward. I have beheld the impressive outlines of her massive religious-education buildings. Over and over I have found myself asking: "What kind of people worship here? Who is their God? Where were their voices when the lips of Governor Barnett dripped with words of interposition and nullification? Where were they when Governor Wallace gave a clarion call for defiance and hatred? Where were their voices of support when bruised and weary Negro men and women decided to rise from the dark dungeons of complacency to the bright hills of creative protest?"

Yes, these questions are still in my mind. In deep disappointment I have wept over the laxity of the church. But be assured that my tears have been tears of love. There can be no deep disappointment where there is not deep love. Yes, I love the church. How could I do otherwise? I am in the rather unique position of being the son, the grandson and the great-grandson of preachers. Yes, I see the church as the body of Christ. But, oh! How we have blemished and scarred that body through social neglect and through fear of being nonconformists.

There was a time when the church was very powerful—in the time when the early Christians rejoiced at being deemed worthy to suffer for what they believed. In those days the church was not merely a thermometer that recorded the ideas and principles of popular opinion; it was a thermostat that transformed the mores of society. Whenever the early Christians entered a town, the people in power became disturbed and immediately sought to convict the Christians for being "disturbers of the peace" and "outside agitators." But the Christians pressed on, in the conviction that they were "a colony of heaven," called to obey God rather than man. Small in number, they were big in commitment. They were too God-intoxicated to be "astronomically intimidated." By their effort and example they brought an end to such ancient evils as infanticide and gladiatorial contests.

Things are different now. So often the contemporary church is a weak, ineffectual voice with an uncertain sound. So often it is an archdefender of the status quo. Far from being disturbed by the presence of the church, the power structure of the average community is consoled by the church's silent—and often even vocal—sanction of things as they are.

But the judgment of God is upon the church as never before. If today's church does not recapture the sacrificial spirit of the early church, it will lose its authenticity, forfeit the loyalty of millions, and be dismissed as an irrelevant social club with no meaning for the twentieth century. Every day I meet young people whose disappointment with the church has turned into outright disgust.

Perhaps I have once again been too optimistic. Is organized religion too inextricably bound to the status quo to save our nation and the world? Perhaps I must turn my faith to the inner spiritual church, the church within the church, as the true *ekklesia* and the hope of the world. But again I am thankful to God that some noble souls from the ranks of organized religion have broken loose from the paralyzing chains of conformity and joined us as active partners in the struggle for freedom. They have left their secure congregations and walked the streets of Albany,

Georgia, with us. They have gone down the highways of the South on tortuous rides for freedom. Yes, they have gone to jail with us. Some have been dismissed from their churches, have lost the support of their bishops and fellow ministers. But they have acted in the faith that right defeated is stronger than evil triumphant. Their witness has been the spiritual salt that has preserved the true meaning of the gospel in these troubled times. They have carved a tunnel of hope through the dark mountain of disappointment.

I hope the church as a whole will meet the challenge of this decisive hour. But even if the church does not come to the aid of justice, I have no despair about the future. I have no fear about the outcome of our struggle in Birmingham, even if our motives are at present misunderstood. We will reach the goal of freedom in Birmingham and all over the nation, because the goal of America is freedom. Abused and scorned though we may be, our destiny is tied up with America's destiny. Before the pilgrims landed at Plymouth, we were here. Before the pen of Jefferson etched the majestic words of the Declaration of Independence across the pages of history, we were here. For more than two centuries our forebears labored in this country without wages; they made cotton king; they built the homes of their masters while suffering gross injustice and shameful humiliation—and yet out of a bottomless vitality they continued to thrive and develop. If the inexpressible cruelties of slavery could not stop us, the opposition we now face will surely fail. We will win our freedom because the sacred heritage of our nation and the eternal will of God are embodied in our echoing demands.

Before closing I feel impelled to mention one other point in your statement that has troubled me profoundly. You warmly commended the Birmingham police force for keeping "order" and "preventing violence." I doubt that you would have so warmly commended the police force if you had seen its dogs sinking their teeth into unarmed, non-violent Negroes. I doubt that you would so quickly commend the policemen if you were to observe their ugly and inhumane treatment of Negroes here in the city jail; if you were to watch them push and curse old Negro women and young Negro girls; if you were to see them slap and kick old Negro men and young boys; if you were to observe them, as they did on two occasions, refuse to give us food because we wanted to sing our grace together. I cannot join you in your praise of the Birmingham police department.

It is true that the police have exercised a degree of discipline in handling the demonstrators. In this sense they have conducted themselves rather "non-violently" in public. But for what purpose? To preserve the evil system of segregation. Over the past few years I have consistently preached that nonviolence demands that the means we use must be as pure as the ends we seek. I have tried to make clear that it is wrong to use immoral means to attain moral ends. But now I must affirm that it is just as wrong, or perhaps even more so, to use moral means to preserve immoral ends. Perhaps Mr. Connor and his policemen have been rather nonviolent in public, as was Chief Pritchett in Albany, Georgia, but they have used the moral means of nonviolence to maintain the immoral end of racial injustice. As T. S. Eliot has said: "The last temptation is the greatest treason: To do the right deed for the wrong reason."

I wish you had commended the Negro sit-inners and demonstrators of Birmingham for their sublime courage, their willingness to suffer and their amazing discipline in the midst of great provocation. One day the South will recognize its real heroes. They will be the James Merediths, with the noble sense of purpose that enables them to face jeering and hostile mobs, and with the agonizing loneliness that characterizes the life of the pioneer. They will be old, oppressed, battered Negro women, symbolized in a seventy-two-year-old woman in Montgomery, Alabama, who rose up with a sense of dignity and with her people decided not to ride segregated buses, and who responded with ungrammatical profundity to one who inquired about her weariness: "My feets is tired, but my soul is at rest." They will be the young high school and college students, the young ministers of the gospel and a host of their elders, courageously and nonviolently sitting in at lunch counters and willingly going to jail for conscience' sake. One day the South will know that when these disinherited children of God sat down at lunch counters, they were in reality standing up for what is best in the American dream and for the most sacred values in our Judaeo-Christian heritage; thereby bringing our nation back to those great wells of democracy which were dug deep by the founding fathers in their formulation of the Constitution and the Declaration of Independence.

Never before have I written so long a letter. I'm afraid it is much too long to take your precious time. I can assure you that it would have been much shorter if I had been writing from a comfortable desk, but what else can one do when he is alone in a narrow jail cell, other than write long letters, think long thoughts and pray long prayers?

If I have said anything in this letter that overstates the truth and indicates an unreasonable impatience, I beg you to forgive me. If I have said anything that understates the truth and indicates my having a patience that allows me to settle for anything less than brotherhood, I beg God to forgive me.

I hope this letter finds you strong in the faith. I also hope that circumstances will soon make it possible for me to meet each of you, not as an integrationist or a civil-rights leader but as a fellow clergyman and a Christian brother. Let us all hope that the dark clouds of racial prejudice will soon pass away and the deep fog of misunderstanding will be lifted from our fear-drenched communities, and in some not too distant tomorrow the radiant stars of love and brotherhood will shine over our great nation with all their scintillating beauty.

Yours for the cause of Peace and Brotherhood,

Martin Luther King, Jr.

Robert Penn Warren
(1905-   )

ROBERT PENN WARREN was born in Guthrie, Kentucky. He received a B.A. from Vanderbilt (1925), an M.A. from the University of California (Berkeley) in 1927, and a B. Litt. (as a Rhodes Scholar) from Oxford University, England, in 1930. He has taught at Southwestern College, Vanderbilt, Louisiana State, Minnesota, Yale, Colorado, and Iowa. The winner of numerous awards, Penn Warren is the author of *All The King's Men* (1946), *World Enough and Time* (1950), *Segregation* (1956), *Flood* (1964), *Who Speaks for the Negro?* (1965), and a number of other works.

"Conversation Piece" is sections five and six of the last chapter of *Who Speaks for the Negro?*

CONVERSATION PIECE

In recognizing the justice of the Negro's demands there are many temptations to sentimentality. One such temptation is to assume that it is all a matter of feeling—that we must consult our feelings in order to do justice. When Martin Luther King, standing on a platform, addressing an off-stage white society, says, "You don't have to love me to quit lynching me," he is disinfecting his doctrine of *agapē* from sentimentality—from the notion of easy solutions by easy love. He is also making a grim and paradoxical joke, which Negroes greatly appreciate—to judge by the titter and applause. The joke frees them; it frees them from the need to be "lovable"— lovable by some set of white standards, i.e., servile—in order not to be lynched.

But the joke is one for the white man to ponder. For it frees him, too: from the need to "love" in order not to lynch. Translated, the joke frees him from the need to love in order to refrain from doing a whole lot of things—such as segregating buses, bombing churches, and conniving in racial convenants in housing developments.

In an ideal world, of course, our feelings would all be good—we "love" all men—and the good feelings would express themselves immediately and effortlessly in good acts. There would be no moral problem—in fact, it might be said that there would be no moral consciousness, therefore no moral life. But in this world, the issue is not, so Dr. King is saying, one of achieving perfection; it is one of achieving a proper awareness of, and attitude toward, our imperfection. In this world, we may aspire to be pure in heart, but we can't wait for that far-off divine event before trying to be reasonably decent citizens who, with all their failings, may believe in justice. Since the odds are that, in this imperfect world, the old human heart remains rather impure, we can scarcely consult it to find out what to do. Rather than depend on our spontaneous and uncriticized feelings we had better consult our intelligence, fallible as it is, to see what is reasonable, decent, socially desirable—and even just—and then, as best we can, act on that.

When, in the South, a white woman says to me, as not a few have said, "I pray to God to change my feelings," she is recognizing the old human split—between her intellectual recognition that makes her pray for a change, and her feelings which she prays that God will change. But if the split exists—and the recognition of such splits is the ground fact of our moral life—there is no ultimately compelling reason why she should wait on the mystic change of feeling before she can take a practical step. To wait for the regeneration of feeling is sentimentality, a self-flattering indulgence and an alibi.

If we want to change feelings we can remember that the performing of an act does a good deal to change the feelings of the performer of the act. In fact, one of the surest ways for an intellectual recognition to change feelings is to put the recognition, in however minimal a way, into action. But it is sentimental, again, to expect immediate, easy, and absolute re-generation of feelings just because you have joined the NAACP or sent a contribution to CORE or marched in a demonstration. It is absurd to expect such cataclysmic, glorious, and easy purgation on the particular point of racial brotherhood, when you know that you have to live in a shifting complex of feelings about mother, father, sister, brother, wife, child, friend, the U.S.A., and God Almighty. Why should you think that feelings on the question of racial brotherhood are to be exempted from the ordinary complexities of life?

We do want to love our fellow men and live at peace with them, we do long for clarity of feeling, we do want as little lag as possible between feeling and action; and as human beings, we are certainly due for a good deal of healthy self-scrutiny and self-criticism. But is it healthy to go into a breast-beating routine of upside-down Phariseeism every time we—white people—discover some complication of feeling a little less than worthy according to the rule book? Or according to some self-appointed snooper with his portable couch? A deeply disturbing awareness of one's sins does not have to be the same thing as the masochistic self-indulgence not infre-quently associated with the white man's (not the Negro's) sense of a communal white guilt—the thing described by Whitney Young as the guilt feeling that makes the white man abase himself before "Malcolm X or James Baldwin or Adam Clayton Powell," and cry out, "Beat me, Daddy, I feel guilty!"

It is not doing the Negro population much of a favor for a white man to indulge himself in a nice warm bubble bath of emotion, no matter how sweet he feels while in the suds. When a white man, fresh from his virgin experience on the picket line or in jail (with his bail money usually handy), begins to tell me how he feels clean for the first time in his life, I wonder if he has bemused himself into believing that the whole demonstration had been mounted exclusively for the purpose of giving him a spiritual cathartic.

Word filters out of Mississippi, in fact, that Negroes now and then express amusement or even resentment at some of the white helpers who seemed to feel that the Summer Project was a quick course in psychotherapy or a religious conversion without tears arranged for their personal convenience. And this reaction is to workers who, after all, had taken their risks. What about the white man who wants the nice feeling without taking the risks? As Ruth Turner put it to me in Cleveland, "The Negro should not be a suffering servant for an American conscience." It is a strange and sad sort of sentimentality we have here—like all sentimentality it is ultimately self-centered, but here the self-centeredness is obscenely cloaked in selflessness, a professed concern for the rights and feelings of others.

Another form of sentimentality appears in the notion of the "debt" to the Negro—the idea that society owes "back wages" for slavery. There is, at first glance, a logic to this, and people as wise and good as Martin Luther King have accepted it.[1] He writes that his "Bill of Rights for the Disadvantaged" finds its "moral justification" in idea of the "debt." But the logic is spurious and the notion is fraught with mischief.

The whole notion of untangling the "debts" of history smacks of fantasy. Would the descendants of an Athenian helot of the fifth century B.C., assuming that such a relationship could be established, have a claim today on the Greek government? And with or without accrued interest? Would the descendant of a mill girl in Lowell, Massachusetts, who died of lint-lungs in 1845, have a claim on Washington, D.C., in 1965? Or would it be Boston? And suppose the issue of the girl has been born, as was often the case in that class, out of wedlock—would that prejudice the claim? Or is debt never due to Caucasians who have been penalized by history?

If we assume that the U.S. Government does owe the Negro citizens back pay, how do we calculate it? Does a statute of limitations ever apply? And in equity what do we do about taxes collected for this purpose from citizens whose ancestors came over after Lincoln had signed the Emancipation Proclamation? Do they get a proportionate rebate? Or does the fact of whiteness make them automatically guilty, too?

And while we are on the subject, let us branch out and try to calculate how many explosion-prone trade guns, ankers of rum, and iron bars the Nigerian government owes what percentage of the twenty million American

1. Martin Luther King, Jr., *Why We Can't Wait* (1963).—*Author.*

Negroes—those things being the common currency the ancestors of the said Nigerians demanded in payment for the ancestors of the said American Negroes whom the ancestors of the Nigerians had bagged in the bush and put up for sale. The whole thing is a grisly farce. Come to think of it, it smacks not of fantasy, but of Bedlam.

But before I proceed from the matter of logic to the matter of mischief, I shall say that I am totally in accord with Dr. King's notion of a "Bill of Rights for the Disadvantaged." We are facing a desperate crisis, and there must be a special crash program—or better, a series of intermeshed programs, governmental and private—involving Negroes and whites. To say, however, that this should be regarded as "back wages" for the Negroes denies the very basis on which such a program should be instituted. The basis for the Negro is his status as a citizen, just as it is for the white beneficiary.

Even after 1865, if the Federal Government, busy with the game of politics and business, had not tragically defaulted on its obligations, the justification for any program for the freedmen—even one involving a period of preparation for the franchise—would not have been in terms of back wages but would have been based on the status of citizenship potential in the situation. And now a hundred years later, the notion of the "debt" is not, as King would have it, a "moral justification"; it is an immoral justification. Immoral because it sets up a false relation between the Negro and society, distinguishing him from the white citizen who needs assistance. To regard the relation as based on a debt is a line of thought that, on one hand, would unman and demean the Negro, and on the other would lead straight to the happy inspiration in some hoodlum's head that the back wages are sitting there in the form of a new TV set and all he has to do is to kick in the show window and collect his pay.

What society may do to relieve the Negro's plight is not payment for work done; it is preparation for work to be done. Society does not owe the Negro *qua* Negro, anything. But it does owe many individual citizens, who happen to be Negro and who happen to be disadvantaged, a chance to work—and to work at something that will fulfill them and will benefit society in general. The whole theory of a debt to the Negro is, as Stokeley Carmichael puts it, "a drip from the Black Muslims."[2]

The point is not that the Negro citizen's rights are special. As a citizen he can expect nothing special. What is special is the fact that because of his situation he cannot fare equally with other citizens. He has the same claim as others, but because here race and class intersect in a long history of mutual aggravation, there is a special difficulty in fulfilling it; the

2. Both Bayard Rustin and James Farmer explicitly repudiate the notion of the "debt."—*Author.*

program to meet his needs might require special tailoring to meet special difficulties.

Anything else would be racism—pure and simple. It would also be condescension. It would be to put the Negro on a reservation, like the Indian—even if a gilded reservation full of child psychologists, reading experts, electronic training laboratories, and computers to feed data into the office of the director.

Another form of sentimentality appears in the notion that the Negro—qua Negro—is intrinsically "better." This betterness is described in many forms, but, strangely enough, you never hear the Negro admired as a better philosopher, mathematician, nuclear physicist, banker, soldier, lawyer, or administrator. It would seem that the betterness is always something that can be attributed to that term. This modern American Noble Savage is admired for athletic prowess, musicality, grace in the dance, heroic virtue, natural humor, tenderness with children, patience, sensitivity to nature, generosity of spirit, capacity to forgive, life awareness, and innocent sexuality. A white man may choose the particular version of the Noble Savage to suit his tastes. Here is Jack Kerouac, in a now well-advertised passage, making his choice:

> At lilac evening I walked with every muscle aching among the lights of 27th and Welton in the Denver colored section, wishing I were a Negro, feeling that the best the white world had afforded was not enough ecstasy for me, not enough life, joy, kicks, darkness, music, not enough night.[3]

It would, I imagine, be a very dull Negro who did not catch here the note of condescension. James Baldwin, who is definitely not dull, caught the tone, and remarked: "I would hate to be in Jack Kerouac's shoes if he should ever be mad enough to read this aloud from the stage of the Apollo Theatre [in Harlem]."[4]

3. *The Subterraneans.—Author.*
4. Some of the most admired qualities of the Negro may be said to be compensatory, the result of deprivation, and may even be, in their origins, a mark not of freedom but of compulsion. Jazz, for instance, is not a product of orgiastic joy but of deprivation—both an expression for, and a conquest of, deprivation. The same would hold for dancing, where the numbed and throttled emotional life would find a "safe" way to appear. Athletic powers may be taken as a "safe" expression of the aggressive impulses. The point here is not that the achievements in themselves do not represent triumphs, but that the naive and romantic admirer is apt to misinterpret the grounding as noble savagery. It is no wonder that Negroes sometimes regard the white who romantically tries to "go Negro" as an object of amusement or contempt: the white man wants something without knowing the price tag.

On the matter of art (and other things) as compensatory, the Negro, again, is not a special case. Many philosophers and psychologists have, for centuries, taken all art to be compensatory in one sense or another—a way of remedying the defects of nature or man's lot.—*Author.*

Over and over again, directly or as irony, we may encounter the Negro's resentment at such white man's praise. For instance, we may remember how Stokely Carmichael resented the praise and even the popularity he found at Bronx High. He read the condescension in it— and worse, the special condescension in the fact that he was being addressed as *the* Negro and not as himself. We may remember the classic example of unconscious condescension in the notion in the old sociology text book, by Park and Burgess, of the Negro as "the lady of the races."

The risk of condescension is always present in any romantic attachment to the simple—or to what, sometimes erroneously, may sometimes be taken as simple: Wordsworth's peasant, child, and idiot; Leatherstocking; the "worker" of the 1930's; folk song. Now that *the* Negro, from Ray Charles to Martin Luther King, is in for special attention, we find special versions of condescension. Even in the admiration, sometimes abject, for a man like King—who is far from peasant, child, idiot, "worker," Indian scout, or box-beater—the paradox of inferiority-superiority, the sense of the complex person (white) recognizing simple worth (black), the psychology of the appeal of the pastoral poem, lurks in the very abjectness of the admiration granted.

Or to take another, a literary example, the now famous Kitten of *One Hundred Dollar Misunderstanding* is a special brand of Noble Savage, or a "naturally" wise and witty milkmaid in a pastoral of our time; and the author, in presenting her, has mobilized all the constellation of inferiority-superiority feelings. In writing his *One Hundred Dollar Misunderstanding*, Robert Gover, is, in fact, very like the Southerner who makes the classic remark about his cook: "Ole Sallie—now I tell you she is a better Christian than any of us. In Heaven, won't any of us be fit to tie her shoe." But that will be in Heaven. Just as Kitten is safely stowed away in a novel.

The admiration for the betterness of the Negro is often little more than a simple turning upside down of the white man's old conviction of the Negro's inferiority. The ineffable fear of what is mysteriously different becomes its inevitably linked opposite, an attraction; loathing becomes desire, strangely mixed. The Negro has been what is called a "contrast conception"[5]—that is, the thing on which the white man may project the opposite of all the fine qualities he attributes to himself. The Negro is the scapegoat, the inner enemy who must be ejected. He is, therefore, officially inferior. But the inner enemy, the secret sharer in darkness who has been ejected, leaves an ache of forbidden yearnings behind him. If the old-time Southern theologians, as Myrdal reminds us, attributed to the black man (as the old-time New England theologians did to the red) a disproportionate

5. Lewis C. Copeland, "The Negro as a Contrast Conception," in *Race Relations and the Race Problem*, ed. Edgar R. Thompson.—*Author.*

dose of Original Sin, unwittingly they encouraged the suspicion that the more Original Sin, the more fun.

This suspicion has not died. In fact, a thousand developments in our post-Protestant society tend to keep that piece of theology alive in various attractive disguises. In the hairy and breathless dark where such mumbo-jumbo takes place, the Negro's Original Sin—i.e., the notion of a superior and more free sexuality—may put on the disguise of superior moral force; which disinfects everything.

Civilization thwarts us, we are starved for instinctual and effective satisfactions—or at least have to locate them well down in a hierarchy of values and subject them to dreary postponement. So we turn to the Noble Savage. Or civilization tarnishes us, for we live in a texture of conflicting values and move in a maze of moral casuistries which block or distort what we regard as our purer and more generous impulses. So we turn to the Noble Savage. Or civilization gives us only false or derivative knowledge, and has cut us off from the well-springs of experience and truth, from nature and from our deeper selves. So we turn to the Noble Savage. He becomes the symbolic vessel of a number of things we yearn for, the image in which we find our vicarious satisfactions. And this modern American Noble Savage is obtruded upon the scene at a moment when the tensions of civilization are unusually high. If we add to this the not uncommon impulse to romantic flight from some personal insufficiency, and the sense, not uncommon among the young today, that society offers no commanding values and that middle-class affluence is the death of the spirit, and the humbling effect of the spectacle of thousands of potent exemplars of courage and dedication among the young Negroes, then we have a heady brew. There is no wonder that to many the Noble Savage appears as a redeemer.

The only trouble with this negrophilism is that it doesn't recognize the Negro as a man. It recognizes him only as a Negro—if sometimes as a Negro Jesus Christ. And that is the worst condescension of all.[6]

At the same time that Negroes may recognize, and resent, this upside-down condescension, some may cling, paradoxically enough, to the very superiority which they, as good psychologists, have just condemned the

6. Faulkner's treatment of Dilsey in *The Sound and The Fury* has sometimes been taken by Negroes as a condescending and offensive rendering, like Aunt Jemima. It is true that Dilsey, taken abstractly and schematically, is a cliché, the soothing Black Mammy, "better" than the white folks. But in the novel, she does not appear schematically and abstractly; she functions there before our eyes, psychologically three-dimensional—even if Faulkner has not given her the same full subjective rendering he gives his main white characters. She is capable of, for instance, resentments; and she is involved in a complicated set of relationships which imply meaning beyond that of the character taken in isolation. See Ralph Ellison's discussion of Faulkner's development of clichés of the Negro, in *Shadow and Act* [see pp. 251–253 in this anthology].—*Author.*

white man for granting. Or is it cynicism to guess that sometimes it may not be the superiority granted that is resented, but the tone of voice of the granting? As various people have pointed out, the same Baldwin (or is it the same one?) who had taken Kerouac not gently to task for his negrophilism can write, in *The Fire Next Time*, a passage shot through with the black mystique, the glorification of the black life-awareness:

> I remember . . . rent and waistline parties where rage and sorrow sat in the darkness and did not stir, and we ate and drank and talked and laughed and danced and forgot all about the "man." We had the liquor, the chicken, the music, and each other, and had no need to pretend to be what we were not. This is the freedom that one hears in gospel songs, for example, and in jazz.

Some Negroes—even Whitney Young—may attribute special virtues to *the* Negro as a result of his slave experience: understanding, compassion, etc. And some, as we have noted, see the Negro as the redeemer of our society.

Now many Negroes, the sung and the unsung, people like Martin Luther King and Ruth Turner, and some nameless ones whom I could name, have exhibited great compassion. And I am confident that the effect of the Negro Revolution may be redemptive for our society—in the sense that Bayard Rustin suggests when he refers to the Negro Movement as a "catalytic." But at the same time, the white *homme moyen et sensuel* may be pardoned for seeing in the slaughter of a poor old woman for no other crime than that she was white and had a hole of a clothing store in Harlem, as something less than practical compassion, or the stomping of an old man on a subway platform as something less than redeemers at work. Negroes do have special reasons and special temptations to arrogate to themselves, as Negroes, special virtues, but no matter how clearly we understand this (and Southerners and Jews, as minorities, may have special reasons for understanding it), we had better stick to the old principle that if any man, black or white, isn't content to pass up a notion of group superiority, moral or any other kind, and to be regarded and judged as an individual man, with individual virtues and defects, there is something wrong with him. This is, of course, a principle which many Negroes are more than anxious to recognize. As Stokley Carmichael backhandedly puts it: "I am sure you know Negroes are bastards, too."

Power, success, and self-indulgence may degrade the human spirit. But it is well to remember that degradation degrades, too. The world is a world of risks.

Whether the Negro as redeemer is taken in the avatar of a Jesus Christ or a Noble Savage, or a combination of both, we have the question of why white society needs redemption. Clearly, redemption is in order, but the diagnosis of the case would seem to have some bearing on the kind of medicine to be prescribed.

The notion is current that history has failed us, specifically Western history, Western culture, the Judeo-Christian tradition. This notion has been with us a long time, and all our literature of this century, especially since World War I, has been shot through with it, with the sense of a crisis of culture. We have been living in the murky atmosphere of a Spenglerian Twilight of the Gods, waiting for the end. The notion was in Pound and Hemingway and Eliot and Auden and a hundred others; and I find it most recently in a college girl down South, of a most conventional upbringing and no intellectual distinction, who said to me: "I don't see what we, the white people, have got to defend or be proud of." For her, as for Pound, civilization—white civilization—is "an old bitch gone in the teeth."

White civilization: for despite whatever was absorbed by Europe of blood or culture from non-white sources, and despite whatever contributions have been made to America by non-whites, when a Negro attacks Western civilization he means *white* civilization. He sets himself apart from, and superior to, the "burning house."

The white man must grant, of course, that Western civilization, white culture, has "failed." We—the white race—have failed to respect the worth of the individual soul and person, to respect the rights of man, to achieve a common liberty, to realize justice, to practice Christian charity. But how do we know that we have failed? We know it only by applying to actuality those very standards which are the central fact of Western civilization. Those standards are, paradoxically enough, the major creation of that civilization which stands condemned by them.

Other civilizations have developed insights and values which demand our respect and admiration, and if we close our minds, our sensibilities, to them we do so at a grave risk to our own fulfillment. But to absorb such values means to absorb them into *something*—that is, into the progressive dialectic of all our values, into, in fact, ourselves. We have to remain ourselves in order to redeem ourselves. To think anything else is, again, sentimentality—a peculiarly destructive form of self-pitying sentimentality.

Only if we recognize the historical cost and significance of those standards by which we judge the failure of our civilization can that civilization have any chance of retrieving its failure. Meanwhile, whatever the values of other civilizations, we—American white men—may remember that, not only our history, but the whole of human history, has been brutal and nasty, as well as grave, noble, and tragic; and looking about us now—at India, China, Russia, Europe, South America and Africa—we may see the grim failure, in terms of their own professions, of all other societies, too. If our failure seems grimmer it is only because our professions were grander, and better advertised. Looking about us, we find no clear and persuasive model for imitation. We must go it alone.

No, not alone, for there are the non-white Americans—specifically the Negro. But if he is to redeem America, he will do so as a creative inheritor of the Judeo-Christian and American tradition—that is, by applying the standards of that tradition—the standards of Western civilization developed and elaborated here. He will point out—as he is now pointing out with anger and irony, with intelligence, devotion, and distinguished courage—that the white man is to be indicted by his own self-professed, and self-created, standards. For the Negro is the Negro American, and is "more American than the Americans." He is, shall we say, the "existentialist" American. He is a fundamentist of Western culture. His role is to dramatize the most inward revelation of that culture.

Even James Baldwin, for all the bitterness of his attacks on the white civilization, attacks that civilization merely because white men "do not live the way they say they do, or the way they say they should." If he preaches his gospel of redemptive sensuality, it sounds very like D. H. Lawrence, one of a long line of traditional "antibodies," we might say, of our culture. If he preaches his gospel of redemptive love, it sounds very like Christian charity. If he threatens us with "the fire next time," that fire is not so much a metaphor for mobs in the street or for political or military action as it is a "cosmic vengeance"—as we recognize who are old enough to have caught the stench of brimstone from many a pulpit of the old-time religion.

It is sentimental to think that the Negro will give us redemption in our spiritual bankruptcy. All he can bring to the question is the "catalytic" of his courage and clarity. If some of that rubs off on the rest of us, then we may redeem ourselves—by confronting honestly our own standards.

For, in the end, everybody has to redeem himself.

Why have we dwelt on the various kinds of sentimentality which the well-intentioned white may indulge in vis-a-vis the Negro? It would seem, in fact, that we should forget that whole business and accept the straight political view which holds that a vote is a vote no matter what motive prompts the casting. True enough: the most self-indulgent sentimentalist may cast a vote for justice—or give a million dollars to Snick, for Mississippi. But in the long haul, attitudes, like means, are important; they can fortify or poison a cause. Furthermore, since all sentimentality is, as we have said, self-referring, the sentimentalist is peculiarly open to disillusionment. For vanity—though sometimes vanity of the most subtly concealed order—is what sustains him, not principle, and vanity is like the wind-sock at a landing field: one end is firmly fixed (to the self, shall we say?), but the other may shift with every breeze.

Why had the host of friends of the Negro disappeared by 1876 and the Great Sell-Out? There are, no doubt, many reasons. But we may guess one.

There is one more kind of sentimentality that the white man cannot afford: a sentimentality about himself. He cannot afford to feel that he is going to redeem the Negro. For the age of philanthropy is over, and it would be a vicious illusion for the white man to think that he, by acting alone, can reach a solution and pass it down to gratefully lifted black hands.

It would be an even more vicious illusion to think that in trying to solve the problem he would be giving something away, would be "liberal," or would be performing an act of charity, Christian or any other kind. The safest, soberest, most humble, and perhaps not the most ignoble way for him to think of grounding his action is not on generosity, but on a proper awareness of self-interest.

It is self-interest to want to live in a society operating by the love of justice and the concept of law. We have not been living in such a society. It is self-interest to want all members of society to contribute as fully as possible to the enrichment of that society. The structure of our society has prevented that. It is self-interest to seek out friends and companions who are congenial in temperament and whose experience and capacities extend our own. Our society has restricted us in this natural quest. It is self-interest to want to escape from the pressure to conform to values which we feel immoral or antiquated. Our society has maintained such pressures. It is self-interest to want to escape from the burden of vanity into the hard and happy realization that in the diminishment of others there is a deep diminishment of the self. Our society has been organized for the diminishment of others.

More than a half-century ago, in *The Souls of Black Folk*, W. E. B. Du Bois called us "this happy-go-lucky nation which goes blundering along with its Reconstruction tragedies, its Spanish War interludes and Philippine matinees, just as though God were really dead." A lot has happened since he said that, but perhaps God is not dead yet.

It would be sentimentality to think that our society can be changed easily and without pain. It would be worse sentimentality to think that it can be changed without some pain to our particular selves—black and white. It would be realism to think that that pain would be a reasonable price to pay for what we all, selfishly, might get out of it.

J. William Fulbright
(1905–   )

FULBRIGHT was born in Sumner, Missouri. He took a B.A. from the
University of Arkansas (1925), another Bachelor's degree from Oxford
University, England (1928), and a law degree from George Washing-
ton University in 1934. He taught at and later became President of the
University of Arkansas, and has been United States Senator from Arkansas
since January 1945. He is the author of *Prospects for the West* (1963),
Old Myths and New Realities (1964), and *The Arrogance of Power*
(1966).

The essay "The Two Americas" is the conclusion to *The Arrogance of
Power*.

THE TWO AMERICAS

There are two Americas. One is the America of Lincoln and Adlai Stevenson; the other is the America of Teddy Roosevelt and the modern superpatriots. One is generous and humane, the other narrowly egotistical; one is self-critical, the other self-righteous; one is sensible, the other romantic; one is good-humored, the other solemn; one is inquiring, the other pontificating; one is moderate, the other filled with passionate intensity; one is judicious and the other arrogant in the use of great power.

We have tended in the years of our great power to puzzle the world by presenting to it now the one face of America, now the other, and sometimes both at once. Many people all over the world have come to regard America as being capable of magnanimity and farsightedness but no less capable of pettiness and spite. The result is an inability to anticipate American actions which in turn makes for apprehension and a lack of confidence in American aims.

The inconstancy of American foreign policy is not an accident but an expression of two distinct sides of the American character. Both are characterized by a kind of moralism, but one is the morality of decent instincts tempered by the knowledge of human imperfection and the other is the morality of absolute self-assurance fired by the crusading spirit. The one is exemplified by Lincoln, who found it strange, in the words of his second Inaugural Address, "that any man should dare to ask for a just God's assistance in wringing their bread from the sweat of other men's faces," but then added: "let us judge not, that we be not judged." The other is exemplified by Theodore Roosevelt, who in his December 6, 1904, Annual Message to Congress, without question or doubt as to his own and his country's capacity to judge right and wrong, proclaimed the duty of the United States to exercise an "internal police power" in the hemisphere on the ground that "Chronic wrongdoing, or an impotence which results in a general loosening of the ties of civilized society, may in America . . . ultimately require intervention by some civilized nation. . . ." Roosevelt of course never questioned that the "wrongdoing" would be done by our Latin neighbors and we of course were the "civilized nation" with the duty to set things right.

After twenty-five years of world power the United States must decide which of the two sides of its national character is to predominate—the humanism of Lincoln or the arrogance of those who would make America the world's policeman. One or the other will help shape the spirit of the age—unless of course we refuse to choose, in which case America may come to play a less important role in the world, leaving the great decisions to others.

The current tendency is toward a more strident and aggressive American foreign policy, which is to say, toward a policy closer to the spirit of Theodore Roosevelt than of Lincoln. We are still trying to build bridges to the communist countries and we are still, in a small way, helping the poorer nations to make a better life for their people; but we are also involved in a growing war against Asian communism, a war which began and might have ended as a civil war if American intervention had not turned it into a contest of ideologies, a war whose fallout is disrupting our internal life and complicating our relations with most of the world.

Our national vocabulary has changed with our policies. A few years ago we were talking of detente and building bridges, of five-year plans in India and Pakistan, or agricultural cooperatives in the Dominican Republic, and land and tax reform all over Latin America. Today these subjects are still discussed in a half-hearted and desultory way but the focus of power and interest has shifted to the politics of war. Diplomacy has become largely image-making, and instead of emphasizing plans for social change, the policy-planners and political scientists are conjuring up "scenarios" of escalation and nuclear confrontation and "models" of insurgency and counter-insurgency.

The change in words and values is no less important than the change in policy, because words are deeds and style is substance insofar as they influence men's minds and behavior. What seems to be happening, as Archibald MacLeish has put it, is that "the feel of America in the world's mind" has begun to change and faith in "the idea of America" has been shaken for the world and, what is more important, for our own people. MacLeish is suggesting—and I think he is right—that much of the idealism and inspiration is disappearing from American policy, but he also points out that they are not yet gone and by no means are they irretrievable:

. . . if you look closely and listen well, there is a human warmth, a human meaning which nothing has killed in almost twenty years and which nothing is likely to kill. . . . What has always held this country together is an idea—a dream if you will—a large and abstract thought of the sort the realistic and the sophisticated may reject but mankind can hold to.[1]

The foremost need of American foreign policy is a renewal of dedication to an "idea that mankind can hold to"—not a missionary idea full of pretensions about being the world's policemen but a Lincolnian idea expressing that powerful strand of decency and humanity which is the true source of America's greatness.

Humanism and Puritanism

I am not prepared to argue that mankind is suffering from an excess of virtue but I think the world has endured about all it can of the crusades of high-minded men bent on the regeneration of the human race. Since the beginning of history men have been set upon by zealots and crusaders, who, far from wishing them harm, have wanted sincerely and fervently to raise them from benightedness to blessedness. The difficulty about all this doing of noble deeds has not been in its motives but in the perverseness of human nature, in the regrettable fact that most men are loutish and ungrateful when it comes to improving their souls and more often than not have to be forced into their own salvation. The result has been a great deal of bloodshed and violence committed not in malice but for the purest of motives. The victims may not always have appreciated the fact that their tormentors had noble motives but the fact remains that it was not wickedness that did them in but, in Thackeray's phrase, "the mischief which the very virtuous do."

Who are the self-appointed emissaries of God who have wrought so much violence in the world? They are men with doctrines, men of faith and idealism, men who confuse power with virtue, men who believe in some cause without doubt and practice their beliefs without scruple, men who cease to be human beings with normal preferences for work and fun and family and become instead living, breathing embodiments of some faith or ideology. From the religious wars to the two world wars they have been responsible for much or most of the violence in the world. From Robespierre to Stalin and Mao Tse-tung they have been the extreme practitioners of the arrogance of power—extreme, indeed, in a way that has never been known and, hopefully, never will be known in America.

There are elements of this kind of fanticism in Western societies but

1. Archibald MacLeish, Address to the Congress of the International Publishers Association, May 31, 1965.—*Author.*

the essential strength of democracy and capitalism as they are practiced in the West is that they are relatively free of doctrines and dogma and largely free of illusions about man and his nature. Of all the intellectual achievements of Western civilization, the one, I think, that is most truly civilized is that by and large we have learned to deal with man as he is or, at most, as he seems capable of becoming, but not as we suppose in the abstract he ought to be. Our economy is geared to human acquisitiveness and our politics to human ambition. Accepting these qualities as part of human character, we have been able to civilize them because we have understood that a man's own satisfaction is more nearly a condition of than an obstacle to his decent behavior toward others. This realism about man may prove in the long run to be our greatest asset over communism, which can deny and denounce but, with all the "Red Guards" of China, cannot remake human nature.

Acceptance of his own nature would seem to be the most natural thing in the world for a man, but experience shows that it is not. Only at an advanced state of civilization do men become tolerant of human shortcomings. Only at an advanced level of civilization, it seems, do men acquire the wisdom and humility to acknowledge that they are not really cut out to play God. At all previous levels of culture men seem to be more interested in the enforced improvement of others than in voluntary fulfillment for themselves, more interested in forcing their fellow creatures to be virtuous than in helping them to be happy. Only under the conditions of material affluence and political democracy that prevail in much of the modern West have whole societies been able and willing to renounce the harsh asceticism of their own past, which still prevails in much of the East, and to embrace the philosophy that life after all is short and it is no sin to try to enjoy it.

Our hold on this philosophy is tenuous. There is a strand in our history and in our national character which is all too congenial to the spirit of crusading ideology. The Puritans who came to New England in the seventeenth century did not establish their faith as a major religion in America but the Puritan way of thought—harsh, ascetic, intolerant, promising salvation for the few but damnation for the many—became a major intellectual force in American life. It introduced a discordant element into a society bred in the English heritage of tolerance, moderation, and experimentalism.

Throughout our history two strands have coexisted uneasily—a dominant strand of democratic humanism and a lesser but durable strand of intolerant puritanism. There has been a tendency through the years for reason and moderation to prevail as long as things are going tolerably well or as long as our problems seem clear and finite and manageable.

But when things have gone badly for any length of time, or when the reasons for adversity have seemed obscure, or simply when some event or leader of opinion has aroused the people to a state of high emotion, our puritan spirit has tended to break through, leading us to look at the world through the distorting prism of a harsh and angry moralism.

Communism has aroused our latent puritanism as has no other movement in our history, causing us to see principles where there are only interests and conspiracy where there is only misfortune. And when this view of things prevails, conflicts become crusades and morality becomes delusion and hypocrisy. Thus, for example, when young hoodlums—the so-called "Red Guards"—terrorize and humiliate Chinese citizens who are suspected of a lack of fervor for the teachings of Mao Tse-tung, we may feel reconfirmed in our judgment that communism is a barbarous philosophy utterly devoid of redeeming features of humanity, but before going into transports of moral outrage over the offenses of the "Red Guards," we might recall that no fewer than two hundred thousand, and possibly half a million, people were murdered in the anti-communist terror that swept Indonesia in 1966 and scarcely a voice of protest was heard in America—from our leaders, from the press, or from the general public. One can only conclude that it is not man's inhumanity to man but communist manifestations of it that arouse the American conscience.

One of the most outrageous effects of the puritan spirit in America is the existence of that tyranny over what it is respectable to say and think of which we spoke in Part I. Those who try to look at the country with some objectivity are often the objects of scorn and abuse by professional patriots who believe that there is something illegitimate about national self-criticism, or who equate loyalty to our fighting men in Vietnam with loyalty to the policy that put them there.

Puritanism, fortunately, has not been the dominant strand in American thought. It had nothing to do with the intelligent and subtle diplomacy of the period of the American Revolution. It had nothing to do with the wise policy of remaining aloof from the conflicts of Europe, as long as we were permitted to do so, while we settled and developed the North American continent. It had nothing to do with the restraint shown by the United States at moments of supreme crisis in the cold war—at the time of the Korean War, for example, in the first Indochina war in which President Eisenhower wisely refused to intervene in 1954, and in the Cuban missile crisis of 1962. And it has had absolutely nothing to do with the gradual relaxation of tensions associated with the test ban treaty and the subsequent improvement of relations with the Soviet Union. I am reminded of "Mr. Dooley's" words about the observance of Thanksgiving: " 'Twas founded by th' Puritans to give thanks f'r bein' presarved fr'm th'

Indyans, an'. . . . we keep it to give thanks we are presarved fr'm th' Puritans."[2]

The crusading puritan spirit has had a great deal to do with some of the regrettable and tragic events of American history. It led us into needless and costly adventures and victories that crumbled in our hand.

The Civil War is an example. Had the Abolitionists of the North and the hotheads of the South been less influential, the war might have been avoided and slavery would certainly have been abolished anyway, peacefully and probably within a generation after emancipation actually occurred. Had the peace been made by Lincoln rather than the Radical Republicans, it could have been a peace of reconciliation rather than the wrathful reconstruction which deepened the division of the country, cruelly set back the cause of the Negro, and left a legacy of bitterness for which we are still paying a heavy price.

The puritan spirit was one of the important factors in the brief, unhappy adventure in imperialism that began with the war of 1898. Starting with stirring slogans about "manifest destiny" and a natural sense of moral outrage about atrocities in Cuba—which was fed by a spirited competition for circulation between the Hearst and Pulitzer newspapers—America forced on Spain a war that it was willing to pay almost any price short of complete humiliation to avoid. The war was undertaken to liberate the Cuban people and ended with Cuba being put under an American protectorate, which in turn inaugurated a half century of American intervention in Cuba's internal affairs. American interference was motivated, no doubt, by a sincere desire to bring freedom to the Cuban people but it ended, nonetheless, with their getting Batista and Castro instead.

The crusading spirit of America in its modern form, and the contrast between the crusading spirit and the spirit of tolerance and accommodation, are illustrated in two speeches made by Woodrow Wilson, one preceding, the other following, America's entry into World War I. In early 1917, with the United States still neutral, he declined to make a clear moral distinction between the belligerents, and called on them to compromise their differences and negotiate a "peace without victory." In the spring of 1918, when the United States had been at war for a year, Wilson perceived only one possible response to the challenge of Germany in the war: "Force, Force to the utmost, Force without stint or limit, the righteous and triumphant Force which shall make right the law of the world, and cast every selfish dominion down in the dust."[3]

Even Franklin Roosevelt, who was the most pragmatic of politicians,

2. Finley Peter Dunne, *Mr. Dooley's Opinions* (1900), Thanksgiving.—*Author.*
3. Speech at Baltimore, Maryland, April 6, 1918.—*Author.*

was not immune from the crusading spirit. So overcome was he, as were all Americans, by the treachery of the Japanese attack on Pearl Harbor that one of America's historic principles, the freedom of the seas, for which we had gone to war in 1812 and 1917, was now immediately forgotten, along with the explicit commitment under the London Naval Treaty of 1930 not to sink merchant vessels without first placing passengers, crews, and ships' papers in a place of safety. Within seven hours of the Japanese attack the order went out to all American ships and planes in the Pacific: "Execute unrestricted air and submarine warfare against Japan." Between 1941 and 1945 American submarines sank 1,750 Japanese merchant ships and took the lives of 105,000 Japanese civilians. So much for the "freedom of the seas."

In January 1943, while meeting with Churchill at Casablanca, President Roosevelt announced that the Allies would fight on until the "unconditional surrender" of their enemies. Roosevelt later said that the phrase just "popped into his mind" but I think it was dredged up from the depths of a puritan soul. Its premise was that our side was all virtue and our enemies were all evil who in justice could expect nothing after their fall but the righteous retribution of Virtue triumphant.

"Unconditional surrender" was an unwise doctrine. Aside from its negativism as a war aim and the fact that it may have prolonged the war, we did not really mean to carry out its implications. As soon as our enemies delivered themelves into our hands we began to treat them with kindness and moderation, and within a very few years we were treating them as valued friends and allies.

The West has won two "total victories" in this century and it has barely survived them. America, especially, fought the two world wars in the spirit of a righteous crusade. We acted as if we had come to the end of history, as if we had only to destroy our enemies and then the world would enter a golden age of peace and human happiness. Some of the problems that spawned the great wars were in fact solved by our victories; others were simply forgotten. But to our shock and dismay we found after 1945 that history had not come to an end, that our triumph had produced at least as many problems as it had solved, and that it was by no means clear that the new problems were preferable to the old ones.

I do not raise these events of the American past for purposes of national flagellation but to illustrate that the problem of excessive ideological zeal is our problem as well as the communists'. I think also that when we respond to communist dogmatism with a dogmatism of our own we are not merely responding by the necessity, as we are told, of "Fighting fire with fire." I think we are responding in a way that is more natural and congenial to us than we care to admit.

The great challenge in our foreign relations is to make certain that the major strand in our heritage, the strand of humanism, tolerance, and accommodation, remains the dominant one. I do not accept the excuse, so often offered, that communist zealotry and intransigence justify our own. I do not accept the view that because they have engaged in subversion, intervention, and ideological warfare, so must we and to the same degree. There is far more promise in efforts to encourage communist imitation of our own more sensible attitudes than in ourselves imitating the least attractive forms of communist behavior. It is of course reasonable to ask why we must take the lead in conciliation; the answer is that we, being the most powerful of nations, can afford as no one else can to be magnanimous. Or, to put it another way, disposing as we do of the greater physical power, we are properly called upon to display the greater moral power as well.

The kind of foreign policy I have been talking about is, in the true sense of the term, a *conservative* policy. It is intended quite literally to conserve the world—a world whose civilizations can be destroyed at any time if either of the great powers should choose or feel driven to do so. It is an approach that accepts the world as it is, with all its existing nations and ideologies, with all its existing qualities and shortcomings. It is an approach that purports to change things in ways that are compatible with the continuity of history and within the limits imposed by a fragile human nature. I think that if the great conservatives of the past, such as Burke and Metternich and Castlereagh, were alive today, they would not be true believers or relentless crusaders against communism. They would wish to come to terms with the world as it is, not because our world would be pleasing to them—almost certainly it would not be—but because they believed in the preservation of indissoluble links between the past and the future, because they profoundly mistrusted abstract ideas, and because they did not think themselves or any other men qualified to play God.

The last, I think, is the central point. I believe that a man's principal business, in foreign policy as in domestic policy and in his daily life, is to keep his own house in order, to make life a little more civilized, a little more satisfying, and a little more serene in the brief time that is allotted him. I think that man is qualified to contemplate metaphysics but not to practice it. The practice of metaphysics is God's work.

An Idea Mankind Can Hold To

Favored as it is, by history, by wealth, and by the vitality and basic decency of its diverse population, it is conceivable, though hardly likely, that America will do something that no other great nation has ever tried to do—to effect a fundamental change in the nature of international relations. It has been my purpose in this book to suggest some ways in which we might proceed with this great work. All that I have proposed in these pages—that we make ourselves the friend of social revolution, that we make our own society an example of human happiness, that we go beyond simple reciprocity in the effort to reconcile hostile worlds—has been based on two major premises: first, that, at this moment in history at which the human race has become capable of destroying itself, it is not merely desirable but essential that the competitive instinct of nations be brought under control; and second, that America, as the most powerful nation, is the only nation equipped to lead the world in an effort to change the nature of its politics.

If we accept this leadership, we will have contributed to the world "an idea mankind can hold to." Perhaps that idea can be defined as the proposition that the nation performs its essential function not in its capacity as a power, but in its capacity as a society, or, to put it simply, that the primary business of the nation is not itself but its people.

Obviously, to bring about fundamental changes in the world we would have to take certain chances: we would have to take the chance that other countries could not so misinterpret a generous initiative on our part as to bring about a calamity; we would have to take a chance that later if not sooner, nations which have been hostile to us would respond to reason and decency with reason and decency. The risks involved are great but they are far less than the risks of traditional methods of international relations in the nuclear age.

If we are interested in bringing about fundamental changes in the world, we must start by resolving some critical questions of our foreign relations: Are we to be the friend or the enemy of the social revolutions of Asia, Africa, and Latin America? Are we to regard the communist countries as more or less normal states with whom we can have more or less normal relations, or are we to regard them indiscriminately as purveyors of an evil ideology with whom we can never reconcile? And finally, are we to regard ourselves as a friend, counselor, and example for those around the world who seek freedom and who also want our help, or are we to play the role of God's avenging angel, the appointed missionary of freedom in a benighted world?

The answers to these questions depend on which of the two Americas is speaking. There are no inevitable or predetermined answers because our past has prepared us to be either tolerant or puritanical, generous or selfish, sensible or romantic, humanly concerned or morally obsessed, in our relations with the outside world.

For my own part, I prefer the America of Lincoln and Adlai Stevenson. I prefer to have my country the friend rather than the enemy of demands for social justice; I prefer to have the communists treated as human beings, with all the human capacity for good and bad, for wisdom and folly, rather than as embodiments of an evil abstraction; and I prefer to see my country in the role of sympathetic friend to humanity rather than its stern and prideful schoolmaster.

There are many respects in which America, if she can bring herself to act with the magnanimity and the empathy which are appropriate to her size and power, can be an intelligent example to the world. We have the opportunity to set an example of generous understanding in our relations with China, of practical cooperation for peace in our relations with Russia, of reliable and respectful partnership in our relations with Western Europe, of material helpfulness without moral presumption in our relations with developing nations, of abstention from the temptations of hegemony in our relations with Latin America, and of the all-around advantages of minding one's own business in our relations with everybody. Most of all, we have the opportunity to serve as an example of democracy to the world by the way in which we run our own society. America, in the words of John Quincy Adams, should be "the well-wisher to the freedom and independence of all" but "the champion and vindicator only of her own."[4]

If we can bring ourselves so to act, we will have overcome the dangers of the arrogance of power. It would involve, no doubt, the loss of certain glories, but that seems a price worth paying for the probable rewards, which are the happiness of America and the peace of the world.

4. John Quincy Adams, July 4, 1821, Washington, D.C. Reported in *The National Intelligencer*, July 11, 1821.—*Author.*

Eric Norden

ERIC NORDEN is a free-lance reporter. [The editor of this anthology has been unable to secure any further information about Mr. Norden.]

"American Atrocities in Viet-Nam" appeared in *Liberation* in February 1966.

AMERICAN ATROCITIES IN VIET-NAM

In the bitter controversy over our Vietnamese policies which has raged across the nation since the President's decision last February to bomb North Viet-Nam, there is only one point which supporters of U.S. policy will concede to the opposition: the sheer, mindnumbing horror of the war. Despite the barrage of official propaganda, reports in the American and European press reveal that the United States is fighting the dirtiest war of its history in Viet-Nam. The weapons in the American arsenal include torture, systematic bombing of civilian targets, the first use of poison gas since World War One, the shooting of prisoners and the general devastation of the Vietnamese countryside by napalm and white phosphorous. Not since the days of the American Indian wars has the United States waged such unrelenting warfare against an entire people.

Torture of prisoners and "suspects" by Vietnamese troops and their U.S. advisers is a matter of public record. "Anyone who has spent much time with Government units in the field," writes William Tuohy, *Newsweek*'s Saigon correspondent, "has seen the heads of prisoners held under water and bayonet blades pressed against their throats. . . . In more extreme cases, victims have had bamboo slivers run under their fingernails or wires from a field telephone connected to arms, nipples or testicles." (*New York Times Magazine*, November 28, 1965.)

Donald Wise, Chief foreign correspondent for the London *Sunday Mirror*, reports that such torture is condoned and even supervised by U.S. officers. "No American is in a position to tell his 'pupils' to stop torturing," Wise writes from Saigon. "They are in no mood to either. . . ." Some of the standard tortures described by Wise include "dunking men head first into water tanks or slicing them up with knives. . . . Silk stockings full of sand are swung against temples and men are hooked up to the electric generators of military HQ's." (London *Sunday Mirror*, April 4, 1965).

The "Viet-Cong" use terror also, of course, but theirs is of a more selective nature, if only to avoid estranging the peasants and villagers on whom they depend for food and shelter. They will kill and mutilate the body of a Government official, but they generally pick an unpopular and corrupt victim whose death is welcomed by the peasants. U.S. and Government troops in the countryside, on the other hand, feel themselves lost in an enemy sea and tend to strike out indiscriminately at real or imagined guerrillas. Thus, no Vietnamese is exempt from mistreatment and torture. As Wise reports, "Inevitably, innocent peasants are kneed in the groin, drowned in vats of water or die of loss of blood after interrogation. But you cannot identify VC from peasants. . . ." In fact, it is assumed that every peasant is a real or potential Viet-Cong rebel. "In a VC-controlled area the yardstick is rough; every man of military age is assumed to be a VC soldier who has thrown away his weapon just before capture. Most areas of Viet-Nam are now VC-controlled. Therefore, most men in the country-side should be presumed to be VC soldiers or sympathizers." (*Ibid.*)

Many U.S. reporters have witnessed torture first-hand. Beverly Deepe, the *New York Herald Tribune's* correspondent in Saigon, writes:

> One of the most infamous methods of torture used by the government forces is partial electrocution—or "frying," as one U.S. adviser called it. This correspondent was present on one occasion when the torture was employed. Two wires were attached to the thumbs of a Viet-Cong prisoner. At the other end of the strings was a field generator, cranked by a Vietnamese private. The mechanism produced an electrical current that burned and shocked the prisoner. (*New York Herald Tribune*, April 25, 1965.)

Electrical torture is employed all over Viet-Nam, even on the battlefront. A small U.S. field generator used to power pack radios is often "modified" for torture purposes and is prized for its high mobility. The device generates sufficient voltage to provide strong and sometimes deadly shocks. According to Malcolm Browne, the A.P. correspondent who won the Pulitzer Prize for his reporting of the war, "The 'ding-a-ling' method of interrogation involves connection of electrodes from this generator to the temples of the subject, or other parts of the body. In the case of women prisoners, the electrodes often are attached to the nipples. The results are terrifying and painful. . . ." (*The New Face of War* by Malcolm Browne, Bobbs-Merrill Co., 1965.)

Less sophisticated methods than electrical torture are also used. According to Beverly Deepe:

> Other techniques, usually designed to force onlooking prisoners to talk, involve cutting off the fingers, ears, fingernails or sexual organs of another

prisoner. Sometimes a string of ears decorates the wall of a government military installation. One American installation has a Viet-Cong ear preserved in alcohol. (*Op. Cit.*)

There is apparently no attempt to disguise such atrocities, even for public relations reasons. Writes Malcolm Browne:

Many a news correspondent has seen the hands whacked off prisoners with machetes. Prisoners are sometimes castrated or blinded. In more than one case a Viet-Cong suspect has been towed after interrogation behind an armored personnel carrier across the rice fields. This always results in death in one of its most painful forms. Vietnamese troops also take their share of enemy heads. . . . (*Op. Cit.*)

U.S. Army Special Forces men pride themselves on their advanced methods of "interrogation," often patterned after Chinese models. In his first-hand account of the Special Forces in action, *The Green Berets*, Robin Moore gives a graphic description of a torture session presided over by a Special Forces officer of Finnish origin who had served with the Nazi Army on the Russian Front in World War Two. (Because of Moore's embarrassing disclosures, his publishers, who had originally presented the book as "truthful . . . a factual account," were forced under pressure from Assistant Secretary of Defense Arthur Sylvester to label the material "fictionalized.")

Although torture of Viet-Cong suspects antedated the arrival in strength of U.S. forces, American technology has given it some interesting twists. The helicopter, introduced by the United States as a vital element in the air war, is now playing a role in the "interrogation" of prisoners. *Houston Chronicle* reporter Jonathan Kapstein reported the innovation, termed "the long step," on his return from an assignment in Viet-Nam.

A helicopter pilot looked up from his Jack Daniels-and-Coke to relate what had happened to a captive he had been flying back from a battle area. A Vietnamese army officer yelled in the ear of the suspected guerrilla who was tied hand and foot. The man did not respond, so the officer and a Vietnamese soldier heaved him, struggling against his ropes, out of the UH-1B helicopter from 2,900 feet. Then over the roar of the engine, the officer began to interrogate another prisoner who had watched wide-eyed. The answers must have been satisfactory, the flier said, because, though kicked and roughly handled, the guerrilla was alive to be marched off when the helicopter landed. . . . (*Nation*, Dec. 21, 1964.)

A prisoner who "cooperates" after watching the exit of his comrade is not always rewarded. *Herald Tribune* Saigon correspondent Beverly Deepe reports an instance when "Two Viet-Cong prisoners were interrogated on an airplane flying toward Saigon. The first refused to answer questions and was thrown out of the airplane at 3,000 feet. The second immediately answered all the questions. But he, too, was thrown out." (*New York Herald Tribune*, April 25, 1965). Sometimes there is not even the pretense of "questioning." Jack Langguth, Saigon correspondent for the *New York Times*, reports a case where "One American helicopter crewman returned to his base in the central highlands last week without a fierce young prisoner entrusted to him. He told friends that he had become infuriated by the youth and had pushed him out of the helicopter at about 1,000 feet." (*New York Times*, July 7, 1965.)

Even if a prisoner is lucky enough to make the full trip, half the fun isn't getting there. Jimmy Breslin, in a dispatch to the *New York Herald Tribune* from South Vietnam, wrote:

> At 12:00 o'clock, a helicopter came in and the shirtless Marine in the tent said it was going to Da Nang. . . . A young redheaded machine-gunner sat in the doorway, chewing on a chocolate cracker from a C-ration tin. He kicked a small spool of wire out of the doorway and made room.
> "We just rode Nuongs, you can tell that by the wire here," he said.
> "Why?" he was asked. Nuongs are Chinese mercenaries from Formosa. . . .
> "They always want the wire for the prisoners," the kid said.
> "Don't you know that? They get a VC and make him hold his hands against his cheeks. Then they take this wire and run it right through the one hand and right through his cheek and into his mouth. Then they pull the wire out through the other cheek and stick it through the other hand. They knot both ends around sticks. You never seen them with prisoners like that? Oh, you ought to see how quiet them gooks sit in a helicopter when we got them wrapped up like that. (*New York Herald Tribune*, Sept. 29, 1965.)

As the tempo of the fighting has increased, many Viet-Cong prisoners are spared the ordeal of torture—they are shot on the spot by their U.S. or Vietnamese captors. Writes *Newsweek*'s Saigon correspondent, William Tuohy:

> Some Viet-Cong suspects do not survive long enough for the third degree. Earlier this year, in an operation along the central coast, a Government detachment failed to flush VC troops suspected of lurking in the area. However, several villagers were rounded up and one man was brought before the company commander. The Vietnamese officer briefly questioned the suspect, then turned to his adviser . . . and said, "I think I shoot this man. Okay?"
> "Go ahead," said the adviser.
> The officer fired a carbine round point-blank, striking the villager below

the chest. The man slumped and died. The patrol moved on. Later, a correspondent asked the adviser, who had seemed a decent enough fellow, why he had given his approval.

. . . "These people could have moved to a Government area. In this war they are either on our side or they are not. There is no in-between." (*New York Times Magazine*, Nov. 28, 1965.)

Houston Chronicle correspondent Jonathan Kapstein reported on his return from Viet-Nam:

In the pleasantly dim officers' club at Vinh Long, South Viet-Nam, a 25-year-old U.S. Army lieutenant described what he had seen one time when soldiers of the Vietnamese 7th Infantry Division captured prisoners. "They had four, all suspected of being Viet-Cong—the first prisoners they had taken in a long time. They lined 'em up and shot the first man. Then they questioned the second. His answers were unsatisfactory, I guess, because they shot him too. . . ." (*Nation*, December 24, 1964.)

As U.S. casualties have mounted even the pretense of preliminary interrogation has been dropped. Captured and wounded Viet-Cong are now executed summarily. Captain James Morris, a U.S. Army Special Forces man, reports the aftermath of an ambush he sprang on a small enemy contingent:

I moved from one dark shape to the other, making sure they were dead. When I moved up on the last one, he raised up, his arms extended, eyes wide. He had no weapon. Cowboy stitched him up the middle with his AR-15. He didn't even twitch. . . . (*Esquire*, August, 1965.)

Pulitzer Prize winning correspondent David Halberstam recounts the treatment accorded a group of Viet-Cong prisoners by Government forces after a "particularly bitter" battle near Bac Lieu:

The enemy were very cocky and started shouting anti-American slogans and Vietnamese curses at their captors. The Marines . . . simply lined up the seventeen guerrillas and shot them down in cold blood. . . . (*The Making of a Quagmire* by David Halberstam. Random House, 1965.)

The treatment of Viet-Cong POW's seems to vary with the severity of American losses in the action preceding their capture. After a platoon of the U.S. 1st Air Cavalry Division was almost wiped out in a battle in the Chu Prong foothills of the Ia Drang valley, Reuters reported:

In one place nearby the Americans found three North Vietnamese wounded. One lay huddled under a tree, a smile on his face. "You won't smile any more" said one of the American soldiers, pumping bullets into his body. The other two met the same fate. (November 18, 1965.)

Chicago Daily News correspondent Raymont R. Coffey, reporting on the same battle, accompanied U.S. relief forces to a clearing littered with dead from the previous day's fighting. He writes:

> It was almost impossible to walk twenty paces without stumbling upon a body. . . . Suddenly a few yards away a wounded enemy soldier lifted one arm weakly and an American sergeant poured a long burst of M-16 rifle bullets into him. "Was he trying to give up, Sarge?" a man asked. "I'd like to find more of these bastards trying to give up," the sergeant said bitterly. No one disagreed with him. . . . (*Chicago Daily News*, November 19, 1965.)

Apart from the moral question, U.S. and South Vietnamese torture and execution of prisoners of war is, of course, in clear violation of international law. Both South Viet-Nam and the United States are signatories to the 1949 Geneva Conventions governing the treatment of prisoners. Article 17 states: "No physical or mental torture, nor any other form of coercion, may be inflicted on prisoners of war to secure from them information of any kind whatever." In a specific provision pertaining to undeclared or civil war, the Conventions prohibit, with respect to prisoners of war, "violence to life and person, in particular murder of all kinds, mutilation, cruel treatment and torture."

The International Red Cross in Geneva, to which the Conventions assigned the right to visit POW's and insure their proper treatment, has publicly protested U.S. treatment of prisoners in Viet-Nam. The *New York Times* declared on December 1, 1965 that "the International Committee of the Red Cross Committee is dissatisfied with the way the United States and South Vietnamese Governments observe their pledge to respect the Geneva Conventions protecting war victims. . . . The Committee's representative in Saigon has been unable to visit prisoners taken by American and South Vietnamese troops despite the affirmative reply of the two governments to its appeal for the observance of the conventions. The Saigon authorities were said to have given repeated assurances that they intended to allow the International Red Cross to visit the prisoners but to date have done nothing more about it." (*New York Times*, November 26, 1965.)

If the United States is not willing to observe the Geneva Conventions itself, it is quick to point an accusing finger at others. When the North Vietnamese Government threatened to try captured U.S. airmen as war criminals, the United States denounced any such move as a violation of the Geneva Conventions and appealed to the International Red Cross. Hans

Henle, a former executive of the Information Service of the International Committee of the Red Cross in Geneva, commented:

> The Viet-Cong fighters are as protected by the Geneva Conventions as the American G.I.s are. Dramatic protests against violations of the Geneva Conventions should have been made when the first Viet-Cong prisoners were shot, when they were tortured, when the American Army started to destroy Viet-Cong hospitals and to cut off medical supply. . . . It is utterly hypocritical to condone wholesale violations of the Red Cross principles on one side and protest reprisals against them. . . . (*New York Times*, International Edition only, October 14, 1965.)

Not content with the present level of inhumanity, some agencies of the United States Government are attempting to turn torture from a political liability to an asset. The Associated Press reported on October 16, 1965, that Senator Stephen Young, who had just returned from a fact-finding mission in Viet-Nam, "says he was told by a member of the Central Intelligence Agency in Viet-Nam that the C.I.A. committed atrocities there to discredit the Viet-Cong. Young said he was told that the C.I.A. disguised some people as Viet-Cong and they committed atrocities. . . ." (Philadelphia *Inquirer*, October 20, 1965.) Young's revelations landed like a bombshell on official Washington. "The C.I.A. and the State Department went into an uproar," the *Herald Tribune* reported. "There was deep distress among State Department officials who feared his reported remarks would have disastrous repercussions abroad." (*New York Herald Tribune*, October 21, 1965.) But Young refused to back down. "The C.I.A. has employed some South Vietnamese," he reiterated, "and they have been instructed to claim they are Viet-Cong and to work accordingly . . . several of these executed two village leaders and raped some women. I know such men have been employed, and I question the wisdom of that."

So, as the war escalates, does the human agony in its wake. The prospect is for more, not less, torture and shooting of POW's. "There comes a time in every war," James Reston writes from Saigon, "when men tend to become indifferent to human suffering, even to unnecessary brutality, and we may be reaching that point in Viet-Nam." (*New York Times*, September 5, 1965.) Frustrated and bitter, U.S. forces in Viet-Nam have dehumanized their enemy, and anesthetized their own conscience. Graham Greene, struck by the ubiquitous photographs of torture in the U.S. press, wrote recently:

> The strange new feature about the photographs of torture now appearing is that they have been taken with the approval of the torturers and published over captions that contain no hint of condemnation. They might have come out of a book on insect life. "The white ant takes certain

measures against the red ant after a successful foray." But these, after all, are not ants, but men. . . . These photographs are of torturers belonging to an army which could not exist without American aid and counsel. . . . The long, slow slide into barbarism of the Western World seems to have quickened. (*The London Daily Telegraph*, November 6, 1965.)

The *New York Herald Tribune* reported on May 23, 1965, that "Near the big coastal city of Hue, U.S. Marines set crops on fire and burned or dynamited huts. . . ." In July, 1965, U.S. Marines fought a Viet-Cong force which had landed in sampans on the island of An Hoa and attacked a Vietnamese navy post there. The two major towns on the island, Longthanh and Xuanmy, had been occupied by the guerrillas. Together the towns had about 1,500 inhabitants. After the Viet-Cong retreated, " the Marines were ordered to burn Longthanh and Xuanmy to prevent the Viet-Cong from reoccupying them. . . ." (*New York Times*, July 11, 1965.) Few Viet-Cong had been killed or captured, but two prosperous villages were razed and, according to U.S. sources, about 100 civilians died from U.S. fire. An A.P. dispatch from the island on July 11, 1965, reported that Americans had called An Hoa "Little Hawaii" because "of its rolling surf and happy people. In one day An Hoa became a little hell."

The two nearby villages of Chan Son and Camne in the Mekong Delta felt the brunt of U.S. "pacification" in August, 1965. Marine patrols near the villages had received light sniper fire from Viet-Cong guerrillas. What happened next was described by U.S. newsmen accompanying the Marines into the villages.

A Marine shouted, "Kill them! I don't want anyone moving!" . . . The Marines burned huts they believed were the sites of sniper fire. A sergeant said orders called for this. . . . [After the firing died down] U.S. Marines found a woman and two children among 25 persons they killed. . . . The woman died of a wound in the side, perhaps from one of the 1,000 artillery shells poured into the area. A wailing child beside her had an arm injury. A grenade hurled by a Marine blasted two children to death in an air-raid shelter. (*New York Times*, August 3, 1965.)

How the Marines reacted to their "victory" was described by a U.P.I. dispatch from Chan Son:

"I got me a VC, man. I got at least two of them bastards." The exultant cry followed a 10-second burst of automatic weapons fire yesterday, and the dull crump of a grenade exploding underground.

The Marines ordered a Vietnamese corporal to go down into the grenade-blasted hole to pull out their victims.

The victims were three children between 11 and 14—two boys and a girl. Their bodies were riddled with bullets.

Their father was still suffering from shock. A husky Marine lifted him on his shoulder and carried him off.

"Oh, my God," a young Marine exclaimed. "They're all kids."

A moment earlier, six children nearby watched their mother die. Her blood left a dark trail in the "air-raid shelter," where the family fled when the Marines attacked. A wrinkled grandmother had pulled her into a more comfortable position to let her die.

The terrified face of a 60-year-old man looked up from a hole; his wailing mingled with the crying of the village children.

In the village, a little boy displayed his sister who was no more than four. She had been shot through the arm.

The Marines had received a few sniper rounds from Chan Son village. . .

The sniper fire was enough for the Marines to open up with everything they had: rifle fire, automatic fire and grenades. A number of women and children were caught in the fire. Five of them were killed and five others wounded.

Shortly before the Marines moved in, a helicopter had flown over the area warning the villagers to stay in their homes. (*New York Herald Tribune*, August 3, 1965.)

Chan Son's neighboring village of Camne fared no better. Morley Safer, a CBS television correspondent accompanying the force occupying the town, reported that U.S. Marines had burned 150 houses in the hamlet, ignoring "the pleas of old men and women to delay the burnings so that belongings could be removed." Safer's report, delivered on "Evening News with Walter Cronkite," August 4, 1965, said that:

"After surrounding the village . . . the Marines poured 3.5 in. rocket fire, M-79 grenade launchers and heavy and light machinegun fire. The Marines then moved in, proceeding first with cigarette lighters, then with flame throwers, to burn down an estimated 150 dwellings." Safer concluded by revealing that "I subsequently learned that a Marine platoon on the right flank wounded three women and killed one child in a rocket barrage. The day's operations netted about four prisoners—old men."

It was unusual for U.S. "pacification" teams to be accompanied by U.S. reporters, and Washington was evidently embarrassed by the widespread publicity given the Chan Son and Camne incidents. Charles Mohr reported from Saigon on subsequent "attempts by public information officers to deemphasize the importance of civilian deaths and the burning of village huts at the hands of U.S. Marines." (*New York Times*, August 9, 1965.) And Secretary of the Navy Paul Nitze publicly supported the burning of villages as a "natural and inevitable adjunct" to defense of U.S. bases in their vicinity. Nitze declared that "Where neither United

States nor Vietnamese forces can maintain continuous occupancy, it is necessary to destroy these facilities." (*New York Times*, August 15, 1965.) The final word was had by a U.S. military spokesman in Saigon who told reporters that "Marines do not burn houses or villages unless those houses or villages are fortified." When a U.S. correspondent commented that the great majority of Vietnamese villages were fortified in one way or another, the spokesman said simply: "I know it."

The Vietnamese peasant is caught in a vicious vise by U.S. "pacification" tactics. If he stays in his village he may die under U.S. fire; if he flees before the advancing troops he may still be rounded up, and shot on the spot as an "escaping Viet-Cong."

Murders of such terrified peasants are a daily occurrence in Viet-Nam, and American G.I.'s are bagging their share of the game. A typical instance was reported by the A.P. from the town of Hoi Vuc, scene of a Marine "search-and-destroy" operation:

"The sweat-soaked young Leatherneck stood over the torn body of a Viet Cong guerrilla with mixed emotions flitting over his face. For Cpl. Pleas David of Tuscaloosa, Alabama, it was a day he would never forget. David had just killed his first man. 'I felt kind of sorry for him as I stood there,' said David, a lanky 17-year-old. 'And he didn't even have a weapon.' . . ." The unarmed "Viet-Cong" was walking along a paddy dike when the four Marines approached him with levelled guns. The frightened Vietnamese saw the guns and threw himself on the ground. As the Marines ran towards him he jumped up and tried to escape. "I let him get 250 yards away and then dropped him with two shots from my M-I," The A.P. quotes the young Marine, adding "The man had been hit squarely in the back. No weapons were found with him. . . ." The Marine was congratulated by his buddies. "Maybe the Viet-Cong will learn some respect for marksmanship. When we see them we hit them," one boasted. Another declared that "David is a good example. . . . Don't think we are killers. We are Marines." (*New York Post*, April 30, 1965.)

It is official U.S. military policy to shoot and ask questions later. Thus, in an operation thirty-five miles outside of Saigon, U.S. troops rushed a peasant shack believed to harbor Viet-Cong. One U.S. Lieutenant hurled a grenade through the door but the inhabitants tossed it back out. According to the A.P., "Another American soldier charged the shack, pulled the pin on a grenade and gave the fuse a few seconds count-down before pitching it in. Following the explosion the G.I. leaped into the shack with his M-14 rifle blazing. Three men and a baby died. Two women were wounded. Shrapnel took off the lower half of one woman's leg." (November 16, 1965.)

Not all G.I.'s enjoy making war on women and children. Some have written agonized letters home. Marine Cpl. Ronnie Wilson, 20, of Wichita, Kansas wrote the following letter to his mother:

> Mom, I had to kill a woman and a baby. . . . We were searching the dead Cong when the wife of the one I was checking ran out of a cave. . . . I shot her and my rifle is automatic so before I knew it I had shot about six rounds. Four of them hit her and the others went into the cave and must have bounced off the rock wall and hit the baby. Mom, for the first time I felt really sick to my stomach. The baby was about two months old. I swear to God this place is worse than hell. Why must I kill women and kids? Who knows who's right? They think they are and we think we are. Both sides are losing men. I wish to God this was over.

But those American G.I.'s who react with shock and horror to their bloody mission are a distinct minority. Most American soldiers in Viet-Nam do not question the orders that lead them to raze villages and wipe out men, women and children for the "crime" of living in Viet-Cong-controlled or infiltrated areas. Extermination of the (non-white) enemy is to them a dirty but necessary job, and few grumble about it. Some have even come to enjoy it. Warren Rogers, Chief Correspondent in Viet-Nam for the Hearst syndicate, reports that:

> There is a new breed of Americans that most of us don't know about and it is time we got used to it. The 18- and 19-year-olds, fashionably referred to as high-school dropouts, have steel in their backbones and maybe too much of what prize fighters call the killer instinct. These kids seem to enjoy killing Viet-Cong. . . . (*New York Journal-American*, September 16, 1965.)

To many critics of the war this "new breed of Americans" bears a disquieting resemblance to an old breed of Germans.

As the United States build-up has grown, there has been an increasing reliance on air attack. Any village in "VC territory" (which now comprises most of the country outside of the big cities) is considered a "free strike" area. U.S. planes rain death over vast areas of the countryside, killing Viet-Cong guerrillas and innocent peasants alike. No attempt is made to discriminate between military and civilian targets. American pilots, the Washington *Post* reported recently, "are given a square marked on a map and told to hit every hamlet within the area. The pilots know they sometimes are bombing women and children." (March 13, 1965.) Supersonic jets and B-52 bombers blanket vast areas of the countryside with 1,000-pound bombs, napalm and white phosphorous. According to *New York Times'* Saigon Correspondent, Charles Mohr.

This is strategic bombing in a friendly, allied country. Since the Viet-Cong doctrine is to insulate themselves among the population and the population is largely powerless to prevent their presence, no one here seriously doubts that significant numbers of innocent civilians are dying every day in South Viet-Nam. (*New York Times*, September 5, 1965.)

The victims of such raids are always reported in the official U.S. enemy casualty lists as "dead Viet-Cong." The accuracy of such reports was revealed by Jack Langguth in a dispatch from Saigon:

As the Communists withdrew from Quangngai last Monday, U.S. jet bombers pounded the hills into which they were headed. Many Vietnamese —one estimate was as high as 500—were killed by the strikes. The American contention is that they were Viet-Cong soldiers. But three out of four patients seeking treatment in a Vietnamese hospital afterward for burns from napalm or jellied gasoline, were village women. (*New York Times*, June 6, 1965.)

Quang Ngai province has been the scene of some of the heaviest fighting of the war. When U.S. and Vietnamese troops could not dislodge the Viet-Cong from their positions it was decided to destroy all villages in the province which were not garrisoned by U.S. or Vietnamese forces. The fate of Duchai, a complex of five fishing villages on the coast, is typical. Neil Sheehan told the story of Duchai in a dispatch to the *New York Times*:

In mid-August United States and Vietnamese military officials decided the Communists were using Duchai as a base for their operations in the area and that it should be destroyed. For the next two months . . . it was periodically and ferociously bombed by Vietnamese and American planes. . . . At least 184 civilians died during Duchai's two months of agony. Some reasonable estimates run as high as 600. . . . When an American visits Duchai these days, villagers . . . tell him horror stories of how many of the 15,000 former inhabitants were killed by bombs and shells. "There," said a fisherman pointing to a bomb crater beside a ruined house, "a woman and her six children were killed in a bomb shelter when it got a direct hit." Duchai's solid brick and stucco houses, the product of genera-tions of hard-earned savings by its fishermen, were reduced to rubble or blasted into skeletons. Five-inch naval shells tore gaping holes in walls, and bombs of 750 to 1,000 pounds plunged through roofs, shattering interiors and scattering red roof-tiles over the landscape. . . . Here and there napalm blackened the ruins. (November 30, 1965.)

Sheehan reported that at least ten other villages in the province had "been destroyed as thoroughly as the five in Duchai" and another twenty-five nearly as badly damaged. Four hundred and fifty other villages have been under intermittent attack by U.S. and Vietnamese planes. "Each month," Sheehan writes, "600 to 1,000 civilians wounded by bombs, shells, bullets and napalm are brought to the provincial hospital in Quangngai town. Officials say that about thirty per cent of these cases require major surgery. A recent visitor to the hospital found several children lying on cots, their bodies horribly burned by naplam." (*Ibid.*)

An American doctor in the Quang Ngai hospital, J. David Kinzie, was moved to protest the horrors of the war in a letter to a U.S. magazine:

I have been in Quang Ngai for six months in general practice at a civilian provincial hospital, and I can remain silent no longer.

There comes a time in a doctor's life, no matter how hardened he has become, and perhaps in every man's life, no matter how cynical he may be, when he must protest as effectively as he can about the suffering of his fellow man. When one's own country is involved in the inhumanity, the responsibility becomes greater. Thus I add my belated voice.

The civilian hospital in our province in central Viet-Nam is good by Vietnamese standards. The patients, already diseased by tuberculosis, anemia, and malnutrition in many cases, are now entering more frequently from direct effects of the war. For example, a pregnant woman demonstrator with a bullet hole in her abdomen, whose fetus died later; a twelve-year-old boy brought in unconscious by relatives who described how artillery blasted their village the night before; a fifty-year-old woman, accused of being Viet-Cong who had been beaten, electrically shocked, and had her hands punctured for three days to extort information; three other civilians also accused of supporting the Viet-Cong were released to the hospital after severe beatings and their innocence determined. Many of the victims' "crimes" consisted merely in living in an area the Viet-Cong had overrun the night before. . . .

Of course, war has always been described as evil, but does this mean that America must add to it? Our military advisers teach Vietnamese modern techniques of killing each other. Our weapons aid in more thorough destruction of themselves. Rather than liberating a people, it seems that these techniques and weapons result in innocent civilians, women, and children being beaten, burned and murdered. . . .

Is America to survive on the blood of Vietnamese civilians? Does this make us great? (*Progressive*, March 1965.)

Thousands of children are dying as a result of United States air strikes. Charles Mohr writes in the *New York* Times:

In [a] delta province there is a woman—who has both arms burned off by napalm and her eyelids so badly burned that she cannot close them. When it is time for her to sleep her family puts a blanket over her head.

The women had two of her children killed in the air strike which maimed her last April and she saw five other children die. She was quite dispassionate when she told an American "more children were killed because the children do not have too much experience and do not know how to lie down behind the paddy dikes." (September 5, 1965.)

Vietnamese villagers, driven to desperation, have occasionally descended en masse on U.S. bases to protest the bombings of their villages. Such demonstrations have been violently repressed. In early September a group of villagers marched on the U.S. air base at Danang demanding an end to air attacks on their villages. The demonstration was dispersed and five participants, selected at random, were arrested. Their punishment was swift. The *Chicago Daily News* reported from Saigon, "At Danang, three persons were executed by a South Vietnamese firing squad. The execution, held in a soccer stadium was postponed at the last minute until midnight . . . . because news photographers refused to obey an order that no pictures be taken until the final shot had been fired. The three were among five persons arrested Monday during a demonstration by about 200 persons in downtown Danang. They were protesting crop damage from artillery fire and air attacks by U.S. forces." (*Chicago Daily News*, September 23, 1965.) The fate of the other two arrested demonstrators was described in a U.P.I. dispatch from Saigon. ". . . the fourth man would be executed later, but at the moment . . . he was described as a "singing bird." The fifth demonstrator, a woman, was sentenced to life in prison although the demonstrations had been so small that few were even aware of it." (*Washington Daily News*, October 4, 1965.)

The essence of U.S. bombing policy was expressed with unusual frankness by a U.S. officer serving with a helicopter unit in the Mekong Delta. Jack Langguth asked the officer what the answer was to Viet-Cong activity. " 'Terror.' he said pleasantly. 'The Viet-Cong have terrorized the peasants to get their cooperation, or at least to stop their opposition. We must terrorize the villagers even more, so they see that their real self-interest lies with us. . . . Terror is what it takes.' " (*New York Times Magazine*, September 19, 1965.)

But in the long run, the bombing only helps the National Liberation Front. According to Senator George McGovern: "To bomb [the Viet-Cong] is to bomb the women and children, the villages and the peasants with whom they are intermingled. Our bombing attacks turn the people against us and feed the fires of rebellion." (*Congressional Record*, June 17, 1965.) Robert Taber, an authority on guerrilla warfare, writes in his new book *The War of the Flea* [published by Lyle Stuart, 1965.]: "The indiscriminate use of air power against presumed Viet-Cong targets does much to explain the alienation of the rural population from the Saigon Government. Country people whose only contact with the government comes in the form of napalm and rocket attacks can scarcely be expected to feel sympathetic to the government cause, whatever it may be. On the other hand, they have every reason to feel solidarity with the guerrillas, usually recruited from their own villages, who share their peril and their hardships."

More than any other single factor, our air war in Viet-Nam is turning the rest of the world against the United States.

All war, of course, is hell. There is no such thing as a "clean war," in Viet-Nam or anywhere else. But even in warfare there are certain observable norms of decency which cannot be disregarded. These were laid down after World War Two in the Charter of the International Military Tribunal, under which the Nuremberg Trials of top Nazi civilian and military leaders were held. Our actions in Viet-Nam fall within the prohibited classifications of warfare set down at Nuremberg under Article Six, which reads:

> . . . The following acts, or any of them, are crimes coming within the jurisdiction of the Tribunal for which there shall be individual responsibility:
>
> a) Crimes against peace: namely, planning, preparation, initiation or waging of a war of aggression, or a war in violation of international treaties, agreements, or assurances, or participation in a common plan or conspiracy for the accomplishment of any of the foregoing.
>
> b) War crimes: namely, violations of the laws or customs of war . . . plunder of public property, wanton destruction of cities, towns or villages, or devastation not justified by military necessity.
>
> c) Crimes against humanity: namely, murder, extermination, enslavement, deportation, and other inhumane acts committed against any civilian population, before, or during the war. . . .

Under the provisions of Article 6 the United States is clearly guilty of "War Crimes," "Crimes against Peace" and "Crimes against Humanity," crimes for which the top German leaders were either imprisoned or executed. If we agree with Hermann Goering's defense at Nuremberg that "In a life and death struggle there is no legality," then no action can or should be taken against the government leaders responsible for the war in Viet-Nam. But if Americans still believe that there is a higher law than that of the jungle, we should call our leaders to account. Otherwise we shall have proved Albert Schweitzer correct when he wrote:

> It is clear now to everyone that the suicide of civilization is in progress. . . . Wherever there is lost the consciousness that every man is an object of concern for us just because he is a man, civilization and morals are shaken, and the advance to fully developed inhumanity is only a question

of time. . . . We have talked for decades with ever increasing lightminded-
ness about war and conquest, as if these were merely operations on a
chessboard; how was this possible save as the result of a tone of mind
which no longer pictured to itself the fate of individuals, but thought of
them only as figures or objects belonging to the material world? (*The
Philosophy of Civilization.*)

The issue at stake in Viet-Nam is not, as President Johnson constantly
claims, what will happen if we leave. It is what will happen to us as a
people, and to our judgment in history, if we stay.

Eldridge Cleaver
(1935–   )

CLEAVER, at the age of twenty-two, began serving a prison sentence in Folsom Prison (California) for possession of marijuana. Later, on a different charge, he was imprisoned in San Quentin. At first becoming a Muslim convert in prison, Cleaver eventually became a follower of Malcolm X. His first book, *Soul on Ice* (1968), was widely acclaimed; a second collection of essays, *Post-Prison Writings and Speeches* (1969), traces the events leading to Cleaver's flight to Algeria.

Cleaver's "Open Letter to Ronald Reagan" is published in *Post-Prison Writings and Speeches*.

OPEN LETTER
TO RONALD REAGAN

California Medical Facility
Vacaville, California
May 13, 1968

The Honorable Ronald Reagan
Governor of the State of California
Sacramento, California

Honorable Sir:

In writing you this letter, I want first of all to make one thing clear: I do not write it to ask a favor of you; I do not write it seeking mercy; I do not write it to complain. Rather, I am writing to you to call to your attention that certain persons who are responsible to you have conspired to violate my rights and are now holding me as a political prisoner at Vacaville Medical Facility, one of the chain of prisons operated by the California Department of Corrections, a state agency, under your control. As the Chief executive of the State of California, I thought you might want to know what the people whom you have appointed to the California Adult Authority have done. And whether you in fact want to know about it or not, as the Chief Executive it is your duty to see to it that the agencies under your control carry out their functions in such a manner as not to violate the rights of any citizen of the State of California, or of any other state or jurisdiction, for that matter. I want to speak to you about a clear instance in which my rights have been violated in a most flagrant and indefensible manner. So it is from that point of view that I write this letter, and it is in that spirit that I hope you will receive it, look into the matter, and then act, or not act, as your reason, conscience, and advisors move you.

I am a political prisoner, and an examination of the circumstances resulting in my imprisonment will reveal this fact to you or to anybody else. I realize that I have asserted an awkward claim, because I know that other people have already examined the circumstances of which I speak and have drawn the conclusion that, indeed, I should be right where I am. But I do not intend to argue their side of the story, which I not only consider wrong, but perfidious and criminal. Because certain people had to do certain things in order for me to be, at this moment, sitting in this cell. People talked about me and my activities and then they issued orders. Other people moved to carry out those orders. Those who fastened the handcuffs to my wrists, the shackles around my legs, the chain around my body, put me into a car, transported me to this place and turned me over to the keepers here, were mere functionaries, automatons, carrying out their "duties" in Adolf Eichmann's spirit. I speak, rather, of the decision makers, those whom you have appointed and charged with making decisions in this area. They are the guilty ones, the conspirators, whose decisions and orders I bring to your attention.

I was on parole in San Francisco, after serving nine years of a fourteen-year sentence in San Quentin, Folsom, and Soledad. I was released on December 12, 1966. My parole agent was Mr. R. L. Bilideau. I was given four years' parole by the California Adult Authority, presumably because, according to their lights, I had been rehabilitated. According to my own lights, I had.

Having gone to prison from Los Angeles, I decided to take my parole to San Francisco, to start anew in a brand new locale, there to stand or fall on my own merit, and to build a brand new life. I did this with ease, with a thirst for life, a driving hunger to be involved in life, the real life that I had watched for so long from the sidelines of a stagnant, deadening, artificial world. I found love, and married it. Her name is Kathleen, my darling wife. While in prison I decided that, upon my release, I would find a way to relate to the struggle of my people for a better life, to plunge myself into that struggle and contribute of myself what I possessed that could be used, without reservation: my life, my fortune, and my sacred honor which, through my struggles to survive the soul-murder of my stay in prison, I found.

After a few false starts, I encountered the Black Panther Party, which I quickly joined, and after proving myself, was appointed to the position of Minister of Information. It is a position which I still hold and of which I am as proud, Governor, as I imagine you are of the office you hold. You may have heard of my party, and I certainly have heard of yours. We visited you in Sacramento last year on May 2nd, and, if I may say so, were very badly received. As I understand it, this was because some of us brought our guns with us, even though your men had theirs with them. Moreover, your men turned their guns on us, although we did not do the same thing to them. We were told that your men had the right to have their guns but that ours didn't. We argued the point, of course, but evidently our arguments fell on deaf ears, because our men with guns were arrested and some of them had to serve a jail sentence. I was arrested also, but quickly released with all charges dropped. Then a judge discovered that I should not have been arrested in the first place because I was there as a reporter, with proper credentials, for *Ramparts* magazine, of which I was then and still am, a staff writer; because I did not have a gun; and because, in reference to my being on parole, I had the written consent of my parole agent to be there. That was the only time in my eighteen months on parole that I was ever arrested. Since that situation was resolved as it was, I think it would be fair to say, Governor, that in those eighteen months I was never arrested for cause.

If the truth were to be told, I was a model parolee, although I gather that I was something of a headache to my parole agent. This was through no fault of my own, but because he was caught up in the contradiction between the presumptions of the parole department and my human rights and my Constitutional rights to engage in political activity. He was always telling me that, although I had a perfect right to be a Black Panther, there were politicians in Sacramento who did not approve of the party. It was his advice that if I wanted to be successful on parole, I be cool. *Be cool?* For nine long years I had been on *ice*. Shit. I was being cool. In fact I was still thawing out, trying to warm up, so that I could really do my thing. Besides, legality was on my side. As for politicians, I was one myself. (I guess I forgot that politics, especially when they start to get deep, get dirty. You can't really count on anything, not even, as in my own case, the Constitution of the United States. Still, I was not *really* counting on that, being aware as I was that some politicians, in the name of upholding the Constitution, violate it, yea, rub it in the mud.)

But I am Minister of Information of the Black Panther Party. And what would be the quality of my soul, politics, and value to my party, to my comrades, and to the people we represent, if (through mere fear of hostile politicians) I abdicated the responsibilities I had accepted and pledged myself to fulfill? Having yourself taken an oath of office, Governor, I'm sure you can understand that. Suppose Jesse Unruh sent you a threatening message demanding that you resign as governor. I know what you would do: you would tell Big Daddy where to go. Well, I did more or less the same thing, but that was, at least it was *supposed* to be, just between me and my parole agent. I chose to stick to my guns. Anyway, I thought that the politicians in Sacramento had better things to do than to be fucking around with parolees, and the party didn't have any plans for visiting the State Capital again. Dispensing information seemed innocuous enough, and besides, I was so busy that I didn't have much time to worry about it.

Huey P. Newton, Minister of Defense of the Black Panther Party, was uptight, on Death Row, and he needed me: District Attorney Coakley of Alameda County was prosecuting my leader for murder, in the name of the People of the State of California, so it was very clear to me that the people needed some information they didn't seem to have: about Huey, about the Black Panther Party, about the Oakland Police Department, about District Attorney Coakley, about black people, about 1968, and the black response to white racism (this was before LBJ decided to give me a hand by issuing his Civil Disorders Report), and about politics—and about how all that jazz was mixed up, interrelated with welfare, police brutality, bad housing, the war in Vietnam—all that shit. All that shit had to be put into a perspective from which the people could see, and understand, and join in the demand that Huey Must Be Set Free! Come See About Huey!

Whew! To tell you the truth, Governor, that shit was wearing me out. I was getting old before my time: I'm twenty-two years old, the age I was when I went to prison, because when I got out, there was a great big gap in my soul that had to be filled. I filled it with the Black Revolution. In practical terms, I filled it with Huey, because Huey is the incarnation of the Black Revolution, if you can dig that.

And then along came the Peace and Freedom Party. Politics. What the hell. We had called them, hadn't we? "Come See About Huey, but the rest of you don't come." No, we were serious, and there was very little time. The Black Revolution was at stake, and we needed every hand we could get, because the people needed information.

O.K. We had asked for it, and here it was: the Peace and Freedom Party. Politics. How do we relate to it? Shit. Do you think we had a hard time coming up with the answer, Governor? If you do, you are as wrong as two left shoes, because it was as simple as "States' Rights" is to George Wallace. He, by the way, came along with his National States' Rights Party, the American Independence Party, at the same time as the Peace and Freedom Party, as I'm sure you are aware. But they didn't come to see about Huey. I think they went to see about the Oakland Police Department and D. A. Coakley. The Peace and Freedom people only needed a little information because they already had a lot of their own. In fact, it would be fair to say that we exchanged information with them. After that, it was just a question of apportioning the work load, which we did, at the Richmond Auditorium, at the Founding Convention of the Peace and Freedom Party. That was in March, and a grand coalition was formed between Browns (Brown Caucus), Whites (White Caucus), and Blacks

(Black Caucus)—that's a little complicated, Governor, I know, but let me leave it like that. If you want more information on that subject, contact the Peace and Freedom people or the Black Panthers or the Mexican-Americans, and they will fill you in. If I could leave here, I would be glad to go get that information for you, because you really should know about it, it's a brand new bag; but this joint I'm in sort of cramps my style. Information-wise.

The notorious, oppressive, racist, and brutal Oakland Police Department is at the heart of the matter. This gestapo force openly and flagrantly terrorizes the black people of Oakland. The Black Panther Party took a position against what the OPD was and is doing to black people. As one of the chief spokesmen for the party, I became well known to the OPD and I was hated by them. I know that they hated me; I've seen murderous hatred burning in their eyes. They hated the whole idea of a Black Panther Party, and they were out to destroy it. We were out, on the other hand, to organize the black community so that it could put an end to the terror. We saw no reason why we shouldn't do this, and nobody else seemed to be doing anything about it. If they were, it was not showing, because things were getting worse and not better. The OPD had increased its patrols of the black community to the saturation point, and become like a sword buried in the heart of the people. The Black Panther Party intended to remove that sword.

In its effort to counter the party's drive, the OPD launched a systematic campaign of harassment by arrest of party members, particularly its leaders. Take a look at the rap sheets of Huey P. Newton, our Minister of Defense, or David Hilliard, our National Captain, or Bobby Seale, our Chairman. You will find a string of phony cases as long as your arm. On October 28, 1967, they attempted to murder Huey, then charged him with murder when one of their own men came up dead. On April 6, 1968, they attempted to murder me, shot me, and did murder a member of our party —Bobby Hutton, seventeen years old. And then they charged me with attempting to murder them!

Governor Reagan, I would call to your attention an old saying: that where there is smoke there is fire; because there is a lot of smoke around the Oakland Police Department. I submit that the smoke is from the frequent use of their guns against the black community. It deserves looking into. As the Governor of the State of California, you would not be stepping out of your place if you looked into Oakland. Besides, it may be easier for you to look into Oakland than for anybody else. I understand that you have many friends and supporters in Oakland and that recently you received a warm welcome by the Republican convention there.

Well, on the night that I was shot and arrested, the OPD came up with the paranoid, fantastic notion that other members of the Black Panther

Party *might* invade the jail and rescue me. (Shit. Anybody *might* do anything!) So they got in touch with the California Adult Authority (did
they, I wonder, get in touch with you?) and asked them to come get me
and take me to San Quentin. The OPD communicated its own panic to the
Adult Authority, because at the absurd hour of 4 a.m., Sunday morning,
April 7, two of its members (a quorum meeting over the telephone; voices
groggy from sleep) ordered my parole revoked and I was taken to San
Quentin, and from there to Vacaville. I have at last been served by the
Adult Authority with three reasons for revoking my parole. Here they are:

1. Eldridge Cleaver violated his parole by being in possession of a gun.

2. Eldridge Cleaver violated his parole by associating with people of
bad reputation.

3. Eldridge Cleaver violated his parole by failing to cooperate with his
parole agent.

Are you outraged, Governor? I am, and I think you should be. Let me
point out why. On what do they base the first charge? The impeccable
word of the Oakland Police Department! (After the Surgeon General of
the United States said to stop, after the Chiefs of Police of both San
Francisco and Los Angeles issued orders to stop, the OPD still hasn't said
that it will stop using mace on the citizens of the state you govern.) This
charge by the Adult Authority amounts to nothing more nor less than an
invasion into the province of the Judiciary. I have been imprisoned without a trial; I have entered a plea of Not Guilty to the charge in the Superior Court; but the Adult Authority has already convicted and sentenced
me. Am I not entitled to a trial?

The second charge—that I associated with people of bad reputation—
is fantastic. Now I realize that all black people have a bad reputation in
the eyes of certain racists, but the Adult Authority here refers to members of the Black Panther Party. My parole officer, Mr. Bilideau, told me,
and I quote him, that "it's all right with us if you are a Black Panther."
We had a full discussion of the matter and he merely cautioned me about
Sacramento politicians who don't like the Panthers. My question is, in
whose opinion does the Black Panther Party have a bad reputation?
Certainly not in the opinion of the black community, and not in the
opinion of all white people. So what's this shit about reputation? Hundreds of people, all over the Bay Area, all over the state, across the nation,
and around the world, have cried out against the persecution of the Black
Panther Party by the Oakland Police Department. As a matter of fact, if
we are going to speak of reputations, the Oakland Police Department has
the worst reputation of any police department in the State of California,
and can only be compared to the racist police in Mississippi and South
Africa. So what is the Adult Authority doing associated with this disreputable police force? Ah, they have a regular thing going. The prisons

of California are bursting with people handed over by the Oakland Police Department. Pure and simple, this bad reputation jazz is nothing but political opinion, uninformed at that.

The third and last charge, that I failed to cooperate with my parole officer, turns my stomach inside out, because it is a lie. Like the other charges, it is an afterthought, conjured up as justification for the precipitous action of ordering me back to prison. (Why is it that when some people see that they have made a serious mistake, instead of moving to correct it and offer relief to the victim of their mistake, they move to fabricate a justification? I know a boxcarful of convicts who are better men than that, who are more than willing to admit that they were wrong.) The last time I saw my parole officer, just a few days before I was arrested, we shook hands, and his parting words to me were: "I want you to do me a favor, Eldridge. When I get a copy of your book, will you autograph it for me?" We both laughed, and I said, "Isn't this a fantastic turn of events? Just think of it: all these years I have been dependent on you guys signing things for me, and now I get a chance to sign something for you! It will be a pleasure!"

I do not know whether or not my parole officer actually submitted such a lying report against me, or whether the Adult Authority merely charged me in his name, because failure to cooperate with one's parole officer is a routine charge lodged against men whose paroles are revoked. It is a cliche, tossed in for good measure. And the Adult Authority operates in such a secret fashion, is cloaked with such an impenetrable shroud of darkness, that nobody knows what goes on in its Star Chamber proceedings. However, if my parole officer did submit that lie, I would be more hurt than surprised, because in my time I have seen enough of the organization men of the Department of Corrections so that nothing they do could surprise me, no matter how nauseating. But you know, Governor, when you have frequent contact with another person for eighteen months, something between you is built up. You get to know each other on a human level, you learn to see inside each other's personalities, and there are certain things that human beings naturally expect from each other, like not to be stabbed in the back. But, alas, it is not so, or else why and from what depth of a sense of betrayal, could Caesar say, Et tu Brute? *Et tu Bilideau?*

Well, there you are, Governor, that is more or less the substance of what I wanted to lay before you. But permit me to add a few remarks. I am finished with the California Department of Correction, with the Adult Authority, with parole officers, with prisons, and all of their world of restraint, confinement, and punishment. I can't relate to them anymore, because I am free. I am a free man, Governor, and I no longer know how to submit and play the part of a debtor to society. What I owe to society is the work that I must do outside these stone walls. My work can't wait, it won't wait, it should not wait. And you, Governor, should welcome me back to my job, because I was dealing with some of the most pressing problems facing not only the State of California but this nation and the world. And the people you can't reach, the dispossessed and oppressed people—whom you can't even talk to, whom you can't understand, and who neither trust nor understand you—are the very people with whom I am on the best of terms, for I am of them, I am one of them. You and I, Governor, have both been working on the same problems, except that you are working from the top down and I am working from the bottom up. The bottom of the world is in motion, Governor, and Bobby Dylan's "empty handed beggar" is at the door, except that his hand is not empty any more. He's got a gun in that hand. And he's stopped begging. In fact, he's nearly stopped talking, because it's becoming clear to him that hardly anybody is listening. When he finally stops talking altogether, he is going to start shooting. This brings to a conclusion what I wanted to talk to you about, and I have nothing else to say, except one question: Have you been listening to me, Governor?

Respectfully submitted,

Eldridge Cleaver,
Minister of Information
Black Panther Party.

Truman Nelson
(1912–   )

TRUMAN NELSON was born in Lynn, Massachusetts. He has contributed articles to the *Saturday Review, Nation,* and *Ramparts,* and is the author of *The Sin of the Prophet* (1952), *Passion by the Brook* (1953), *John Brown Reader* (1959), and *The Right of Revolution* (1968).

"No Rights, No Duties" is Chapter Three of *The Right of Revolution.*

NO RIGHTS, NO DUTIES

Thomas Jefferson, when queried about the authority, legal and otherwise, for his revolutionary assertion that people have a right to overthrow their government under certain conditions, said:

> All its authority rests then on the harmonizing sentiments of the day, whether expressed in conversation, in letters, printed essays, or the elementary books of public right, as Aristotle, Cicero, Locke, Sidney, etc. . . . it was intended to be an expression of the American Mind.

It was just as plainly understood by the founding fathers that all government is a contract, and if it gives no rights, or even diminished rights, you owe it no duties. What allegiance, really, can this government demand of a group commonly known as *second-class citizens?* The same is true of *paupers* and *minors.* They are never given the equal protection of the laws. The poor are confined by economic attrition in slums where violations of housing and health codes are carried on with impunity every day. They could not exist as slums, otherwise. The minors, healthy young boys under voting age, are forced into an involuntary servitude in the military establishment, which demands of them that they kill or be killed in countries far away for purposes which they consider irrelevant to the point of madness. As minors, they have no rights that a legislator needs to respect.

The American people as a whole, even the affluent, seem to have lost control over their own politics. They know that faceless men at the levers of power in the Pentagon can throw a switch to oblivion for the world without even considering asking for the consent of the governed. Many of us are finally getting this straight in our heads, but they have got to us lower down and made us political eunuchs. We are so squeezed by our "responsibility to the free world" that we cannot have a free thought but what we are warned that the whole "free world" will go down if we act on it.

Political emasculation is not our only organic change. The simple facts of the Newark rebellion reveal that the total organism of American life is rotting faster and faster into putrefaction. The stinking decay grows in our guts, and when we try to cure it, they break in our hands. One of our most sacred rights, that of the individual, *individualism*, forsooth, is now debased and swept away with the full connivance of the elected powers.

The crimes, if any, in Newark, were carried out by individuals. A few armed men, estimated by the police as not over ten men, with names, personalities, and motives of their own (men feeling perhaps, that they owed no more duty to this government than the Irish did to the British Government in the beginning of their revolution) fired at our police and our soldiers. A whole people was punished for this. Mortal punishment in a rain of fire went sweeping into the apartment houses and killing the innocent.

It is nowhere known for certain if any snipers were killed by the police, and it never will be known because the police have moved into simple warfare where the trajectory of function is to find the locus of the enemy and flush him out with firepower. And to act, with the greatest immediacy, not against a suspected individual, but against a flawed totality. Thus our nationalism has reached its apogee. No longer can a man stand and bargain with his government over the extent of his rights and duties, his innocence or guilt, as our forefathers did, even with their God.

This new point of view, the consciousness now formed which demands that we punish collectively for individual guilt, we are acting out all over the world. The most important task assigned to us as a nation, the leading and generating fact of our lives, is the war we are carrying on in Vietnam, a war against a total people, wherein it is a routine function to bomb and burn a whole village because it is suspected that one or two of the active enemy are located there, or have always lived there.

How can we think that in performing this, which even our apologists characterize as a cruel and *dirty* war, that our actions will not stain through our whole consciousness and benumb and degenerate us in our wholeness and make us act toward ourselves as we do toward others?

The fact is, what the rich man does to the poor man, what the landlord does to the tenant, what the merchant does to the consumer, what the boss does to the worker, what the policeman does to the suspect, what the jailor does to the helpless criminal in his power is only a local reflection of what we are doing as a nation abroad with our armies. And as the merchants, police, judges, landlords, bosses, jailors increase at home, while our soldiers escalate their presence abroad, so does the scope and intensity of their action against their victims.

And all the time we are told that to suffer this is part of the *duty* we must pay for our *rights*. That these acts which they say they perform only as a cruel necessity are saving us from being the victims of evil men, somewhere else, or evil systems, over there . . . who will only use us for their gratification. That if they let up for a moment their heavy-handed control of our lives, it will provide the vicious and unprincipled a chance to oppress the innocent. So, although some individuals may question some of the acts performed by those in power . . . they must continue to rule us for the greater good.

This means that they, our overlords, are all virtuous, all compassionate, all understanding public servants who took up the cross to suffer and sacrifice in carrying out their tasks and duties to us . . . that it is their duty to curtail our rights because they are carrying out a responsibility to law and order and the greatest good.

We, on the other hand, have to accept their acts of usurpation and control as our *duty* and promise on our oaths that we will unquestioningly obey their commands as spoken and enforced by their myriads of overseers, spies, interrogators, and whippers-in, from the President to the local draft board and social worker. And cheerfully recognize their rights to the lion's share of our daily labor so they can carry out their duty to control us with a maximum efficiency and have a gracious surrounding in which they can unwind, after a wearisome day of holding us in an appropriate system of checks and balances.

And we must carry out, proudly and cheerfully, our right to mark, every four years, a cross beside some names printed on a ballot . . . names of men either completely unknown to us, or only too well known as scoundrels, windbags, and embezzlers who have lived all their lives on the public payrolls and prospered well beyond the million mark. And although we know, from the experiences of ourselves, our fathers, and grandfathers, that regardless of the inane speeches they utter, promising change, they will do the same as the men in office before them and before them and before them, and they will plead the same crisis of the Republic, plead the same urgencies and imperatives about the obscene Vietnam War of 1967 as they did about the obscene Mexican War of 1847, and in about the same words.

We must also perform the right and duty of serving voluntarily in the courts, and sitting in judgment on other frail humans; knowing that by the time the government prosecutor and the government judge get through with the case we will still not know much about the guilt or innocence of the accused or be able to do anything about it if we did. All we have to do is be the face of the rubber stamp which the clerk pounds on the face of the man on trial which says, The people find you guilty and sentence you to prison and torture for your life's duration.

And finally, we must always consider it part of our rights and duties that, no matter how decent, how politically and economically advanced, how humane, gentle, and loving we know people in other nations to be, and no matter if the cause they are fighting and dying for is to overthrow the yoke of centuries of exploitation and despotism, we must be prepared at a moment's notice to look on them as deadly enemies threatening the very foundations of our homes and be prepared to burn them, starve them, torture them, kill them, and do the same to all others who do not regard them as deadly enemies because of government fiat, even though these others may be our own sons, brothers, fathers, lovers, and friends. Laws, lawmakers, or law-enforcers who do this are not to be considered laws, nor lawmakers, nor law-enforcers, and should be resisted as any usurpation or usurper should be, at all times.

The self-evident American right of revolution lies in this: that an unconstitutional law is not a law. An unconstitutional law can be defined, in revolutionary terms, as one against the people en masse, and for special privilege. It should be just as opposable when it is against a *people*, living within the confines of the United States. It is thus clearly not agreed on by all the people.

An officer of the government is as any officer "of the law" only when he is proceeding according to law. When he is killing a woman in an apartment house that may or may not be the location of a sniper, he is not acting in a lawful way. The moment he ventures beyond the law he becomes like any other man. He forfeits the law's mantle of immunity and protection. He may then be resisted like any other trespasser. A law that is palpably against the peace and security of all the people, such as all the racist laws on the books of the Southern States, laws limiting the rights and privileges of privacy and movement of the blacks in the Northern states, the laws against the Indians in the Western States, and those against the poor in all the states, is really not a law at all, consitutionally, and is thus void and confers no authority on anyone, and whoever attempts to execute it, does so at his own peril.

Common sense, the conscience of the mass, will tell you if this doctrine is not valid; then anyone with police power can usurp authority, and sustained by these unconstitutional laws, can treat people as he pleases. Many have already done this, are doing this, and still we wonder why we can't get these usurpers off our backs. A self-proclaimed "law-making body" or "law-enforcing agency" can beat, rape, torture or kill at will— as such bodies do now, in Mississippi, and have for over a century—and the people have no right to resist them. It simply does not make sense.

The best of our founding fathers wanted the law to make sense . . . wanted a "government and policy on such plain and obvious general principles, as would be intelligible to the plainest rustic. . . ."

The true revolutionary, then and now, holds that the Declaration and the Constitution contemplate no submission by the people to gross usurpation of civil rights by the government, or to the lawless violence of its officers. On the contrary, the Constitution provides that the right of the people to keep and bear arms shall not be infringed. This constitutional right to bear arms implies the right to use them, as much as the constitutional right to buy and keep food implies the right to eat it.

The Constitution also takes it for granted that, as the people have the right, they will also have the sense to use arms, whenever the necessity of the case justified it; this is the only remedy suggested by the Constitution, and is necessarily the only remedy that can exist when the government has become so corrupt that it can offer no peaceful solution to an intolerable way of life.

It is no answer to this argument on the right of revolution to say that if an unconstitutional act be passed, the mischief can be remedied by a repeal of it, and that this remedy can be brought about by a full discussion and the exercise of one's voting rights. The black men in the South discovered, generations ago, that if an unconstitutional and oppressive act is binding until invalidated by repeal, the government in the meantime will disarm them, plunge them into ignorance, suppress their freedom of assembly, stop them from casting a ballot and easily put it beyond their power to reform their government through the exercise of the rights of repeal.

A government can assume as much authority to disarm the people, to prevent them from voting, and to perpetuate rule by a clique as they have for any other unconstitutional act. So that if the first, and comparatively mild, unconstitutional and oppressive act cannot be resisted by force, then the last act necessary for the imposition of a total tyranny may not be.

The right of the government "to suppress insurrection" does not conflict with this right of the people to resist the execution of laws directed against their basic rights. An insurrection is a rising against the law, and not against usurpation. The actions, for example, of native fascist groups can be demonstrated by their own public acts and statements to be designed for privilege for themselves and to be defamatory and oppressive to other groups among the people. The black people don't want the police to shoot into white working-class apartments either.

The right of resistance to usurping laws is in its simplest form a natural defense of the natural rights of people to protect themselves against thieves, monomaniacs, and trespassers who attempt to set up their own personal, or group, authority against the people they are supposed to serve. It is the threat of the power of the people to remove them by force that keeps officeholders from perpetuating themselves. Not that they are any worse than other men, but the rewards are great and most of them act as though they were trying to discover the utmost limit of popular acquiescence to their self-exploitation and small tyrannies. In sum, if there is no right of revolution there is no other right our officials have to respect.

By no means am I saying that this is the prevailing concept of our organic law among the leaders and pundits of the country. Although they might, if pressed hard enough, give lip service to it. Arthur Schlesinger said in the *Atlantic Monthly* that the American concept of the right of revolution was the greatest idea we have given to the world:

> First and foremost stands the concept of the inherent and universal right of revolution . . . proclaimed in the Declaration of Independence: the doctrine that "all men are created equal . . . possessing inalienable rights to life, liberty and the pursuit of happiness" with the corollary that governments derive their just powers from the consent of the governed and that therefore the people have a right to supplant any government "destructive of these ends" with one they believe most likely to effect their safety and happiness. True, the history of England provided precedents to the men of 1776, and the Age of Enlightenment supplied intellectual support; but the flaming pronouncement, followed by its vindication on the battlefield, made the doctrine ever afterwards an irrepressible agency "in the course of human events." Europe was the first to respond . . . A series of revolts overturned, or strove to overturn, illiberal governments through most of the Continent, and hastened popular reforms in other lands to forestall popular upheavals. These convulsions all had their internal causes but in every instance the leaders derived inspiration from America's achievement of popular rule, as well as from its freely expressed interest in their similar aspirations.

"The Declaration of Independence is our Creed," Supreme Court Justice Douglas said, in an article on "The U.S. and the Revolutionary Spirit." He said we should not be afraid to talk revolution and to voice our approval of it. He tells us to become the active protagonist of the independence of all people. Go up against the darkness and pain of continuing feudalism. "There is a political feudalism where a dynasty has the trappings of a parliamentary system but manipulates it for the benefit of a ruling class . . . Revolution in the twentieth century means rebellion against another kind of feudalism . . . economic feudalism . . . the United States should promote democratic revolutions against these conditions of economic feudalism."

Going back, we find John Locke's dictum, in his essay on government, that when the natural rights of man are violated, the people have the right and the duty of suppressing or changing the government. "The last recourse against wrongful and unauthorized force is opposition to it."

It is the massiveness of the display of force against them that has brought the black people to their revolutionary flash point more than anything else. They know, as soon as they hear the sounds of masses of police sirens that their little insurrection, or their little rebellion, or their small act of resistance will turn into a massacre, not of the enemy, but of themselves. But yet they go on resisting until the local police sirens are replaced by the clank of tanks, or personnel carriers; the clubs, the police revolvers are superseded by bayonets and death-spitting machine guns. And still their exultation grows, an exultation that is absolutely inexplicable to the whites, seeing them surrounded by the massacre of their own people. Sartre speaks of this; of how the Frenchmen of the Resistance never felt freer than when they were under the attacks of the Nazi S. S. How the more they were condemned to silence, the more they felt that they were approaching liberation.

These rebellions by the blacks are a minority action: they cannot succeed militarily, and nobody thinks they will. The whole process is a *telling* revolution, a way of stating something buried under centuries of apathy and indifference far worse than omnipresent opposition. A *Life* magazine interview with a black sniper reveals this. He is not trying to kill cops and Guardsmen. When they are struck down it is by accident. He is trying, he says, to tell "our people we are here." And in the process, "the firing of five or six shots in the air is enough to draw cops thick as fleas on a dog and still give time to get away." Then the people take what they want.

But it is much more than that: the black insurrection-white massacre method of telling revolution is in some ways comparable to the Buddhists burning themselves to tell of their to-the-death commitment to their country's revolution.

I always felt that an enormous amount of time, money, and effort was wasted in the last years of the civil-rights crisis, while the leaders, black and white, were trying to convince the American black man that he was really a downtrodden Hindu, a palpitating mass of ingrained and inborn submission, a victim of a caste society which stretches back, almost to prehistory. The Hindu, or to be more specific, the followers of Gandhi, were victims in a land so impoverished and barren that a lifetime of starvation was, and still is, their common lot . . . a land where living is so hard that men want a God so they can hate him as the father and ordainer of their degradation.

The American black man is a citizen in a rich land, with a citizen's rights and duty to resist, resist all attempts to deprive him of its manifold blessings. Even if he doesn't *want* to resist, he must; it is his duty, as it is the duty of all honest whites to urge him and support him in the process. Why should he have been urged to go through all this Hinduizing to regain the rights he already had in 1776? He was here then and fought alongside of the whites out of the same revolutionary morality, for the same revolutionary rights he is dying for right now . . . the idea that men before the law are exactly equal and that no man can take away these equalities except as forfeiture for a crime adjudged and confirmed by ancient and democratic due process.

Legally he has always had these rights. They were taken away from him by force and fraud. When the racist laws were written and enforced and then upheld finally by the Supreme Court of the United States, it was the lawbreaker and should have been resisted. The black man did resist these racist laws, but in vain. Police, militia, Federal troops beat him until he went down, over and over again, a victim of blood and violence, his land looted, his home burned, his daughter raped, his son lynched, his babies starved, his progeny for generations suffering automatically the same fate.

When he was finally handed the weapon of "soul force" he tried it; no one can deny that he honestly gave it a try. But we are living in a lunatic society, a racist society that will never stop hiring cops and soldiers to beat him until he stops them . . . or we stop the hiring. If we say the black man is a citizen, then he has a clear duty to resist tyranny and dictatorship, legally and peacefully if he can, forcibly if he must. He is the birthright possessor of the same rights we have. He cannot give them up if he wants to. He was not born to be a victim to test the longevity of our desire to oppress him.

Take a good look at the *Life* magazine for July 28, 1967. Look at it before it lies dog-eared in the dentist's office, or slides to oblivion in the trash trucks. Before the eyes of one of its reporters and cameramen, a police cruiser drew up on a littered street, surrounded by stores so gutted and debased that they are simply valueless: they are not stores anymore, they are piles of trash. A twenty-four-year-old black man took a six-pack of beer from one of them. He saw the cops. He had been arrested before, so he ran.

A yellow-helmeted cop with a shotgun leaped out of the cruiser. He aimed the gun with *his kind* of all deliberate speed and shot the black man dead . . . for a six-pack of beer! And the spreading pellets from the murderous blast tore their way into the soft flesh of Joe Bass, Jr., a black shoeshine boy, twelve years old, with nothing in his hands. He was struck in the neck and the thigh and fell bleeding to the pavement, his eyes open and staring ahead, his body almost finding a restful embrace in the dirty asphalt.

The Newark policeman, his shotgun still at the ready, turns away from the murdered Billy Furr, the looter of a six-pack of beer. There is no anguish in his face, his mouth is relaxed, almost soft as he reaches into the side pocket of his blue shirt for a cigar. The story is told accurately and compassionately, even to the point of telling how when little Joey was struck down fifty sobbing black men and women tried to get to him, to help him, and were clubbed back by a small squad of police with rifle butts. But the name of the murderer in the blue uniform shirt is not reported. And it is possible he will never be known, and his face will be forgotten, for the police in this country, when they are acting against the black people, are usually faceless and nameless and omnipotent, infallible and unpunishable, like Yahweh.

There was the Boston Massacre and there was the Newark Massacre. The last took place yesterday, in our time, in our country; the men who carried it out bore our faces, the bullets that found their way anonymously into black bodies were paid for, in part by us. It is our consciousness, our heritage, vibrating in the air we breathe.

Let us examine again the rules we live by . . . the life, liberty and pursuit of happiness guarantees. These rules say, if these guarantees are not forthcoming . . . "that whenever any form of government shall become destructive of these ends, it is the right of the people to alter or abolish it, and to institute a new government."

Certainly, no one in his right mind will deny that this form of government has been highly destructive to the life, liberty, et cetera of the black people. This, above all things, is self-evident. The black people are still in a social, economic, and political bondage. After a great war was fought to free them, they are not free. There is no excuse for the brute fact that our parliamentary system has not been able to bring them into the mainstream of American life. Not only that, their story can only be told in times of upheaval and self-slaughter. And even after these take place, the only comment made on it, or the only ones asked about it, are old crocks like Senator Dirksen, someone who is supremely irrelevant to what is going on, anywhere, and who yet is considered one of the two or three leading spokesmen of our government. All he can say is that we, the whites, are "getting impatient with this disregard of law and order." This fact alone, that Dirksen is speaking for it, shows the complete idiocy and futility of the Congress.

We say over and over again that the solving of the race question will take time, but there is no excuse for this. We establish new forms of government because it took too much time before, in the old form, to resolve an accursed question of human suffering. New governments are not to create a continuation of the same wrongs and social stultifications that made the new form a bloody imperative. We have had long enough . . . enough, enough to see ourselves as white-skinned racists creating and maintaining a society where some get all the good of it while others deeply suffer . . . where the good of one comes out of the evil put upon another . . . where we exist in a prison of our white skin as inescapable as that of our black neighbors. What we do to the black people, daily, makes me want to secede from the white race! It makes me, down deep, hate myself, and my color. All decent whites especially the young whites, abhor having to bear the burden of racist guilt their fathers have placed upon them.

And they hate white racist America and their own fathers for sustaining it, for stealing from them what should have been a birthright of human brotherhood, alienating them from young blacks by white cruelty to them, in their white image. For setting up impassable barriers between young whites and young blacks, areas of suspicion coming from a constant betrayal. They want to clasp hands with the blacks, if only in admiration of the dignity, patience, and restraint they have shown up to this breaking point. If we let them alone they will offer them love and support for their bloody struggle to rise to a level of liberation and privilege which whites accept as due to them by their birth alone.

And we adults: we hate white racist America because it has blocked out of the culture of our time the unfettered expression of the wisdom of a people to whom the meaning of life has had to be privation, suffering and alienation, but who have lived, somehow, with moments of ecstasy, with spurts of infectious and inexplicable joy. White racist America makes me ashamed of my own country, which not only presents to a vibrant, revolutionary world the complacent facade of a sluttish society whose mass ideal is the unlimited consumption of all possible goods and services . . . but has lost all of its revolutionary virtues in an hour when the darker people are finally climbing into the light, and are forced to seek elsewhere the encouragement which some of our revolutionary fathers meant for us to bestow upon mankind. And in the losing of this revolutionary virtue, we have turned despicably into our opposites and are murdering revolutionaries all over the world.

And all the time we are doing this we are telling the little white children, and some of the little black children, that Abe Lincoln said in 1848: "Any people anywhere being inclined and having the power, have the right to rise up and shake off the existing government, and form a new one that suits them better. This is a most valuable and sacred right, a right we hope and believe is to liberate the world."

And we are teaching high school students, black and white, that Abe Lincoln, the great emancipator, said, in his First Inaugural Address: "This country, with its institutions, belongs to the people who inhabit it. Whenever they shall grow weary, of the existing government, they can exercise their constitutional right of amending it, or their revolutionary right to dismember, or overthrow it."

They tell us that we have this great and basic right, but if we so much as suggest the use of it, we are punished . . . we are imprisoned. So that it serves as an entrapment, a vicious provocation to smoke out radicals and revolutionaries. Why do they say this . . . why do they so piously quote the forefathers and then blame and hurt people under an unforgivable longevity of oppression . . . obviously getting worse instead of better . . . for trying to act under it?

The United States House of Representatives has just demonstrated its imbecility and outright betrayal of the Bill of Rights, which it has sworn to uphold, by passing a bill which makes traveling from one state to another and saying anything that might be, after the fact, twisted into a connection with a riot, a criminal offense. It carries a fine of ten thousand dollars or imprisonment for five years, or both.

It was written by a white racist from Florida and forced onto the floor by the white racist from Mississippi, who said, the insurrections in the black ghettos were "organized conspiracies backed by the Communists . . . if you vote against this bill, what are you going to say when you go home and meet the policeman and fireman who risked their lives, and in many instances, lost them. . . ." As if it was not already clear that the lawless, conspiratorial, rioting element in the community is the police themselves.

This does not mean that the Southern racist congressmen were responsible for the bill. Charles W. Sandman, Jr., a Republican from New Jersey, was one of its most ardent supporters and said the police in Newark had told him that rioters had crossed the Hudson River in buses, were picked up in cars and taken to the center of Newark, where the trouble occurred. There is no proof in existence that this did occur, while on the other hand it is well known that the police will say anything that will develop their own positions. So the bill was passed by a vote of 347 to 70 . . . and they were not all Southern congressmen who voted for it.

This is how we put off, again and again, truth and resolution for some dishonest and shoody solution. And then we snivel and hurt the helpless when the chickens come home to roost. It was not outside agitators behind the guns of Newark . . . it could be the inflammatory boasts and texts of our daily education. Now they will have to prevent Thomas Jefferson, in the form of his writings, from crossing state lines, for he said: "What country can preserve its liberties if their rulers are not warned from time to time that this people preserve the spirit of resistance. Let them take arms. . . ."

Or if the agitator from New Jersey crosses the line into Pennsylvania, he will find the Pennsylvania Declaration of Rights already there, saying: "The Community hath an indubitable, inalienable, and indefeasible right to reform, alter or abolish government in such manner as shall be by that community judged most conductive to the public weal."

Henry Clay of Kentucky, the Great Commoner, said: "An oppressed people are authorized, whenever they can, to rise and break their fetters."

John Adams, the second President of the United States, said: "It is an observation of one of the profoundest inquiries into human affairs that a revolution of government is the strongest proof that can be given by a people, of their virtue and good sense."

His son, also a President of the United States, said: "In the abstract theory of our government, the obedience of the citizen is not due to an unconstitutional law: he may lawfully resist its execution."

And Henry D. Thoreau, a good revolutionary, an artist of the revolutionaries, said: "All men recognize the right of revolution, that is the right to refuse allegiance to and to resist, the government where its tyranny or its inefficiency are great and unendurable."

In Maryland its Declaration of Rights reads: "Whenever the ends of government are perverted, and public liberty manifestly endangered, and all other means of redress are ineffectual, the people may, and of right ought to, reform the old or establish a new government; the doctrine of nonresistance against arbitrary power and oppression is absurd, slavish and destructive of the good and happiness of mankind."

General and President U. S. Grant said: "The right of Revolution is an inherent one. When people are oppressed by their government, it is a natural right they enjoy to relieve themselves of the oppression if they are strong enough, either by withdrawing from it, or by overthrowing it and substituting a government more acceptable."

And Emerson, talking of affairs in Kansas, when white settlers in 1856 had to knuckle down to racist tyrants and live like people in the black ghettos today, said:

I think there never was a people so choked and stultified by forms. We adore the forms of law, instead of making them vehicles of wisdom and justice. Language has lost its meaning in the universal cant. . . . *Representative Government* is really misrepresentative. *Democracy, Freedom,* fine names for an ugly thing. They call it attar of roses and lavender,—I call it bilge water. They call it Chivalry and Freedom; I call it the stealing of all the earnings of a poor man and the earnings of his little girl and boy, and the earnings of all that shall come from him his children's children forever. But this is union and this is Democracy, and our poor people, led by the nose by these fine words, dance and sing, ring bells and fire cannon, with every new link of the chain which is forged for their limbs by the plotters in the Capital. . . . What are the results of law and Union? There is no Union. The judges give cowardly interpretation to the law, in direct opposition to the known foundation of all law, *that every immoral statute is void!* If that be law, let the ploughshare be run under the foundations of the Capitol—and if that be Government, extirpation is the only cure. I am glad that the terror at disunion and anarchy is disappearing. . . .

Now I submit that somewhere, every day in this country, some schoolboy is reading about these men; that their words, revolution and all, are passing into their consciousness. This being undeniably true . . . how can we stop these dangerous thoughts from crossing state lines, color lines, or lines of any kind? We could not stop them from entering the icy legal mind of Mr. Justice Jackson, late of the Supreme Court, who gave, in 1950, the most concrete modern juridical opinion of the right of revolution based on the Declaration of Independence.

> . . . we cannot ignore the fact that our own government originated in revolution, and is legitimate only if overthrown by force can sometimes be justified. That circumstances sometimes justify it is not Communist doctrine, but an old American belief. The men who led the struggle forcibly to overthrow lawfully constituted British authority found moral support by asserting a natural law under which their revolution was justified, and they bravely proclaimed their belief in the document basic to our freedom. Such sentiments have also been given ardent and rather extravagant expression by Americans of undoubted patriotism.

So there it is, deep in the hide of the Republic, and you can talk about it all you want, having a revolution, that is, just as long as it is in a classroom, and you are white. But don't say it, as William Epton[1] did, on the streets of Harlem before a group of silent men, whose eyes have a tiny glow like the stirring of a long-banked fire.

---

1. William Epton, a black man, was arrested in New York City for advocating the overthrow of organized government. Epton's speech, delivered on July 18, 1964, was spurred by the killing of a fifteen-year-old black boy, who was shot by Thomas Gilligan, a white police lieutenant.—*Editor.*

THE BILL OF RIGHTS*

Article I
Congress shall make no law respecting an establishment of religion, or prohibiting the free exercise thereof; or abridging the freedom of speech, or of the press; or the right of the people peaceably to assemble, and to petition the Government for a redress of grievances.

Article II
A well regulated Militia, being necessary to the security of a free State, the right of the people to keep and bear Arms, shall not be infringed.

Article III
No Soldier shall, in time of peace be quartered in any house, without the consent of the Owner, nor in time of war, but in a manner to be prescribed by law.

Article IV
The right of the people to be secure in their persons, houses, papers, and effects, against unreasonable searches and seizures, shall not be violated, and no Warrants shall issue, but upon probable cause, supported by Oath or affirmation, and particularly describing the place to be searched, and the persons or things to be seized.

* The Bill of Rights, the first ten amendments to the Constitution of the United States, was proposed on September 25, 1789, and declared in force on December 15, 1791.—*Editor.*

Article V

No person shall be held to answer for a capital, or otherwise infamous crime, unless on a presentment or indictment of a Grand Jury, except in cases arising in the land or naval forces, or in the Militia, when in actual service in time of War or public danger; nor shall any person be subject for the same offence to be twice put in jeopardy of life or limb; nor shall be compelled in any criminal case to be a witness against himself, nor be deprived of life, liberty, or property, without due process of law; nor shall private property be taken for public use, without just compensation.

Article VI

In all criminal prosecutions, the accused shall enjoy the right to a speedy and public trial, by an impartial jury of the State and district wherein the crime shall have been committed, which district shall have been previously ascertained by law, and to be informed of the nature and cause of the accusation; to be confronted with the witnesses against him; to have compulsory process for obtaining witnesses in his favor, and to have the Assistance of Counsel for his defence.

Article VII

In Suits at common law, where the value in controversy shall exceed twenty dollars, the right of trial by jury shall be preserved, and no fact tried by a jury, shall be otherwise re-examined in any Court of the United States, then according to the rules of the common law.

Article VIII

Excessive bail shall not be required, nor excessive fines imposed, nor cruel and unusual punishments inflicted.

Article IX

The enumeration in the Constitution, of certain rights, shall not be construed to deny or disparage others retained by the people.

Article X

The powers not delegated to the United States by the Constitution, nor prohibited by it to the States, are reserved to the States respectively, or to the people.

PB-5923-705-SB
75-71T

71 72 73 74   7 6 5 4 3 2 1